Assessing Adults with Intellectual Disabilities

 University of
Chester

ARROWE PARK
LIBRARY

This book is to be returned on or before the last date stamped below. Overdue charges will be incurred by the late return of books.

EDITED BY
JAMES HOGG AND ARTURO LANGA

Assessing Adults with Intellectual Disabilities

A SERVICE PROVIDERS' GUIDE

BPS Blackwell

© 2005 by The British Psychological Society and Blackwell Publishing Ltd
except for editorial material and organization © 2005 by James Hogg and Arturo Langa

BLACKWELL PUBLISHING
350 Main Street, Malden, MA 02148-5020, USA
9600 Garsington Road, Oxford OX4 2DQ, UK
550 Swanston Street, Carlton, Victoria 3053, Australia

The right of James Hogg and Arturo Langa to be identified as the Authors of the Editorial
Material in this Work has been asserted in accordance with the UK Copyright, Designs, and
Patents Act 1988.

First published 2005 by The British Psychological Society and Blackwell Publishing Ltd

3   2009

Library of Congress Cataloging in Publication Data

Assessing adults with intellectual disabilities : a service providers'
    guide / edited by James Hogg and Arturo Langa.
       p. cm.
    Includes bibliographical references and index.
    ISBN 978-1-4051-0220-9 (pbk. : alk. paper)
    1. People with mental disabilities—Psychological testing.
  2. People with disabilities—Functional assessment.   3. Medical care
  —Needs assessment.   4. Developmental Disabilities—diagnosis—Adult.
  5. Dementia—diagnosis—Adult.   6. Mentally Disabled Persons
  —Adult.   7. Needs Assessment—Adult.   I. Hogg, J. (James)   II. Langa, Arturo.
RC570.2.A85   2005
362.2—dc22

2005011634

A catalogue record for this title is available from the British Library.

Set in 10/12pt Adobe Garamond
by Graphicraft Limited, Hong Kong
Printed and bound in Malaysia
by KHL Printing Co Sdn Bhd

For further information on
Blackwell Publishing, visit our website:
www.blackwellpublishing.com

CONTENTS

CONTRIBUTORS

Ms Gillian Anderson
Consultant Clinical Psychologist
Kirklands Hospital
Mental Health / Learning Disabilities Division
Fallside Road
Bothwell
Glasgow G71 8BB
UK

Professor Robert A. Cummins
School of Psychology
Deakin University
221 Burwood Highway
Melbourne
Victoria 3125
Australia

Dr Lauren R. Charlot
Assistant Professor of Psychiatry
University of Massachusetts Medical School
Program Director, Neuropsychiatric Disabilities Unit
UMASS Memorial Healthcare
Worcester, MA 06155
USA

Professor Eric Emerson
Professor of Clinical Psychology
Institute for Health research
Lancaster University
Lancaster LA1 4YT
UK

Professor James Hogg
Research Professor
White Top Research Unit
University of Dundee
Springfield House
15/16 Springfield
Dundee DD1 4JE
UK

Dr Sunny Kalsy
Consultant Clinical Psychologist
South Birmingham Primary Care NHS Trust
Birmingham Learning Disabilities Services
66 Anchorage Road
Sutton Coldfield B74 2PH
UK

Dr Arturo Langa
Consultant Psychiatrist / Lead Clinician
Department of Psychiatry / Learning Disabilities Service
Kirklands Hospital
NHS Lanarkshire
Fallside Road
Bothwell
Glasgow G71 8BB
UK

Professor Edwin J. Mikkelsen
Associate Professor of Psychiatry
Harvard Medical School
Medical Director, The MENTOR Network
Consultant, Massachusetts Department of Mental Retardation
USA

Professor Chris Oliver
Professor of Clinical Psychology
School of Psychology and South Birmingham Primary Care NHS Trust
University of Birmingham
Edgbaston
Birmingham B15 2TT
UK

Professor Carla Vlaskamp
Healthcare Psychologist
University of Groningen

Grote Rozenstraat 38
Groningen
Netherlands

Mr Robert M. Walley
Consultant Clinical Psychologist
Department of Psychology
Edenhall Hospital
Musselburgh
East Lothian EH21 7TZ
UK

Professor Patricia Noonan Walsh
NDA Professor of Disability Studies
John Henry Newman Building D-005
University College Dublin
Belfield
Dublin 4
Ireland

Dr Kirk Zimbelman
Consultant Clinical Psychologist
Department of Psychology
Learning Disability Service
NHS Lanarkshire
Kirklands Hospital
Bothwell
Glasgow G71 8BB
UK

Introduction: assessment in perspective

James Hogg and Arturo Langa

1 Introduction

In the late 1980s, a volume on the assessment of people with intellectual disabilities began by drawing attention to the 'far-reaching changes in virtually every aspect of society's approach to people with serious development disabilities, including those with mental handicap' that had taken place during the preceding 15 years (Hogg & Raynes, 1987, p. 1). These authors went on to note the impact of normalization philosophy and the accompanying running down of large-scale institutions, with their replacement by smaller-scale community residences. For children, their inclusion in the educational system was also noted, leading to new conceptions of educational practice. These changes were at that time taking place across most English-speaking countries.

With respect to assessment, the authors went on to note, 'The emphasis on explicit intervention, whether for educational or training purposes, has brought the need for usable and technically accessible assessment instruments to the fore, with respect to both determining the present status and competence of an individual and establishing the direction intervention should take' (p. 2). Such intervention was invariably intended to be individualized, and a variety of approaches with much in common developed to provide frameworks in which assessment was conducted (e.g. individual programme plans, individual service plans, goal planning, essential lifestyle planning and care management).

In the intervening period between the present volume and its predecessor, our conception of the process by which people with intellectual disabilities are supported has evolved further. Person-centred planning (O'Brien & Lovett, 1992) has become a dominant approach to developing such support with three characteristics that distinguish it from prevailing planning methods. As noted by Mansell and Beadle-Brown (2004), person-centred planning

- emphasizes the aspirations and capacities expressed by the service user or an advocate rather than the imposition of service goals and constraints;
- draws on the informal support network available to a person, as well as the support offered by services;
- emphasizes the support required to achieve goals rather than what can be offered by services.

Mansell and Beadle-Brown (2004) go on to note, despite the considerable difficulties in implementing person-centred planning, 'There is no serious alternative to the principle that services should be tailored to individual needs, circumstances and wants' (p. 3). What role, then, does formal assessment have in shaping such a tailored response to 'needs, circumstances and wants'? There are in addition two more specific questions that may be framed:

- First, can systematic assessment contribute to the overall process by which a person-centred strategy is developed?
- Second, at what point is specialist assessment called for with respect to difficulties that are not unique to people with intellectual disabilities, but which will unquestionably affect their personal fulfilment?

In preparing the present volume, we have identified priority areas related to both these questions as they affect adults with intellectual disabilities. Since complex issues underpin both, contributors have dealt with each from two perspectives: conceptual issues in part I, and practical strategies and assessment instruments in part II. Clearly, the relevance of assessment to a given individual in any of the areas covered will indeed be determined by that person's needs, circumstances and wants.

With respect to the first question, that of assessment contributing to an overall process affecting a person's life, this is considered in three key areas: the overall assessment of quality of life, with a particular emphasis on *subjective* perception of an individual's own quality of life (chs. 1 and 9); the process by which the aspiration to become and remain in employment can be effected (chs. 2 and 10); and, the complex maintenance of the well-being and development of people with profound and multiple intellectual disabilities (chs. 3 and 11).

The concept of quality of life has become pervasive in society generally, but specifically so with respect to people with intellectual disabilities. In the field of disability generally, quality of life has frequently been invoked in a negative sense to justify termination of the lives of individuals with extreme complex health needs, leading Wolfensberger (1994) to demand its abandonment. As a standard to be attained (a 'good' quality of life), however, the concept is evoked pervasively with authors in the present volume using it with respect to the benefits of employment and the need for support for people with challenging behaviour. Cummins, in chapter 1, however, demonstrates the complexity of the concept, making special reference to the way in which judgements of quality of life are determined by context and a variety of psychological mechanisms that permit us to maintain stability through homeostatic regulation of a consistent level of subjective quality of life. In chapter 9 he reviews some of the plethora of quality of life instruments that have appeared since the 1990s. For service providers his critiques are cautionary; because an instrument is published and available in no way implies that it is reliable and valid, and hence is no guarantee that it can provide an index of the effectiveness of a service. With respect to determining subjective quality of life, his analysis of how this can be attained carries an important message to those undertaking person-centred planning. For many people with intellectual disabilities, particularly those with significant communication difficulties and complex needs, Cummins's analysis clearly points up challenges that have yet to be met.

Enhanced quality of life also emerges as an important outcome of the successful employment and maintenance of employment in Noonan Walsh's chapter 2. She places employment of people with intellectual disabilities firmly within the framework of international and national rights. Self-determination and choice are judged to underpin enhanced quality of life. Importantly, the social and lifespan context in which employment is located is described. For Noonan Walsh the assessment process adds value to such opportunities presented by choice by determining the supports people with intellectual disabilities need to work in the community. The approach to assessment advocated is essentially strategic and diverse (ch. 10). Norm-referenced tests are noted, but greater emphasis is given to both criterion-referenced assessment and functional analysis supported by observational methods, always set against the guiding principle of the individual's choice and as a means of determining the level and nature of required support.

The challenge of facilitating choice in the interest of person-centred planning is particularly salient in supporting people who do not communicate in conventional ways, including those with profound intellectual disabilities and multiple complex needs. Vlaskamp, in chapter 3, characterized the complexity of people with this degree of need. She delineates the wide range of professionals who must, in the interest of comprehensive support, be involved in assessment. She contrasts multidisciplinary with interdisciplinary assessment, the latter not entailing parallel streams of assessment, but an interaction between professionals in the process, leading to a holistic view of the person. To achieve this, norm-referenced tests are explicitly rejected, people with profound intellectual and multiple disabilities having insufficient in common with the populations on which such tests were standardized (ch. 11). Instead, a wide range of criterion-referenced assessments are described, including developmental, motor, sensory, communication instruments and techniques, all such assessment being undertaken within an expert, interdisciplinary context.

The second question raised above relates to the need for specialist assessments when a person's circumstances and behaviour present barriers to leading a full life. Five principal areas were identified where there is a need for specialist assessment to underpin appropriate support. Specifically we consider mental health problems (chs. 4 and 12), challenging behaviour (chs. 5 and 13), offending behaviour and alleged offending (chs. 6 and 14), dementia in people with intellectual disabilities (chs. 7 and 15) and complex behavioural phenotypes (chs. 8 and 16).

There are compelling reasons for highlighting these areas. Over the same period that an ideology of individualized support for people with intellectual disabilities has emerged, so has an increasing awareness of the complex difficulties that they may experience. There is now a body of research and practice that was not available when our earlier volume was prepared, but which can inform support in the wider context of person-centred planning. Key summaries of available knowledge have appeared for mental health (Bouras, 1999), challenging behaviour (Emerson, 2001), offending (Clare & Murphy, 1998), dementia (Janicki & Dalton, 1999) and syndromes associated with intellectual disabilities that profoundly influence behaviour (O'Brien & Yule, 1995). Though separated for the purposes of discussion, all five of these areas bear complex relations to the others that research and practice are still far from delineating. The occurrence of difficulties in any one of these areas, however, will have profound implications for realization of the individual's aspirations.

It is important to note there is no single explanation of what leads to a given behaviour in any of these areas. Environmental, genetic and physiological influences may all be involved. The balance between such influences will shift for any given individual exhibiting a particular difficulty or constellation of difficulties. At one end of the continuum a given challenging behaviour may arise because of a specific set of environmental influences; at the other, behaviour associated with the onset of dementia will fundamentally reflect underlying physiological changes in the brain. For these reasons, comprehensive assessment will approach the behaviour from several standpoints. Mikkelsen, Charlot and Langa, in chapter 4, dealing with the assessment of mental health difficulties, and Emerson, in chapter 5, in a discussion of challenging behaviour, all consider strategic approaches to difficult behaviours. These range from the functional analysis of the relation between environmental events and behaviour through to wider diagnostic and instrument-based assessments. In the respective chapters in part II on mental health and on challenging behaviour (i.e. ch. 12 by Charlot & Mikkelsen, and ch. 13 by Zimbelman), the focus is specifically on the use of reliable and valid instruments through which to assess the presence of such difficulties. Taken with their respective part I chapters, however, these instruments should be seen as contributors to the overall process of assessment described in chapters 4 and 5.

While definitional issues as to what constitutes 'challenging behaviour' or a 'mental health problem' still confront us, offending or alleged offending behaviour by people with intellectual disabilities presents particular difficulties. The complex processes by which people are considered to have offended in such a way that they become involved in the criminal justice system are considered by Anderson in chapter 6. Here she also indicates the inherent problems of establishing the prevalence of offending among people with intellectual disabilities and the implications of these problems for assessment. In chapter 14, assessment is reviewed in relation to various phases of engagement in the criminal justice system. Initial screening to establish *whether or not* people alleged to have committed an offence have intellectual disabilities is covered, as is the assessment of their competence to be engaged in criminal justice proceedings. Approaches to the important processes of risk assessment and management are reviewed. The limited available information on assessment in relation to specific offences such as sex offending is also reviewed.

A further highly significant challenge to the implementation of person-centred planning is the occurrence of dementia in people with intellectual disabilities. In contrast to the emphasis on the developmental potential of people with intellectual disabilities to engage in activities to which they aspire, here loss of function characterizes the progress of the disease. In chapter 7, Oliver and Kalsy emphasize the importance of formal assessment to ensure an early response to change rather than absorbing the deficits through increased support. The importance of assessment is further emphasized by the possibility that the diagnosis may be found not to be dementia and may be treatable. In chapter 15, recently developed approaches to assessment are described. Awareness of the availability of such instruments on the part of all those concerned with middle-aged and older people with intellectual disabilities is a key to the early response to a diagnosis of dementia.

Similarly, the awareness on the part of staff of patterns of behaviour associated with particular genetically determined syndromes should now be a key element of their knowledge. In recent years an increasing number of such syndromes or behavioural phenotypes have been identified. In a very real sense, any analysis of such syndromes cuts across several of the areas considered in this book (i.e. a given syndrome may be associated with mental health difficulties, challenging behaviour, possibly offending behaviour, profound and complex needs and certainly dementia, as in the case of Down syndrome).

This last point provides that justification for undertaking any assessment, i.e. that it has a meaningful outcome which will provide direction to how we can best support an individual. This in turn implies a certain degree of specificity. In contrast to Hogg and Raynes (1987), global measures of intelligence or adaptive behaviour are only considered in relation to the specific assessment of an individual rather than as providing general information to characterize a person. Thus, reference to intelligence tests such as the Wechsler Adult Intelligence Scale and adaptive behaviour scales such as the Vineland Adaptive Behavior Scales is made in the context of specific assessment topics (e.g. ch. 16 on behavioural phenotypes, rather than under a heading 'intelligence tests' or 'adaptive behaviour assessment').

The overall function of both the strategic approaches covered in this volume, and the more specific, often problem-orientated areas in which assessment is considered, should be seen as means by which positive support can be put in place. The techniques reported aim to enable a person to overcome barriers to meeting their aspirations. For this reason, effective professional assessment should be seen as complementary to person-centred planning, an essential adjunct to 'the principle that services should be tailored to individual needs, circumstances and wants' (Mansell & Beadle-Brown, 2004, p. 3).

Our original intention was to include information on tests and assessments in the appendices to each chapter in section 2. However, since publishers' details and websites can change in a short time, it was decided to omit this information. Readers are advised to undertake their own web-based searches in order to secure the most up-to-date information on material cited in the text.

REFERENCES

Bouras, N. (ed.) (1999) *Psychiatric and Behavioural Disorders in Developmental Disabilities and Mental Retardation*. Cambridge: Cambridge University Press.

Clare, I. C. H. & Murphy, G. H. (1998) Working with offenders or alleged offenders with intellectual disabilities. In E. Emerson, C. Hatton, J. Bromley & A. Caine (eds.), *Clinical Psychology and People with Intellectual Disabilities*. Chichester: Wiley, pp. 154–176.

Emerson, E. (2001) *Challenging Behaviour: Analysis and Intervention in People with Severe Intellectual Disabilities*. Cambridge: Cambridge University Press.

Hogg, J. & Raynes, N. V. (1987) Assessing people with mental handicap: Introduction. In J. Hogg & N. V. Raynes (eds.), *Assessment in Mental Handicap: A Guide to Assessment, Practices, Tests and Checklists*. London: Croom-Helm, pp. 1–11.

Janicki, M. P. & Dalton, A. J. (eds.) (1999) *Dementia, Aging, and Intellectual Disabilities: A Handbook*. Philadelphia, PA: Brunner/Maze.

Mansell, J. & Beadle-Brown, J. (2004) Person-centred planning or person-centred action? Policy and practice intellectual disability services. *Journal of Applied Research in Intellectual Disabilities*, 17, 1–9.

O'Brien, G. & Yule, W. (1995) *Behavioural Phenoypes*. London: MacKeith.

O'Brien, J. & Lovett, H. (1992) *Finding a Way Toward Everyday Lives: The Contribution of Person Centred Planning*. Harrisburg, PA: Pennsylvania Office of Mental Retardation.

Wolfensberger, W. (1994) Let's hang up 'Quality of Life' as a hopeless term. In D. Goode (ed.), *Quality of Life for Persons with Disabilities: International Perspectives and Issues*. Cambridge, MA: Brooklyn, pp. 285–321.

PART I

Conceptual issues in assessment

CHAPTER 1

Issues in the systematic assessment of quality of life

Robert A. Cummins

1 Introduction

In recent years, quality of life (QOL) has emerged as an important and controversial topic in the field of intellectual disability (Schalock et al., 2002). As one consequence, increasing attention has been focused on the issue of measurement, with all the attendant problems of reliability and validity (Cummins, 1997a). Such assessments have traditionally been made by measuring objective living conditions. So, for example, much attention has been paid to standard of accommodation, patterns of time expenditure, extent of interaction with the general community, and so on. Such data are usually in the form of counts or frequencies.

The best-known scales of this type are PASS and PASSING devised by Wolfensberger and colleagues (Wolfensberger & Glenn, 1975; Wolfensberger & Thomas, 1983). Ratings on instruments of this type are made by caregivers, staff members or researchers, almost never by the people who are the target of concern, and the data are used as some form of objective index of deficit relative to general population norms.

There are several problems in the interpretation of such data, and their contemporary usefulness in Western countries is now limited. These measures, driven by the ideology of 'normalization', were most relevant when attention could be drawn to the extremely deprived institutional environments that were commonplace in Australia, North America and Europe only a few decades ago. Now, however, the institutions have largely closed, most people with an intellectual disability live in community housing of some description, and attention can be paid to higher-order aspects of life quality than simply the living environment (Felce, 1998). There is also an interpretative problem with normalization data, in that they are based on a standard vision of normality, and, as such, they ignore individual preferences. In the general population, many people choose to live under circumstances that do not accord with the standards assumed by the normalization technology. It therefore fails to recognize that individuals who are intellectually disabled can experience a high quality life under living conditions that deviate substantially from society norms.

Certainly the material circumstances of living will always be relevant to the attainment of a high-quality life. But how people feel about their quality of life is the ultimate test of a life worth living (Schalock, 1997). And in circumstances where basic material needs are met, authors generally agree that the relationship between objective life circumstances and how people feel about their life is minimal (e.g. Cummins, 2000a; Headey, 1981; Spilker, 1990). Personal well-being in these terms is referred to as subjective well-being or subjective quality of life.

1.1 Subjective QOL

The measurement of subjective QOL is a controversial topic, most particularly for people with an intellectual disability (Ager & Hatton, 1999; Hatton & Ager, 2002). In a recent review of QOL assessment for people with an intellectual disability, Hensel (2001) concluded, 'There is a strong argument for abandoning the use of QOL measures, and in particular, subjective measures such as satisfaction, as a means of judging services and determining resource allocation' (p. 323). This strong assertion is based on the following concerns: (a) subjective QOL is stable and so not liable to reflect environmental variation; (b) proxy responding is likely to be invalid; (c) major problems exist in the delivery and interpretation of subjective scales of measurement; (d) Hatton (1998) has argued that adopting a QOL agenda based on subjective measures disenfranchises peoples with severe/profound levels of intellectual disability. Let me address these concerns.

In two earlier papers (Cummins, 2001, 2002b) I addressed the issues raised by Hatton and Ager, and provided a detailed argument that subjective QOL measurement is useful precisely *because* it is so stable. As background to this discussion, we (Cummins et al., 2002; Cummins & Nistico, 2002) have proposed that subjective QOL is held under homeostatic control. In other words, it is held within a narrow range of values in a manner analogous to the homeostatic maintenance of blood pressure and body temperature. These medical 'vital signs' are crucial diagnostic indices for pathology precisely because they are normally so predictable. So it is also for subjective QOL. The normal range has been described (Cummins, 1995; Cummins et al., 2002) and deviations from this range, invariably downward, are indicative of homeostatic failure.

The problems of proxy responding and measurement procedures, highlighted by Hensel (2001), are technical issues. They require that care be taken with the process of data collection. They are certainly not so intractable that all efforts at measurement should be abandoned, and solutions to the identified problems will be discussed later. On one point, however, Hensel and I agree. This is that subjective QOL should not be used as the sole means of judging service delivery. Such measurement is mainly useful to detect homeostatic failure. Therefore, given the power of the adaptive process, services considered substandard through the use of objective criteria may not be bad enough to cause chronic homeostatic failure. Because of this, QOL assessments for the purpose of judging services and for determining resource allocation should employ both subjective and objective measurement.

1.2 Quality of Life assessment

Objective QOL variables are those that can be simultaneously observed by a number of people, and involve estimates of frequencies or quantities. For example, these can include the number of friends a person has or the degree of disability. While all such estimations involve various degrees of judgment, they constitute a form of measurement that, at least in theory, and with sufficiently careful attention, could yield a high degree of agreement among people making the rating.

Subjective variables, on the other hand, can only be directly experienced by individuals themselves, such as the degree of felt happiness or satisfaction. Consequently, the only valid method of measurement is to ask the individuals concerned how they feel about various aspects of their lives. It is not generally valid to infer subjective QOL either from ratings made by other people (i.e. proxy responses – see later), or from objective measures.

Numerous studies have shown that, except under unusual circumstances, there is remarkably little relationship between objective and subjective variables due to the operation of homeostasis (see Cummins, 2000a, for a review). For example, the correlation between subjective QOL and wealth is generally very low (Cummins, 2000b). Perhaps more surprising is the low degree of correspondence when objective and subjective measurements are made in relation to a similar life domain. For example, there is a generally low correlation between the extent of material possessions and satisfaction with wealth (e.g. Flanagan, 1978), or between physical health and perceived health (e.g. DeStefano & Richardson, 1992). The reason for these discrepancies lies in a plethora of psychological mechanisms that allow most people to maintain a feeling of personal well-being despite adverse circumstances. Many of these mechanisms are dispositional and include various processes of adaptation, selective-attention and social comparison, which act in concert to maintain the average level of subjective QOL at around 75% of the measurement scale maximum (Cummins et al., 2003).

The scales that measure subjective QOL are described in chapter 9. They all use the technique that asks people how they feel about their lives, and this can be operationalized by questions of satisfaction directed to various life domains. For example, 'How satisfied are you with your health?', with the response recorded on a Likert scale. While at a surface level this may seem fairly straightforward, it is actually not. There are numerous pitfalls in instrument construction, administration, and data analysis. Some of these will now be discussed.

2 Issues in Instrument Construction

2.1 Instrument content

Which aspects of life (domains) should be chosen to represent subjective QOL? Reviews on this issue have found considerable common ground (Cummins, 1997b; Felce & Perry, 1995; Cummins et al., 2002). Nevertheless, authors invariably use an idiosyncratic mixture of items and rarely provide their rationale. This is an unfortunate situation. It means that there is no agreed, simple scale, with which to measure the subjective QOL construct. This measurement problem is compounded by the very poor state of psychometric investigation into most scales. Many do not even have a published factor analysis. As a consequence, the data collected by these various instruments are not strictly comparable. This means that any reviewer of the subjective QOL literature who combines studies that have used different instruments is at risk of drawing false conclusions.

2.2 Combining objective and subjective indicators

Objective and subjective indicators normally have a very low degree of relationship with one another (for a review see Cummins, 2000a). They are also conceptually distinct, since objective is tangible and subjective is not. Consequently, combining such indices into a single index is invalid, since the derived score cannot be simply interpreted. The Quality of Life Questionnaire (QOLQ) (Schalock & Keith, 1993) can be used as an example. As detailed in chapter 9, this instrument comprises four subscales, and each uses a combination of objective and subjective items.

Rapley and Hopgood (1997) conducted a study of convergent validity on 34 people with an intellectual disability living in community-based residences. The other instruments were two objective scales (Raynes et al., 1989a, 1989b, Indexes of participation in domestic life and community), a subjective scale (Neighborhood Sense of Community Index, Pretty et al., 1994), and the Adaptive Behavior Scale (ABS) (Nihira et al., 1975). The ABS Part 1 measures the individual's effectiveness in coping with the natural and social demands of the environment, while Part 2 measures maladaptive and undesirable behaviour. (For a full discussion of ABS Part 2 see ch. 13.)

The pattern of correlations shown in table 1.1 indicates the dominance of the objective items within the QOLQ. Correlations are positive with the two objective scales and with adaptive behaviour (ABS Part 1). However, correlations are non-significant, or even negative, with the subjective scale. It is particularly instructive that the 'Social Belonging' subscale failed to correlate significantly with 'Sense of Community'. These results show how the subjective measures have been swamped by the inclusion of objective items in the same scale. Measures of objective and subjective life quality must be made separately.

2.3 Measuring perceived importance

Some scales have used the perceived importance of scale items as a weighting factor for item satisfaction (e.g. Comprehensive Quality of Life Scale, Cummins, 1997c). That is, they ask 'How satisfied are you with x?', and then ask 'How important to you is x?' A combined variable is then created by multiplying the two values together (satisfaction score [mult] importance score).

Table 1.1 The Quality of Life Questionnaire (QOLQ): Convergent Validity

	Participation in Domestic Life	Community Participation	Sense of Community	ABS Part 1	ABS Part 2
QOLQ Total score	.67**	.35**	[minus].17	.30**	[minus].27
Competence	.66**	.35*	[minus].35*	.09	–
Empowerment	.48**	.06	.00	.34*	–
Satisfaction	.55**	.16	[minus].02	.40**	–
Social Belonging	[minus].19	.27	.17	[minus].12	–

This procedure has considerable intuitive appeal. It seems reasonable to enhance the weighting of satisfaction from a life-area the respondent considers highly important. Unfortunately, however, such a procedure is logically and psychometrically flawed.

People can regard areas of their life as important for a wide variety of reasons. For example, they may see something as important because they do not have it and want it (e.g. an expensive car), or because they have it and do not want it (e.g. chronic pain), or because they have it and wish to retain it (e.g. political power). The logical link to satisfaction between these alternatives is very mixed.

At a psychometric level, Trauer and MacKinnon (2001) have empirically demonstrated the invalidity of using such multiplicative composites (importance [mult] satisfaction), which are actually interaction terms, as dependant variables. Additionally, Lau and Cummins (submitted) have demonstrated that variables rated on importance form a fragile factorial structure. Such fragility is consistent with the variety of reasons people may regard something as important to them. I conclude that perceived importance is an ambiguous variable and most certainly should not be used to weight satisfaction. Further discussion of this matter can be found in a Web document (Cummins, 2003).

2.4 Normative scale reference

The criteria for judging a life of high quality should be the same for all people. Unfortunately, this is not evident in the majority of subjective QOL scales for people who have an intellectual disability. Such scales tend to set the bar too low. For example, these scales commonly include items on autonomy and community integration. The implication is that high autonomy and living in a community setting are linearly related to high life quality. This, however, is false. People who are not disabled generally have high levels of these variables, and yet would not regard either as very relevant to their life quality. In other words, such scales use a different, lower, criterion for judging high life quality than would be applied to the general community of non-disabled people. This is an undesirable situation. It means that the scales measure degrees of deficit rather than life quality. A scale to measure autonomy measures autonomy, not life quality.

2.5 Alternative scale formats and procedures

In an effort to create scales that are less cognitively demanding than conventional Likert scales, authors have experimented with various alternatives. The most popular among these is a row of stylized faces ranging from unhappy to happy. The implicit assumption is that pointing to faces, in order to indicate relative levels of satisfaction or happiness, is a simpler task than verbal responding. Perhaps this is true, but the assumption has not been tested by any study of which I am aware. Moreover there are good reasons to be cautious. First, there is no standard form of such scales, each author assuming that his or her own depiction of a happy/sad face captures the essential elements required for recognition of the affective difference. The essential graphical criteria, which form the basis for such depictions, are assumed to be universal and so not defined. This is likely to be highly contestable, most certainly for the depiction of affective states intermediate between overtly happy and sad. Second, while differences between artists' depictions of happy/sad may be unimportant for non-disabled people, the essential elements of the faces become more relevant as the respondents' cognitive ability decreases. As is well known, people with an intellectual disability have more difficulty than non-disabled people in the recognition of facial expressions (e.g. Adams & Markham, 1991; McAlpine et al., 1991).

A different approach has been provided by Dagnan and Ruddick (1995). Within a group of mild/moderately disabled people they found two alternative formats to provide reliable data. These were a visual analogue scale anchored by visual images such as happy/sad faces, and a 'three-point personal questionnaire'. This latter device comprises three possible paired response options; for example, 'very satisfied / not satisfied', 'not satisfied / quite satisfied', and 'quite satisfied / very satisfied'. The respondent selects a preferred response from *each* of the three combinations. The advantage of this method is that the responses can be used to create a 4-point scale. That is: 4 = very, quite, very; 3 = very, quite, quite; 2 = not, quite, quite; 1 = not, not, quite. Any other combination is considered inconsistent responding. The authors found both of these methods yielded reliable data. However, both are more time-consuming than using Likert scales. So whether the additional effort is worthwhile, in terms of yielding data with greater validity and reliability beyond a simple Likert scale, remains to be determined.

An alternative procedure for the delivery of subjective QOL questionnaires is to employ people with an intellectual disability as trained interviewers (Bonham et al., 2004). The rationale is that such people are better able to rephrase questions than a non-disabled interviewer. While this may seem to be a sympathetic technique, the serious problems of rephrasing identified by Rapley and colleagues (see later) apply equally here. Until convincing validation studies have been published to support the use of this technique, it cannot be recommended.

3 Issues in Test Administration

3.1 Pre-testing for respondent acquiescence and comprehension

A major challenge for subjective QOL measurement in the areas of intellectual disability is asking questions that lie within the cognitive capacity of the respondent. For them, comprehension at an abstract level, which is inherent in subjective measurement, is difficult or even impossible. This has clear implications for test construction. It means that questions must be as simple as possible, sentences must be kept short, negatives must be avoided, and so on. In other words, close attention must be paid to all the technical issues that make comprehension easier. But even after attending to such matters, there remains the fundamental issue of whether respondents are simply going to agree fully with whatever question they are asked, and also whether they are able to comprehend the question. These matters can, and must, be resolved using pre-testing.

Pre-testing involves screening for both acquiescence and performance competence. Testing for acquiescence may involve just a single question, such as that used by Kishi et al. (1988): 'Do you choose who lives next door?' However, since random responding will produce a 50% hit-rate for such a binary choice, more than one such question is recommended. Testing for acquiescence can also be built into the interview (see Finlay & Lyons, 2002, for a review). This may involve the inclusion of nonsense questions, pairs of questions that are opposite in meaning, asking questions using multiple formats, and informant checks on objective data. Data analysis should also involve screening for response sets as part of quality control (see later).

The ability of respondents to use Likert scales can be tested using the protocol described by Cummins (1997c) in relation to the ComQol-ID scale. If people are unable to complete the prescribed series of tasks, it can reasonably be inferred that they would not be capable of validly responding to questions that require them to estimate degrees of a subjective variable, such as degrees of satisfaction. If they are allowed to remain in the tested sample, they may respond in either a random or an acquiescent manner, thereby introducing either random or systematic error variance.

A carefully conducted study by Hensel et al. (2002) is exemplary in showing how such screening should take place. Their screening occurred in three stages as follows:

- A variety of professionals were asked to identify people with an intellectual disability 'who would be interested in taking part in the research and who were able to communicate verbally' (p. 98).
- The researchers then followed the protocol suggested by Arscott et al. (1998) to establish both verbal understanding and informed consent. In the presence of a staff member who knew the nominated person well, the research procedure was explained. The person was then asked the following questions in order to establish his or her understanding:
  - What will I be talking to you about?
  - How many times will I want to talk to you?
  - Are there any good things about talking to me?
  - Are there any bad things about talking to me?
  - What can you do if you decide you don't want to talk to me anymore?

Using a criterion of at least three appropriate responses, six people, or 14% of the original sample, were eliminated from the study.

- The ComQol-ID scale (Cummins, 1997c) pre-test was employed and a further five people were eliminated. In all, 11 people, or 26% of the original sample, were discovered to be unable to complete the required task, and this was despite the original search profile requiring that people were able to communicate verbally. The importance of such careful screening can hardly be exaggerated.

3.2 Verbal scale administration

When people have difficulty reading a questionnaire on their own, test administrators often resort to reading it aloud to the respondent, with the implicit assumption that such a procedure is psychometrically equivalent. It is not. The most obvious problem is that the respondents are not autonomous and their responses are not private. They are being asked to express their feelings in the presence of another person and, typically, this will create a tendency for them to respond more positively than they would otherwise have done (e.g.

Shields & Wooden, 2002). More important, however, the verbal presentation may make the task of comprehension more difficult for the following reasons:

- They must show a high level of attention each time the assessor speaks.
- They cannot easily rerun the text for themselves, as they could if they were reading.
- They must be able to transcend issues of accent and inflection, and be able to match the speed of speech delivery with their own speed of cognitive processing.
- If they are required to remember the response options, these must be recalled and matched with their understanding of the question.

In this context, the Quality of Life Questionnaire (Schalock & Keith, 1993) is instructive. The interviewer reads each question aloud, followed by the response options, which differ from question to question. The person being interviewed then provides a verbal response. For example, the interviewer reads, 'How successful do you think you are compared to others?', and follows this with the response options of 'Probably more successful than the average person,' 'About as successful as the average person,' and 'Less successful than the average person.' While this procedure overcomes the problem of literacy levels, it clearly introduces a high cognitive demand that would, in some instances, be challenging even for people who are not intellectually disabled. Consider the following example: 'What about opportunities for dating or marriage?' The response provision is, 'I am married, or have the opportunity to date anyone I choose,' 'I have limited opportunities to date or marry' and 'I have no opportunity to date or marry.'

When the respondent cannot understand the question or recall the response options, these problems may be compounded by allowing the interviewer to paraphrase. This permission is made explicit in the QOLQ manual, as 'You may paraphrase items and repeat them as often as necessary to ensure the respondent's understanding of the item content' (p. 14). This procedure is likely to generate two forms of error variance. The first is derived from interviewers paraphrasing questions in novel ways, thereby leading to different questions being asked from those intended. This has been documented in the administration of the QOLQ by Houtkoop-Steenstra and Antaki (1997).

The second problem arises from a form of induced acquiescence first reported by Rapley and Antaki (1995) and Antaki and Rapley (1996). These authors undertook a detailed analysis of the verbal interactions between interviewer and interviewee while the QOLQ was being administered. They discovered that, when an initial answer was not immediately accepted by the interviewer, continued dialogue very often resulted in the interviewees changing their response. That is, the process of repeating and paraphrasing an item in different ways following a response was likely interpreted by the interviewees as an indication that their initial response was wrong or unacceptable. So they change it. This finding has deep ramifications, not only for the use of the QOLQ, but as a broader issue of attempting to elicit elaborated responses from people with an intellectual disability.

As an extension of this research, Antaki (1999) has shown that, during these interactions between the interviewer and the respondent, the interviewers tend to redesign the questions in such a way that the respondent ends up getting a higher score than would otherwise be the case. Overall it seems clear this research has exemplified the considerable dangers to scale validity caused by interpretative interaction over the meaning of scale items and responses.

3.3 Proxy responding

It is now well documented that people with a severe level of intellectual disability cannot respond for themselves to either the Quality of Life Questionnaire (see Campo et al., 1996) or the ComQol-ID scale (Cummins, 1997c). This raises the issue of whether responses should be provided by someone else answering 'on behalf of' the person with the disability. Such responses are called 'proxy', 'third-party' or 'vicarious' and it is now well established that the data provided through this means bear little relationship to how the person actually feels, even when the respondent knows the person very well (see Cummins & Baxter, 1994; Cummins et al., 1997; Stancliffe, 1999). Proxy responses to questions of subjective QOL are invalid (see Cummins, 2002a, for a review).

4 Issues in Data Screening

As has been stated, any subjective QOL data set, derived from people with an intellectual disability, is highly likely to contain some consistently high scores derived from people who have employed an acquiescent response mode. Unless such data are removed from the data-set prior to analysis, they will form a subset of high scores that will systematically distort both difference and relationship statistics.

An example of these dangers has been provided by Kazdin et al. (1983). Engaging a sample of people with a range of intellectual disability from borderline to severe, they report good convergent validity between a number of depression scales. These results, however, require scrutiny. The authors report no pre-testing for respondent competence. This is of special concern, since the sample included people with a severe level of intellectual disability. Further, the authors report correlations of [minus].42 to [minus].47 between IQ and the depression scales. Since there is no good reason to expect higher depression in people with lower IQ, the more likely explanation is acquiescent responding by people in the severe category. That is, the people with the lowest IQ consistently responded at the top of any scale presented to them. This acquiescent response strategy gave the impression of both high depression and convergent validity between the depression scales.

5 Scales for People with Severe and Profound Disability

Self-responding to subjective QOL scales is not an option for people who have a severe or profound level of intellectual disability. They can only have their QOL estimated by other means.

One alternative is to measure happiness through behaviour. For such a purpose, Green and Reid (1996) define happiness as 'any facial expression or vocalization typically considered to be an indicator of happiness among people without disabilities including smiling, laughing, and yelling while smiling' (p. 69).

Some measure of success has been reported using such behavioural techniques (e.g. Green & Reid, 1999). But care does need to be taken. As noted by Green and Reid (1996), there are three major methodological issues:

- The extent to which the manifest behaviours reflect an inner state of happiness cannot be known with certainty. However, as long as the indicative behaviours are restricted to the most obvious associated behaviours in non-disabled people, the technique has strong face validity.
- Reliability of measurement is an issue that can be largely resolved by limiting the 'happiness' criteria to overt behaviour displays. Green and Reid (1996) did this and found an acceptable level of inter-rater agreement.
- The issue of whether the manifest behaviour represents happiness, or is intended to serve some other purpose, is a major concern. For example, the act of smiling may occur for social or operant reasons, such as attempting to avoid displeasing someone who is attempting to be humorous, even though the person may not, actually, be feeling happy.

Green and Reid suggest this last concern is unlikely to be an issue for people who are profoundly intellectually disabled. They exhibit few behaviours that are under apparent social control. It may, however, be an issue for people with higher levels of cognitive functioning. For example, Yu et al. (2002) found no difference in the levels of observed happiness between people with profound or severe levels of disability when the measures were taken at work. However, when the two groups were compared during leisure activities 'provided by staff for the participants' enjoyment' (p. 423), the happiness ratings of those with severe ID were four times those of individuals in the group with profound ID. Of course, it is not possible to know whether the cognitive advantage of the former group allowed them to experience greater happiness at leisure. It does seem prudent, however, to regard the observational measurement technique as potentially less valid for people with higher levels of cognitive functioning.

The final approach, to be mentioned here, is the determination of preference between available options, with the aim of structuring people's environment in a way to maximize their overall quality of life. A detailed and thoughtful description of a methodology for determining choice preference is provided by Green et al. (1988). These authors found no correlation between preferences determined by their systematic, observational approach and preferences based on caregiver opinion. A clear implication of this study is that carers should place little confidence in making informal judgements about choice and preference.

6 Conclusion

Several recommendations emerge from the preceding review:

1. *Questions must be kept simple and unambiguous.* Questions must refer to just one unambiguous topic, be phrased in the positive, and contain no words that lie outside common usage of the client group.
2. *The response options must be understood before questioning commences.* Use a simple, standard response choice, and ensure that the interviewee is familiar with the response options before questioning commences.
3. *Verbal presentations must be tightly controlled.* The interviewer must *not* attempt to reinterpret questions or responses. A question can be repeated if it is not heard in the first

instance but, if no response or an indeterminate response is provided, the interviewer should proceed to the next item.

4. *Subjective and objective items must not be combined to form a scale.* While it may be useful to measure both objective and subjective data, each form of data must be confined within separate scales.

5. *Satisfaction responses should not be weighted by perceived importance.* This procedure is logically and psychometrically invalid.

6. *Pre-testing, to establish respondent competence, is essential.* While this may be viewed as undesirable, because of the additional testing time involved, it is absolutely necessary in order to exclude people who cannot understand the task they are being asked to perform.

7. *Data must be screened for acquiescent response patterns.* Journal editors should insist that authors of empirical reports describe their data-screening methodology.

Chapter 9 of this volume constitutes a review of selected instruments used to measure the QOL of people with an intellectual disability. The recommendations above will be incorporated within the criteria for judging the relative usefulness of these instruments.[1]

NOTE

1 I thank Ann-Marie for her assistance in the preparation of this chapter.

REFERENCES

Adams, K. & Markham, R. (1991) Recognition of affective facial expressions by children and adolescents with and without mental retardation. *American Journal on Mental Retardation*, **96**, 21–28.

Ager, A. & Hatton, C. (1999) Discerning the appropriate role and status of 'quality of life' assessment for persons with intellectual disability: A reply to Cummins. *Journal of Applied Research in Intellectual Disabilities*, **12**, 335–339.

Antaki, C. (1999) Interviewing persons with a learning disability: How setting lower standards may inflate well-being scores. *Qualitative Health Research*, **9**, 437–454.

Antaki, C. & Rapley, M. (1996) 'Quality of Life' talk: The liberal paradox of psychological testing. *Discourse and Society*, 7, 293–316.

Arscott, K., Dagnan, D. & Kroses, B. S. (1998) Consent to psychological research by people with an intellectual disability. *Journal of Applied Research in Intellectual Disabilities*, **11**, 77–83.

Bonham, G. S., Basehart, S., Schalock, R. L., Marchand, C. B., Kirchner, N. & Rumencap, J. M. (2004) *Consumer Based Quality of Life Assessment: The Maryland Ask Me! Project*. Mental Retardation. *Mental Retardation*, **42**, 338–355.

Campo, S. F., Sharpton, W. R., Thompson, B. & Sexton, D. (1996) Measurement characteristics of the quality of life index when used with adults who have severe mental retardation. *American Journal on Mental Retardation*, **100**, 546–550.

Cummins, R. A. (1995) On the trail of the gold standard for life satisfaction. *Social Indicators Research*, **35**, 179–200.

Cummins, R. A. (1997a) Self-rated quality of life scales for people with an intellectual disability: A review. *Journal of Applied Research in Intellectual Disabilities*, **10**, 199–216.

Cummins, R. A. (1997b) Assessing quality of life. In R. Brown (ed.), *Quality of Life for People with Disabilities*. Cheltenham: Stanley Thornes, pp. 116–150.

Cummins, R. A. (1997c) *Comprehensive Quality of Life Scale – Intellectual/cognitive disability*. Manual (5th ed.). Melbourne: School of Psychology, Deakin University (pp. 1–81).

Cummins, R. A. (2000a) Objective and subjective quality of life: An interactive model. *Social Indicators Research*, 52, 55–72.

Cummins, R. A. (2000b) Personal income and happiness: A review. *Journal of Happiness Studies*, 1, 133–158.

Cummins, R. A. (2001) Self-rate quality of life scales for people with an intellectual disability: A reply to Ager and Hatton. *Journal of Applied Research in Intellectual Disabilities*, 14, 1–11.

Cummins, R. A. (2002a) Proxy respond for subjective well-being: A review. *International Review of Research in Mental Retardation*, 25, 183–207.

Cummins, R. A. (2002b) The validity and utility of subjective wellbeing: A reply to Hatton and Ager. *Journal of Applied Research in Intellectual Disabilities*, 15, 261–268.

Cummins, R. A. (2003) *Caveats to Using the Comprehensive Quality of Life Scale* (http://acqol.deakin.edu.au/instruments/index.htm).

Cummins, R. A. & Baxter, C. (1994) Choice of outcome measures in service evaluations for people with an intellectual disability. *Evaluation Journal of Australasia*, 6, 22–30.

Cummins, R. A., Eckersley, R., Pallant, J., van Vugt, J. & Misajon, R. (2003) The development of a national index of subjective wellbeing: The Australian Unity Wellbeing Index. *Social Indicators Research*, 64, 159–190.

Cummins, R. A., Gullone, E. & Lau, A. L. D. (2002) A model of subjective well being homeostasis: The role of personality. In E. Gullone & R. A. Cummins (eds.), *The Universality of Subjective Wellbeing Indicators: Social Indicators Research Series*. Dordrecht: Kluwer, pp. 7–46.

Cummins, R. A., McCabe, M. P., Romeo, Y., Reid, S. & Waters, L. (1997) An initial evaluation of the Comprehensive Quality of Life Scale – Intellectual Disability. *International Journal of Disability, Development and Education*, 44, 7–19.

Cummins, R. A. & Nistico, H. (2002) Maintaining life satisfaction: The role of positive cognitive bias. *Journal of Happiness Studies*, 3, 37–69.

Dagnan, D. & Ruddick, L. (1995) The use of analogue scales and personal questionnaires for interviewing people with learning disabilities. *Clinical Psychology Forum*, 79, 21–24.

DeStefano, T. J. & Richardson, P. (1992) The relationship of paper-and-pencil wellness measures to objective physiological indexes. *Journal of Counseling and Development*, 71, 226–230.

Felce, D. (1998) The determinants of staff and resident activity in residential services for people with severe intellectual disability: Moving beyond size, building design, location and number of staff. *Journal of Intellectual and Developmental Disability*, 23, 103–119.

Felce, D. & Perry, J. (1995) Quality of life: Its definition and measurement. *Research in Developmental Disabilities*, 16, 51–74.

Finlay, W. M. L. & Lyons, E. (2002) Acquiescence in interviews with people who have mental retardation. *Mental Retardation*, 40, 14–29.

Flanagan, J. C. (1978) A research approach to improving our quality of life. *American Psychologist*, 33, 138–147.

Green, C. W. & Reid, D. H. (1996) Defining, validating, and increasing indices of happiness among people with profound multiple disabilities. *Journal of Applied Behavior Analysis*, 29, 67–78.

Green, C. W., & Reid, D. H. (1999) A behavioral approach to identifying sources of happiness and unhappiness among individuals with profound multiple disabilities. *Behavior Modification*, 23, 280–294.

Green, C. W., Reid, D. H., White, L. K., Halford, R. C., Brittain, D. P. & Gardner, S. M. (1988) Identifying reinforcers for persons with profound handicaps: Staff opinion versus systematic assessment of preferences. *Journal of Applied Behavior Analysis*, 21, 31–43.

Hatton, C. (1998) Whose quality of life is it anyway? Some problems with the emerging quality of life consensus. *Mental Retardation*, **36**, 104–115.

Hatton, C. & Ager, A. (2002) Quality of life measurement and people with intellectual disabilities: A reply to Cummins. *Journal of Applied Research in Intellectual Disabilities*, **15**, 254–260.

Headey, B. (1981) The quality of life in Australia. *Social Indicators Research*, **9**, 155–181.

Hensel, E. (2001) Is satisfaction a valid concept in the assessment of quality of life of people with intellectual disabilities? A review of the literature. *Journal of Applied Research in Intellectual Disabilities*, **14**, 311–326.

Hensel, E., Rose, J., Stenfert Kroses, B. & Banks-Smith, J. (2002) Subjective judgments of quality of life: A comparison study between those people with intellectual disability and those without disability. *Journal of Intellectual Disability Research*, **46**, 95–107.

Houtkoop-Steenstra, H. & Antaki, C. (1997) Creating happy people by asking yes–no questions. *Research on Language and Social Interaction*, **30**, 285–313.

Kazdin, A. E., Matson, J. L. & Senatore, V. (1983) Assessment and depression in mentally retarded adults. *American Journal of Psychiatry*, **140**, 1040–1043.

Kishi, G., Teelucksingh, B., Zollers, N., Park-Lee, S. & Meyer, L. (1988) Daily decision-making in community residences: A social comparison of adults with and without mental retardation. *American Journal on Mental Retardation*, **92**, 430–435.

Lau, A. L. D. & Cummins, R. A. (submitted) Why perceived importance is not worth measuring: Quality of life among stroke survivors in Hong Kong.

McAlpine, C., Kendall, K. A. & Singh, N. N. (1991) Recognition of facial expressions of emotion by persons with mental retardation. *American Journal on Mental Retardation*, **96**, 29–36.

Nihira, K., Foster, R., Shellhaas, M. & Leland, H. (1975) *American Association on Mental Deficiency Adaptive Behavior Scale*. Washington, DC: American Association on Mental Deficiency.

Pretty, G. M. H., Andrews, L. & Collett, C. (1994) Exploring adolescents' sense of community and its relationship to loneliness. *Journal of Community Psychology*, **22**, 346–358.

Rapley, M. & Antaki, C. (1995) A conversation analysis of the 'acquiescence' of people with learning disabilities. *Journal of Community and Applied Social Psychology*, **6**, 207–227.

Rapley, M. & Hopgood, L. (1997) Quality of life in a community-based service in rural Australia. *Journal of Intellectual and Developmental Disability*, **22**, 125–141.

Raynes, N. V., Sumpton, R. C. & Pettipher, C. (1989a) *The Index of Community Involvement*. Manchester, UK: Department of Social Policy and Social Work, University of Manchester.

Raynes, N. V., Sumpton, R. C. & Pettipher, C. (1989b) *The Index of Participation and Domestic Life*. Manchester, UK: Department of Social Policy and Social Work, University of Manchester.

Schalock, R. L. (1997) The conceptualization and measurement of quality of life: Current status and future considerations. *Journal of Developmental Disabilities*, **5**, 1–21.

Schalock, R. L., Brown, I., Brown, R., Cummins, R. A., Felce, D., Matikka, L., Keith, K. D. & Parmenter, T. (2002) Conceptualization, measurement, and application of quality of life for persons with intellectual disabilities: Report on an international panel of experts. *Mental Retardation*, **40**, 457–470.

Schalock, R. L. & Keith, K. D. (1993) *Quality of Life Questionnaire*. Ohio: IDS Publishing.

Shields, M. & Wooden, M. (2002) The importance of where you live for life satisfaction. Paper presented at the 4th Australian Conference on Quality of Life, Deakin University, Toorak.

Spilker, B. (1990) Introduction. In B. Spilker (ed.), *Quality of Life Assessments in Clinical Trials*. New York: Raven Press, pp. 3–9.

Stancliffe, R. J. (1999) Proxy respondents and reliability of the quality of life questionnaire empowerment factor. *Journal of Intellectual Disability Research*, **43**, 185–194.

Trauer, T. & MacKinnon, A. (2001) Why are we weighting? The role of importance ratings in quality of life measurement. *Quality of Life Research*, **10**, 579–585.

Wolfensberger, W. & Glenn, L. (1975) *Program Analysis of Service Systems (PASS): A Method for the Quantitative Evaluation of Human Services. Field Manual* (3rd ed.). Toronto: National Institute on Mental Retardation.

Wolfensberger, W. & Thomas, S. (1983) *PASSING (Program Analysis of Service Systems' Implementation of Normalization Goals): Normalization Criteria and Ratings Manual.* Toronto: National Institute on Mental Retardation.

Yu, D. C. T., Spevack, S., Hiebert, R., Martin, T. L., Goodman, R., Martin, T. G., Harapiak, S. & Martin, G. L. (2002) Happiness indices among persons with profound and severe disabilities during leisure and work activities: A comparison. *Education and Training in Mental Retardation and Developmental Disabilities*, 37, 421–426.

CHAPTER 2

Outside the box: assessment for life and work in the community

Patricia Noonan Walsh

1 Introduction

> Jim, aged 19, grasps the wooden peg with his right hand, moving it slowly across the well-worn board. He falters, glancing at the face of the psychologist seated across the table. Here – is this right? Jim hesitates . . . he raises an eyebrow and glances at his companion to check. But this is not a game. If he completes the task surely and swiftly according to the norms prescribed by a local employment service agency, Jim may well celebrate adulthood by moving to a sheltered workshop. Just last month, an occupational therapist travelled with him between home and the workshop to observe Jim's prowess using the city buses. Jim knows he will soon leave school, although he is not sure what he will do next year, or the year after that. Nor does he understand why the perplexing array of boxes, boards, pegs, pens, puzzles and switches presented to him this morning are worth the effort. But he is an obliging young man, and keeps at it. After some moments, he finds a slot for the peg that seems to fit. There! Jim leans back and grins with satisfaction.

In countries with formal service systems, thousands of people like Jim were stuck for years or decades in a furrow not of their making. In Europe, many worked for their adult lives as long-term *trainees* completing contract assembly or production jobs for a token weekly wage. To fit such schemes, European adults with disabilities underwent assessment to determine their suitability for special vocational and other day activity programmes. Living far longer than expected when they entered service systems, many resilient older adults have been relabelled as retired people or pensioners without spending a single day in the ordinary workforce.

During the last decades of the twentieth century, striking changes in legislation and policy redirected employment pathways for people with intellectual disabilities. Federal laws in the United States passed by Congress and subsequently re-authorized gradually widened access to meaningful work. For example, PL (Public Law) 106–170, or the Work Incentives Improvement Act, required networks to serve people with significant disabilities, a group hitherto excluded from such initiatives (Croser, 2002). National governments in Australia, Israel and elsewhere have created incentive programmes making it worthwhile for private agencies to train and recruit employees with disabilities (Bickenbach, 2001).

Today in Europe, a rights-based model of disability specifies equality of opportunity as the benchmark, supplanting an earlier model in which the person was the locus of the problem rather than a social and physical environment (Quinn, 1999). The European Union endorses a rights-based rather than a welfare-based model of disability as the engine of its social policy for this population of citizens (Commission of the European Communities, 1998). Through the lens of equity, Jim is viewed not as a dependent misfit who will never pay taxes. Rather, he is a European citizen whose existing political, economic, educational and vocational resources to date may be found wanting as they do not give him a chance to take a full part in community life. National policy and practice guidelines aim to promote the quality of life and social inclusion of adults with intellectual and other developmental disabilities; for example, in England (Department of Health, 2001), Scotland (Scottish Executive, 2000), Ireland (Government of Ireland, 1996) and elsewhere. Once funded, policies may drive initiatives to build employment and other community supports for adults.

New models of support are worthy of a refreshed look at assessment. Formerly, care providers assessed needs for a set menu of goods and services devised to help people with disabilities make good their deficits as best they could. Men and women with intellectual disabilities who proved that they could not use public transport were collected in a special van emblazoned with the benefactor's logo. Those who failed tests presumed to predict their future contribution to workshop productivity were sidetracked entirely from the critical path to employment and rolled to dead-end dayrooms. While these practices persist in all too many cities and towns, current approaches increasingly focus on individualized supports so that adults with intellectual disabilities may choose and experience satisfying, ordinary leisure and work opportunities. Even so, what does assessment mean? What is being assessed, and for what purpose?

Such questions provoke a debate on employment itself. Is full employment the only qualifier for full citizenship? If a person with significant limitations travels to an office park to carry out a micro-task laboriously with intensive support for a few hours a week, holding down a 'real job', is it worth the effort? Perhaps not financially, but it may be if she enjoys these sessions very much and her family and friends are gratified. In the context of domains of the quality of life construct (Schalock & Verdugo, 2002, table 9.2), for example, employment plays many parts. It may express an aspect of the individual's 'material well-being', a performance indicator within 'personal development', a measure of 'self-determination' or even 'rights'. Arguably, conferring the right to employment on all individuals regardless of their type or level of disability makes any assessment score redundant in deciding whether or not a person can work: the procedure is useful if it helps effect an optimal fit of person and job.

This chapter adopts a contextual approach to current issues in the assessment of adults with intellectual disabilities. First, it introduces themes important for understanding the needs of individuals within their families, communities and the wider environment. Next, it offers a brief history of how men and women with intellectual disabilities were typically assessed as prospective residents or employees in the recent past. Third, it asks whether the box of various assessment tools carried forward into the twenty-first century will prove worth the trouble of transporting them. Finally, some strategies are presented for those charged with assessing needs and providing supports.

2 Current Themes

If not always expressed in day-to-day practice, current policies focus on attaining an enhanced quality of life for people with intellectual disabilities based on individual needs and preferences in the context of their own homes, families and cultures. These themes recur in government policy documents and the mission statements of many service-provider agencies.

2.1 Quality of life

With appealing simplicity, quality of life has gained global currency as the leading personal and political target for all citizens, including those with disabilities, or who are otherwise disadvantaged in their own countries. But quality of life has also emerged as a 'potentially unifying construct in setting the goals for services and measuring their impact on the character of people's day-to-day lives' (Felce, 1997, p. 126). It measures the effectiveness of supports by how well they achieve desired personal outcomes for people with intellectual or other disabilities. On an applied level, quality of life indicators have yet to be attained in service systems of many countries (Rapley & Beyer, 1998). Conceptually, critics debate the reliability of measures of subjective well-being – for example, how to understand directly the experiences of people with severe intellectual disabilities or with few communication skills (Hatton, 1998). Nonetheless, consensus is emerging. Quality of life is a multidimensional construct; both subjective and objective components must be assessed; and it is a suitable yardstick to appraise outcomes of services for individuals with developmental disabilities. For a full discussion of both the complexity of conceptualizing and measuring quality of life, see chapter 1.

2.2 Self-determination

Self-determination has emerged from civil rights movements to form a key element in conceptualizing quality of life. For people with intellectual disabilities, it is widely held that good practice means offering personalized, flexible supports to individuals in core areas of adult life so that they may make personal choices – about how to lead one's life, with whom to live, where to work. Evidence suggests that people who live or work in community-based settings are more self-determined, have higher autonomy, have more choices and are more satisfied than their peers – matched for age and intelligence – living or working in congregate settings (Wehmeyer & Bolding, 2001). These authors conclude that assessment may itself promote self-determination, and that assessment is an important feature in the environment of people with intellectual disabilities, playing an influential role as mediator in promoting the availability of employment opportunities.

2.3 Community supports

How can individuals with intellectual disabilities achieve desired outcomes? Community supports describe the scaffolding of personal, technical, financial and social struts erected to enable an individual to live and prosper in the community. A closely related idea is that the community itself through its members and structures has the capacity to support individuals where they are. Certainly, this aspiration is founded on demographic reality. It is striking that most people with intellectual disabilities are to be found at home, living with their families or in other community settings. Braddock et al. (2001) present an overview of where people with intellectual disabilities live in five prosperous, industrialized countries – Australia, Canada, England, the United States and Wales. Nearly all children and many adults live in family homes, although an age-related trend towards moving away is apparent and thus older adults are less likely to live at home. *Community* is a term applied as often to the ultimate outcomes envisaged for people with intellectual disabilities as it is to the means of achieving these outcomes on their behalf.

While interventions can enhance personal control among persons who have more complex needs, or who have significant communication difficulties, many will continue to need particular support in order to exercise preferences (Stancliffe et al., 2000). Nevertheless, best practices have been developed in applied areas; for example, ensuring that individuals may express their preferences for entering employment and may then rely on high-quality supports to keep it. A new paradigm of assessment for prospective employees with intellectual disabilities incorporates the individual's life direction and wishes into vocational assessment as a priority (DiLeo, 1996).

2.4 Summary

If enhanced *quality of life* is the answer sought by policy-makers and service providers, then the question is, 'How will you appraise the outcomes of what you do on behalf of people with disabilities?' A core element in this construct is *self-determination*, a disposition more readily attained if individuals have supports with the intensity and form best suited to their needs. Assessment helps to identify needs for *support*, ideally in a way that widens the individual's zone of proximate development and helps him or her to gain a foothold and move forward. It may be defined for clinicians and other practitioners as the process by which information is gathered in order 'to guide the design and implementation of constructional and socially valid intervention' (Emerson, 1998, p. 114). Within this paradigm, the assessment process adds value if it leads to greater self-determination (Wehmeyer & Bolding, 2001). But assessment provoked rather different outcomes in the twentieth century. The next section provides an overview of some dominant models of assessment.

3 A Brief History

Not so long ago, psychometric assessment tools were the practising psychologist's stock-in-trade: mainly portable and always standardized. Assessment itself is a distinctive contribution of professional psychology to understanding the behaviour of people with intellectual and other developmental disabilities and in shaping interventions on their behalf.

3.1 Institutional care

In the last century, institutions, often of outlandish size, grew to become the dominant form of residence and employment for people with intellectual and other disabilities in the UK, where the number of those 'requiring care' in institutions rose sevenfold in the decades between the two world wars (Race, 1995, p. 50), Ireland (Robins, 1986), the United States and other developed countries (Braddock & Parish, 2001). Ironically, the development of psychological assessment tests in the early part of the twentieth century served to consolidate the dominant, congregate and medical models of care for people with intellectual disabilities. Until recently, thousands of children with intelligent quotient (IQ) scores – initially developed by Binet to describe a child's current functioning – of less than 50 were excluded from formal education in the UK and other European countries (McConkey, 1997). Since the mid-1990s, Irish psychologists have argued in court that children with severe and profound disabilities could not benefit from an entitlement to school due to their low IQ scores and mental age (judgment by Mr Justice Rory O'Hanlon in Re: *O'Donoghue vs the State*, 1993).

3.2 A dark chapter

It is sobering to recall that in the middle of the twentieth century, assessment of ability was turned to a malign purpose with nightmarish consequences. While harrowing to read, it is impossible to ignore accounts of how special tests were devised in both the USA and Nazi Germany to target feeble-mindedness (Black, 2003). Assessors asked questions tapping the individual's acquired knowledge about the names of capital cities and the days of the week, but ultimately the subjective appraisal of the interviewer prevailed. Positive identification of being feeble-minded served as a prelude, first, to eugenic sterilization, and later in the case of Germany to outright euthanasia of many thousands of children and adults with disabilities (Friedlander, 1995).

3.3 Traditional assessment

In the recent past, thousands of adults with intellectual disabilities were assessed for their suitability to enter available forms of residential or day services using what Sturmey (1996) terms a traditional or structural model of assessment. This model aims to diagnose and classify, to identify a problem and predict its future course. Sturmey offers examples from psychoanalytical therapy and biological psychiatry in which *non-observables* – a developmental stage or a personality trait – inferred from observed behaviour may be attributed with causing a person's current performance. Traditional assessment approaches focused on how to predict future performance from the competence manifested today according to diagnostic and other norms (Sturmey, 1996; see table 2.1 below). Jim's success on a timed test of hand–eye

Table 2.1 Examples of Some Models of Assessment

Target	Model of assessment	Source
Placement in sheltered, special work settings	Diagnostic or structural	Sturmey (1996)
Rehabilitation	Transferable Skills Analysis	Dunn & Growick (2000)
Transition from school to work	• A developmental tool to enable strategic thinking about the individual's vocational future • Identify specific skill deficits to inform decisions	National Information Center for Children and Youth with Disabilities (1990) Agran & Morgan (1991)
Identify needed community supports	Functional, individualized	Pancsofar & Steere (1997) Parsons et al. (1997)

coordination depends on whether the score he obtains falls within certain norms. The score is assumed to predict his future performance, not with fitting wooden pegs into holes, but various work-assembly tasks.

Many of the rigid boxes ferried through clinics, wards and dayrooms by psychologists in the 1960s, 1970s and 1980s helped to seal the futures of unsuspecting men and women. They contained instruments devised to measure an individual's performance, compute a score and compare it with scores obtained by a normative sample. Regrettably, one size did not fit all. A woman plucked from a ward for assessment by a stranger, puzzled by an outsized paper doll, challenged to chart the route of a hypothetical air journey – when she had never played with the former, nor had a hope of taking the latter – might fail to reach even the lowest rung.

3.4 Functional approaches

By contrast, a functional approach to assessment encompasses environmental features (table 2.1). A functional behavioural assessment aims to identify the relationship between an individual's behaviour and the environmental conditions that serve to maintain that behaviour (Sturmey, 1996). Parsons et al. (1997) developed a protocol for determining choice-making skills to assist a small number of older adults with severe disabilities in expressing leisure preferences. These authors point out that the ideology recognizing the right to make choices must be translated into practical strategies for evaluating and training such skills. Pancsofar and Steere (1997) contrast the traditional vocational assessment question 'Is this person employable?' (p. 99) with the more relevant 'What will it take to obtain a job that maximally enhances the quality of his or her life?' (p. 108). These authors outline an assessment process coupling situational assessment with an individual profile.

Elsewhere, the traditional approach to assessment may be contrasted with a more holistic process, albeit incorporating some functional elements (Russell, 1995), or with the probing of personal experiences such as the person's creative engagement in leisure and other social activities (Hogg, 1995). Today's assessors helping an individual to plan the future and to specify the supports needed may choose from a bank of person-centred planning resources; for example, *futures planning* (Mount, 1995).

3.5 Transition to adulthood

The transition to adulthood is a defining moment in each person's life, albeit celebrated diversely across cultures. Young adults with intellectual disabilities especially rely on support to negotiate this developmental stage (May, 2000). Vocational assessment can smooth the way. It can help to inform both the individual and the prospective employers about personal capacities and thus help to harmonize jobs and workers. Successful methods include interviews (with the young person, family members and advocates), observing the individual in a work setting, reviewing records of performance, visiting the work site and devising trial work periods (Wehman & Walsh, 1999).

In the United States, federal laws mandate transition planning as an element in the educational programme of each second-level student engaged in special educational services – (National Information Center for Children and Youth with Disabilities, 1990). The authors of this guide for parents and professionals recognize the diverse needs of individuals with disabilities, and list an array of vocational assessment strategies: interest inventories, job try-outs, work samples, observations, situational assessments and curriculum-based vocational assessment, in addition to more traditional aptitude and achievement tests (p. 6). They conclude that vocational assessment can help the young adult, family members and advocates to think strategically about his or her vocational future and to make informed decisions.

It seems that transition planners choose assessment tools widely. Agran and Morgan (1991) cite research to indicate a move from prediction-related transitional assessments towards those identifying specific skill deficits, and conclude that teachers and employment training personnel use a variety of procedures to make transition decisions.

3.6 Rehabilitation

Rehabilitation is a process more commonly applied to the needs of individuals who have neurological, psychiatric or physical disabilities, or disabilities other than intellectual ones. If the individual has incurred the disabling condition in adulthood, he or she may well have previous work experience but will nonetheless need support in modifying present employment or learning new skills. To help to assess vocational learning needs, the Transferable Skills Analysis (TSA) approach has gained broad acceptance (table 2.1). Dunn and Growick (2000) describe major components of the theory of skill transfer and methods of performing the analysis. These authors recommend that job placement procedures be scrutinized for validity and use, rather than their ease or their apparent link with vocational theories.

3.7 Community supports

In the wake of a shift from services to supports, from welfare to rights, from dependency to self-determination, adults with intellectual disabilities increasingly take part in and indeed direct the assessment process in order to determine their need for supports to live and work in the community. A report on Horizon – an EU programme funding employment and training initiatives throughout the member states – presents aims and recent changes in assessment systems used by employment service agencies for people with disabilities (Employment Support Unit, 2000). Here assessment is conceptualized as a channel that is fluid and adaptable to individual needs and self-perception. Particular reference is made to identifying barriers and support requirements. Specific assessment, tracking and review models are described.

3.8 Summary

If assessment is a process that potentially facilitates men and women with intellectual disabilities to determine how they will lead satisfying adult lives in the community, then it is a worthy calling for psychologists at the start of the new century to pursue. To create bottom-up, person-centred strategies and thus express global and national policies, there is much to learn from colleagues in developing countries (McConkey, 1997). Specifically, psychologists can learn to work through family members and others – employers, neighbours – who directly support people with intellectual disabilities in the community and who may be well placed to lead assessment processes.

4 Why Assess?

While the taxonomy of assessment tools is daunting, Emerson (1998) simplifies matters by suggesting that the questions underlying most assessments are of three types, asking first if something *is the case* about an individual, second, what he or she *can do* (and hence what support is required to perform a given task), and third, *why* he or she behaves in a certain way. He urges assessors to be clear about

- Why is this question being asked?
- To what purposes will information be put?
- Who will use the information?
- Are results likely to be of real benefit to the individual? (Emerson, 1998)

Each question is relevant for those involved in assessing adults with intellectual disabilities for their participation in leisure or employment opportunities.

4.1 Employment: Why assess?

Assessment helps would-be workers find employment with the best fit to their needs and preferences. The fabric of an ordinary life as an adult in the community is threaded with some element of productive work, either at home or in the labour force. Employment is the default option for men and women with intellectual disabilities, as a critical path to social inclusion as well as to heightened income, higher self-esteem, companionship and a host of other positive benefits. For example, friendships at work may lead to an enhanced probability of psychological well-being (Ohtake & Chadsey, 1999).

In developing countries, ordinary employment may be elusive, especially for those with severe disabilities, notwithstanding the pressures on women and men with intellectual disabilities to help to earn their own and their family's livelihood (Sutton & Walsh, 1999). Those who find work are likely to do so in traditional agriculture, production or forms of self-employment. Three women with various disabilities may form the workforce of a village industry packing matches into boxes in a rural province in Viet Nam. Their supervisor is a local woman who buys the raw materials, delivers the products to a wholesaler and manages the finances. She sustains herself and her family in this way.

In countries with developed market economies and formal service systems, congregate, special vocational training and employment settings dominate even now. National and regional funds ostensibly aimed at vocational integration maintain, instead, a separate and unequal system of employment. Men and women who are deemed unsuited for work – those with substandard skills, or with profound levels of intellectual disability, with autism, with challenging behaviour – may enter formal day programmes for activation, leisure and life skills; still others do nothing at all. While just 1,400 Irish adults with intellectual disabilities are engaged in supported or open employment, for example, more than 6,000 attend sheltered workshops or special vocational training (Mulvany & Barron, 2003, table 3.9). Yet while only a minority of European adults with disabilities enter open or supported employment, EU policies favour the social and vocational inclusion of people with disabilities and other marginalized groups.

Assessment of adults, especially with reference to their employment, has evolved in step with changing approaches in the EU member states, North America and Australia towards policies promoting the employment of people with disabilities (Thornton & Lunt, 1997). Responsibilities for policy and services include providing specialist help for those whose needs cannot be met in the mainstream specialist employment support services. Groups formerly not thought of in terms of employment provision or provided for in separate spheres have been seen as clients for employment-integrating measures. These include people with severe disabilities and those with psychiatric impairment.

4.2 Supported employment

Supported employment – work in the ordinary labour force with personal or technical supports for a real wage – has flourished for more than two decades in North America (Kiernan & Schalock, 1997) and more recently throughout Europe (Walsh & Beyer, 1999). It is important to take into account manifest benefits for individuals in terms of their quality of life, increased personal income, as well as benefits for wider society, for the efficacy of service provider agencies and for those funding such services through taxes (Beyer & Kilsby, 1998). A fundamental issue is whether it may be assumed that employment will bring benefits to the lives of people with intellectual disability and particularly to the individual being assessed. At the level of society, the relative costs and benefits outcomes of supported employment are not fully understood and it is likely that many factors will prove to contribute to its costs.

While diversity in supported employment programmes allows for their best fit to local conditions, it also has implications for evaluating programmes. Continuous quality improvement (CQI) presents an alternative to traditional evaluations of social services by emphasizing continuous quality improvement undertaken from within organizations providing employment and training supports. In evaluating outcomes for supported employees with disabilities in five European countries, Walsh et al. (1999) describe a cross-cultural evaluation applying CQI and based on locally relevant principles and values emphasizing customer-defined quality, teamwork, clarity of mission, and shared information. The overall project aimed to define culturally fitting approaches to evaluation, as well as build a network of support across culturally diverse environments.

4.3 Benefits for individuals

Assessment processes should be devised to benefit the individual. Self-appraisal of the person's own capacities and of various options presented in the environment is indicated in order to make real choices. With support, individuals may gain greater control over how employment services are delivered, including choices about type of occupation, professional training staff, training methods and career development (West & Parent, 1992). Self-instructional training may be an effective element in training for adults with intellectual disabilities in work settings that takes no more time than traditional, external training (Whitman et al., 1987).

4.4 Real-world assessment

Assessors should set their sights on identifying what skills or adaptations will enable a person to function in real-world settings (Emerson, 1998, p. 121). If the individual has all the skills needed to carry out daily life to everyone's satisfaction, well and good – at least for the present. But if target skills are needed to tackle the next step in the individual's living or working zone, then these deficits should drive a developmental process of acquisition and consolidation. It is important to ascertain the purpose or social validity of assessment procedures and to select methods that will generate the information needed to answer underlying questions (Emerson, 1998). Methods of functional assessment, ecological inventory, repeated direct observation, discrepancy analysis are described as appropriate ways of collecting accurate information about skills already possessed, skills to be learned, and adaptations to be made. These methods may be applied to leisure and other community settings as well as to employment. Ecological inventory, for example, extends to workplace environments and the outcomes of the individual's experiences there. Evidence indicates that greater *typicalness* of employment led to better outcomes for individuals (Mank et al., 1997).

In practice, assessment may itself be a beneficial intervention. O'Reilly et al. (2000) highlighted the possible consequences of deficits in skills required for keeping a job placement. Using a problem-solving approach to teach social skills to workers with brain injuries in supported employment settings, they conclude that assessment is part of intervention – in this case, support for the employee – in the supported workplace. The authors show how social skills can be selected, operationally defined, and rated, explaining how task analyses can serve as objective measures, and how social skills performance can be assessed at baseline, intervention, generalization, and follow-up probes. Ongoing support can take the form of social skills training conducted in a setting removed from the employment site in which new skills are acquired and are then generalized to the workplace.

4.5 Fine-tuning

An individual may benefit from highly specialized supports devised from a detailed analysis of the tasks required in a work setting. Lee et al. (2001) examined the effects of training on selection behaviour of two individuals with severe intellectual disabilities across two different vocational tasks designs:

- a site-based or traditional approach
- a more efficient motion-economy-based approach

Selection behaviour was affected by task efficiency, only when efficiency was made more salient by pairing task cues with work incentives. The authors note that enhanced productivity is likely to lead to more satisfying and better-paid work opportunities for individuals with severe intellectual disabilities, who are often under-represented in employment settings. In addition, technological applications have the potential to enhance work outcomes for individuals with intellectual disabilities, as assessment tools and also in assisting individuals to make independent choices about their lives (Siegel, 1999).

4.6 Summary

Assessment plays a critical role in determining the supports that people with intellectual disabilities need to live and work in the community. The process should be directed by the individual and be carried out in the real world. Problems are likely to arise if the purpose of the assessment process is not in harmony with the procedures chosen to bring it to pass. In the next section, strategies to address some of these discordant events are presented.

5 Strategies

The assessment process extends in the real world – ideally – and also in real time. At its core is the complex interplay of an individual within the nested ecologies of family, community, culture and the political and economic environment (Hogg, 1995). At any level, assessment may be flawed with predictable, negative impact. Three problems may confront service providers or advocates for people with intellectual disabilities (table 2.2).

First, the assessment may be carried out as a once-off or dutiful task, perhaps ticking boxes on an intake or review sheet in the files. Any practitioner of a certain age has trawled through the archives to find evidence that, indeed, Margaret, an older woman with intellectual disabilities, has duly been assessed for her social skills competence, and failed to meet the

Table 2.2 Some Strategies to Address Problematic Assessment Practices

Level	If assessment	Likely impact	Strategies
Wider environment	is a once-off or rarity	Changes in the person and environment will be ignored	Consider assessment as a lifelong, fluid process involving the person in context
Service system	is fragmented	A patchwork of information will amass	Consider a cohesive assessment process drawing on multiple sources of information but centred on the individual
Individual	drives intervention or placement	The process will overshadow and ultimately replace a focus on outcomes	Recall the purpose of assessment: to inform valid interventions on the person's behalf

grade – in 1981. Fixing placement decisions in stone ignores two fundamental truths – that people change, and that times change. Who foresaw, when institutions began to close their doors a generation ago, that men and women with intellectual disabilities might aspire to buy their own apartments, fly to Majorca or seek jobs in call centres? Who knows whether Margaret has or has not learned to use a mobile phone in the last few years?

Assessment may be used as a fixative in the work life of an adult if service providers are merely relieved that they have secured any sort of job for an individual with distinctive needs for support. For example, people with autism may require long-term, intensive supports to sustain fruitful employment. Datlow Smith et al. (1995) designed a practical guide aimed at achieving successful employment and community integration for individuals with autism. The authors describe the strengths and limitations of traditional and standardized assessments, and recommend greater use of non-standardized assessments including criterion-referenced and informal methods. Such methods, coupled with regular reviews of individual capacity and preferences, might form a useful strategy to replace sporadic assessment processes.

Second, fragmented assessments may result in an unreliable patchwork of information (table 2.2). Luiselli et al. (2001) note in their survey of national service centres in the United States that relatively little is known about the types of assessment instruments used with individuals with autism. This report draws attention to the lack of information about the types of assessment instruments used routinely by practitioners. Developing cohesive, co-ordinated assessment processes is a priority at service system level. A central resource of assessment instruments used by employment service agencies can support information sharing (Employment Support Unit, 2000). A second strategic safeguard is to ensure that the person who will ultimately benefit, or perhaps an advocate, leads all assessment processes and has access to the findings in a way he or she best understands.

If equity were to prevail, then Jim would be the focus of any assessment process. As the customer, Jim would always be in the right, although his occupational therapist, psychologist, school curriculum, local job market and national policies might be some of the suspects rounded up for scrutiny if he fails to secure the life he wishes to lead.

Finally, the paraphernalia and demands of assessment procedures – boxes, appointments, computing scores, timetabling, multidisciplinary meetings and documentation – absorb considerable energy. The noise may muffle the voice of the individual. If process overrides outcomes, then the purpose of the assessment recedes and, paradoxically, the very activities devised to serve become tyrants (table 2.2). Many service agencies and consultants today pride themselves on seamless, high-quality assessment cycles completed on time within days or weeks of a set target, year after year. The process is flawless – but what about tangible outcomes for men and women in terms of achieving a satisfying, ordinary life? A prudent strategy is to ensure that outcomes are the target and that assessment and other processes are the means to this end.

6 Conclusion

As this century unfolds, men and women with intellectual disabilities will continue to gain ground in shaping their own lives with support from family members, advocates and professional workers. This chapter suggests that contextual models of leisure and work are valuable in understanding the complex interactions of individuals with their environments at different stages of adult life. The main purpose of assessment is to help to identify personal capacities and preferred living and working options, and the types and intensity of supports needed to achieve desired outcomes. Assessment plays a critical role in determining the supports needed to live and work in the community. Accordingly, the process should be directed by the individual, with appropriate supports, and be carried out in the real world. Those charged with providing services should aspire to timely, cohesive and productive assessment strategies.[1]

NOTE

1 I thank Elaine MacDonald, Department of Psychology at the National University of Ireland, Dublin, for her assistance in preparing this chapter.

REFERENCES

Agran, M. & Morgan, R. L. (1991) Current transition assessment practices. *Research in Disabilities*, **12**, 113–126.

Beyer, S. & Kilsby, M. (1998) Financial costs and benefits of two supported employment agencies in Wales. *Journal of Applied Research in Intellectual Disabilities*, **11**, 303–319.

Bickenbach, J. (2001) Disability human rights, law, and policy. In G. Albrecht, K. D. Seelman & M. Bury (eds.), *Handbook of Disability Studies*. Thousand Oaks, CA: Sage, pp. 565–584.

Black, E. (2003) *War against the Weak: Eugenics and America's Campaign to Create a Master Race*. New York: Four Walls Eight Windows.

Braddock, D. & Parish, S. (2001) Disability history from antiquity to the Americans with Disabilities Act. In G. L. Albrecht, K. D. Seelman & M. Bury (eds.), *Handbook of Disability Studies*, Thousand Oaks, CA: Sage, pp. 11–68.

Braddock, D., Emerson, E., Felce, D. & Stancliffe, R. J. (2001) Living circumstances of children and adults with mental retardation or developmental disabilities in the United States, Canada, England and Wales and Australia. *Mental Retardation and Developmental Disabilities Research Reviews*, 7, 115–121.

Commission of the European Communities (1998) *A New European Community Disability Strategy.* Document 98/0216 (CNS). Brussels: Commission of the European Communities.

Croser, M. D. (2002) Federal disability legislation: 1975–1999. In R. L. Schalock, P. C. Baker & M. D. Croser (eds.), *Embarking on a New Century: Mental Retardation at the End of the Twentieth Century.* Washington, DC: AAMR, pp. 3–16.

Datlow Smith, M., Belcher, R. G. & Juhrs, P. D. (1995) *A Guide to Successful Employment for Individuals with Autism.* Baltimore, MD: Brookes, pp. 17–43.

Department of Health (2001) *Valuing People: A New Strategy for Learning Disability for the Twenty-first Century.* London: Stationery Office.

DiLeo, D. (1996) Changing values and best practices for employment consultants. In D. DiLeo & D. Langton (eds.), *Facing the Future: Best Practices in Supported Employment.* St. Augustine, FL: Training Resource Network, pp. 90–93.

Dunn, P. L. & Growick, B. S. (2000) Transferable skills analysis in vocational rehabilitation: Historical foundations, current status, and future trends. *Journal of Vocational Rehabilitation*, 14, 79–87.

Emerson, E. (1998) Assessment. In E. Emerson, C. Hatton, J. Bromley & A. Caine (eds.), *Clinical Psychology and People with Intellectual Disabilities.* Chichester: John Wiley, pp. 114–124.

Employment Support Unit (2000) *Horizon: Models of Assessment of Employability Seminar.* Birmingham, UK: Employment Support Unit, pp. 10–48.

Felce, D. (1997) Defining and applying the concept of quality of life. *Journal of Intellectual Disability Research*, 41, 126–135.

Friedlander, H. (1995) *The Origins of Nazi Genocide.* Chapel Hill: University of North Carolina Press.

Government of Ireland (1996) *A Strategy for Equality.* Report of the Commission on the Status of People with Disabilities. Dublin: Government Publications.

Hatton, C. (1998) Whose Quality of Life is it anyway? Some problems with the emerging Quality of Life consensus. *Mental Retardation*, 36, 104–111.

Hogg, J. (1995) Assessment methods and professional directions. In N. Malin (ed.), *Services for People with Learning Disabilities.* London: Routledge, pp. 219–235.

Kiernan, W. E. & Schalock, R. L. (1997) How we got to where we are. In W. E. Kiernan & R. L. Schalock (eds.), *Integrated Employment – Current Status and Future Directions.* Washington, DC: AAMR, pp. 5–16.

Lee, D. L., Belfiore, P. J. & Tro-Zambrana, W. (2001) The effects of mastery training and explicit feedback on task design preference in a vocational setting. *Research in Developmental Disabilities*, 22, 333–351.

Luiselli, J. K., Campbell, S., Cannon, B., DiPietro, E., Ellis, J. T., Taras, M. & Lifter, K. (2001) Assessment instruments used in the education and treatment of persons with autism: Brief report of a survey of national service centers. *Research in Developmental Disabilities*, 22, 389–398.

Mank, D., Cioffi, A. & Yovanoff, P. (1997) Analysis of the typicalness of supported employment jobs, natural supports, and wage and integration outcomes. *Mental Retardation*, 35, 185–197.

May, D. (ed.) (2000) *Transition and Change in the Lives of People with Intellectual Disabilities.* London: David Fulton.

McConkey, R. (1997) Intellectual disability: A psychological assessment. In R. Fuller, P. N. Walsh & P. McGinley (eds.), *A Century of Psychology: Progress, Paradigms and Prospects for the New Millennium.* London: Routledge, pp. 69–84.

Mount, B. (1995) *Capacity Works.* Manchester, CT: Communitas.

Mulvany, F. & Barron, S. (2003) *National Intellectual Disability Database Committee: Annual Report 2002.* Dublin: Health Research Board (www.hrb.ie).

National Information Center for Children and Youth with Disabilities (1990) Vocational assessment: A guide for parents and professionals. *Transition Summary.* No. 6, December 1990. Washington, DC: NICHCY, PO Box 1492, Washington, DC 20013, USA.

O'Reilly, M. F., Lancioni, G. E. & O'Kane, N. (2000) Using a problem-solving approach to teach social skills to workers with brain injuries in supported employment settings. *Journal of Vocational Rehabilitation,* 14, 187–194.

Ohtake, Y. & Chadsey, J. G. (1999) Social disclosure among coworkers without disabilities in supported employment settings. *Mental Retardation,* 37, 25–35.

Pancsofar, E. L. & Steere, D. E. (1997) The C.A.P.A.B.L.E. process: Critical dimensions of community-based assessment. *Journal of Vocational Rehabilitation,* 8, 99–108.

Parsons, M. B., Harper, V. N., Jensen, J. M. & Reid, D. H. (1997) Assisting older adults with severe disabilities in expressing leisure preferences: A protocol for determining choice-making skills. *Research in Developmental Disabilities,* 18, 113–126.

Quinn, G. (1999) The human rights of people with disabilities under EU Law. In P. Alston (ed.), *The EU and Human Rights.* Oxford: OUP, pp. 281–326.

Race, D. (1995) Historical development of service provision. In N. Malin (ed.), *Services for People with Learning Disabilities.* London: Routledge, pp. 46–78.

Rapley, M. & Beyer, S. (1998) Daily activity, community participation and quality of life in an ordinary housing network: A two-year follow-up. *Journal of Applied Research in Intellectual Disabilities,* 11, 34–43.

Robins, J. (1986) *Fools and Mad.* Dublin: Institute for Public Administration.

Russell, O. (1995) Professional and planning issues in assessment. In N. Malin (ed.), *Services for People with Learning Disabilities.* London: Routledge, pp. 207–218.

Schalock, R. L. & Verdugo, M.-A. (2002) *Handbook on Quality of Life for Human Service Practitioners.* Washington, DC: American Association on Mental Retardation.

Scottish Executive (2000) *The Same as You? Review of Services for People with Learning Disabilities.* Edinburgh: Scottish Executive.

Siegel, J. (1999) Utilizing technology for the inclusion of individuals with mental retardation. In P. Retish and S. Reiter (eds.), *Adults with Disabilities: International Perspectives in the Community.* Mahwah, NJ: Lawrence Erlbaum, pp. 287–308.

Stancliffe, R. J., Abery, B. H. & Smith, J. (2000) Personal control and the ecology of community living settings: Beyond living-unit size and type. *American Journal on Mental Retardation,* 105, 431–454.

Sturmey, P. (1996) *Functional Analysis in Clinical Psychology.* Chichester: John Wiley.

Sutton, B. & Walsh, P. N. (1999) *Inclusion International's* Open Project on Inclusive Employment. *Journal of Vocational Rehabilitation,* 12, 195–198.

Thornton, P. & Lunt, N. (1997) *Employment Policies for Disabled People in Eighteen Countries: A Review.* York: Social Policy Research Unit, University of York.

Walsh, P. N. & Beyer, S. (1999) Guest editors' introduction. *Journal of Vocational Rehabilitation,* 12, 127–129.

Walsh, P. N., Mank, D., Beyer, S., McDonald, R. & O'Bryan, A. (1999) Continuous quality improvement in supported employment: A European perspective. *Journal of Vocational Rehabilitation,* 12, 165–174.

Wehman, P. & Walsh, P. N. (1999) Transition from school to adulthood: A look at the United States and Europe. In P. Retish & S. Reiter (eds.), *Adults with Disabilities: International Perspectives in the Community.* Mahwah, NJ: Lawrence Erlbaum, pp. 3–31.

Wehmeyer, M. & Bolding, N. (2001) Enhanced self-determination of adults with intellectual disability as an outcome of moving to community-based work or living environments. *Journal of Intellectual Disability*, **45**, 371–383.

West, M. & Parent, W. S. (1992) Consumer choice and empowerment in supported employment services: Issues and strategies. *Journal of the Association for Persons with Severe Handicaps*, **17**, 47–52.

Whitman, T. L., Spence, B. H. & Maxwell, S. (1987) A comparison of external and self-instructional teaching formats with mentally retarded adults in a vocational training setting. *Research in Developmental Disabilities*, **8**, 371–388.

CHAPTER 3

Interdisciplinary assessment of people with profound intellectual and multiple disabilities

Carla Vlaskamp

1 Introduction

A key objective of assessment is to determine the progress an individual is making developmentally or in response to the aims of parents and professionals. There is, however, a category of persons for whom progress or development in the generally accepted sense is lacking. People with profound intellectual and multiple disabilities progress as they get older, but not always towards goals seen as important in our society. Some people with profound intellectual and multiple disabilities even have such profound cerebral lesions that, based on neurological evidence, no functional adaptation is said to be possible (Robertson & Murre, 1999). On the other hand, most parents and most direct support staff believe firmly in the abilities of people with profound intellectual and multiple disabilities, even when these seem to run counter to clinical or educational assessment. Whatever the opinions on possibilities for development, progress or adaptation, people with profound intellectual and multiple disabilities form a very vulnerable group with a strong need for personal assistance in everyday tasks.

In this chapter, I shall describe the cognitive, motor, sensory, physical and communicative characteristics of people with profound intellectual and multiple disabilities. And in chapter 11, I shall consider the implications of such a complex pattern of disabilities for diverse assessments. There I shall also consider the need for integrated interdisciplinary assessment, a plea for which ends the present chapter.

2 People with Profound Intellectual and Multiple Disabilities

There is no standardized terminology with which to describe the individuals with whom this chapter is concerned. We have adopted a current term, 'profound intellectual and multiple impairment', though at the time of writing 'profound and multiple learning disabilities' and 'profound and complex needs' have currency in the United Kingdom and 'profound retardation and multiple disabilities' is employed in the US. All may be regarded as improvements on early usage such as 'vegetative human organism' (Rice & McDaniel, 1966). Nor are there agreed international criteria to determine inclusion in this group. With respect to the American Association on Mental Retardation and World Health Organization criteria current until their more recent versions, profound intellectual disability would be taken to indicate a measured IQ under 20. Fryers (1984, p. 154), in reviewing the classification of people with profound intellectual disabilities, comments:

> The information (intelligence tests) provide is . . . of rather doubtful value, since it is not clear that it represents, in different groups and populations, any common biological characteristics or educational potential. Since in most practical situations, rigorously administered test results are not available, for most relevant population and even research projects may find them impossible to provide . . . , an IQ definition becomes spurious.

The alternative of using a single *developmental* criterion is also dismissed by this author, who goes on to state:

> Since this group is characterised by the profound degree and multiplicity of disabilities, whatever else, it is probably spurious to attempt to measure and use for classification either one element alone or all elements combined into a single score; these procedures serve neither epidemiological needs for category standardisation nor practitioner needs for individual guidance and monitoring. (p. 155)

Nevertheless, the attempt to place people with profound intellectual and multiple disabilities within a developmental framework, albeit not reducing the developmental marker to a single score, has been compelling. Such a framework has typically derived from developmental psychology, placing the level of cognitive functioning in the sensorimotor stage of development (0–18 months). The impetus for such a view came from the classic studies of Mary Woodward in her examination of the applicability of Piagetian stage concepts in individuals with intellectual disabilities (Woodward, 1959). The importance of Woodward's work and the direction it gave to research into the assessment and abilities of people with profound intellectual and multiple disabilities cannot be overemphasized. The view that members of this population were 'un-assessable' and 'in-educable' gave way to a detailed examination of their behaviour and development within the relatively well-worked-out framework of developmental psychology. Contrast such a view of people who have profound intellectual and multiple disabilities with the implications of the term noted above, 'vegetative human organism'.

As we shall see, the developmental framework is multidimensional, assessment generating profiles of ability rather than a single score such as mental age. Typically, people with profound intellectual and multiple disabilities assessed as falling within this framework will be at the preverbal stage of communication, though some will have limited spoken or signed expressive language, and limited communicative comprehension. Understanding of causality and space will be limited, and adaptive, and self-help abilities will be at such a level that the support they require will be pervasive.

I shall later discuss the limitations placed on developmental assessment of people with profound intellectual and multiple disabilities by the multiplicity of their impairments. However, taken with the developmental perspective these further imply the need for a multidimensional concept of this group for purposes of classification (Nakken & Vlaskamp, 2002). Within such a framework it is possible to distinguish different, if overlapping subgroups (e.g. those with profound intellectual disabilities and sensory impairments but whose motor impairment does not prevent ambulation, and those with profound intellectual disabilities and significant motor impairment precluding ambulation). Although there are no scientific grounds for reserving this term for only one specific target group, it is the latter group for whom the term 'profound intellectual and multiple disabilities' is most commonly used in the literature.

3 Additional, Multiple Impairments

A profound intellectual disability almost always occurs concomitantly and is indeed the consequence of neurological impairments arising from trauma or genetic influences (Arvio & Sillanpää, 2003) (e.g. encephalopathy and/or cerebral visual impairment with implications for overall functioning). Typically, their care needs are pervasive, being provided by family carers or paid staff. Central nervous system (CNS) damage results in severe or profound motor disorders (e.g. spastic quadriplegia). Obvious consequences of such CNS damage are that most people with profound intellectual and multiple disabilities are wheelchair users, frequently have limited use of hands and arms and have difficulties in maintaining postural balance. Both gross motor and fine motor functions, then, are profoundly disturbed.

Causation is varied and often not determined. Chromosomal abnormalities, degenerative diseases, inborn errors of metabolism, congenital brain damage and the results of serious infections or trauma can all lead to profound intellectual and multiple disabilities. On average, a proper diagnosis can be established for about half of the people affected (van Karnebeek et al., 2002).

In addition to the intellectual and physical disabilities just noted, further concomitant impairments should also be mentioned as they, too, have significant implications for assessment. Extensive 'additional' impairments include sensory impairments, seizure disorders, chronic pulmonary infections, and skeletal deformations. Some of these impairments (e.g. cortical blindness and some forms of seizure disorders), are primary (they stem from the same extensive brain disorder that also caused the intellectual and motor disorders). Others, such as skeletal deformations and pulmonary infections, are secondary disorders.

With respect to assessment, then, it is essential to assess not only intellectual and physical functioning, but also these additional disabilities. Even though a person with profound intellectual and multiple disabilities cannot be understood as a simple combination of results of assessment of different impairments, it is still necessary to know what her disabilities and potential entail in order to understand how these may affect the overall functioning of the person.

People with profound intellectual and multiple disabilities, then, form a heterogeneous group in terms of central nervous system integrity, physical growth, development and behavioural repertoires. Notwithstanding this huge diversity, people with profound intellectual and multiple disabilities are comparable in the degree of profound intellectual and severe or profound motor disabilities, and may be considered to constitute the most disabled group of people in the populations of individuals with intellectual disabilities.

4 Assessing People with Profound Intellectual and Multiple Disabilities

The assessment of people with profound intellectual and multiple disabilities presents special challenges. If we begin by considering the assessment of their understanding of the world (their cognitive ability) we encounter a wide range of barriers to the conventional types of assessment that are feasible with more able individuals lacking complex difficulties. We shall consider these barriers with respect to the impact of physical and sensory impairments on cognitive development and assessment, and health-related problems.

4.1 Cognitive assessment

As noted above, a significant proportion of people with profound intellectual and multiple disabilities have severe or profound physical impairments. In the early stages of development most items assessing cognition are heavily dependent upon motor behaviour, particularly fine motor behaviour. This is the case whether we consider standardized developmental tests, such as the Bayley Scales of Infant Development (Bayley, 1967) or more flexible forms of assessment such as the Piagetian-based Užgiris–Hunt Scales of Ordinal Development (Dunst, 1980; Užgiris & Hunt, 1975), or, in more advanced development, symbolic functions (Lowe & Costello, 1976). Due in part to the additional motor impairments, commonly used standardized tests such as the Bayley Scales do not lead to a valid estimation of a level of developmental level or cognitive functioning. The lack of choice of development instruments is discussed more fully in chapter 11. In passing, it should be added that while global assessment using such instruments is rarely valid, individual items may have value in assessing some aspect of functioning. For example, both forms of assessment noted above involve items related to sensory functioning such as visual tracking, orienting to sound and reaching for objects, all of which fall within the range of some individuals with profound intellectual and multiple disabilities.

4.2 Sensory impairments

Apart from motor impairments, people with profound intellectual and multiple disabilities frequently have sensory impairments. The prevalence of visual and hearing impairments is higher among people with intellectual disabilities generally (Warburg, 2001), but people with profound intellectual and multiple intellectual disabilities have a much higher prevalence than those with mild intellectual disabilities (van Schrojenstein Lantman-de Valk et al., 1994, 1997; Janicki & Dalton, 1998; Evenhuis et al., 2001; Woodhouse et al., 2000). Visual impairments are more frequent than hearing disorders. According to studies in the Netherlands (van Gelderen,

2000; Inspectie voor de Gezondheidszorg, 2000), an estimation of at least 85% of the people with profound intellectual and multiple disabilities have visual impairments, in many cases caused by damage to the visual cortex in the occipital lobe (cortical blindness). People with cortical blindness are not blind in the sense that they have no vision, but have visual impairments because their perception of light images is inaccurate and inconsistent. Visual functioning in people with profound intellectual and multiple disabilities can be enormously variable both within the same person even within short time intervals, and between different people (Pagliano, 2001). For example, some people are attracted to bright lights and bright colours, while others may be photophobic. Depth vision is often poor because it requires cerebral coordination of binocular vision. People may become overwhelmed by a visual experience while others may lack visual information because of additional problems such as motivation, stress, fatigue and medication.

Often, up-to-date information on functional visual abilities is lacking. A systematic screening of visual functioning of people with profound intellectual and multiple disabilities is not one of the standard routines of service providers (Inspectie voor de Gezondheidszorg, 2000). Not knowing if a person with profound intellectual and multiple disabilities has cortical blindness has consequences for communication with that person. The approach of other people or events in the environment may not be noticed by the person and may occur quite unexpectedly. Inability to detect objects visually may lead to insecurity and possibly behavioural or mental health difficulties.

It is equally important to obtain up-to-date information on the functional hearing abilities of a person with profound intellectual and multiple disabilities. Cortical hearing loss may be more common in people with profound intellectual and multiple disabilities than previously thought, but its prevalence is lower than for cortical visual impairments. In a Dutch survey, 25–33% of the people with profound intellectual and multiple disabilities were diagnosed with auditory impairments, but due to the lack of systematic screening it is suspected that a substantial number of cases may have remained unidentified (Evenhuis et al., 2001). Lack of attention, restricted responses to auditory signals and responses to speech that vary in relation to environmental factors, as well as the use of an inappropriate volume, are all signs of a hearing impairment. As these are also behaviours that might be seen when a person is confused, frustrated, isolated or depressed, a hearing impairment is often difficult to diagnose.

Visual and auditory impairments are not the only sensory impairments that may occur. Dysfunction of taste and smell is relatively common (Bromley, 2000) but mostly ignored. The tactile and cutaneous senses that include the receptors of touch, pressure, temperature and pain are frequently thought to be impaired to some degree (Dunn, 1999; Oberlander et al., 1999). Some dramatic anecdotal examples can be given of cases in which the person apparently could not express pain and suffered from third-degree burns, gastric ulcers or open wounds as a result. Although tactile and cutaneous senses are essential for the person, little attention is paid to the actual functioning of these senses.

Such sensory impairments present similar barriers to those offered by physical impairments when it comes to the use of developmental tests. Such tests are heavily loaded with sensory, particularly visual, items. Again any valid global estimate will not be possible for most individuals and only a limited subset of items may have relevance. However, only where we have reliable information on the sensory abilities of a person is any form of assessment involving a particular modality meaningful.

4.3 Health status influences

People with profound intellectual and multiple disabilities frequently also have additional physical disorders. Seizure disorders are a very frequently occurring form of co-morbidity in people with profound intellectual and multiple disabilities. Figures higher than 50% are reported in the literature (Hogg, 1992; Arts, 1999). The occurrence of seizures is mostly caused by disorders following antenatal adverse factors or perinatal damage, metabolic disorders or the consequences of encephalitis or meningitis (Arts, 1999). The possibilities for treatment of seizure disorders have improved strongly in recent years, due to improvement of anticonvulsant medication, surgical techniques and advanced diagnostic techniques. But especially in people with profound intellectual and multiple disabilities, finding the balance between the results of medication and their side effects is difficult. People with profound intellectual and multiple disabilities often use other drugs in addition to anticonvulsant drugs (Hogg, 1992), and their sensitivity to side effects is greater (Arts, 1999). This may have consequences for their behaviour: they may become agitated, suffer from sleeplessness or be dull during the day.

People with profound intellectual and multiple disabilities have an overall risk of developing several medical complications. An estimated 70% exhibit gastro-oesophageal reflux (Böhmer et al., 1999), a chronic partial regurgitation of stomach contents upwards into the oesophagus. It may not only cause gastritis and lead to vomiting and feeding irritability, but also to recurrent pneumonia, or other chronic respiratory disorders. If treatment is not given because staff are unaware of the cause of these health problems, it will also lead to refusal of food, and agitated or challenging behaviour (Böhmer et al., 1999).

Sleep disorders are also widespread among people with profound intellectual and multiple disabilities. For example, Quine (1991) has found a larger proportion of sleep disorders among children with intellectual impairments and cerebral palsy (71%) compared to children with intellectual impairments without cerebral palsy. As noted, additional loss of vision, a common disorder among people with profound intellectual and multiple disabilities, also leads to significant increase in sleep disorders (Tröster et al., 1996).

Difficulties with feeding are prevalent among people with profound intellectual and multiple disabilities, and may lead to dehydration and malnourishment (Beange et al., 1995). Difficulties with mental health may occur, although it is hard to diagnose and treat such problems. Many people with profound intellectual and multiple disabilities exhibit significant challenging behaviours, particularly making disruptive sounds, self-injurious behaviour and eating inappropriate objects or substances (Hogg & Lambe, 1988; Hogg, 1992).

Physical impairments and medical complications often lead to the need for medication. Anticonvulsants, medication to prevent reflux, and drugs with a sedative effect are used frequently (Hogg, 1992; Böhmer et al., 1999). Apart from these types of medication, almost all people with profound intellectual and multiple disabilities have medication on a daily basis for a whole range of medical conditions, including constipation or respiratory problems (Inspectie voor de Gezondheidszorg, 2000).

4.4 Assessing communication

Of all the challenges faced in educating and supporting people with profound intellectual and multiple disabilities, problems in communication are to the fore. Physical and sensory impairments, together with the impact of profound intellectual disability, will have constrained the development of communication along its typical course. Communication will characteristically be preverbal, involving signals such as reflex responses, sounds and facial expressions and bodily movements (Ware, 1997). Language in any form (e.g. speech, signing or use of symbols) will be limited or non-existent. The communicative repertoire is not only limited, but may include idiosyncratic ways of communicating. The repertoire may include physiological signals such as a rise in body temperature, muscle relaxation, or a change in the level of alertness. Sometimes these signals are so subtle that they go unnoticed. Even if we do notice these signals, we do not always comprehend their meaning. A wink or blink, the same vocal sounds or the same movement of an arm can have different meanings in different situations. Crying, for example, is not always an expression of sadness, nor is being quiet an expression of being content or wanting rest (Vlaskamp, 1999). The significance of crying or being very quiet may vary across situations. Therefore, the responsibility for interpreting these signals in accordance with the feelings and meanings of a person with profound intellectual and multiple disabilities is considerable (Porter & Ouvry, 2001). People with profound intellectual and multiple disabilities have a high dependence on the interpretations of others to make themselves understood. They use (to us) inconsistent ways of communication, leading to ambiguity of meaning, but are unable immediately to contradict or clarify our interpretation. People with profound intellectual and multiple disabilities rely on parents and professionals for the interpretation of their communicative signals, opening up the possibility of misinterpretation and inappropriate response (Grove et al., 1999).

5 Multidisciplinary Assessment

The multiplicity of barriers to effective assessment of people with profound intellectual and multiple disabilities indicates the need for a large number of different disciplines to be involved in assessment. For educational and developmental intervention and support to be effective, assessment must be multidimensional. From the perspective of people with profound intellectual and multiple disabilities, their parents and advocates, there will be a need to deal with a variety of medical professionals, including the general practitioner, paediatrician, neurologist, dietician, clinical psychologist and nurse. A physiotherapist is needed to assess and facilitate motor functioning related to positioning and mobility, prevent contractures, and minimize abnormal reflexes and reactions. A speech and language therapist is needed to enhance communication and to support parents and staff to improve eating and drinking and cope with difficulties arising from dysphagia. In order to ensure that the relation between the person and the environment is optimal, an occupational therapist is required to design adaptations identified through assessment. By improving the person–environment fit (e.g. finding the most comfortable position, reducing problems related to eating and drinking, and providing a range of adapted equipment), well-being can be immeasurably enhanced.

Assessment, too, must address the needs and wishes of people with profound intellectual and multiple disabilities. The need to initiate contact – for structure, security and predictability – must be addressed, as well as ensuring stimulation, variation and challenges in their lives. Building and maintaining meaningful relationships with significant others are crucial, enabling them to be heard and to control their own lives. People with profound intellectual and multiple disabilities should have the opportunity to exert an influence on those around them and be co-determiners of what happens with and to them – however dependent they may be on others for support in their daily existence. Communicative consistency may be difficult to achieve and maintain across several relationships. However, only through such consistency can people with profound intellectual and multiple disabilities make their needs known and have them properly addressed.

6 Interdisciplinary Assessment

How should this multiplicity of professional assessments be integrated in order to provide the best interventions and support for people with profound intellectual and multiple disabilities? These professionals have all been trained in different approaches to service provision, with one of the biggest differences being that teachers and direct-support personnel are trained in an educational model, while therapists and other health-care professionals are trained in a health-care model. There are philosophical, theoretical and managerial differences between these models, and most methods and models used perpetuate single-discipline thinking within the system. Professionals rarely collaborate in ways that result in an effective, integrated programme. When professionals do not assume responsibility for the synthesis, integration, application and generalization of fragmented, sometimes even conflicting, programme components, they inadvertently shift the responsibility of synthesis and integration on to the very people they are trying to support: individuals with profound intellectual and multiple disabilities (Rainforth & York-Barr, 1997).

Assessment, then, should be looked at as a process rather than as a set, rigid, procedure. It is an essential prerequisite to the development and evaluation of individual educational and therapeutic programmes. Assessment is a tool for changes in desired, agreed directions, making it a normative process. Assessment provides the necessary knowledge on which decisions for change are built. Within the overall framework of such planning, particular concerns may initiate assessment. For example, professionals may be unsure about the meaning of agitated behaviour, disagree on the meaning of affective behaviour or the perceived needs of a person with profound intellectual and multiple disabilities. In some instances, professionals may need to resolve disagreements through further assessment. Solving these problems means making underlying ideas and views on the current actions explicit. Some problems exist because of false or insufficient ideas of objectives in supporting a person with profound intellectual and multiple disabilities. Assessment should aim at replacing such ideas by better informed ones.

This exchange can take place in discussing the theoretical and normative assumptions of all professionals involved, and introducing alternative theories, views or explanations. In this exchange, the ideas of parents and other close relatives can make an important contribution. The first step in assessment is therefore to gather data on the content and formal aspects of current activities with respect to an individual. This information is primarily based on knowledge collected from direct-support staff and is supplemented by information found in files and reports supplied by parents and/or other carers. This information does not consist of skills categories alone, as such an approach tends to omit information about everyday experience. Nevertheless, skills categories, especially concerning sensory abilities, are very important and should be the subject of assessment by professionals. But behaviours, communication and needs can only be understood in terms of the total context of events, processes, relationships and routines. Differences members of the staff team have about concepts and opinions can become clear within this overall context.

In order to illustrate this process more fully I describe below the case of a young man with Cornelia de Lange syndrome:

Edward is a young man with Cornelia de Lange syndrome. He has profound intellectual and severe motor disabilities. He is unable to speak, use sign language or symbols. Staff says that he is physically very fragile: he suffers from chronic pulmonary infections, has periods in which he vomits regularly, and has chronic constipation. He is tactilely hypersensitive, especially when touching his feet, his back and his face. His sense windows to the outside world are unstable and fragile. Once he has his attention fixed on a certain object or situation, it is difficult to enable him to change his focus, and he may well be overwhelmed by the experience. Edward has a mild visual impairment. Because of problems with food digestion, Edward is fed by a percutane extraperitoneal gastrostomy (PEG) tube. Edward is described as outgoing and cheerful. Staff believe that a lot can be done to stimulate and activate him. He needs a stable attitude towards his world, and therefore his environment should be reliable and understandable; he needs to expand his ways of communicating and he needs more activities, especially those that involve music.

From six months of age, his cheerful mood has been subject to sudden changes. He has heavy outbursts of anger and periods of inconsolable crying. During these periods of anger or crying he bangs his head on the wall, bites his hands, rubs and pokes his eyes, and vomits. Once he starts, it is difficult to stop him. No one knows the cause of these sudden spells. Parents find it very difficult to deal with this behaviour. Edward's mother is especially saddened by the fact that Edward does not want to be touched during these periods of anger and sadness.

During a meeting with all involved, it becomes clear that staff are ambivalent towards Edward. Therapists stressed that Edward is still young and possibilities for development should be addressed here and now. They find it hard to motivate Edward during therapy. Maybe his spells are related to the beginning of puberty? Direct-support personnel stress that they work on several areas of development, and find it hard to set priorities. Also, Edward's mood changes are hard to deal with, and interfere with staff's efforts to stimulate his developmental abilities. When Edward has a crying spell, he is not sensitive to anything or anybody. Direct-support personnel think that Edward is under a lot of strain and they are pleased by a reduction in therapy hours. The GP wants a short-stay admission in the hospital, to exclude a physical cause for Edward's behaviour. He points out that gastro-oesophageal reflux is a frequent disorder in those with profound intellectual and multiple disabilities. Parents stress their son's need for a stable and responsive environment; they think there has been too great a turnover of personnel and believe this has caused Edward's unstable frame of mind.

As shown in this example, professionals tend to relate to one another within a disciplinary framework with its accompanying language and role system. The family itself has alternative explanations for the behaviour. Each presents a fragment of a whole, not an overall view, of the individual. A functional and above all interdisciplinary assessment is recommended. The assessment process should lead to intervention strategies that occur in natural contexts.

7 Developing a Profile from Assessment

The first step in this assessment process is to identify a personal profile. Drawing up such a profile starts with what the person can do, enjoys doing and needs to do because of environmental demands, individual preferences, or for health-care reasons. The process involves taking the person's life history, his or her personal characteristics, the feelings and motives attributed to him or her, and the quality of his or her relationship with support staff. The profile cannot be drawn up unless there is also knowledge of the present situation: which activities, therapies, and skills are offered, by whom and why. Only when all involved have used their knowledge or gathered information and discussed individual viewpoints, and/or observed the person, are there sufficient data for drawing up an overall profile of that person.

Some of the data can be gathered through instruments, by systematic observations or video analysis, discussed more fully in chapter 11, where relevant instruments will also be reviewed. Some information will be based purely on the experience of parents or direct-support personnel. In any case, the drawing up of a profile forces stakeholders to make their priorities explicit in the data gathered. To draw up a good profile, those involved are asked to put into words what to them may be considered obvious. This means discussing competing principles and ideas: Is Edward understimulated or overstimulated? Is there a physical cause for his problems or a lack of secure and responsive people around him? From the profile, a perspective can be articulated. The perspective is actually a normative framework that professionals can use to guide their activities. It indicates a desired situation or advisable change in the future; it makes clear what we should aim at. Drawing up a perspective also means that a professional takes responsibility for the person with profound intellectual and multiple disabilities. A perspective may be vague or only feasible in the long term, but most importantly sets the direction of travel. The perspective can be drawn up only if all stakeholders contribute from their own professional expert analyses. A direction can be taken only if there is a consensus. This does not mean that deliberations go on until there is a joint statement, as in such cases we run the risk that the perspective is about what is desired by or feasible for professionals, not what is desirable for the person with profound intellectual and multiple disabilities. Reaching consensus often means taking chances, cutting knots, making informed choices (Vlaskamp, 1993, 1997).

8 Assessment and Intervention

Assessment of people with profound intellectual and multiple disabilities cannot be isolated from interventions. Assessment is an ongoing process; the results of the interventions should be looked at with an assessor's 'eye'. Establishing goals, both long term and short term, should meet certain requirements. Assessment means that it is known how the person with profound intellectual and multiple disabilities reacts to the activities offered or the opportunities to engage in relationships or experiences. The person should have the opportunity to react to his or her environment, to correct or approve, to steer and guide in the right direction. This is only possible when direct-support personnel and therapists work very accurately and precisely to establish transparent goals, including an accurate description of how, when and by whom activities are to be carried out. The use of objectives such as goal attainment scaling (GAS) (Kiresuk, 1994) can be used as a method to document change as a function of the intervention planned.

The unique functioning and the large number of professionals involved stress the need for a collaborative interdisciplinary assessment. The foundation of the assessment process is that all the parties concerned, support staff, therapists, activity supervisors/instructors, parents and other supporters contribute their part to the integrated and interactive whole of understanding the person with profound intellectual and multiple disabilities. The complexity of developmental disabilities and the interrelated nature of these developmental domains should prompt professionals to work together, share a sense of equal participation in and responsibility for the outcome of the assessment process. It is important to remember that this type of assessment is dynamic and ongoing; the information is checked, rechecked and revised as individual abilities, needs and desires change.

9 Conclusion

Each individual with profound intellectual and multiple disabilities represents a unique configuration of abilities and constraints to functioning, as well as a possibly idiosyncratic communicative repertoire. The more disabled the person is, the more likely it is that the assessor will need personal skills rather than relying entirely on assessment instruments. Assessment will consist of judgements made by all involved in supporting the person with profound intellectual and multiple disabilities. Assessment of people with profound intellectual and multiple disabilities is therefore inherently bound to characteristics of the assessors, and those assessors are also the ones to test their assessment results in practice. To discover their abilities in an interdisciplinary and dynamic way, to assess the meaning and significance of what people with profound intellectual and multiple disabilities do, is a vehicle for understanding them and forms a basis for our interventions. It also acknowledges the participation of the person with profound intellectual and multiple disabilities in the assessment process.

REFERENCES

Arts, W. F. M. (1999) Epilepsie. In H. Evenhuis & L. Nagtzaam (eds.), *Wetenschap en geneeskunde voor mensen met een verstandelijke handicap: Een nieuw ontgonnen gebied in de Nederlandse gezondheidszorg*. Den Haag: NOW, pp. 45–51.

Arvio, M. & Sillanpää, M. (2003) Prevalence, aetiology and co-morbidity of severe and profound intellectual disability in Finland. *Journal of Intellectual Disability Research*, 47, 108–112.

Bayley, N. (1967) *Manual for the Bayley Scales of Infant Development*. New York: Psychological Corporation.

Beange, H., Gale, L. & Stewart, L. (1995) Project re-nourish: A dietary intervention to improve nutritional status in people with multiple disabilities. *Australia and New Zealand Journal of Developmental Disabilities*, **20**, 165–174.

Böhmer, C. J. M., Niezen-de Boer, M. C., Klinkenberg-Knol, E. C., Devillé, W. L. J. M., Nadorp, J. H. S. M. & Meuwissen, S. G. M. (1999) The prevalence of gastro-oesophageal reflux disease in institutionalized intellectually disabled individuals. *American Journal on Gastroenterology*, **94**, 804–810.

Bromley, S. M. (2000) Smell and taste disorders: A primary care approach. *American Family Physician*, **61**, 427–337.

Dunn, W. (1999) The sensorimotor systems: A framework for assessment and intervention. In F. P. Orelove & D. Sobsey (eds.), *Educating Children with Multiple Disabilities: A transdisciplinary approach*. Baltimore, MD: Paul Brookes, pp. 35–79.

Dunst, C. J. (1980) *Clinical and Educational Manual for Use with the Uzgiris and Hunt Scales of Infant Psychological Development*. Austin, TX: Pro-ed.

Evenhuis, H., Theunissen, M., Denkers, I., Verschuure, H. & Kemme, H. (2001) Prevalence of visual and hearing impairment in a Dutch institutionalized population with intellectual disability. *Journal of Intellectual Disability Research*, **45**, 457–464.

Fryers, T. (1984) *The Epidemiology of Severe Intellectual Impairment: The Dynamics of Prevalence*. London: Academic Press.

Gelderen, I. van (2000) Sensory impairment and its correlation with the aetiology of handicaps in people with severe multiple handicaps and intellectual disability. Paper presented at the 11th congress of the IASSID, Seattle.

Grove, N., Bunning, K., Porter, J. & Ollson, C. (1999) See what I mean: Interpreting the meaning of communication by people with severe and profound intellectual disabilities. *Journal of Applied Research in Intellectual Disability*, **12**, 190–203.

Hogg, J. (1992) The administration of psychotropic and anticonvulsant drugs to children with profound intellectual disability and multiple impairments. *Journal of Intellectual Disability Research*, **36**, 473–488.

Hogg, J. & Lambe, L. (1988) *Sons and Daughters with Profound Retardation and Multiple Handicaps Attending Schools and Social Education Centres: Final Report*. London: Mencap.

Inspectie voor de Gezondheidszorg (2000) *Ernstig meervoudig gehandicapt en dán? Een onderzoek naar de kwaliteit van zorg voor mensen met meervoudige complexe handicaps*. Den Haag: Inspectie voor de Gezondheidszorg.

Janicki, M. P. & Dalton, A. J. (1998) Sensory impairments among older adults with intellectual disability. *Journal of Intellectual and Developmental Disability*, **23**, 3–11.

Karnebeek, C. D. M. van, Scheper, F. Y., Abeling, N. G., Alders, M. Barth, P. G., Hoovers, J. M. N., Koevoets, C., Wanders, R. J. A. & Hennekam, R. C. M. (2002) Aetiology of mental retardation or borderline cognitive delay in 281 children referred to a tertiary care centre: A prospective study. In C. D. M. van Karnebeek (ed.), *Mental Retardation: Diagnostic Studies on Aetiology*. Amsterdam: University of Amsterdam Press, 76–109.

Kiresuk, T. J. (ed.) (1994) *Goal Attainment Scaling: Applications, Theory and Measurement*. Mahwah, NJ: Lawrence Erlbaum.

Lowe, M. & Costello, A. J. (1976) *Manual for Symbolic Play Test: Experimental Edition*. Windsor: NFER.

Nakken, H. & Vlaskamp, C. (2002) Joining forces: Supporting individuals with profound multiple learning disabilities. *Tizard Learning Disability Review*, **7**, 10–16.

Oberlander, T. F., O'Donell, M. E. & Montgomery, C. J. (1999) Pain in children with significant neurological impairment. *Journal of Developmental Behavior Pediatrics*, **20**, 235–243.

Pagliano, P. (2001) *Using a Multisensory Environment: A Practical Guide for Teachers*. London: David Fulton.

Porter, J. & Ouvry, C. (2001) Interpreting the communication of people with profound and multiple learning difficulties. *British Journal of Learning Disabilities*, **29**, 12–16.

Quine, L. (1991) Sleep problems in children with mental handicap. *Journal of Mental Deficiency Research*, **35**, 269–290.

Rainforth, B. & York-Barr, J. (1997) *Collaborative Teams for Students with Severe Disabilities: Integrating Therapy and Educational Services*. Baltimore, MD: Paul Brookes.

Rice, H. K. & McDaniel, M. W. (1966) Operant behavior in vegetative patients. *Psychological Record*, **16**, 279–281.

Robertson, I. H. & Murre, J. M. J. (1999) Rehabilitation of brain damage: Brain plasticity and principles of guided recovery. *Psychological Bulletin*, **125**, 544–575.

Schrojenstein Lantman-de Valk, H. M. J. van, Akker, M. van den, Maaskant, M. A., Haveman, M. J., Urlings, H. F. J., Kessels, A. G. H. & Crebolder, F. J. M. (1997) Prevalence and incidence of health problems in people with intellectual disability. *Journal of Intellectual Disability Research*, **41**, 42–51.

Schrojenstein Lantman-de Valk, H. M. J. van, Haveman, M. J., Maaskant, M. A. & Kessels, A. G. H. (1994) The need for assessment of sensory functioning in ageing people with mental handicap. *Journal of Intellectual Disability Research*, **38**, 373–379.

Tröster, H., Brambring, M. & Burg, J. van der (1996) *Early Child Development and Care*, **119**, 1–14.

Užgiris, I. Č. & Hunt, J. McV. (1975) *Assessment in Infancy: Ordinal Scales of Psychological Development*. Champaign, IL: University of Illinois Press.

Vlaskamp, C. (1993) Development and evaluation of individual educational programmes for profoundly multiple handicapped residents. *Issues in Special Education and Rehabilitation*, **8**, 45–51.

Vlaskamp, C. (1997) The implementation of a care programme for individuals with profound multiple disabilities. *European Journal on Mental Disability*, **4**, 3–12.

Vlaskamp, C. (1999) *Een eigen perspectief: Een programma voor mensen met ernstige meervoudige beperkingen* Assen: Van Gorcum.

Warburg, M. (2001) Assessment of visual acuity. *Journal of Intellectual Disability Research*, **45**, 424–438.

Ware, J. (1997) *Educating Children with Profound and Multiple Learning Difficulties*. London: David Fulton.

Woodhouse, J. M., Griffiths, C. & Gedling, A. (2000) The prevalence of ocular defects and the provision of eye care in adults with learning disabilities living in the community. *Ophtalmic Physiology and Optics*, **20**, 79–89.

Woodward, M. (1959) The behaviour of idiots interpreted by Piaget's theory of sensorimotor development. *British Journal of Educational Psychology*, **29**, 60–71.

CHAPTER 4

The assessment of mental illness in individuals with intellectual disabilities

Edwin J. Mikkelsen, Lauren R. Charlot and Arturo Langa

1 Introduction

A thorough assessment process is fundamental to the diagnosis of behavioural disorders as they present in individuals with cognitive impairments, as well as the treatment that follows. The lack of a comprehensive evaluation can lead to errors that are then magnified in the subsequent diagnostic and therapeutic phases of treatment. The urgency of clinical situations can put pressure on assessors to hurry through the early data collection phases of the assessment process, and move directly to making a psychiatric diagnosis. In emergency situations this may, to some extent, be necessary. However, if the crisis nature of a situation dictates immediate decision-making, this does not preclude the assessor from also implementing a prospective data collection system that will allow for the full clarification of behavioural and diagnostic issues as time progresses.

For purposes of this chapter, we have divided the assessment process into the following phases, which are conceptually sequential. However, in practice they frequently overlap considerably.

- *Description of the problematic behaviour*: Clear description of the problematic behaviour in a manner that can be readily understood by others, and which can be empirically measured to the extent possible.
- *Data collection*: The development of a data collection system that allows one to assess the frequency of the behaviour, as well as the intensity of the behaviour.
- *Hypothesis generation*: The descriptive and quantitative data should be used to generate alternative hypothesis, which may explain the aberrant behaviour. This phase is frequently overlooked as assessors rush towards formulating a diagnosis so that treatment can commence.
- *Diagnostic phase*: This phase entails the process of establishing the differential diagnosis, and then arriving at a working diagnosis on which active treatment will be predicated.

- *Evolution of the diagnosis over time*: Although the assessment process initially proceeds in a more or less linear manner, it should not be viewed as terminating when treatment begins. Rather, there is an ongoing, reciprocal interaction between treatment and assessment. The efficacy of various treatment approaches provides new data that either tend to confirm or refute the original working hypothesis and, likewise, the assessment data will impact on the treatment plan as it evolves.

Prior to discussing this five-stage process in more detail, we shall review basic factors, which influence the diagnostic process.

2 General Diagnostic Considerations

The ability to arrive at a reliable psychiatric diagnosis in individuals with intellectual disabilities is affected by several factors.

2.1 Developmental effects of psychiatric disorders and the use of behavioural equivalents

A variety of developmental effects on psychopathology in people with intellectual disabilities have been described (Charlot, 1998; Hurley, 1996) including a tendency to decompensate rapidly under stress, to misconstrue events due to cognitive limitations, to have concrete thinking, and to have poor fantasy/reality distinctions. It is important when evaluating an individual with intellectual disabilities to take into account the ways in which that individual's developmental stage impacts on his or her behaviour and thinking. Sometimes, developmentally appropriate but primitive behaviours or thinking can be mistaken for psychotic ideation (Hurley, 1996). For example, a person with intellectual delay who has similar cognitive features to a typically developing preschool-age child may be seen to talk out loud to herself when anxious. This 'self talk' may seem bizarre if one does not apply a developmental perspective. Important considerations when evaluating a person with cognitive delay are summarized in table 4.1.

An additional source of information about the ways cognitive and other developmental features may affect surface manifestations of psychiatric illness can be found in the current American Psychiatric Association (1994) Diagnostic and Statistical Manual (DSM-IV), in which age effects are described for a number of syndromes (Charlot, 1998). Using the example of depression, DSM-IV notes that children may present more often with irritable mood, withdrawn behaviour, somatic complaints and conduct problems. These variations in phenomenology are consistent with findings for people with intellectual disabilities and depression (Charlot et al., 1993; Meins, 1994; Evans et al., 1999; Johnson et al., 1995; Reiss & Rojhan, 1993). Adults with intellectual disabilities present more as children without disabilities do when depressed, most likely due to the impact of developmental features.

Researchers were initially surprised to find that it was quite common for a person with intellectual disabilities and depression to be irritable and aggressive (Charlot et al., 1993; Meins, 1994; Reiss & Rojan, 1993). Of note is the fact that aggression and other agitated behaviours appear to have diagnostically non-specific surface features that may be a final common pathway for a wide array of underlying problems (Gardner, 2002). Problematic behaviours,

Table 4.1 Developmental Effects on Cognitive Processes that May Impact on Psychiatric Evaluation of Individuals with ID

Magical thinking
Fantasy reality distinctions are poor, not due to psychotic thinking, but due to stage of cognitive development. Individual may be talking to people not present, not because of hallucinations, but because he or she is fantasizing. Wishes may be expressed as beliefs, and can be misconstrued as delusions.

Pre-logical thinking
Thinking that is typical of preschool-aged children and most individuals with severe to moderate ID, and may seem 'tangential', rambling. This is not uncommon in conversations with preschool-aged children, not due to psychosis, but to lack of appreciation of logical relations between subjects.

Concrete thinking
Thinking and reasoning are grounded in the here and now, what can be seen, counted, observed, etc. Example Mental Status Exam question: What does this saying mean: 'People in glass houses should not throw stones'? Patient with ID answered: 'Because the stones would break the glass'. Concrete thinking may also be seen as a sign of a thought disturbance and can be seen in adults with organic brain syndromes.

Egocentrism
Tendency for children to construe reality based only on what they experience. This is related to cognitive capacities in very young children, but is sometimes confused with 'narcissism' (a psychopathologic tendency to be overly self-centered). Preschool-aged children often fail to comprehend that others may see or experience things differently. Individuals with ID may sometimes have difficulty understanding the impact of their behaviour on others due to cognitive limitations, rather than being 'oppositional'.

such as self-injury, aggression and irritability, are often referred to as 'challenging behaviour'. Ross and Oliver (2002) investigated the possible relationship between challenging behaviours and symptoms of depression. They utilized the Mood, Interest and Pleasure Questionnaire (MIPQ) within a total cohort of 53 adults with severe or profound intellectual disabilities. They were able to identify a group with low mood (N = 12) that they could then compare with a group that had higher scores (N = 12). The index of challenging behaviours indicated no differences between the two groups with regard to self-injury, aggression or disturbing behaviour. However, a second analysis for the entire group indicated that those who displayed challenging behaviour scored significantly lower on the MIPQ. A somewhat related study (Tsiouris et al., 2003) indicated that challenging behaviours, such as self-injury or aggression, were not significantly associated with depressive disorders. Because people with intellectual disabilities have a limited behavioural repertoire, they may become aggressive when anxious, depressed, sick, angry or as a way to control events (Charlot et al., 1993, 2002). This appears to be true both for people with intellectual disabilities as well as typically developing children (Puig-Antich, 1982). When trying to make a psychiatric diagnosis, it is important not to get overly focused on aggressive behaviour if this is the 'chief complaint'. The assessor will need to look past this problem to assess fully the individual's overall functioning. Other areas to explore include mood, sleep patterns, eating patterns, motor behaviour, thinking, concentration and other aspects of the person's mental status. In this way, the assessor can ascertain if there are any changes suggesting a departure from that individual's usual behaviour that are occurring in conjunction with the onset of or increase in aggressive behaviour. Another important consideration is that people with intellectual disabilities usually do not refer themselves for psychiatric assessment, and a significant proportion of the data that will be gathered will come from informant reports (Charlot et al., 1993). Research has shown that dependence on informant reports when performing a psychiatric evaluation tends to lead to an overemphasis on externalizing behaviours (Rapoport & Ismond, 1996). Problems such as anxiety and depression can sometimes be underestimated because of this. Although there is no easy answer, it is important to keep this in mind when acting as an informant or when conducting a psychiatric evaluation of a person with intellectual disabilities.

One potential way to ameliorate some of these diagnostic assessment problems is to use behavioural equivalents. These were first described by Sovner and Hurley, and later elaborated by Lowry, who has described 'symptomatic behaviours' seen in depression and mania (Lowry & Sovner, 1992; Sovner & Hurley, 1982a, 1982b). Although it is not always possible, in many instances behaviours that may be seen in individuals with cognitive impairment, which are a likely manifestation of a given psychiatric symptom, can be noted. Charlot and Fletcher (in preparation) have developed a structured interview tool containing behavioural descriptors or equivalents for a number of DSM-IV Axis I syndrome symptoms, including those suggested by Sovner and Hurley and by Lowry for depression and mania. In this structured interview, possible behavioural equivalents for symptoms of generalized anxiety disorder (GAD), obsessive-compulsive disorder, post-traumatic stress disorder and schizophrenia are provided as a guide to the assessor's interview with multiple familiar informants. In table 4.2, behavioural equivalents for GAD from the Charlot Semi-structured Interview for Individuals with Developmental Disabilities (CSI-DD) are listed (Charlot and Fletcher, in preparation).

Table 4.2 Examples from the Charlot Semi-structured Interview for Individuals with Developmental Disabilities (CSI-DD), Including Behavioural Equivalents for DSM-IV Symptom Criteria for Diagnostic Category of Generalized Anxiety Disorder*

All symptoms must be serious and persistent, interfering with normal routines.
Note any behaviours described by informants that appear to be a behavioural manifestation of the symptoms, but are not already listed. Ask informants if the individual displayed . . .
This may be demonstrated in some of the following ways:

1. EXCESSIVE ANXIETY AND WORRY (for at least one month)
   _____ appears anxious much of the time, has a fearful expression, or reports feeling anxious
   _____ appears apprehensive regarding events or activities; i.e. work, family, health, etc.
   _____ appears 'needy' and clinging
   _____ experiences nightmares (associated with anxiety)
   _____ crying or whimpering in a fearful manner
2. DIFFICULTY CONTROLLING WORRY (for at least one month)
   _____ hard to sooth or comfort this person
   _____ appears anxious, tense or agitated, despite efforts to provide support
3. RESTLESSNESS/TENSENESS, (for a least one month)
   _____ hand-wringing (also seen in Retts' disorder)
   _____ tense facial expression or furrowed brow
   _____ reports feeling anxious, nervous, worried, afraid or scared

Source: Charlot and Fletcher (in preparation)

2.2 Reliability of diagnostic assessment methods

It is very important that a diagnostic system has reliability. If one assessor uses the system and makes a particular diagnosis, it is important that almost any assessor would apply the scheme assessing the same person and arrive at the same conclusion. A system must be reliable or its validity cannot be established. Spitzer (1980) described a number of common sources of unreliability in the assessment of children with psychiatric disorder, most of which can be applied to any clinical population, but are particularly salient for individuals whose assessment is heavily dependent on informant reports. Spitzer's observations regarding unreliability in diagnostic assessment are summarized in table 4.3.

Although there may not be any simple solutions to the problem, when evaluating individuals with limited language skills, some steps can be taken. Multiple sources of clinical information can be used to arrive at a diagnosis. As suggested, using clear operational definitions

Table 4.3 Spitzer's Sources of Unreliability in Psychiatric Assessment

Information variance
When there are multiple informants, information given about the patient may differ from one informant to another.

Recommended approach
Clinicians should recognize that informants tend to emphasize aggressive, disruptive behaviours and under-report anxiety, depression, etc. Multiple sources of information can be used to increase reliability, including rating scales, chart reviews and direct patient observations.

* * *

Observation variance
Different clinicians may draw different conclusions, even if they have been given the same information.

Recommended approach
It may help for clinicians to use behavioural equivalents to improve the reliability of symptom identification in people with ID.

* * *

Criterion variance
Even when clinicians are using the same classification system (i.e. ICD-10 or DSM-IV), they may use different thresholds for making a particular diagnosis.

Recommended approach
Using structured or semi-structured interview tools that include recommended threshold or intensity criteria could reduce this type of reliability problem

Source: Spitzer (1980)

of symptoms and behavioural criteria can be helpful, as well as having concrete guides regarding thresholds for labelling a behaviour a symptom. Symptom severity criteria could also be used (i.e. problem is present throughout most of each day, duration of the problem, patient not able to work because of the problem, etc.). Psychiatric evaluations need to be longer when informants must provide a substantial proportion of the clinical data.

2.3 Validity of psychiatric syndromes in special clinical population

Validation of psychiatric syndromes includes several steps. First, there must be a comprehensive description of the symptoms of the syndrome and its associated features. A means reliably to assess for the presence of these phenomena must be developed. When considering individuals with intellectual disabilities, developmental effects should also be described. Studies of family history, laboratory findings and treatment outcome can then provide external validation. It is not until these steps have been taken that rates of disorder within a given population can be established (Cantwell, 1996).

Most DSM-IV psychiatric syndromes have not been validated in individuals with intellectual disabilities. Validation of syndromes with core features that are more 'internalized' is likely to be more difficult than for externalizing disorders. It will be important to deal with the fact that psychiatric evaluation of people with intellectual disabilities often relies heavily on the use of informant reports, which, in turn, results in an increased emphasis on externalizing behaviour problems. In individuals with developmental disabilities, a further challenge will be to examine the extent to which genetic syndromes commonly resulting in intellectual disability and other developmental disabilities are also associated with specific psychiatric sequelae. (See also chs. 8 and 16 on behavioural phenotypes.) Individuals with intellectual disabilities may also be at risk for missed medical diagnoses, with high rates of physical health and medication side-effect problems that mask or mimic acute psychiatric illness (Ryan & Sunada, 1997; Charlot et al., 2002). There have been efforts to provide guidance for assessors in applying the ICD-10 classification of mental illness (see page 58) to the diagnosis of these disorders in individuals with intellectual disability (World Health Organization, 1992). A related guide has also been developed by an expert group in the United Kingdom and in Ireland (Royal College of Psychiatrists, 2001). This system utilizes three axes. The first axis addresses the severity of the intellectual disability, the second axis addresses causation and the third axis is used to note specific mental health problems.

A variety of factors impact on the diagnosis of mental health problems in people with intellectual disabilities. These include intelligence, verbal ability, decreased ability for abstract thought, suggestibility, non-specific effects of central nervous system impairment and diagnostic overshadowing. Each will be considered in the following sections.

2.3.1 Intelligence and verbal ability
In those individuals who are functioning in the mild to borderline range of intelligence it should be relatively easy to utilize standard diagnostic criteria, such as those found DSM-IV. However, as intelligence decreases through the moderate range and into the severe to profound area, it can become increasingly difficult to establish a reliable psychiatric diagnosis. Depending on the aetiology of the intellectual disability, there may also be selective impairments in expressive abilities. Many of the DSM-IV

diagnoses require access to the individual's internal state of mind to fulfil the criteria. Examples of major DSM-IV diagnostic criteria that require this type of information are discussed below. Although these examples relate specifically to the DSM-IV, they are also relevant to the International Classification of Diseases (ICD-10).

2.3.1.1 Obsessive-compulsive disorders (OCD)

Most assessors who work with individuals who have development disabilities acknowledge that obsessive-compulsive behaviours are a relatively frequent phenomenon. The DSM-IV criteria for obsessions almost all rely on the individual's capability to describe his or her own internal state to a significant degree. Specifically, the four major criteria for obsessions are:

• 'recurrent and persistent thoughts, impulses, or images that are experienced . . . as intrusive and inappropriate and that cause marked anxiety or distress
• these thoughts or impulses should not be simply excessive worries about real-life problems
• the person attempts to ignore or suppress these thoughts or impulses
• the individual recognizes that these thoughts are a product of his own mind'

The criteria for compulsions (DSM-IV, pp. 417–436) would, at first, appear to be somewhat easier to meet, as they are for the most part observable phenomena. However, DSM-IV notes that the compulsive behaviour must be 'aimed at preventing or reducing distress or preventing some dreaded event or situation' and 'the person feels driven to perform in response to an obsession or according to rules that must be applied rigidly'. Thus one cannot make a valid DSM-IV based diagnosis of obsessive-compulsive behaviour without verbal access to some relatively sophisticated thoughts on the part of the individual.

OCD has been studied extensively in clinical populations of adults without intellectual disabilities, and more has been learned about its phenomenology. Of note is the fact that certain subtypes seem to occur more frequently than others. For example, fears about contamination and associated cleaning rituals appear to be the most common form of OCD symptoms reported by outpatients without intellectual disabilities. Some subtypes occur less frequently, and may actually be more treatment resistant, such as having the need for symmetry and hoarding behaviours. Although research is limited, there is some suggestion that people with intellectual disabilities may present with different phenomenology than individuals with OCD in the general population. McDougle et al. (1995) reported on 50 individuals with OCD symptoms and autistic disorder, comparing them to 50 individuals without intellectual disabilities who also exhibited OCD. Those with an autistic disorder were more likely to present with hoarding, ordering and touching rituals, as well as self-injurious behaviour (SIB) than subjects without intellectual disabilities. King (1993) actually proposed a theory that self-injurious behaviour may sometimes be a compulsive behaviour. He cited research showing strong correlations between other symptoms of OCD and SIB, as well as other repetitive movement problems (stereotypies) (Bodfish et al., 1995; Powell et al., 1996). Also, in some cases, people who engage in SIB that appears compulsive in nature will try to restrain themselves. This is similar to reports from people without intellectual disabilities who describe a desire to resist compulsions. In a similar manner to children, people with intellectual disabilities and OCD may lack insight into the pathologic nature of their symptoms (Vitiello et al., 1989).

2.3.1.2 General anxiety disorder Similar difficulties exist for general anxiety disorder in that the primary criteria require some ability to self-report to fulfill three of the following six criteria (DSM-IV, pp. 432–436):

- 'restlessness or feeling keyed up or on edge
- being easily fatigued
- difficulty concentrating
- irritability
- muscle tension
- sleep disturbance'

The text notes, 'only one item is required in children'. However, using only one of these (i.e. sleep disturbance or irritability) would seem to make the diagnosis meaningless, as these individual symptoms can be observed in so many other syndromes. Some likely developmental features of anxiety are noted in table 4.2.

2.3.1.3 Psychotic disorder There are also difficulties in using the DSM-IV criteria for psychotic disorder (pp. 273–290) in that one cannot document the presence of delusions and hallucinations without confirmatory feedback from the individual, and these are integral to a diagnosis of schizophrenia.

2.3.1.4 Depressive disorders There are some DSM-IV diagnoses, such as major depressive disorder, in which criteria are directly applicable to individuals with intellectual disabilities. In the case of major depressive disorder (pp. 339–345), this is because many of the essential criteria include the phrase 'As indicated by either subjective report or observation made by others'. However, the criteria for dysthymic disorder again require more subjective reporting from the individual. McBrien (2003) has extensively reviewed the issues related to establishing a diagnosis of depression in individuals with intellectual disabilities. She notes a distinction between those with mild to moderate intellectual disability, as opposed to those who function in the severe to profound range, which is consistent with our experience.

2.3.1.5 Intermittent explosive disorder Intermittent explosive disorder (IED) is another DSM-IV diagnosis (pp. 345–349) that relies heavily on observable phenomena, and this may explain why it is so commonly used in this population. These criteria for intermittent explosive disorder are:

- 'Several discrete episodes of failure to resist aggressive impulses that result in serious assaultive acts or destruction of property
- the degree of aggressiveness expressed during the episodes is grossly out of proportion to any precipitating psycho-social stressor
- the aggressive episodes are not accounted for by another mental disorder'

The problem here, of course, is that the diagnosis is so descriptive that it could be used for individuals who actually have the behaviour due to another disorder, such as a psychotic disorder, but the lack of verbal access to the individual's thought process makes it impossible to establish another diagnosis. These factors may contribute to the relative over-reliance on this purely descriptive diagnosis for individuals with developmental disabilities who also present with aggressive behaviour.

In the section on 'mental retardation' in DSM-IV, the authors do note the difficulty in establishing some diagnostic criteria for different disorders in this population, and suggest the use of the qualifying phrase 'not other specified' in these situations. As with any syndrome diagnosis, it is important to look at other factors relative to differential diagnosis that may include consideration of age at onset, clinical history and course of illness, familial patterns of illness, and contextual factors. For example, a diagnosis of IED should be reserved for situations in which the symptoms seen cannot be better explained by another diagnosis.

2.3.2 Decreased ability to think abstractly

In addition to the difficulties in verbal expression, the ability to think abstractly also decreases with declining intelligence. The resulting concreteness of interpretation and expression can further impair an adequate assessment of the individual's internal state of mind. For example, it is not uncommon to inquire about hallucinations using simple terminology that one would think the individual can understand, and obtain an affirmative response. Then, upon further inquiry, it is ascertained that the individual's response was affected by their concreteness and that they were actually affirming hearing a voice when someone was actually calling them from another room. The same type of misinterpretation can occur with inquiries into delusional and/or paranoid ideation. Thus it is extremely important to account for this in one's assessment.

2.3.3 Suggestibility

Mikkelsen and Stelk (1999) have reviewed the forensic literature with regard to legal issues related to individuals with developmental disabilities who also commit criminal offenses. (See also discussions of suggestibility and its assessment in chs. 6 and 14.) In this context there are a number of studies indicating that individuals with developmental disabilities can be quite prone to respond to questions in a manner that they believe will please the interviewer. This has obvious implications with regard to criminal interrogations, but also has relevance for more routine psychiatric clinical assessments.

2.3.4 Nonspecific effects of central nervous system impairment

The DSM-IV criteria were largely developed by consensus of diagnostically related expert panels, and then field-tested for reliability. For the most part, the clinical database upon which these criteria were derived involved adults and children of average intelligence. As indicated above, one usually encounters relatively little difficulty in directly applying these criteria to individuals who function in the borderline to mild range of intellectual deficiency. However, as one approaches the severe to profound range of intellectual disabilities it can become difficult fully to assess thought processes. This is primarily related to the decrease in expressive ability, as many individuals who function in this range have no productive speech, or have only limited means of communication.

It has been well documented that individuals with intellectual disabilities can experience the entire range of psychiatric disorders that are encountered within the general population. However, it also seems plausible that as one reaches the profound end of the spectrum of intellectual disability, there very well could exist disorders that are not fully accounted for in the DSM-IV. Examples of these potential types of disorders would include basic diffuse dysregulation of impulses, mood and thought processes.

2.3.5 Diagnostic overshadowing   The phenomenon of diagnostic overshadowing has been extensively reviewed by Jopp and Keys (2001), who define this concept in the following manner: 'Diagnostic overshadowing is a tendency that professionals have to inaccurately assess the degree of concomitant psychopathology evidenced by people with cognitive deficits, when compared to people without such deficits' (p. 417). In their attempt to better understand this process, they reviewed 12 studies that investigated 'moderators of diagnostic overshadowing' (p. 416). In essence, the term 'diagnostic overshadowing' refers to the difficulty that assessors encounter in assessing the contributions of multiple factors to a given clinical presentation, and the related tendency to respond to this complexity by diagnostic oversimplification, which can lead to the exclusion of co-morbid diagnoses.

A clear example of this is provided by Reiss et al. (1982). Here psychologists were asked to compare identical schizophrenic symptomatology in 'average', 'alcoholic' and 'mentally retarded' descriptions. The results indicated that the psychologists 'were generally more likely to rate an individual as having a single diagnosis, rather than multiple diagnoses' (Jopp & Keys, 2001, p. 417) and that individuals with developmental disabilities were 'rated significantly less likely than individuals in either of the other groups to have a concomitant mental illness' (p. 417).

3 Systematic Identification of Mental Health Problems

The extensive educational and research efforts carried out in the 1980s and 1990s with regard to clarifying the existence of mental illness in individuals with developmental disabilities has, to some extent, ameliorated these issues, though this review suggests that the difficulty still persists.

3.1 Description of the problematic behaviour

A fundamental distinction can be made between behaviours that have evolved on a learned or operant basis, as opposed to behaviours that are the outgrowth of an endogenous psychiatric disorder. Learned behaviours are often understandable, but are frequently not productive from a cost–benefit ratio standpoint. For example, hitting oneself to gain the attention of a caregiver serves a purpose, but the cost is high and is not guaranteed to produce the desired result. These behaviours are often the outgrowth of accidental learning and may respond to behavioural intervention. In this chapter, the term 'pathological' is used to refer to behaviours that have no apparent benefit to the individual.

The purpose of a clear description of the behaviour is not to lead to an immediate determination of the aetiology of the behaviour, but rather to provide the type of information that can contribute to this determination as the assessment process continues. The best way to accomplish this is to begin with a thorough description of the overt behaviour that attracted one's attention, the antecedent conditions that preceded the incident, approximately how long the behavioural incident lasted, how it evolved and resolved, and what events followed. This task can appear to be more daunting than it actually is. The following examples (tables 4.4, 4.5) are relatively brief, yet show how significant information is provided.

Table 4.4 Negative Behavioural Interaction and its Resolution: 1

Overt behaviour
John approached his peer, Bill, and began slapping him forcefully on the back with his open right hand. He gave him three sharp hits in the course of a few seconds and then walked away.

Antecedent context
Bill did not appear to irritate John. However, Bill is frequently verbally abusive to John.

Evolution and resolution of incident
John walked away after hitting Bill. Bill did not physically retaliate, but yelled out loudly so that he drew staff's attention. John was directed to a quiet area of the residence without resistance. He indicated that Bill 'had been nasty to me'.

Table 4.5 Negative Behavioural Interaction and its Resolution: 2

Overt behaviour
Henry began striking out at the air. Bill was walking through the room, and when Henry saw him he moved towards him and began to direct the blows towards him.

Antecedent context
Henry was turning his head to the right and speaking loudly, although no one could be seen in his immediate area and the observer heard no one speaking to him.

Evolution and resolution of incident
When Henry was approached by staff, he continued to strike out, but could be directed to a quiet area. He continued to strike out at the air and to speak loudly, as if he were talking to someone. After approximately 20 minutes, he began to calm down.

These brief examples provide information to assist the assessor in differentiating learned behaviours and those that are the outgrowths of an underlying psychiatric disorder. Example 1 suggests an aggressive incident that was an outgrowth of a *premeditated* act of aggression – whereas the particulars of Example 2 are more suggestive of aggression that is the result of a psychotic process involving a response to presumed auditory and visual hallucinations. Over time, the collection of a number of these brief examples of behaviour can begin to provide the basis on which to construct a comprehensive diagnostic formulation.

For most individuals, the type of overt behaviour will cluster into a finite number of behavioural subtypes, making it possible to categorize the behaviour and then track the frequency and duration by subtype. For example: unprovoked aggression – hits; unprovoked aggression – bites; provoked aggression – hits, self-injurious behaviour, head to object, self-injurious behaviour, bites, and so on.

An example of a fairly comprehensive listing of the types of overt behaviour that can be recorded is contained in table 4.6.

Table 4.6 Behavioural Information

Subjective	*Objective*
1. Depressed mood	1. Aggression towards staff
2. Suicidal ideation	a. Hitting
3. Self-destructive ideation	b. Biting
4. Sleep disorder	c. Kicking
5. Appetite disturbance	d. Pulling hair
6. Non-compliance	e. Other
7. Decreased work performance	
8. Crying	2. Aggression towards clients
9. Somatization	a. Hitting
10. Easy fatigability/apathy	b. Biting
11. Withdrawn behaviour	c. Kicking
12. Screaming	d. Pulling hair
13. Psychotic ideation	e. Other
14. Hallucinations	
	3. Aggression towards self
	a. Head hits
	b. Biting self
	c. Gouging eyes
	d. Pulling hair
	e. Other
	4. Property destruction
	5. Denotative behaviour
	6. Clothes ripping
	7. Enuresis
	8. Encopresis
	9. Smearing faeces
	10. Weight changes
	11. Eating disturbance
	12. Sleep
	13. Crying
	14. Self-induced vomiting
	15. Pica
	16. Suicide attempts
	17. Suicide gestures
	18. Other

3.2 Data collection

The subclassification of the aberrant behaviour into clusters makes it easier to track the frequency of the behaviours. The ultimate purpose of the data collection process is to provide as many clues as possible to aid in the diagnostic process, as well as to provide important information on the severity of the disorder. This severity-intensity factor will figure predominantly in later discussions concerning the calculation of the risk–benefit ratio of potential pharmacological, behavioural and other treatment interventions. With regard to the frequency data, one is interested in more than just the total and overall frequencies of the behaviour over time. Specifically, the assessor should be able to analyse the frequency data with regard to both the inter- and intra-day distribution, as well as the duration of the episodes.

An example where this type of specific information was of value in discerning the aetiology of the behaviour is as follows:

> Mary was a 26-year-old female with severe intellectual disabilities. She engaged in severe self-injurious behaviour, which often took the form of her biting her fingers quite severely. The average frequency of the self-injurious behaviour was fairly consistent from week to week and month to month. However, when the data were analysed for intra-day distribution, it became apparent that the majority (in excess of 90% of episodes of hand-biting) consistently occurred during the hours of 6.00–7.00 p.m.

This observation then raised the question as to what was occurring in Mary's life between the hours of 6.00–7.00 p.m. It emerged that this was a very chaotic time when the individuals on her unit were showered. It was also revealed that staff members were not always as sensitive to the temperature of the water as they should be, and that Mary had a variant of Raynaud's disease. Hence, if the water was too cool, she could experience pain in her fingertips. This led to a change in Mary's treatment plans so that she received an individual, warm bath in a tub. The result of this was that the self-injurious behaviour decreased dramatically in both frequency and severity.

Although this data collection method can appear to be an extremely time-consuming process, it can be effectively accomplished with a simple calendar/log approach. An example of this would simply involve adding a date and time to the example provided in the descriptive section above. Another (even more abbreviated) example is as follows:

8.15–8.25 a.m.:	Verbal aggression
Antecedent:	Difficulty getting organized for transition to day programme
Terminated:	Left for day programme
6.30–7.00 p.m.:	Verbal aggression and property destruction (throwing objects)
Antecedent:	Exploded when prompted to help clean up after evening meal
Terminated:	Allowed me to help to get the work organized

Analysis of the data collected provides valuable information for the subsequent tasks involved in the assessment process. Preliminary examples of questions that can be answered by the analysis are as follows:

- Is there a periodicity to the frequency distribution that would be suggestive of a clinical mood disorder?

- Does the behaviour occur at almost exactly the same time each day, suggesting an environmental precipitant?
- Does the behaviour occur only in one setting; e.g. in the day habilitation programme and not in the residence, suggesting an environmental precipitant?
- Does the behaviour occur on what appears to be a totally random basis, suggesting psychiatric illness, such as psychosis or an intermittent explosive disorder?
- Does the overt behaviour occur in conjunction with more subjective behaviours, such as depressed mood or apparent hallucination activity, suggesting that it may be related to an underlying psychiatric disorder?

Although the accurate reporting of frequency is important, it can be misleading without additional information on intensity. Intensity can be much harder to measure in an objective manner compared to frequency; that is, what one rater might consider to be a 'hard hit' could to another rater appear to be a 'mild' or a 'moderate hit'. In order to assist in the assessment of intensity/severity, Mikkelsen and McKenna (1999) have developed a 10-point continuum to assist in the rating of severity, as based on empirical verifiable evidence (table 4.7). The data on frequency and severity can then be easily graphed by using the 10-point intensity continuum as the horizontal axis, and frequency as the vertical axis. Frequencies can be reported on an absolute basis or can be collapsed into the 10-point continuum illustrated in table 4.8.

Different behaviours can then be displayed on the same graph by using abbreviations, such as aggression and self-injurious behaviour.

The monitoring of more subjective symptoms, such as mood, is much more problematic. Although these ratings are inherently subjective, one can make the process as objective as possible by developing a consensus among the members of the clinical team with regard to the behavioural criteria for different states of mood and then using a simple 5-point scale that would have '0' for normal mood, '−1' for mild depression, '−2' for significantly depressed mood, '+1' for mildly elevated mood, and '+2' for hypomanic-manic symptomatology. These data can be tracked on a daily or shift basis, and can then be chronicled by using a linear calendar/log approach that simply has bars extending one or two blocks above the line for

Table 4.7 Behavioural Severity Rating Continuum

1. Behaviour causes mild, infrequent annoyance to self or others.
2. Behaviour causes severe disruption to quality of life of self or others.
3. Significant verbal aggression, periodic mild property destruction.
4. Frequent destruction of property.
5. Frequent self-injurious or aggressive behaviour barely leading to tissue damage.
6. Frequent self-injurious or aggressive behaviour that leads to tissue damage.
7. Disfiguring self-mutilation or disfiguring aggression towards others.
8. Self-injurious or aggressive behaviour leading to reversible loss of physical function (i.e. fractures, repairable detached retina, loss of consciousness, concussion) to self or others.
9. Self-injurious or aggressive behaviour leading to irreversible loss of physical function (enucleation, paralysis) to self or others.
10. Self-injurious or aggressive behaviour leading to loss of life to self or others.

Table 4.8 Frequency Continuum Scale

1. One episode per 6 months or less
2. One episode every 3–6 months
3. One episode every 1–3 months
4. One episode every 1–4 weeks
5. One episode every week
6. Two–three episodes every week
7. Six–seven episodes every week
8. One–two episodes every day
9. Two–five episodes every day
10. Greater than five episodes every day

the positive excursions from euthymia, while blocks extending below the horizontal line indicate degrees of depression. A group that studies bipolar disorder at the US National Institute of Mental Health has developed this type of charting over several years, and the instrument is referred to as the National Institute of Mental Health Life Chart Methodology (NIMH-LCM) (Leverich & Post, 1998). This methodology was developed to measure the excursions of mood in adults of average intelligence who have manic-depressive illness. The NIMH rating system uses 4-point excursions above the horizontal axis for manic symptomatology and excursions below the axis for depressive symptoms. For both depressive and manic symptoms the four points are labelled

- mild
- low moderate
- high moderate
- severe

The example cited for a severe rating of manic symptoms is 'family and friends want me in the hospital'. An example of a descriptor for mild elevation is 'very energetic, enhanced functioning or slightly disorganized'.

Although the rating of mood is necessarily somewhat subjective, there are overt behaviours that can also be monitored, and which provide additional objective information that can assist in establishing a diagnosis of a mood disorder. These include overt behaviours, such as crying, meal refusals and non-compliance. Many of these ancillary behaviour correlates of affective disorders can be found in table 4.6. Examples of descriptors for the extreme points on the depressive continuum are severe, 'largely unable to function because of depression', and mild, 'low mood, but essentially no impairment in usual functioning'.

As noted above, this methodology was developed for use with verbal individuals of average intelligence who are capable of self-report. However, the methodology can be modified for use with individuals who are not verbal and who have significant cognitive handicaps (King & McCartney, 1999; Lowry, 1997). In these situations the ratings are determined by observers, rather than by the individual themselves. Examples of the modification of this methodology for use with an individual with developmental disabilities are shown in table 4.9 with respect to mania and depression.

Table 4.9 Modification of Observational Methodology for Individuals with Intellectual Disabilities: Mania and Depression

3a: Mania

Severe: Restless (unable to sit at least 50% of the time). Significant sleep disturbance. Inability to focus on activities, and high-intensity aggression. Perseveration on upcoming events or routines for sustained periods of time without being able to be redirected.

Moderate high: Restless movement paired with a steady gait and head up, energized, excessive laughing. Some sleep disturbance. Excessively focused on eating/drinking. Hard to redirect to or away from activities. Clear speech with a perseverative quality. High intensity head-bangs or hand bites. Not able to be engaged in preferred TV shows.

Moderate low: Running outside the house, repetitive touching of objects (the stove, behind the furnace, light switches, etc.). Displaying mild to moderate head-bangs or hand bites that are paired with laughter. Perseverative speech paired with a demanding tone. Intrusive to staff's space (hand grabbing, face grabbing).

Mild: Moving from one room to another, talking clearly, able to follow redirection with minimal cues. Short periods of perseveration. Easily engaged in conversation or activities.

3b: Depression

Severe: Awake, slumped over when sitting, head down, unsteady when walking, drooling. Mumbling when talking, unable to be understood. Minimal or no verbal interaction with staff.

Moderate high: Perseveration on negative issues, focus on abandonment issues. Hard to redirect, little–no eye contact, intrusive to staff's space, whining paired with perseveration. Requires labour-intensive staff redirection to complete activities of daily living. May appear restless with an overall tiredness (looking like he wants/needs to sleep but is unable to). Excessive napping (more than 2 hours during the day). Moderate–high consecutive incidents of aggression.

Moderate low: Perseveration on upcoming issues, reaching/grabbing for staff with low energy. Intermittent verbal interaction that is done in a whispering voice. Unresponsive to staff's questions or processing, few independent verbalizations. Not able to be engaged in preferred TV shows.

Mild: Quiet, whispering when talking, flat, plain affect and mood. Requires staff cues to interact. Greasy or dishevelled in appearance, whining during shower routine.

Measurement of sleep is also an extremely important behavioural dimension that can be objectively monitored. The sleep data can then be reported in terms of the monthly range, average hours per night, the number of nights with less than four hours of sleep, and number of nights awake for the entire night.

3.3 Hypothesis generation

This phase of the assessment process is frequently overlooked, leading assessors prematurely to form conclusions as to the etiology of a behavioural disorder. Once this conclusion is reached, there is considerable risk of assessment bias as the subsequent data that do not fit with the hypothesis tend to be ignored or underweighted. In addition, more effort may be expended searching for data that confirms the premature hypothesis to the exclusion of evidence of equal weight that would support an alternate hypothesis. Unless the diagnosis is extremely obvious, it is useful to attempt to generate at least three working hypotheses derived from the existing subjective observations and objective data. A two-column ledger sheet can then be utilized for each hypothesis to list the observations that either support or do not support each hypothesis. A notation can also be made of additional clarifying information to be collected in the future.

This period of reflection on the data is also a useful time specifically to review information that might suggest a primary medical or behavioural contribution to the aberrant behaviour. An added advantage of this process is that it can keep the team alert to the fact that the behaviour may well have multiple contributions, which need to be addressed by different treatment modalities.

3.4 Diagnostic phase

The process of establishing a psychiatric diagnosis for individuals with intellectual disabilities parallels the process that is used for individuals within the general population. The cornerstone of this process is a detailed history with regard to the evolution of the individual's symptoms over time. This history is placed in the context of a thorough developmental history that includes the aetiology of the individual's intellectual disability, the rate of acquistion of basic developmental milestones, and a description of the highest level of functioning the individual attained before the onset of the psychiatric symptoms. An extensive family history with regard to the incidence of psychiatric illness in first-degree relatives may also shed some light on genetic considerations that can help to clarify a complicated differential diagnosis. The response patterns of family members to specific psychotropic medications may also inform the selection of specific pharmacological treatments.

However, the diagnostic process can also be more complex than that commonly employed with the general population. The first of these potential complications relates to the factors that may impede the ability of the individuals being evaluated to provide a thorough description of their own experience of the symptoms. The primary factors in this regard are their receptive and expressive verbal abilities, as discussed above. However, these limitations should not lead the assessor to ignore the individuals as potential informants. Every attempt should be made to capture their description of their own feelings in their own words, no matter how limited their verbal abilities may be. In those situations where individuals are non-verbal, meaningful observations can still be made with regard to observations related to

- general level of alertness
- motor activity level
- degree of spontaneous interaction with others
- stereotypic mannerisms
- preoccupation with internal stimuli
- the presence of any self-injurious behaviour or its sequela, such as scarring
- the presence of any aggressive behaviour
- any indication that the individual may be experiencing medication side effects in the form of abnormal motor movements

In addition to interested family members, many individuals with intellectual disabilities will also have caregivers who may provide valuable information with regard to establishing a psychiatric diagnosis. These caregivers will usually fall into two broad groups comprising those who work with the individuals in the residential setting and those who work with them in their day programme or at their worksite. Ideally, an attempt should be made to obtain information from both groups of providers. Of particular interest is any discrepancy between the reports of these individuals, as problems that exist only at the residence or only at the work site (to the exclusion of the other) is a clue that environmental factors may be a major determinant of the problematic behaviour. In addition to these traditional sources of information, one will also have available the precise behavioural data described in section 1 above.

4 Advances in the Diagnosis of Mental Illness in Individuals with Developmental Disabilities

Since the 1980s there has been substantial progress in the refinement of the diagnostic assessment of individuals with developmental disabilities who also experience mental illness. This progress has been the most striking in the area of affective illness. A key impetus to this progress was the publication by Sovner and Hurley (1983), in a well-respected psychiatric journal, which clearly established the presence of affective disorders in individuals with developmental disabilities. Since that time, there have been numerous articles addressing the diagnosis of both depressive disorders (Charlot, 1997; Mikkelsen, 1997) and bipolar disorders (Pary et al., 1999). As already noted (section 3.2), the NIMH Life Charting Methodology has also been modified for use with individuals with developmental disorders who also have a bipolar disorder (King & McCartney, 1999; Lowry, 1997).

Progress has also been made in the diagnostic process with regard to anxiety disorders (Stavrakaki & Mintsioulis, 1997; Khreim & Mikkelsen, 1997) and obsessive-compulsive disorder (Gedye, 1996). As a result of these clinical advances, the diagnostic process has become much more sophisticated (Silka & Hauser, 1997; Hauser, 1997). The interface between psychiatric diagnosis and treatment has been the subject of three recent extensive 'best practice publications' (Reiss & Aman, 1998; Szymanski et al., 1999; Rush & Frances, 2000). In addition to the clinical advances in diagnosis and assessment, there have also been efforts to develop rating scales that would aid in the assessment process. Of interest in this regard is a publication by Gedye (1998), which is a series of symptom-based checklists that facilitate the assessment process by providing a context for integrating the observation of discrete behaviours in a manner that may then lead to a diagnostic hypothesis. This series of checklists has not been rigorously studied, but it does contain a great deal of common sense, practicality and appeal.

The most well-developed and intensively studied rating scale instruments are the Aberrant Behavior Checklist (Aman & Singh, 1986, 1994), the Reiss Screen for Maladaptive Behaviors (Reiss, 1988), and its child and adolescent version, The Reiss Scales (Reiss & Valenti-Hein, 1994), The Psychopathology Instrument for Mentally Retarded Adults (PIMRA) (Matson, 1997), and The Psychiatric Assessment Schedule for Adults with Developmental Disabilities (PAS-ADD) (Moss et al., 1996a, 1996b). (See ch. 13 for a detailed discussion of the principal instruments for assessing challenging behaviour.) There have also been efforts made to modify well-accepted scales from general psychiatry for use with individuals who have developmental disabilities. For example, the Zung Self-Rating Anxiety Scale has been adapted in such a manner (Lindsay et al., 1994), and a similar modification of the Beck Anxiety and Depression Inventories is in development (Lindsay et al., 2004). The specifics of the primary ratings scales will be discussed in chapter 12.

5 Evolution of the Diagnosis over Time

Establishing a psychiatric diagnosis in difficult to diagnose individuals should be seen as an evolving process. In particular, the response to treatment interventions will provide useful information with regard to the validity of the working diagnosis. For example, if the working diagnosis is that of a depressive disorder and the symptoms substantially remit following treatment with an antidepressant medication, that response would tend to support the diagnosis of a primary depressive disorder. However, if the individual developed manic symptoms when treated with the antidepressant and then subsequently displayed a sustained, long-term response to a mood stabilizer such as lithium or valproic acid, that would suggest that the depressive symptoms may have represented the depressed phase of a bipolar disorder (Mikkelsen et al., 1997).

In a related fashion, if there have been several unsuccessful medication trials, that might suggest that a behavioural component may be overlooked. Conversely, if several well-reasoned behavioural strategies have not been effective, one might be overlooking a more biologically driven disorder. Thus, one is continually re-evaluating the diagnostic formulation with the progression of time and the addition of new information.

6 Conclusion

A thorough assessment for mental illness in individuals with developmental disabilities is multifaceted and includes considerations of behavioural, medical, environmental and psychiatric contributions. The foundation of the diagnostic process is a clear description of the maladaptive/pathological behaviour that is supported by as much objective data as possible. Efforts should be made to document symptoms that are subjective in nature in as reliable a manner as possible. These data are then utilized to generate a hypothesis to explain the aberrant behaviour, which can include both behavioural and psychiatric considerations. This process will, in turn, lead to the establishment of both a differential diagnosis and a working diagnosis for treatment planning.

The last two decades have seen substantial progress in the refinement of the diagnosis of psychiatric disorders in individuals with developmental disabilities. This progress has been aided by the development of specific rating instruments and scales, which will be discussed in more detail in chapter 12.

REFERENCES

Aman, M. G. & Singh, N. N. (1986) *Aberrant Behaviour Checklist Manual.* East Aurora, NY: Slosson Educational Publications.

Aman, M. G. & Singh, N. N. (1994) *Aberrant Behaviour Checklist Community Supplementary Manual.* East Aurora, NY: Slosson Educational Publications.

American Psychiatric Association (1994) *Diagnostic and Statistical Manual of Mental Disorders* (4th ed.). Washington, DC: American Psychiatric Association.

Bodfish, J. W., Crawford, T. W., Powell, S. B., Parker D. E., Golden, R. N. & Lewis, M. H. (1995) Compulsions in adults with mental retardation: Prevalence, phenomenology, and comorbidity with stereotypy and self-injury. *American Journal of Mental Retardation,* **100**, 183–192.

Cantwell, D. P. (1996) Classification of child and adolescent psychopathology. *Journal of Child Psychology and Psychiatry,* **17**, 3–12.

Charlot, L. R. (1997) Irritability, aggression, and depression in adults with mental retardation: A developmental perspective. *Psychiatric Annals,* **27**, 190–197.

Charlot, L. R. (1998) Developmental effects on mental health disorders in persons with intellectual disabilities. *Mental Health Aspects of Intellectual Disabilities,* **1**, 29–38.

Charlot, L. R., Abend, S., Silka, V. R., Kuropatkin, B. B., Garcia, O., Bolduc, M. & Foley, M. (2002) A short-stay inpatient psychiatric unit for adults with developmental disabilities. In J. Jacobsen (ed.), *Model Programs for Individuals with Developmental Disabilities and Psychiatric Disorders.* Kingston, NY: NADD, pp. 35–54.

Charlot, L. R., Doucette, A. D. & Mezzecappa, E. (1993) Affective symptoms in institutionalized adults with mental retardation. *American Journal of Mental Retardation,* **98**, 408–416.

Charlot, L. R. & Fletcher, K. (in preparation) Use of behavioral equivalents to assess inpatients with intellectual disabilities and mood and anxiety disorders: Results from a pilot investigation.

Evans, L. M., Cotton, M. M., Enfield, S. L. & Florio, T. (1999) Assessment of depression in adults with severe or profound intellectual disability. *Journal of Intellectual and Developmental Disability,* **24**, 147–160.

Gardner, W. (2002) Understanding challenging behaviours. In D. M. Griffiths, W. I. Gardner & J. A. Nuget (eds.), *Behavioural Supports: Individual Centered Interventions: A Multimodal Functional Approach.* Kingston, NY: NADD, pp. 35–54.

Gedye, A. (1996) Issues involved in recognizing obsessive-compulsive disorder in developmentally disabled clients. *Seminars in Clinical Neuropsychiatry,* **1**, 142–147.

Gedye, A. (1998) *Behavioral Diagnostic Guide for Developmental Disabilities.* Vancouver: Diagnostic Books.

Hauser, M. J. (1997) The role of the psychiatrist in mental retardation. *Psychiatric Annals,* **27**, 170–181.

Hurley, A. D. (1996) The misdiagnosis of hallucinations and delusions in persons with mental retardation: A neurodevelopmental perspective. *Seminars in Clinical Neuropsychiatry,* **1**, 122–133.

Johnson, C. R., Handen, B. L., Lubetsky, M. J. & Sacco, K. A. (1995) Affective disorders in hospitalized children and adolescents with mental retardation: A retrospective study. *Research in Developmental Disabilities,* **16**, 221–231.

Jopp, D. A. & Keys, C. B. (2001) Diagnostic overshadowing reviewed and reconsidered. *American Journal on Mental Retardation,* **106**, 416–433.

Khreim, I. & Mikkelsen, E. J. (1997) Anxiety disorders in adults with mental retardation. *Psychiatric Annals,* **27**, 175–181.

King, B. (1993) Self-injury by people with mental retardation: A compulsive behavior hypothesis. *American Journal on Mental Retardation,* **98**, 93–112.

King, R. & McCartney, J. (1999) Charting for a purpose: Optimal treatment of bipolar disorder in individuals with developmental disabilities. *Mental Health Aspects of Developmental Disabilities*, **2**, 1–9.

Leverich, G. S. & Post, R. M. (1998) Life charting of affective disorders. *CNS Spectrums*, **3**, 21–31.

Lindsay, W. R., Law J. & McLeod, F. (2004) Intellectual disabilities and crime: Issues in assessment, management, and treatment. In A. Needs & G. Towl (eds.), *Applying Psychology to Forensic Practice*. Oxford: British Psychological Society and Blackwell, pp. 97–114.

Lindsay, W. R., Michie, A. M., Baty F. J., Smith, A. H. W. & Miller, S. (1994) The consistency of reports about feelings and emotions from people with intellectual disability. *Journal of Intellectual Disability Research*, **38**, 61–66.

Lowry, M. A. (1997) Unmasking mood disorders: Recognizing and measuring symptomatic behaviors. *Habilitative Mental Healthcare Newsletter*, **16**, 1–6.

Lowry, M. A. & Sovner, R. (1992) Severe behaviour problems associated with rapid cycling bipolar disorder in two adults with profound mental retardation. *Journal of Intellectual Disabilities Research*, **36**, 269–281.

Matson, J. L. (1997) *The PIMRA Manual* (2nd ed.). Worthington, OH: IDS.

McBrien, J. A. (2003) Assessment and diagnosis of depression in people with intellectual disability. *Journal of Intellectual Disability Research*, **47**, 1–13.

McDougle, C. J., Price, L. H., Volkmar, F. R., Goodman, W. K., Ward-O'Brien, D., Nielsen, J., Bregman, J. & Cohan, D. J. (1995) Clomipramine in autism: Preliminary evidence of efficacy. *Journal of the American Academy of Child and Adolescent Psychiatry*, **31**, 746–750.

Meins, W. (1994) Symptoms of major depression in mentally retarded adults. *Journal of Intellectual Disabilities Research*, **39**, 41–45.

Mikkelsen, E. J. (1997) Risk-benefit analysis in the use of psychopharmacologic interventions for difficult-to-diagnose behavioural disorders in individuals with mental retardation. *Psychiatric Annals*, **27**, 207–212.

Mikkelsen, E. J., Albert, L. G., Emens, M. & Rubin, E. (1997) The efficacy of antidepressant medication for individuals with mental retardation. *Psychiatric Annals*, **27**, 198–206.

Mikkelsen, E. J., McKenna, L. (1999) Psychopharmacologic algorithms for adults with developmental disabilities and difficult-to-diagnose behavioural disorders. *Psychiatric Annals*, **29**, 302–314.

Mikkelsen, E. J. & Stelk, W. J. (1999) *Criminal Offenders with Mental Retardation: Risk Assessment and the Continuum of Community-Based Treatment Programs*. Kingston, NY: NADD.

Moss, S. C., Prosser, H. & Goldberg, D. P. (1996a) Validity of the schizophrenia diagnosis of the Psychiatric Assessment Schedule for Adults with Developmental Disability (PAS-ADD). *British Journal of Psychiatry*, **168**, 359–367.

Moss, S. C., Prosser, H., Ibbotson, B. & Goldberg, D. P. (1996b) Respondent and informant accounts of psychiatric symptoms in a sample of patients with learning disability. *Journal of Intellectual Disability Research*, **40**, 457–465.

Pary, R. J., Levitas, A. S. & Hurley, A. D. (1999) Diagnosis of bipolar disorder in persons with developmental disabilities. *Mental Health Aspects of Developmental Disabilities*, **2**, 1–13.

Powell, S. B., Bodfish, J. W., Crawford, T. W. & Lewis, M. H. (1996) Self-injury and self-restraint: Occurrence and motivational significance. *American Journal on Mental Retardation*, **101**, 41–48.

Puig-Antich, J. (1982) Major depression and conduct disorder in prepuberty. *Journal of the American Academy of Child and Adolescent Psychiatry*, **21**, 188–123.

Rapoport, J. L. & Ismond, M. A. (1996) *DSM-IV Training Guide for Diagnosis of Childhood Disorders*, New York: Brunner Mazel, pp. 3–31, 191–236.

Reiss, S. (1988) *The Reiss Screen for Maladaptive Behavior Test Manual*. Worthington, OH: IDS.

Reiss, S. & Aman M. G. (eds.) (1998) *Psychotropic Medications and Development Disabilities: The International Consensus Handbook*. Columbus, OH: Ohio State University Nisonger Center.

Reiss, S., Levitan, G. & Szyszko, J. (1982) Emotional disturbance and mental retardation: Diagnostic overshadowing. *American Journal of Mental Deficiency*, **86**, 567–574.

Reiss, S. & Rojhan, J. (1993) Joint occurrence of depression and aggression in children and adults with mental retardation. *Journal of Intellectual Disabilities Research*, **37**, 287–294.

Reiss, S. & Valenti-Hein, D. (1994) Development of a psychopathology rating scale for children with mental retardation. *Journal of Consulting Clinical Psychology*, **62**, 28–33.

Ross, E. & Oliver C. (2002) The relationship between levels of mood, interest and pleasure and 'challenging behaviour' in adults with severe and profound intellectual disability. *Journal of Intellectual Disabilities Research*, **46**, 191–197.

Royal College of Psychiatrists (2001) *DC-LD*: Diagnostic criteria for psychiatric disorders for use with adults with learning disabilities/mental retardation. Occasional Paper OP48. London: Gaskell.

Rush, A. J. & Frances, A. (eds.) (2000) Treatment of psychiatric and behavioral problems in mental retardation: Expert consensus guideline series. *American Journal on Mental Retardation*, **105**, 159–228.

Ryan, R. & Sunada, K. (1997) Medical evaluation of persons with mental retardation referred for psychiatric assessment. *General Hospital Psychiatry*, **19**, 274–280.

Silka, V. R. & Hauser, M. J. (1997) Psychiatric assessment of the person with mental retardation. *Psychiatric Annals*, **27**, 162–169.

Sovner, R. & Hurley, A. D. (1982a) Diagnosing depression in the mentally retarded. *Psychiatric Aspects of Mental Retardation Reviews*, **1**, 1–3.

Sovner, R. & Hurley, A. D. (1982b) Diagnosing mania in the mentally retarded. *Psychiatric Aspects of Mental Retardation Reviews*, **1**, 9–11.

Sovner, R. & Hurley, A. D. (1983) Do the mentally retarded suffer from affective illness? *Archives of General Psychiatry*, **40**, 61–67.

Spitzer, R. L. (1980) Classification of mental disorders and DSM-III. In H. I. Kaplan, A. M. Freedman & B. J. Sadock (eds.), *Comprehensive Textbook of Psychiatry III*. Baltimore, MD: Williams & Wilkins, pp. 76–84.

Stavrakaki C. & Mintsioulis, G. (1997) Implications of a clinical study of anxiety disorders in persons with mental retardation. *Psychiatric Annals*, **27**, 182–189.

Szymanski, L. & King, B. H., principal authors and the Work Group on Quality Issues (1999) Practice parameters for the assessment and treatment of children, adolescents, and adults with mental retardation and comorbid mental disorders. *Journal of the American Academy of Child and Adolescent Psychiatry*, **38**, 5–35.

Tsiouris, J. A., Mann R., Patti, P. J. & Sturmey, P. (2003) Challenging behaviours should not be considered as depressive equivalents in individuals with intellectual disability. *Journal of Intellectual Disabilities Research*, **47**, 14–21.

Vitiello, B., Spreat, S. & Behar, D. (1989) Obsessive-compulsive disorder in mentally retarded patients. *Journal of Nervous and Mental Diseases*, **177**, 232–236.

World Health Organization (1992) *ICD-10 Guide for Mental Retardation*. ICD-10-MR, Geneva: World Health Organization.

CHAPTER 5

Issues in the assessment of challenging behaviour

Eric Emerson

1 Introduction

Assessment it is not an end in itself. Most people do not particularly enjoy being assessed and many carers complain bitterly about the seemingly unending round of assessments to which they and their adult son or daughter are subjected. Assessment should be the process by which information is collected in as efficient a manner as possible to help guide either:

- the development of efficient and effective services for people with intellectual disabilities and challenging behaviour, or
- the design and implementation of constructional and socially valid interventions for individuals

This being the case, it is crucial that we are very clear about the aims of the assessment (including understanding of the broader context in which the assessment is taking place) and the most appropriate and efficient ways of achieving those aims. There are three broad types of questions that may lead to the need to 'assess' challenging behaviour:

- What are the characteristics of people who use a particular service? (Alternatively, is this person eligible for this service?)
- How effective is a particular service or set of supports in meeting the needs of users with challenging behaviour?
- Why does this person show challenging behaviour and what can be done to support them?

This chapter will address these three types of assessment in turn. As well as clarifying the essential aim of assessment, it is also important to be clear from the outset about the following:

- Who will act on the information provided by the assessment?
- What possible courses of action are open to them?
- What types of information *they* need to make constructive action more likely?

Time answering these questions will be time well spent. Otherwise, these is a significant risk of developing an approach to the assessment of challenging behaviour that, regardless of the 'scientific' credibility of the assessment strategy, asks the wrong questions or asks them in ways that have little or no credibility to the people who are capable of making things happen. Taking account of the local organizational context within which decisions are made is fundamental to what has been called *utilization-focused* evaluation or assessment (Patton, 1986).

The process of clarifying the aims of assessment will draw attention to the inherently political nature of assessment. Assessment is not a neutral activity. Any assessment undertaken should at least contain the possibility of bringing about significant consequences for people with intellectual disabilities and significant others in their lives. Being clear about these potential consequences is essential if practice is to proceed within a professionally and ethically justifiable framework.

2 Assessing the Characteristics of People who Use a Given Service

Many health and personal social services in the UK are rationed. As a result, it is often important for commissioners and managers to determine through service audit whether the available resources are being targeted at those in greatest need. It is also necessary at times to set thresholds of 'need' above which people become eligible for particular types of support. Severity of challenging behaviour often constitutes an important dimension of 'need'.

Assessing severity of challenging behaviour for these two purposes requires the collection of information that:

- is credible to key decision makers;
- can be collected with the minimum of resources across a range of potential settings;
- allows simple decisions to be made.

Bliss (2002), for example, describes the use of the Learning Disability Casemix Scale (Pendaries, 1997). This is a simple informant checklist that contains 14 items relating to adaptive behaviour and 9 items relating to challenging behaviour. Each item is scored on either a 4- or 5-point scale. Bliss (2002) used this scale to review the severity of intellectual disability and challenging behaviour among people waiting to receive services from a specialist challenging behaviour service and following that review to establish explicit eligibility criteria. It has also been used successfully to assess levels of adaptive and challenging behaviour among people with intellectual disabilities living in supported accommodation (Bliss et al., 1999).

3 Assessing the Outcomes of Services or Interventions

Over recent years there has been an increasing emphasis on issues of accountability within health and social care services. One manifestation of this trend has been the attention now paid to attempting to evaluate the actual outcomes of services for people with intellectual disabilities. Assessing the outcomes of services or interventions for people with challenging behaviour, however, raises some complex issues.

It is clear that challenging behaviours often have wide-ranging personal and social consequences. These may include: impairing the health and/or quality of life of the person, those who care for them and those who live or work in close proximity; abuse, inappropriate treatment, exclusion, deprivation and systematic neglect (Emerson, 2001). It has been argued, therefore, that the 'success' of intervention strategies should be judged against their impact in not just reducing the frequency or severity of challenging behaviour, but also in bringing about significant 'lifestyle' changes in the types of areas listed above (e.g. Carr et al., 1999; Emerson, 2001; Fox & Emerson, 2001; Meyer & Evans, 1993; Symons et al., 1999).

For example, Fox and Emerson (2001) used case vignettes to investigate the relative salience of a range of outcomes across different 'stakeholder' groups, including people with intellectual disabilities, the parents of people with intellectual disabilities, various professions, managers and front-line staff. They reported that reduction in the severity of challenging behaviour was considered the most important outcome of intervention for only approximately 50% of these stakeholder groups. Alternative outcomes considered to be the *most* important by stakeholder groups included increased friendships and relationships, changes in the perceptions of individuals by others, learning alternative ways of getting needs met, increased control and empowerment (Fox & Emerson, 2001).

As a result, it is likely that any approach to assessing the outcomes of services for people with challenging behaviour will need to measure (1) changes in the severity of challenging behaviour, and (2) changes in those aspects of lifestyle that may be legitimately linked to challenging behaviour. Fox and Emerson (2002) have provided a practical guide to the task of identifying these broader outcomes of intervention.

Assessing severity of challenging behaviour in this context requires the collection of information:

- that is credible to key decision-makers,
- that can be collected with the minimum of resources across a range of potential settings;
- that is sufficiently sensitive to detect the types of change in challenging behaviour that may be expected to occur as a result of intervention.

Unfortunately, the available evidence-base is somewhat contradictory on the matter of what degree of change may be expected to occur as a result of intervention. While a large number of small case series have been published illustrating the *possibility* of highly significant short- to medium-term reductions in challenging behaviour (Carr et al., 1999; Emerson, 2001), such results need to be tempered with caution given the more pessimistic results of longitudinal epidemiological studies (e.g. Emerson et al., 2001).

It appears likely that instruments such as the Learning Disability Casemix Scale (Pendaries, 1997), while appropriate for general use in service audit, may be insufficiently sensitive to monitor changes over time as a result of intervention. More sensitive general measures of the overall severity of challenging behaviour include the Aberrant Behavior Checklist (Aman et al., 1995) and the Challenging Behaviour Scales (Wilkinson, 1989). For example, the Aberrant Behavior Checklist (Aman et al., 1995) has been used to assess change in severity of challenging behaviour as a result of the intervention of community-based specialist teams

(Lowe et al., 1996) and placement in different forms of community-based supported accommodation (Robertson et al., 2004). In chapter 13 assessment instruments that meet specified psychometric criteria are discussed in detail.

4 Understanding Challenging Behaviour

As we have seen, the initial step in any assessment is to clarify its essential purpose. The most common form of assessment undertaken with people with challenging behaviour has as its manifest aim to understand why the person is acting in the way they are, and subsequently to design supports and interventions that may help them to act in different ways in the future. However, four types of problems are commonly encountered when professional or advisory staff are asked to assess why someone may be showing challenging behaviour.

First, it is extremely unusual for a person with intellectual disabilities to refer themselves for help. Commonly, referral decisions are made by significant others (e.g. professionals, care staff, relatives), often without discussing this with the person themselves. The first step in any referral, therefore, is to determine wherever possible the person's own understanding of the reason for referral and to ensure, wherever appropriate, that they have consented to such a referral being made.

Second, the nature of the problem may have been incompletely conceptualized by the referring agency. Thus, for example, the explicit reasons for referrals (e.g. the elimination of troublesome behaviour) are often non-constructional and may well fail to address the broader social impact of challenging behaviour on lifestyle (see Fox & Emerson, 2002).

Third, many referrals in relation to challenging behaviour contain hidden agendas. The 'real' reasons underlying such referrals can include enlisting the help of external agencies to document the extent of the challenge in order to support arguments for additional resources or the person's exclusion from their home, school or workplace.

Finally, it is important to be clear about the particular questions that you will (and will not) address. Take, for example, the question '*Why* is this person showing severe self-injurious behaviour?' While it may be appropriate for a clinical psychologist to attempt to determine what behavioural or psychological processes may underlie the person's self-injury, it is probably beyond their competence and resources to do more than simply draw attention to the potential roles of neurobiological factors.

As a result, it is important to *clarify* and *document* as early as possible in the assessment process the actual purpose of the assessment you will be undertaking and to negotiate any changes between your aims and the requested reason for referral with the referring agency and wherever possible with the person themselves. This will help to minimize problems of misunderstanding about what you are trying to achieve and potential confusion about the sources and types of information you consider legitimate and relevant to answering the basic question(s) posed by the referring agency.

There are a number of detailed guides to the assessment of challenging behaviour (e.g. Carr et al., 1994; Demchak & Bossert, 1996; Durand, 1990; Feldman & Griffiths, 1997; McBrien & Felce, 1994; Miltenberger, 1998; O'Neill et al., 1997; Pyles & Bailey, 1990; Zarkowska & Clements, 1994). Any intervention-linked assessment of challenging behaviour is likely to have four distinct aims. These are:

- Identify what it is that the person does which is challenging.
- Describe the impact of challenging behaviour upon the person's quality of life.
- Attempt to understand the process(es) underlying the person's challenging behaviour.
- Identify possible alternatives to replace challenging behaviour. (Emerson, 1998)

These activities need to be undertaken, however, in the context of what we know from the existing evidence-base to be likely explanations for challenging behaviour. A large number of studies have been undertaken in an attempt to understand the processes underlying challenging behaviours (for further detail, see Emerson, 2001). The vast majority of this work has been conducted within either behavioural or neurobiological paradigms. Behavioural approaches view challenging behaviour as an example of *operant behaviour*. That is, challenging behaviour is seen as functional and in a general sense adaptive. It can be thought of as a way through which the person exercises control over key aspects of their world. Behavioural accounts are interested in the consequences of challenging behaviour and aspects of the context in which these behaviours occur.

The environmental consequences that maintain challenging behaviour are termed 'reinforcers'. Two types of relationship between behaviour and reinforcers are important. *Positive* reinforcement refers to an increase in the rate of a behaviour as a result of the contingent *presentation* of a positively reinforcing event (e.g. self-injury may lead to the comforting attention of a carer). *Negative* reinforcement refers to an increase in the rate of a behaviour as a result of the contingent *withdrawal* or prevention of occurrence of a negatively reinforcing event (e.g. self-injury may lead to the withdrawal of academic demands in the classroom). Of course, not all behaviour is shaped by environmental consequences. Some behaviours appear to be maintained by consequences internal to the person (e.g. masturbation may lead to orgasm; clenching teeth may reduce pain). Such behaviours may be thought of as examples of operant behaviour maintained by a process of *automatic or perceptual reinforcement*, in which the reinforcing stimuli are private or internal to the person. Contextual factors operate in two ways: they may *establish the motivational base* that underlies behaviour; or they may *provide information or cues* to the individual concerning the probability of particular behaviours being reinforced. There is now extensive evidence to support the idea that many examples of challenging behaviours are maintained by their environmental consequences (Emerson, 2001).

Neurobiological theories have focused on the role of three classes of endogenous neurotransmitters in modulating behaviour: dopamine, serotonin (5-Hydroxytryptamine) and the opioid peptides (in particular β-endorphin).

- *Dopamine*: The dopaminergic system is closely involved in the regulation of motor activity. Evidence suggests that abnormalities in aspects of this system may be involved in the development and maintenance of some forms of self-injurious behaviour.
- *Serotonin*: The serotoninergic system is closely linked with a number of processes including arousal, reactivity to aversive stimuli, appetite control, anxiety and depression. Some evidence suggests that there may be a link between serotonin and aggression, and, perhaps, serotonin and some forms of 'obsessional' self-injurious behaviour.
- β-*Endorphin*: β-endorphin (which is closely related to morphine) is released in response to repeated trauma. It has been suggested that self-injurious behaviour leads to the release of β-endorphin, which, through its analgesic and euphoria-inducing properties, automatically reinforces self-injury.

5 Identifying Challenging Behaviour: What Does the Person Do that Is Challenging?

Challenging behaviours are often described by carers and care staff in very general terms. The first step in any process of assessment, therefore, is to clarify the how, what, where and when of challenging behaviour. Usually, the information needed to answer these questions will come from interviews with people who are in close contact with the person, e.g. family members or care staff. It may also be useful, both as a prompt during interviewing and as a basis for evaluating change (see above), to use an existing checklist of challenging behaviour. If the behaviour is very frequent or highly predictable it is also important to spend some time observing the behaviour.

Describing what the person does that is challenging has two aims. First, it provides a *detailed* descriptions of the *different forms* of challenging behaviour shown by the person . Most people who show challenging behaviour do so in several different ways. Second, we need to know about the *sequence of behaviours* which lead up to an episode of challenging behaviour. Challenging behaviours rarely occur 'out of the blue'. More commonly they follow a sequence during which the person's behaviour escalates from more appropriate (e.g. turning away) to less appropriate (e.g. hitting out) ways of attempting to exercise control. Knowledge about sequences can be helpful in (1) developing guidelines for managing challenging behaviour, and (2) identifying possible alternatives that could replace challenging behaviour.

Preliminary information about the frequency and location of challenging behaviour will come from interviews. However, it is nearly always important to collect additional information. How that additional information is collected will depend upon the nature of the behaviour and the resources at your disposal. One of the main purposes of collecting this information will be to evaluate the impact of any intervention. As a result, it will be important to ensure that any additional recording you introduce is sufficiently 'user friendly' that its implementtion could be sustained over potentially long periods of time. This means you should

- keep things as simple as possible;
- develop new systems in partnership with the people who will be collecting the information and (for care staff) their managers;
- make sure that the information generated by any new recording system is regularly fed back to the people collecting it.

5.1 Low-frequency / high-impact behaviours

Some forms of challenging behaviour are relatively infrequent but have very serious consequences when they do occur (e.g. serious assault). In such cases, archival information is often available (e.g. from case notes, staff communication books, incident report forms). If so, check out the likely accuracy of this information with the people who actually fill in the records. Possible problems include inconsistent reporting between informants, and inconsistent reporting over time due to changes in the reporting system or administrative or managerial changes. If archival information is unavailable or of dubious reliability, it will be necessary to develop a new recording system. At a minimum you will need to define what you will record as constituting an episode of challenging behaviour in such a way that different informants would be able to agree that an episode has or has not occurred; decide on what other information you need and whether it is viable to collect it.

5.2 High-frequency behaviours

It is not possible to monitor each instance of high-frequency challenging behaviours. Rarely will any useful information be available in existing records. As a result, it will nearly always be necessary to develop a new recording system. Recording systems for high-frequency behaviours will need to sample occurrences of the behaviour.

5.2.1 Sampling by rate or intensity   It is often possible to set a threshold in terms of the intensity or rate of behaviour that defines an 'episode'. So, for example, a recording system could monitor episodes of self-injurious head hitting that lead to bleeding (i.e. sampling by intensity), or episodes in which the person hit themselves 10 or more times in any given 30-minute block of time (i.e. sampling by rate). This approach is commonly taken when using scatter plots (Touchette et al., 1985). These are particularly useful for collecting information on the frequency, timing and contextual control of episodes of challenging behaviour. Carers simply note whether a clearly defined episode of challenging behaviour has occurred within a given interval. Intervals are usually set at 30 or 60 minutes.

5.2.2 Sampling over context and/or time   An alternative approach is to restrict recording to particular settings and/or times (e.g. over the lunchtime period every other week). The 'how and what' of recording will depend on the resources available and the nature of the behaviour. Options will include measuring the

*   rate of behaviours (i.e. frequency over a given period of time);
*   the duration of behaviours (i.e. the percentage of time allocated to specific activities);
*   the intensity or impact of behaviours. (Murphy, 1986)

5.3 Describing the impact of challenging behaviour

It is important to try to determine the impact of the person's challenging behaviour on their lifestyle. This information is important for

*   prioritizing targets for intervention;
*   evaluating the social validity of interventions (see above).

Fox and Emerson (2002) provide practical guidance on this task.

5.4 Understanding the processes underlying challenging behaviour

Effective intervention is dependent on first identifying the processes underlying challenging behaviour, often called 'functional assessment'. The assessment process typically follows a sequence

Table 5.1 Structured Interview to Determine the Immediate Impact and Contextual Control of Challenging Behaviour

Ask each question separately for each form of challenging behaviour shown by the person.

1 What are the activities or settings in which the behaviour typically occurs?
2 What typically happens when the behaviour occurs (i.e. what do you or others typically do)?
3 Are there particular events or activities that usually or often occur just before an instance of challenging behaviour? Please describe.
4 Are there particular events or activities that you usually avoid because they typically result in challenging behaviour? Please describe.
5 Are there particular events or activities that you encourage because they DO NOT result in challenging behaviour? Please describe.
6 What does .... appear to be communicating with their challenging behaviour? Please describe.
7 Does their challenging behaviour appear to be related to a specific medical condition, diet, sleep pattern, seizure activity, period of illness or pain? Please describe.
8 Does their challenging behaviour appear to be related to their mood or emotional state? Does this change following an episode of challenging behaviour? Please describe.
9 Does the behaviour appear to be influenced by environmental factors (noise, number of people in the room, lighting, music, temperature)? Please describe.
10 Does the behaviour appear to be influenced by events in other settings (e.g. relationships at home)? Please describe.

Source: Modified from Demchak and Bossert (1996)

in which preliminary information, often of dubious reliability and validity, is validated through comparison with the results of more rigorous assessment.

In the descriptive phase of a functional assessment we are interested in describing the *immediate* social and environmental impact of the person's challenging behaviour. Through this, we are attempting to identify the *reinforcement contingencies* that are maintaining the behaviour(s); and the *setting events* or contextual factors that provide the motivational basis for challenging behaviour. This descriptive information is often gathered through a combination of structured interview, rating scales and observation.

- *Structured Interview*: Demchak and Bossert (1996) suggest 10 simple questions that can be used as a basis for a structured interview (see table 5.1).
- *Rating Scales*: There are a small number of rating scales that purport to identify the behavioural processes underlying challenging behaviour. Of these, the Motivation Assessment Scale (Durand & Crimmins, 1992) is probably the most commonly used. Unfortunately, while simple to use, such scales have dubious reliability and validity (Thompson & Emerson, 1995).
- *Observation*: Wherever practicable, it is useful to validate the information collected through interview or rating scales by observation. For high-frequency behaviours this should always be possible. The aim of such observations is to describe the relationships between Antecedents, Behaviour and its Consequences. These A-B-C observations need to be conducted by *trained observers* who are familiar with the types of processes or relationships

Table 5.2 Relationships between Contextual Factors, Challenging Behaviours and Consequent Events which May Suggest Particular Behavioural Processes

Socially mediated positive reinforcement	Does the person's challenging behaviour sometimes result in them receiving more or different forms of contact with others (e.g. while the episode is being managed or while they are being 'calmed down') or having access to new activities?
	Is the behaviour more likely when contact or activities are potentially available but not being provided (e.g. situations in which carers are around but are attending to others)?
	Is the behaviour less likely in situations involving high levels of contact or during preferred activities?
	Is the behaviour more likely when contact or activities are terminated?
Socially mediated negative reinforcement (escape or avoidance)	Do people respond to the behaviour by terminating interaction or activities?
	Is the behaviour more likely in situations in which demands are placed upon the person or they are engaged in interactions or activities they appear to dislike?
	Is the behaviour less likely when disliked interactions or activities are stopped?
	Is the behaviour less likely in situations involving participation in preferred activities?
	Is the behaviour more likely in those situations in which they *may* be asked to participate in interactions or activities they appear to dislike?
Positive automatic reinforcement	Is the behaviour more likely when there is little external stimulation?
	Is the behavior less likely when the person is participating in a preferred activity?
	Does the behaviour appear to have no effect upon subsequent events?
Negative automatic reinforcement (de-rousal)	Is the behaviour more likely when there is excessive external stimulation or when the individual is visibly excited or aroused?
	Is the behavior less likely when the individual is calm or in a quiet, peaceful environment?
	Does the behaviour appear to have no effect upon subsequent events?

that may underlie challenging behaviour. Simply asking carers or care staff to complete the archetypical free-form A-B-C chart is of little or no value. Carr et al. (1994) suggest using index cards to record occurrences of challenging behaviour. Information should be collected on at least 10 episodes of *each form* of challenging behaviour shown by the person.

Once sufficient information has been collected, *each episode of each form* of challenging behaviour should be reviewed to see if it is consistent with any of the four main behavioural processes that may underlie the person's challenging behaviour. Table 5.2 gives some questions that should help to identify possible categories for particular episodes of behaviour.

Through the process of categorizing episodes of challenging behaviours (e.g. by sorting the cards into piles or pinning them on a notice board in clusters), we want to answer several questions:

- Is it possible to assign the majority of episodes of each form of challenging behaviour to these categories?
- What appears to be the main function of each form of challenging behaviour? Does it also appear to serve other functions?
- If a specific behaviour serves several functions, is there anything about the context in which the behaviour occurs that predicts which function is operating?
- Do different forms of challenging behaviour appear to serve the same or different functions?

The answers to these questions will form a series of hypotheses or ideas about the function(s) of the challenging behaviour(s) shown by the person. In some instances it may be wise to test these ideas before progressing to intervention. There are two main ways of doing so:

- *Descriptive analysis* involves very detailed naturalistic observation of the challenging behaviour(s) shown by the individual and the events that are thought to be maintaining it (Emerson et al., 1996).
- *Experimental (functional) analysis* involves undertaking a brief 'mini-experiment' during which aspects of the person's context that are related to the hypothesized maintaining processes are manipulated (e.g. Carr et al., 1994; Demchak & Bossert, 1996; O'Neill et al., 1997).

5.5 Identifying possible alternatives to challenging behaviour

The aim of a constructional intervention is to replace challenging behaviour with other, more appropriate, behaviours. One aim of the assessment process, therefore, is to identify possible alternatives to challenging behaviour. Some possible strategies are listed below:

- Look at the sequence of behaviours that lead up to challenging behaviour. Are there any earlier links in the chain that could be built on? For example, if the person often tries to 'wave away' unwanted demands before finally resorting to aggression, perhaps a manual sign based on waving could be used as a functionally equivalent replacement to challenging behaviour.
- Ask carers and care staff what they think the person should do in the situations that are likely to lead to their challenging behaviour.
- Undertake a general assessment of the person's existing skills and, in particular, their methods of communication.

6 Conclusions

This chapter has addressed a range of conceptual and practical issues associated with three approaches to the assessment of challenging behaviours shown by people with intellectual disabilities. However, it is important that we keep in mind that assessment is not an end in itself. Rather, it is the process by which information is collected in as efficient a manner as possible to help guide either the development of efficient and effective services for people with intellectual disabilities and challenging behaviour, or the design and implementation of constructional and socially valid interventions for individuals. Both of these types of activities exist in particular organizational and political contexts. It is crucial that important aspects of these contexts are taken into account if the information collected during any approach to assessment is to be useful in enhancing or defending the quality of life of people with intellectual disabilities and challenging behaviour.

REFERENCES

Aman, M. G., Burrow, W. H. & Wolford, P. L. (1995) The aberrant behavior checklist-community: Factor validity and effect of subject variables for adults in group homes. *American Journal on Mental Retardation*, **100**, 283–292.

Bliss, E. V. (2002) A psychology service for adults with learning disabilities and challenging behaviour: Caseload management. *Clinical Psychology*, **10** (February), 23–26.

Bliss, E. V., Emerson, E., Quinn, H. & Thomas, D. (1999) *NW Audit of Quality in Residential Supports*. Manchester, UK: Hester Adrian Research Centre, University of Manchester.

Carr, E. G., Horner, R. H., Turnbull, A. P., Marquis, J. G., McLaughlin, D. M., McAtee, M. L., Smith, C. E., Ryan, K. A., Ruef, M. B. & Doolabh, A. (1999) *Positive Behavior Support for People with Developmental Disabilities*. Washington, DC: American Association on Mental Retardation.

Carr, E. G., Levin, L., McConnachie, G., Carlson, J. I., Kemp, D. C. & Smith, C. E. (1994) *Communication-Based Intervention for Problem Behavior: A User's Guide for Producing Positive Change*. Baltimore, MD: Brookes.

Demchak, M. A. & Bossert, K. W. (1996) *Assessing Problem Behaviours*. Washington, DC: American Association on Mental Retardation.

Durand, V. M. (1990) *Severe Behavior Problems: A Functional Communication Training Approach*. New York: Guilford.

Durand, V. M. & Crimmins, D. B. (1992) *The Motivation Assessment Scale*. Topkepa, KS: Monaco.

Emerson, E. (1998) Working with people with challenging behaviour. In E. Emerson, C. Hatton, J. Bromley & A. Caine (eds.), *Clinical Psychology and People with Intellectual Disabilities*. Chichester: Wiley, pp. 127–153.

Emerson, E. (2001) *Challenging Behaviour: Analysis and Intervention in People with Learning Disabilities* (2nd ed.). Cambridge: Cambridge University Press.

Emerson, E., Alborz, A., Kiernan, C., Reeves, D., Mason, H., Swarbrick, R., Mason, L. & Hatton, C. (2001) Predicting the persistence of severe self-injurious behavior. *Research in Developmental Disabilities*, **22**, 67–75.

Emerson, E., Reeves, D., Thompson, S., Henderson, D. & Robertson, J. (1996) Time-based lag sequential analysis in the functional assessment of severe challenging behaviour. *Journal of Intellectual Disability Research*, **40**, 260–274.

Feldman, M. A. & Griffiths, D. (1997) Comprehensive assessment of severe behavior problems. In N. N. Singh (ed.), *Prevention and Treatment of Severe Behavior Problems: Models and Methods in Developmental Disabilities*. Pacific Grove, CA: Brooks/Cole, pp. 23–48.

Fox, P. & Emerson, E. (2001) Socially valid outcomes of intervention for people with mental retardation and challenging behavior: A preliminary descriptive analysis of the views of different stakeholders. *Journal of Positive Behavior Interventions*, **3**, 183–189.

Fox, P. & Emerson, E. (2002) *Positive Outcomes*. Brighton: Pavilion.

Lowe, K., Felce, D. & Blackman, D. (1996) Challenging behaviour: The effectiveness of specialist support teams. *Journal of Intellectual Disability Research*, **40**, 336–347.

McBrien, J. & Felce, D. (1994) *Working with People who Have Severe Learning Difficulty and Challenging Behaviour.* Clevedon: BILD.

Meyer, L. H. & Evans, I. M. (1993) Meaningful outcomes in behavioral intervention: Evaluating positive approaches to the remediation of challenging behaviors. In J. Reichle & D. P. Wacker (eds.), *Communicative Alternatives to Challenging Behavior.* Baltimore, MD: Paul H. Brookes, pp. 407–428.

Miltenberger, R. G. (1998) Methods for assessing antecedent influences on challenging behaviors. In J. K. Luiselli & M. J. Cameron (eds.), *Antecedent Control: Innovative Approaches to Behavioral Support.* Baltimore, MD: Paul H. Brookes, pp. 47–66.

Murphy, G. H. (1986) Direct observation as an assessment tool in functional analysis and treatment. In J. Hogg & N. Raynes (eds.), *Assessment in Mental Handicap.* London: Croom Helm.

O'Neill, R. E., Horner, R. H., Albin, R. W., Storey, K. & Sprague, J. R. (1997) *Functional Analysis and Program Development for Problem Behavior.* Pacific Grove, CA: Brooks/Cole.

Patton, M. Q. (1986) *Utilization-Focused Evaluation.* Sage: London.

Pendaries, C. (1997) Pilot study on the development of the learning disability Healthcare Resource Groups. *British Journal of Learning Disabilities,* **25,** 122–126.

Pyles, D. A. M. & Bailey, J. S. (1990) Diagnosing severe behavior problems. In A. C. Repp & N. N. Singh (eds.), *Perspectives on the Use of Nonaversive and Aversive Interventions for Persons with Developmental Disabilities.* Sycamore, IL: Sycamore, pp. 381–401.

Robertson, J., Emerson, E., Pinkney, L., Caesar, E., Felce, D., Meek, A., Carr, D., Lowe, K., Knapp, M. & Hallam, A. (2004) Quality & costs of community-based residential supports for people with mental retardation and challenging behavior. *American Journal of Mental Retardation,* **109,** 332–344.

Symons, F. J., Koppekin, A. & Wehby, J. H. (1999) Treatment of self-injurious behavior and quality of life for persons with mental retardation. *Mental Retardation,* **37,** 297–307.

Thompson, S. & Emerson, E. (1995) Inter-observer agreement on the Motivation Assessment Scale: Another failure to replicate. *Mental Handicap Research,* **8,** 203–208.

Touchette, P. E., McDonald, R. F. & Langer, S. N. (1985) A scatter plot for identifying stimulus control of problem behavior. *Journal of Applied Behavior Analysis,* **18,** 343–351.

Wilkinson, J. (1989) Assessing the challenge: Development of the challenging behaviour scales. *Mental Handicap Research,* **2,** 86–104.

Zarkowska, E. & Clements, J. (1994) *Severe Problem Behaviour: The STAR Approach.* London: Chapman & Hall.

CHAPTER 6

People with intellectual disabilities who offend or are alleged to have offended

Gillian Anderson

1 Introduction

The advent of community care policy in the early 1970s and the move to implementing social models of care for people with intellectual disabilities led to closure of large-scale institutions and provision of services and support in more local settings. As a consequence, the issue of meeting the needs of individuals with intellectual disabilities who offend or are alleged to have offended has come into an increasingly sharper focus. As well as the community care agenda, changes to the ethos of services for people with intellectual disabilities (Department of Health, 2001; Scottish Executive 2000) led to greater media attention on offenders, particularly sex offenders, returning to community settings. Mental health legislation itself also led to a more restrictive policy resulting in people with intellectual disabilities receiving increasing attention from service providers and research workers alike.

How people with intellectual disabilities are dealt with when they offend, or are alleged to have offended, is dependent on a variety of overarching factors. The provisions and workings of the country's criminal justice system, mental health legislation, the remits of social service and health agencies, not to mention society's attitudes, will interact to influence the course responses take. It is beyond the scope of this chapter to cover even the principal English-speaking countries from these perspectives. We concentrate, therefore, on Great Britain generally, with some specific references to the Scottish criminal justice system. Nevertheless, the issues discussed, such as the problems of determining prevalence of offending among people with intellectual disabilities, are universal. Similarly, issues related to assessment, which are dealt with in chapter 14, section 2, are also applicable across a wide range of countries, with issues such as risk assessment and police interviewing equally crucial to providing justice for people with intellectual disabilities.

Before describing the characteristics and needs of people with intellectual disabilities who offend or are alleged to have offended, it is important to define the population of interest, and the prevalence of offending behaviour within that population. How broadly or narrowly the population is defined will have a bearing on this estimate of prevalence (Holland et al.,

2002). The characteristics and needs of the population are then detailed, while finally the current situation with respect to the political and legal context will be discussed along with the service responses to the needs identified.

2 Defining the Population

It is relevant first to define this population. In addition to use of the term *intellectual disability*, which is essentially synonymous with terms such as *mental retardation* and *mental handicap* in the earlier descriptions, we also in this field encounter *mental impairment* and *mental disorder* in British legislation. Despite general agreement regarding the characteristics of the population (i.e. significant impairment of intellectual functioning and of adaptive behaviour with onset before adulthood; British Psychological Society, 2001), definitional inconsistencies between the USA, Canada, the UK and Continental Europe should be noted (McBrien, 2003; Hayes, 1996a). In addition, many of the people included in population studies do not always meet the criteria for intellectual impairment required for a classification of intellectual disability (McBrien, 2003; Hayes, 1996a). Inclusion of offenders, or those who are alleged to have offended, with intellectual functioning in the borderline or low-average range (Wechsler, 1999a) therefore inflates prevalence estimates. In addition, intellectual ability is only one of the main criteria used to assess intellectual disability (Murphy et al., 1995; Winter et al., 1997). Very few studies attempt to measure adaptive functioning (Mason & Murphy, 2002a) or ascertain the extent of developmental delay. Other studies employ administrative classification (Lyall et al., 1995a; McNulty et al., 1995), identifying people through their contact with intellectual disability services, self-report, attendance at special school, or through use of specifically devised assessment procedures (Murphy et al., 1995). Most studies use a combination of these methods because of the difficulties of administering a full assessment to address the presence of all relevant criteria. Methodological differences in studies and reports make comparisons with respect to presence of intellectual disability very difficult, and identification of prevalence almost impossible (McBrien, 2003; Simpson & Hogg, 2001).

How, then, is the term 'offending' defined? In law, criminal offending is not only a product of the act itself but is also defined by intent and knowledge of possible consequences of the act. In England and Wales this is known as *mens rea*. There is also a process through which people who have committed alleged offences will proceed before a criminal prosecution is mounted. At any stage in this process a person may be diverted by being transferred to another service or path without trial, conviction or sentence. Initially this will depend on whether a prosecution is deemed to be in the public interest. This is taken forward through either the Crown Prosecution Service in England and Wales, or through the Procurator Fiscal in Scotland.

People with intellectual disabilities are often viewed as not fulfilling the criteria of *mens rea*, and their behaviour is not deemed to be offending. It is more likely that people with mild intellectual disabilities (American Psychiatric Association, 1994; British Psychological Society, 2001) will meet these criteria than those with more severe impairment (British Psychological Society, 2001). This underlines the fact that the group in question is far from homogeneous. Where people do not meet the criteria for *mens rea* the distinction between offending behaviour and challenging behaviour often becomes blurred (Emerson, 1995).

Differentiation between offending behaviour and challenging behaviour does not necessarily lie in the topography of the behaviour itself, but in the process that underlies entry or otherwise into the criminal justice system (Holland et al., 2002).

Additionally, diversion in response to intellectual disability is not the only way that people will be prevented from entering the criminal justice system. Most offending or are alleged offending remains unreported or undetected (Holland et al., 2002), regardless of whether the perpetrator has intellectual disabilities. For those with intellectual disabilities, there are other factors that will influence reporting and police investigation. These factors include victim characteristics (Holland et al., 2002), with a lesser likelihood of reporting where the victim is another person with an intellectual disability or a female member of staff supporting the perpetrator (Thompson, 1997a); the type of offence, theft and criminal damage being widely tolerated, with staff in some circumstances stating they would hesitate to report a rape (Lyall et al., 1995a); lack of policies and procedures for dealing with offending behaviour within the service (Lyall et al., 1995b); and the assumption that the person does not understand that his or her behaviour is deemed to be offending nor the consequences for others of their behaviour (Holland et al., 2002).

Staff who support people with intellectual disabilities in service settings typically have the responsibility of reporting an alleged offence to the police. However, such reporting tends to be infrequent, with many instances going unreported (Lyall et al., 1995a, 1995b). Where a report is made to the police, it is often the case that they make the decision not to proceed, often on the basis of absence of *mens rea*.

While it is theoretically possible to define the population of interest, as outlined above, differences in terminology, methodology and issues relating to definitions of offending behaviour do make it difficult to identify this population with any precision (McBrien, 2003; Lindsay & Macleod, 2001). In practice, there are two main ways in which the population is identified: first, identifying those in receipt of services who are alleged to have offended or have been the subject of police investigations (McBrien, 2003; Holland et al., 2002); second, identifying those within the criminal justice system who may be classified as having intellectual disabilities (McBrien, 2003; Holland et al., 2002). We discuss below the difficulties both methods have associated with them.

3 Prevalence of People with Intellectual Disabilities who Have Offended or Are Alleged to Have Offended

Historically, a link between intellectual disability and offending behaviour has frequently been proposed (Holland et al., 2002), leading to individuals who offended or were alleged to have offended being isolated in colonies and institutions throughout their lives. There is little evidence to suggest that that such treatment led to any changes in their behaviour (Murphy, 2000). Contemporary discussion has still not resolved the issue of whether people with intellectual disabilities are at greater risk for committing crimes than their peers in the general population. For example, Hayes (1996a) claims that people with learning disabilities are overrepresented in Western criminal justice systems, including in prisons. While in Britain very few people with intellectual disabilities who enter the criminal justice system are imprisoned (Murphy et al., 1995), this is not necessarily the case elsewhere. For example, in a carefully conducted study of the prison population in Ireland, 28.8% of prisoners were found to have intellectual disabilities as defined by an IQ<70. In part, this extraordinarily high figure relative to the British figures presented is an outcome of the Irish criminal justice system. The Irish prison system receives all people remanded or sentenced by the courts with no system or procedure existing to identify an offender with intellectual disabilities (Murphy et al., 2000).

In reality, it is probably the perception of risk of offending that is an issue rather than its high prevalence (Murphy, 2000). This is true of the public perception of the risk posed by people with mental health problems as well as those with intellectual disabilities (Steadman et al., 1998). A contrary view is that people with intellectual disabilities actually pose less risk than other potential offenders due to limited ability to conceal crimes, lack of ability in planning, and the fact they are more likely to have some staff supervision (Murphy, 2000). As we shall see in the following sections, a definitive answer to the question 'Do people with intellectual disabilities offend more or less than those without intellectual disabilities?' has yet to be answered.

3.1 Factors influencing prevalence estimates

Prevalence rates will be affected by the methods used to define presence of an intellectual disability. Such methods vary across studies from use of self-report (Murphy et al., 1995) to asking for information about special educational needs and attendance at special schooling (Winter et al., 1997) and the use of a standardized assessment tool. Tools that have been used include the Wechsler Adult Intelligence Scale – Revised or WAIS-R (Wechsler, 1981) (usually a shortened form) or British Ability Scales (Murphy et al., 1995; Winter et al., 1997; Mason & Murphy, 2002a), and measurement of adaptive functioning using an accepted instrument such as the Vineland Adaptive Behavior Scales (Sparrow et al., 1984; Mason & Murphy, 2002a). Short forms of the WAIS-R are used in most cases (Murphy et al., 1995; Winter et al., 1997; Mason & Murphy, 2002a), but unfortunately there is no standard applied to the use of a shortened version of this assessment (McBrien, 2003). It is suggested by McBrien (2003) that the Wechsler Abbreviated Scale of Intelligence or WASI (Wechsler, 1999b) should always be used if a short form of intellectual assessment is required. A further confounding factor is the inclusion of people whose intellectual functioning is deemed to be 'borderline' (WAIS-III, Wechsler, 1999a). For example, in a number of studies a cut-off IQ of above 70 is used (e.g. Mason & Murphy, 2002a, 2002b), which may lead to the inclusion of people who do not have an intellectual disability.

In addition to the method of assessment to identify presence of an intellectual disability, the point in the criminal justice system at which people are identified will have a bearing on the prevalence rates estimated. Examples of differing prevalence rates are given below. In two studies in England, between 4.4% (Lyall et al., 1995a) and 9% (Gudjonsson et al., 1993) of people interviewed by police in connection with an alleged or suspected offence were screened or assessed as having a potential intellectual disability. A study of those who appeared in two magistrate courts in England identified 1.4% as having intellectual disabilities (French et al., 1995), although much higher percentages were found in two studies in Australia: 14.2% (Hayes, 1993) and 36.0% (Hayes, 1996b). Mason and Murphy (2002a) reported that 5.7% who have contact with probation services were assessed as having an intellectual disability. This was following initial screening where 21% were screened and 5.7% were identified following further assessment. Finally, in a study by Brooke et al. (1996) 0.77% of all remand prisoners were assessed as having an intellectual disability.

3.2 Context defining prevalence

When estimating prevalence of people with an intellectual disability at risk of offending there are two principal groups of concern. First, those who are already known to service providers who are suspected of having offended (Lyall et al., 1995b; Holland et al., 2002; McBrien, 2003). Second, those unknown to services, but are identified at some stage during the criminal proceedings (Hayes, 1996a; Murphy, 2000; Holland et al., 2002; McBrien, 2003).

Suspected offending behaviour by people known to services has been the subject of a number of studies (Lyall et al., 1995a, 1995b). Methods have included surveying staff for information about people using the service who are suspected of having offended or of having had contact with the criminal justice system (Lyall et al., 1995a; McNulty et al., 1995). Here, too, service responses to the alleged offending were studied, including whether a report was made to the police, whether the alleged offence was investigated and the outcome of any such investigations (Lyall et al., 1995b). It was estimated that between 2% (Lyall et al., 1995a) and 5% (McNulty et al., 1995) of people receiving services will have had contact with the criminal justice system in relation to alleged offences.

The other method of estimating prevalence is through assessing people within the criminal justice system for the presence of an intellectual disability (Murphy et al., 1995; Brooke et al., 1996; Mason & Murphy, 2002a). The prevalence here ranges from 0% in a study by Murphy et al. (1995), in which further assessment following self-reported intellectual disability was undertaken, up to 21% in Mason and Murphy (2002a), in which self-report and British Ability Scale subscales were employed. Prevalence also varies according to the method of measurement used (McBrien, 2003) and the point at which individuals are assessed within the criminal justice system. Both these last points are discussed further below.

Greater consistency in identifying individuals with intellectual disabilities may be achieved in future with the introduction of new forms of assessment of intellectual disability. Work in Britain and Australia has been underway for some time to identify a screening tool that will screen for presence of intellectual disability (Mason & Murphy, 2002b; Hayes, 2000, 2002). Mason and Murphy (2002b) and Hayes (2002) note that these screening instruments may be overinclusive (i.e. they are likely to produce more false positives than false negatives). This is seen to be justified as it would, one hopes, reduce the likelihood of excluding people with intellectual disabilities.

3.3 Types of offences

Some evidence suggests that people with intellectual disabilities are over-represented in committing certain crimes. Offences of a sexual nature and fire setting are identified as activities in which people with intellectual disabilities, usually men, are over-represented (Cullen, 1993; Day, 1993). Elsewhere, however, people with intellectual disabilities are involved in a wide spectrum of criminal activity (Hayes, 1996a) comparable with the rest of the population (Cooper, 1995). At present there is insufficient information to clarify the relationship between intellectual disabilities and specific crime profiles (Clare & Murphy, 1998).

3.4 Gender and offending

As in the wider population, it is males who commit most offences among people with intellectual disabilities. Kearns and O'Connor (1988), for example, report that men commit far more offences against the person than do women. Women are not highly represented within the group and much of the work on individuals with an intellectual disability who offend has focused on male perpetrators. There is little information about women's characteristics, but there is some information on how their treatment might differ from that of men within the system, with a greater chance of their receiving intrusive punitive treatments or medication (Holland et al., 2002). This may reflect more the views of society about women offenders than about women with intellectual disabilities per se. What is different for women with intellectual disabilities whose behaviour leads to involvement with the criminal justice system is that they are often placed in mixed-sex environments, particularly in secure accommodation, because there is not a critical mass of such women to justify a single-sex service. This leaves them vulnerable to various forms of abuse within the system and by other service users.

There is some information to suggest that the reasons women with intellectual disabilities become involved with the criminal justice system are due to sexual misdemeanours, violence and theft (Day, 1993) – information based, however, on data collected prior to 1970. Nevertheless, this is a very neglected area, with inadequate information to clarify whether women with learning disabilities are more likely to be involved in particular types of offending than other women.

3.5 Ethnicity

There is little information on the relative probability of members of minority ethnic groups with intellectual disabilities being represented within criminal justice systems in Britain or in other parts of the world (see Holland et al., 2002). It is also important to note that with respect to recently developed screening tools for people with intellectual disabilities, they may tend to screen in people from some ethnic groups who do not have intellectual disabilities (Hayes, 2002). Indeed, this is specifically intended with regard to Hayes' own instrument in order to identify individuals who may for linguistic or cultural reasons have problems in dealing with police questioning.

3.6 Conclusion

There is still no accepted way of adequately estimating the prevalence of people with intellectual disabilities who offend or are at risk of offending (McBrien, 2003). It is probable, however, that there is greater representation of this group at some points in the criminal justice system than at others. For example, from the literature it would appear that people with intellectual disabilities are more highly represented in the numbers questioned in relation to crimes, and in the probation service, but not in prison. According to Murphy (2000) this provides some evidence for the diversion of people with intellectual disability from the criminal justice system to other forms of intervention or support. There is not a great deal of information about exactly where individuals do end up, although Murphy (2000) suggests that it may be more likely that people return to community settings due to the low and reducing number of people with intellectual disabilities detained under mental health legislation.

4 Characteristics of Offenders and Alleged Offenders

Several studies have investigated the characteristic of people with intellectual disabilities who have offended or are alleged to have offended (Lindsay, 2002; Clare & Murphy, 1998; Lindsay & Macleod, 2001; Holland et al., 2002). There are many similarities in the characteristics of this group with those of offenders in the general population. That is, they tend to be young, male (Thompson, 1997b), have experience of social disadvantage (Day, 1988; Winter et al., 1997), have unstable environments, including financial instability and frequent changes of principal carer (Clare & Murphy, 1998). Of note for this population is the finding that intellectual competence can be a protective factor for children facing chronic adversity (Garmezy & Masten, 1994). Additionally, there is often a history of offending within the family, and a higher likelihood of behavioural difficulties in childhood (Day, 1988). Mental health needs also tend to be more prevalent in this population (Day, 1988; Winter et al., 1997), although given some of the other characteristics noted, this is not surprising.

There is little research on how the characteristics of this population compare with the wider population of people with intellectual disabilities. As outlined earlier, this population is not homogeneous and so it would perhaps be naïve to assume that this group would necessarily be more like others with intellectual disabilities than, for example, the population of other offenders.

The information that is available suggests that generally this population tends to be more intellectually able; that is, there are very few people who would be described as having severe intellectual disability within the criminal justice system (Winter et al., 1997; Murphy, 2000). Some with severe intellectual disabilities may be questioned by police, but usually this would progress no further.

There is little research on the issue of how those with an intellectual disability who come into contact with the criminal justice system differ from those with an intellectual disability who do not. Winter et al. (1997) compared the characteristics of a small group of suspects who reported having an intellectual disability with people of similar age, gender and intellectual ability, who had been described as having an intellectual disability from childhood. The main differences found were that the group of suspects were more likely to have experienced psychosocial disadvantage and recently experienced homelessness, illicit drug use, and major life events. The group of suspects were also less likely to have had contact with local health or social services.

5 The Needs of People with Intellectual Disabilities who Offend or Are Alleged to Have Offended

The needs of people with intellectual disabilities entering the criminal justice system are broadly comparable to those without intellectual disabilities who enter this system. These include health needs, requirements for social care and housing provision as well as, where relevant, the support of alcohol and drugs services. Care management or coordination is essential (Clare & Murphy, 1998). There is a general view that needs cannot be met in prison (Clare & Murphy, 1998; Murphy, 2000), and that custodial sentences should not be considered for this population. In the US the specific issue of people with intellectual disabilities receiving the death penalty has been of particular concern (Beail, 2002; Perske, 1991). Differences in the US legal system also mean that people with intellectual disabilities are more likely to be tried relative to other Western jurisdictions (Holland et al., 2002).

The specific needs of those with intellectual disabilities who offend or are alleged to have offended relate to individual assessment of the offending behaviour, and risk, with the outcome of such assessment leading to the appropriate service response (ch. 14, section 2). The needs relating to specific aspects of the person's presentation, such as autistic spectrum disorder and mental health problems, should always be addressed as part of the global assessment of need.

6 Service Response to People who Offend or Are Alleged to Have Offended

There is a consensus with respect to policy in supporting people with intellectual disabilities who have offended or are alleged to have offended. The Reed report (Department of Health & Home Office, 1994) exemplifies these principles arguing that mentally disordered offenders who need care and treatment should receive it from health and personal social services rather than in the criminal justice system. Such support should be individualized and as far as possible be in the community, not institutional settings. Security should be no more than is justified and should maximize rehabilitation and an independent life. The service should be delivered as near to the person's home and family as possible.

Reviews of services and recommendations for supporting people with intellectual disabilities in both England (Department of Health, 2001) and Scotland (Scottish Executive, 2000; Scottish Office, 1999) have confirmed this position in the wider context by recommending individualized, person-centred services based on assessment and support to meet individual needs. This focus is community based, with secure and institutional services being seen as a last resort. New mental health legislation in Britain will, however, have an effect on the treatment of some people with intellectual disabilities, and this may lead to more restrictive interventions.

The service response to people with intellectual disabilities can initially be very limited. Services can, at times, act as judge and jury, with perpetrators being punished through removal of rights and privileges or relocation to a more restrictive environment without reference to the criminal justice system. This is not, however, a function that should be exercised by health or social care services and may be viewed as an infringement of a person's rights (Lyall et al.,

1995b). In some cases lack of appropriate intervention can lead to an escalation of offending behaviour with eventual involvement by criminal justice services, more profound effects on victims and greater restrictions being placed on perpetrators. It is possible that early intervention could prevent such consequences. There is no specific reliable information regarding potential gains from early intervention, because of the problems with retrospective reporting and the difficulties accessing accurate records. There is an important role here for sound policies within services to deal with difficulties relating to offending (Lyall et al., 1995b). There also requires to be an agreed response available to people entering the criminal justice system who have not been previously known to services.

Where the behaviour of an individual leads to greater concern, this is often in the first instance followed by involvement of health or social care services (Murphy, 2000). This type of service response has traditionally led to hospital admission in local in-patient services for people with intellectual disabilities or occasionally mental health facilities. This effectively entails a diversion from the criminal justice system and does not necessarily lead to access to appropriate assessment and service provision. In the longer term, problems may come to light at the time of planned discharge from such retracting in-patient services, leading to delays in discharge and sometimes overly restrictive service provision.

Police involvement is often the first stage of any specific criminal justice involvement, particularly where the individual has not been previously known to services. This is another point at which diversion from continuation in the criminal justice system can occur. The police may not feel confident about dealing with people with intellectual disabilities, whether perpetrator or victim. Diversion from later stages of criminal justice procedures may follow even where the police make a referral for prosecution or at trial or conviction.

Services for people with intellectual disabilities tend to be defined in terms of specific groups, such as those with challenging behaviour, mental health needs, people who offend and those with complex physical needs (Scottish Executive, 2000; Department of Health, 2001). In practice, however, many people requiring services will fall into a number of different categories or groups. People with autism can offend and can experience mental health problems. Should those who commit acts of aggression be labelled as violent offenders or as presenting with challenging behaviour? The level of cognitive impairment is often the factor that determines placement, with those showing severe impairment more likely to be placed in challenging behaviour services, and those with milder impairments more likely to be referred to services for offenders (Holland et al., 2002; Clare & Murphy, 1998).

Though there is recognition of the importance of developing integrated provision, for several reasons services are relatively patchy and at different stages of development across the UK. Continued institutional care, lack of risk assessment processes and procedures, and an absence of any need to develop robust community services have until relatively recently characterized service provision. In some areas, services for people with intellectual disabilities who offend are attached to the local mental health forensic services, while in other areas they are part of the learning disability health services.

Because of recent high profile cases relating to offenders returning to community settings, there has been a greater focus on the development of secure and semi-secure services for this population. As noted above, the policy direction and the view of most service commissioners is that services for mentally disordered offenders that include people with an intellectual disability should provide the least restrictive environment, with the emphasis on development of robust community services. Unfortunately, the political environment and the public reaction to this can lead to such developments being put aside in favour of more secure settings, which have their own difficulties when it comes discharge. Nevertheless, there is no 'gold standard' service. Some of the appropriate service responses have been identified by Mansell et al. (1993), which was largely concerned with people with challenging behaviour and mental health needs.

7 Conclusion

First, in order to begin to provide an appropriate service, it is important to define accurately the population that will be served. The difficulties in doing so have been outlined above. Second, services require skilled staff to assess the needs of individuals and to ensure systems of risk assessment and management are in place and not vulnerable to staff turnover or service change. Third, there need to be appropriate interfaces between the various services involved in providing services to individuals, interfaces that cross organizational structures and professional boundaries. Finally, services must have adequate assessment tools at their disposal for use with this population (tools described in ch. 14 section 2). Beyond these requirements account must be taken of global needs with respect to housing, employment and keeping the restrictions placed on individuals to the necessary minimum. This last requirement is particularly difficult, as people in secure environments do not always have access to situations where they may be required to use skills they have learned as part of their support/treatment or care plans.

REFERENCES

American Psychiatric Association (1994) *Diagnostic and Statistical Manual of Mental Disorders* (4th ed.). Washington, DC: American Psychiatric Association.

Beail, N. (2002) Commentary: Constructive approaches to the assessment, treatment and management of offenders with intellectual disabilities. *Journal of Applied Research in Intellectual Disabilities*, **15**, 179–182.

British Psychological Society (2001) *Learning Disability: Definitions and Contexts*. Leicester: British Psychological Society.

Brooke, D., Taylor, C., Gunn, J. & Maden, A. (1996) Point prevalence of mental disorder in unconvicted male prisoners in England and Wales. *British Medical Journal*, **313**, 1524–1527.

Clare, I. C. H. & Murphy, G. H. (1998) Working with offenders or alleged offenders with intellectual disabilities. In E. Emerson, C. Hatton., J. Bromley & A. Caine (eds.), *Clinical Psychology and People with Intellectual Disabilities*. Chichester: John Wiley, pp. 154–176.

Cooper, A. J. (1995) Review of the role of two anti-libidinal drugs in the treatment of sex offenders with mental retardation. *Mental Retardation*, **33**, 42–48.

Cullen, C. (1993) The treatment of people with learning disabilities who offend. In K. Howells & C. R. Hollin (eds.), *Clinical Approaches to the Mentally Disordered Offender*. Chichester: Wiley, pp. 145–163.

Day, K. (1988) A hospital based treatment program for male mentally handicapped offenders. *British Journal of Psychiatry*, **153**, 635–644.

Day, K. (1993) Crime and mental retardation: A review. In K. Howells & C. R. Hollin, *Clinical Approaches to the Mentally Disordered Offender*. Chichester: Wiley, pp. 111–143.

Department of Health (2001) *Valuing People: A New Strategy for Learning Disability for the Twenty-First Century.* London: Department of Health.

Department of Health & Home Office (1994) *Review of Health and Social Services for Mentally Disordered Offenders and Others Requiring Similar Services.* Vol. 7: *People with Learning Disabilities (Mental Handicap) and Autism.* (The Reed Report.) London: Department of Health & Home Office.

Emerson, E. (1995) *Challenging Behaviour: Analysis and Intervention in People with Learning Disabilities.* Cambridge: Cambridge University Press.

French, A., Brigden, P. & Noble, S. (1995) *Learning Disabled Offenders in Berkshire: Research Report on Mentally Disordered Offenders and Others Requiring Similar Services (The Reed Committee) Centrally Assisted Initiatives.* Windsor: East Berkshire NHS Trust.

Garmezy, N. & Masten, A. S. (1994) Chronic adversities. In M. Rutter, E. Taylor & L. Hersov (eds.), *Child and Adolescent Psychiatry: Modern Approaches* (3rd ed.). Oxford: Blackwell, pp. 191–208.

Gudjonsson, G., Clare, I. C. H., Rutter, S. & Pearse, J. (1993) *Persons at Risk During Interviews in Police Custody: The Identification of Vulnerabilities.* The Royal Commission of Criminal Justice: Research Study 12. London: HMSO.

Hayes, S. (1993) *People with an Intellectual Disability and the Criminal Justice System: Appearance before Local Courts.* Research report 4. Sydney: NSW Law Reform Commission.

Hayes, S. (1996a) Recent research on offenders with learning disabilities. *Tizard Learning Disability Review,* 1, 7–15.

Hayes, S. (1996b) *People with an Intellectual Disability and the Criminal Justice System: Appearances before Local Courts.* Research report 5. Sydney: NSW Law Reform Commission.

Hayes, S. (2000) *Hayes Ability Screening Index Manual.* Sydney: University of Sydney.

Hayes, S. C. (2002) Early intervention or early incarceration? Using a screening test for intellectual disability in the criminal justice system. *Journal of Applied Research in Intellectual Disabilities,* 15, 120–128.

Holland, T., Clare, I. C. H. & Mukhopadhyay, T. (2002) Prevalence of 'criminal offending' by men and women with intellectual disability and the characteristics of 'offenders': Implications for research and service development. *Journal of Intellectual Disability Research,* 46, 6–20.

Kearns, A. & O'Connor, A. (1988) The mentally handicapped criminal offender. A 10 year study of two hospitals. *British Journal of Psychiatry,* 152, 848–851.

Lindsay, W. R. (2002) Integration of recent reviews on offenders with intellectual disabilities. *Journal of Applied Research in Intellectual Disabilities,* 15, 111–119.

Lindsay, W. R. & Macleod, F. (2001) A review of forensic learning disability research. *British Journal of Forensic Practice,* 3, 4–10.

Lyall, I., Holland, A. J. & Collins, S. (1995a) Offending by adults with learning disabilities: Identifying need in one health district. *Mental Handicap Research,* 8, 99–109.

Lyall, I., Holland, A. J. & Collins, S. (1995b) Offending by adults with learning disabilities and the attitudes of staff to offending behaviour: Implications for service development. *Journal of Intellectual Disability Research,* 39, 501–508.

Mansell, J. L., Beaumont, K., Henwood, M., Hewitt, P., Holland, A., Johnson, D., Mallon, G., Metcalf, M., Searle, P., Pugsley, K. & Cooper, E. (1993) *Service for People with Learning Disabilities and Challenging Behaviour or Mental Health Needs: Report of a Project Group.* London: HMSO.

Mason, J. & Murphy, G. H. (2002a) People with intellectual disabilities on probation in the UK: An initial study. *Journal of Community and Social Psychology,* 12, 44–55.

Mason, J. & Murphy, G. (2002b) People with an intellectual disability in the criminal justice system: Developing an assessment tool for measuring prevalence. *British Journal of Clinical Psychology,* 41, 315–320.

McBrien, J. (2003) The intellectually disabled offender: Methodological problems in identification. *Journal of Applied Research in Intellectual Disabilities,* 16, 95–105.

McNulty, C., Kissi-Deborah, R. & Newsom-Davies, I. (1995) Police involvement with clients having intellectual disabilities: A pilot study in South London. *Mental Handicap Research*, 8, 129–136.

Murphy, G. (2000) Policy and service development trends: Forensic mental health and social care services. *Tizard Learning Disability Review*, 5, 32–35.

Murphy, G., Harnett, H. & Holland, A. J. (1995) A survey of intellectual disabilities amongst men on remand in prison. *Mental Handicap Research*, 8, 81–98.

Murphy, M., Harrold, M., Carey, S. & Mulrooney, M. (2000) *A Survey of the Level of Learning Disability among the Prison Population in Ireland: Final Report* (http://www/irishprisons.ie/learning_disability_report.pdf).

Perske, R. (1991) *Unequal Justice: What Can Happen when Persons with Retardation or Other Developmental Disabilities Encounter the Criminal Justice System*. Nashville, TN: Abingdon.

Scottish Executive (2000) *The Same As you? A Review of Services for People with Learning Disabilities*. Edinburgh: Scottish Executive.

Scottish Office (1999) *Health, Social Work and Related Services for Mentally Disordered Offenders in Scotland*. Edinburgh: Scottish Office Department of Health.

Simpson M. K. & Hogg, J. (2001) Patterns of offending among people with intellectual disability: A systematic review. Part 1: Methodology and prevalence data. *Journal of Intellectual Disabilities Research*, 45, 384–396.

Sparrow, S. S., Balla, D. A. & Cicchetti, D. V. (1984) *Vineland Adaptive Behavior Scales: Interview Edition, Survey Form Manual*. Minnesota: American Guidance Service.

Steadman, H. J., Mulvey, E. P., Monhan, J., Robbins, P. C., Appelbaum, P. S., Grisso, T., Roth, L. H. & Silver, E. (1998) Violence by people discharged form acute psychiatric inpatient facilities and by others in the same neighbourhoods. *Archives of General Psychiatry*, 55, 393–401.

Thompson, D. (1997a) Profiling the sexually abusive behaviour with intellectual disabilities. *Journal of Applied Research in Intellectual Disabilities*, 10, 125–139.

Thompson, D. (1997b) Men with intellectual disabilities who sexually abuse: A review of the literature. *Journal of Applied Research in Intellectual Disabilities*, 10, 140–158.

Wechsler, D. (1981) *Wechsler Adult Intelligence Scale – Revised*. New York: Psychological Corporation.

Wechsler, D. (1999a) *Wechsler Adult Intelligence Scale (UK)* (3rd ed.). London: Psychological Corporation.

Wechsler, D. (1999b) *Wechsler Abbreviated Scale of intelligence (WASI)*. New York: Psychological Corporation.

Winter, N., Holland, A. J. & Collins, S. (1997) Factors predisposing to suspected offending by adults with self-reported learning disabilities. *Psychological Medicine*, 27, 595–607.

CHAPTER 7

The assessment of dementia in people with intellectual disabilities: context, strategy and methods

Chris Oliver and Sunny Kalsy

1 Introduction

Since the 1980s there has been a significant increase in clinical and research interest in the assessment of dementia in people with intellectual disability. The most influential factor that has contributed to this increase in interest is the enhanced life expectancy of people with intellectual disability and the corresponding rise in the number of people who have Down syndrome who are surviving into their fifth decade and are consequently at high risk for developing dementia (Eyman et al., 1991; see Carr, 1994, for a review). Aylward et al. (1997) have estimated the prevalence of dementia in people with Down syndrome to be 10% to 25% in the age band of 40 to 49 years, 20% to 50% in the age band of 50 to 59 years and 30% to 75% in those over 60 years of age. There is now a wealth of neuropathological, neuropsychological and related evidence that individuals who have Down syndrome are at high risk for developing Alzheimer disease (Oliver & Holland, 1986; Berg et al., 1993; Holland & Oliver, 1995). As a result of the changing demographics and the evidence for an association between Down syndrome and Alzheimer disease, the vast majority of research into the cognitive and behavioural manifestation of dementia in people with intellectual disability has focused on individuals who have Down syndrome. Consequently, there has been a focus on the presentation of dementia that is associated with Alzheimer disease as opposed to other disease processes such as multi-infarct and Lewy body dementia (Mann, 1993). Thus, although the following discussion is concerned with people with intellectual disabilities in general, the special focus of this chapter will be on Down syndrome, reflecting the high prevalence of dementia in relatively younger people with Down syndrome and a general interest in this topic.

'Dementia' is a general term used to describe a collection of illnesses with a similar pattern of symptoms manifesting as a global deterioration of functioning, and Alzheimer disease is the most common form of dementia accounting for about half of all cases (Katzman, 1976).

In terms of prevalence, it is estimated that over 5% of the general population over 65 years are affected, with prevalence increasing with advancing age to as much as 50% by age 90 (Zec, 1993). The prevalence of other forms of dementia include vascular dementia 20%, dementia with Lewy bodies 15%, and fronto-temporal dementia 5% (Jorm et al., 1987). A practical approach to the diagnosis of dementia begins with the clinical recognition of a progressive decline in memory, a decrease in the individual's ability to perform activities of daily living, psychiatric problems, personality changes and problem behaviours. While the clinical presentation of dementia may vary, depending on the aetiology, the diagnostic features are constant and are well described in the *Diagnostic and Statistical Manual of Mental Disorders*, 4th edition (DSM-IV; Knopman et al., 2001).

Research into the assessment and the course of dementia in individuals with Down syndrome has focused on both cognitive and behavioural change. Early descriptions of dementia were largely anecdotal and primarily focused on emerging skills deficits and behavioural excesses (Crapper et al., 1975; Ellis et al., 1974; Reid et al., 1978; Ropper & Williams, 1980). In the late 1970s and early 1980s cross-sectional age group studies employed some neuropsychological assessments to assess the earlier signs of memory loss and other cognitive signs (e.g. Thase et al., 1984; Wisniewski et al., 1978). These studies commonly employed newly developed or adapted neuropsychological assessments. This strategy reflected the paucity of available test instruments for individuals who had intellectual disability and, arguably, the shift of focus of psychology within the area of intellectual disability from research into cognitive processes to behavioural change. Parallel effects of this shift of focus are becoming evident in the attempts to study cognitive profiles associated with severe intellectual disability in genetically determined syndromes. It is notable that few of the assessment methods and paradigms adopted in early studies of Down syndrome are employed today, an exception being the work of Dalton (Dalton et al., 1974; Dalton & Crapper, 1977; Dalton & Fedor, 1998), and there is still an obvious need for the development of sensitive and specific assessment methods with robust psychometric properties that can document dementia-associated change in people with intellectual disabilities.

The need for assessments is becoming more evident as research and service agendas evolve. Intervention trials aimed at slowing the dementing process in people with Down syndrome are underway in the UK and USA, but are to some extent hampered by the lack of available outcome measures. Clinically, there is a need to address the problems associated with diagnosis that are in turn related to implications for proactive service planning and provision. There is good evidence that dementia in individuals with Down syndrome is associated with difficulties for carers and increasingly limited life experiences (Oliver et al., 2000). Alongside differential diagnosis these service-related issues are important reasons for developing and conducting assessments relevant to dementia.

2 Problems of Diagnosis and the Need for Formal Assessment

There are numerous problems associated with the informal 'clinical' assessment of dementia in the presence of pre-existing intellectual disability (Oliver, 1999). The most apparent are the physical and social changes in an older individual's life that can lead to behavioural change that might be interpreted as, or mask, dementia. Significant life events for all adults who have intellectual disability, and people with Down syndrome specifically, are likely to occur around the same time that the early signs of dementia might be at high risk for development. For those who have Down syndrome it is likely that parents were in their thirties or forties when the individual was born (Penrose, 1966) thus making the loss of a parent likely at an earlier stage. Alongside this significant life event there may be corresponding change of living environments and relationships that might contribute to a presentation of skill loss. Additionally, for individuals who have Down syndrome there are a number of medical, psychological and physical problems that can give rise to skill loss and thus may mimic dementia. Hypothyroidism, cataracts, hearing loss, depression and other conditions can occur and contribute to deterioration in performance and lead to lower test results (Thase, 1982; Lai, 1992; Burt et al., 1992; van Schrojenstein Lantman-de Valk et al., 1994). It is important that these issues are given attention alongside any psychological assessment of dementia in people with intellectual disability generally, and Down syndrome specifically.

The reliance on clinical judgement with no use made of formal assessments gives rise to a number of significant problems. The first is that there are very few standard taxing situations that may be experienced by an individual with intellectual disability over time in order to allow an appraisal of more subtle signs of potential decline. Many individuals with an intellectual disability are likely to be unemployed and living in sheltered environments in which there is the expectation that individuals will need support. Under these circumstances acquired deficits, and particularly the more subtle early signs of dementia, may be absorbed by the environment by more support being made available. Thus, with an insidious increase of lower expectations of an individual, it is difficult to identify a skill loss. Additionally, with higher levels of staff turnover in care environments identification of the critical issue of change, as opposed to performance at a given point in time, is compromised as carers may not be aware of 'baseline' performance. Finally, reliance on informants being able to tease out dementia-specific cognitive deficits against a background of both global and non-dementia-specific deficits is unlikely to be productive.

These issues of physical change, differential diagnosis and responsive environmental change make the diagnosis of dementia and, in particular, identification of the early signs of dementia, difficult. In addition, the task is made more difficult by the fact that any informal assessment of cognitive or behavioural 'state' at a given point in time requires comparison to previous performance to identify change. Given the potential variability of pre-existing degree of intellectual disability in a client group, it is clear that the identification of change is further hampered as information about past performance is often based on poor information. The implications of these issues are that formal assessment is essential to diagnosis and that assessment of change over time is a more critical diagnostic issue for people with intellectual disability than the general population.

3 Problems Associated with Formal Assessments

In the majority of the empirical literature on dementia assessment, there is an implicit assumption that the course and profile of cognitive decline is the same for people with an intellectual disability and the general population. Consequently, the assessment methods that have been developed have drawn heavily on the mainstream dementia literature. While there is no empirical evidence that the course of decline in individuals with intellectual disability is different from that seen in the general population, it is possible that cognitive functioning might show different patterns of deficit given a potential interaction between pre-existing neurological impairment and dementia. Recent research into specific cognitive deficits in younger people who have Down syndrome provides the basis for such an interaction (Jarrold et al., 2000). However, in the longitudinal studies that have been published to date there is strong evidence that the neuropsychological impairments experienced by individuals with Down syndrome who develop Alzheimer disease are similar to those seen in the general population and there is a similar sequence of decline (Burt et al., 1995; Devenny et al., 1996; Lai & Williams, 1989; Oliver et al., 1998).

The most significant problems for the assessment of specific neuropsychological deficits associated with dementia are the variability of intellectual disability and the problems associated with administering neuropsychological tests to those with severe or profound intellectual disability who may not understand verbal instructions (Aylward et al., 1997; Crayton & Oliver, 1993; Oliver, 1999). Given that there will be significant variability in the degree of intellectual disability in those requiring assessment, the development of sufficiently large normative datasets for tests of specific cognitive domains is problematic. There is good evidence that degree of intellectual disability is significantly positively correlated with poor performance on, for example, tests of short-term memory, apraxia and word finding in younger adults who have Down syndrome (Crayton et al., 1998). This means that poor performance on a neuropsychological test that might indicate dementia might easily be attributable to intellectual disability. The clear implication of this problem is that sequential testing is necessary in order to identify decline in an individual from a previous baseline. The second problem of individuals not being able to comply with test instructions either because of receptive language abilities or not understanding the test situation means that psychological testing can be extremely difficult if not impossible. In combination with the likely scenario that a baseline measure is not available when an individual first presents with change that might indicate dementia, this problem has led to a heavy reliance on informant-based measures.

4 Retrospective and Prospective Assessment Strategies

There are a number of strategies that might be adopted with regard to the assessment of dementia in people with intellectual disability (Oliver, 1999). Clinically the most common strategy is to attempt to review past assessments that have known psychometric properties and repeat the assessment. Of the limited past assessments that might be available, those selected may be chosen because they have subscales that assess cognitive domains predicted to decline in the presence of dementia and because they have more robust psychometric properties. In practice, few assessments are available and the school records and case files that are kept are usually of poor quality with regard to psychometric assessments. Additionally, measures of adaptive behaviour have become more commonly used than cognitive assessments, and change on these measures is unlikely in the early stages of dementia. The major problem therefore with a retrospective strategy is that when an individual presents for assessment with the question of dementia, there are usually few assessments available that might serve as a baseline record.

The retrospective strategy, which entails waiting for adults with Down syndrome to present with cognitive or behavioural change that might indicate dementia, has other problems related to the properties of tests that might be available for repeat assessment. First, while the degree of change between the past assessment and the contemporary assessment may be immediately evident, the speed of change cannot be appraised. Consequently, there may have been a very slow change over many years, which is unlikely to indicate dementia, or a change that has taken place over a small number of years, which is more likely to indicate a dementing process. Second, there may be very few items in the initial test relevant to dementia. This is particularly true of the limited attention paid to memory assessment in some test batteries. Third, the pre-existing intellectual disability might mean that the initial test score is very low, which, when combined with test error, means that floor effects may be evident and consequently decline may not be appraised.

For these reasons there have been repeated calls for a prospective strategy which ensures that adults with an intellectual disability who are at high risk for developing dementia have a baseline assessment as they approach the high-risk age band. In practice this strategy probably applies only to adults who have Down syndrome, as the risk of dementia in others who have an intellectual disability is similar to that in the general population.

If a prospective strategy is adopted, then a decision needs to be taken regarding whether direct assessment is undertaken or informant-based measures are used. Additionally, there needs to be consideration given to whether measures used for the general population are employed or whether adapted measures that have been developed in the last two decades have sufficiently robust psychometric properties to be of use.

The prospective strategy can overcome some of the problems outlined above. However, other problems arise from deploying this approach. First, the strategy entails a proactive approach by service providers with the accompanying cost and labour resources. There will also be the need to rule out other potential causes that might underlie any change, and the problem of floor effects is still evident. In order to offset some of the resource issues, it is tempting to employ informant-based measures alone. However, the issue of inter-rater reliability discussed below combined with the change in informant over time may lead to the collection of data that are of poor quality. Given these concerns there is a strong argument that may be made to support a prospective strategy for those individuals with an intellectual disability who are at higher risk for developing dementia that uses neuropsychological tests alongside measures of behavioural deficits that might be indicative of dementia.

The major benefits of employing neuropsychological assessments are related to the reliability, validity, sensitivity and specificity of the tests that might be deployed. It is certainly true that this form of test is more intrusive and demanding and often entails the paradigm of testing to failure. There are also greater costs associated with this method of testing, simply in terms of time and resources. However, these issues are outweighed by the benefit to the individual of early diagnosis, with the attendant possibility of planning future services.

Given the arguments made above of the assessment issues relevant to the appraisal of dementia in individuals with intellectual disability who are at higher risk for dementia, there is a strong case to be made for a prospective strategy that entails laying down a baseline of relevant psychological assessments prior to any referral been made. Additionally, the assessments need to be conducted across reasonably long intervals in order to gauge any change. It might be argued that the periods between the assessments should become shorter as age rises and thus risk increases. These issues are perhaps unique to the assessment of dementia in individuals who are at higher risk.

The above discussion leads to the conclusion that neuropsychological assessment is an important, if not critical, component of the process of diagnosis of dementia in people with intellectual disability. However, it is equally important that some measure of behavioural change is also employed. The diagnostic criteria for dementia, and particularly the later stages of dementia, indicate that behavioural change will continue to be evident after cognitive decline. Thus the assessment of dementia in adults with intellectual disability should focus on both cognitive and behavioural change.

5 Assessment Methods

5.1 Diagnostic interviews and 'global' performance assessments

Although the issues discussed above indicate a need for neuropsychological assessment of specific cognitive domains, a complete assessment strategy might usefully include broad-ranging assessments that are comparatively brief to complete. These assessments have the advantage of covering a number of behavioural and cognitive domains and, when repeated, can give a snapshot of overall decline. Two different approaches are diagnosis and performance-based assessments. While at an early stage of adaptation, the CAMCOG shows promise (Hon et al., 1999) as a diagnostic instrument, although the caveats outlined in the introduction apply. Similarly, the Severe Impairment Battery (Saxton et al., 1993) has been applied only to a limited sample of adults with Down syndrome (Witts & Elders, 1998), but has the advantage of a low floor with the potential for catering for individuals with severe intellectual disability and those who have showed significant decline.

5.2 Neuropsychological assessment

For a prospective strategy to be beneficial it is clear that the earliest signs of dementia should be carefully appraised. Inevitably, this means focusing on memory deficits (Oliver et al., 1998). There is good evidence in the empirical literature from cross-sectional studies that older adults who have Down syndrome do not perform as well on memory tasks as younger adults with Down syndrome and this is consistent with the data on age-related risk for Alzheimer disease (Wisniewski et al., 1978; Thase et al., 1982; Zigman et al., 1987; Crayton et al., 1998). This finding is not replicated in others who have an intellectual disability. This cross-sectional approach has recently been supplemented by a number of longitudinal studies that demonstrate that a decline in the memory function precedes decline in other areas and later significant skill loss (Lai & Williams, 1989; Oliver et al., 1998).

In addition to the early signs of memory loss, there is also evidence that there is a deterioration in learning and orientation. In combination, these empirical findings clearly indicate that neuropsychological assessment should appraise these areas. However, the studies that have addressed cognitive function have all used different methods to assess memory, learning and orientation in adults with Down syndrome. While this has to some extent enhanced the validity of the finding that memory is compromised, it also means that there are very limited normative data for a small number of tests. The second issue that is relevant is that in many of the cross-sectional and longitudinal studies noted earlier it is clear that either some participants evidence floor effects or participants with a more severe degree of intellectual disability were excluded from the study. Given that a low floor but reasonably high ceiling to maximize sensitivity is desirable, the choice of memory tests is somewhat limited. One assessment that does have the advantages of a reasonably large normative dataset, and a training procedure to ensure the participant is able to be assessed, is the match-to-sample test developed by Dalton & McMurray (1995). On balance, this test may prove to be the most useful that is currently available. Finally, the Rivermead Behavioural Memory Test (Wilson & Ivani-Chalian, 1995) warrants comment. Although there are limited data available for individuals with intellectual disability, two studies do indicate that this assessment may be useful for those with moderate or mild intellectual disability (Hon et al., 1998; Martin et al., 2000).

In addition to assessment of memory, it is important to use a test that has a sufficiently low floor to be able to include individuals with severe or moderate intellectual disability and for which there are normative data. It is also important that the test can be used when there has been decline to floor on a memory assessment in order to appraise further deterioration. As is the case for memory assessments within the empirical literature, a wide variety of methods for assessing apraxia, aphasia and agnosia are evident. Consequently, there are few tests that have sufficient normative data and have had validity evaluated. One exception is the dyspraxia scale that has been employed in a longitudinal study (Dalton & Fedor, 1998), has good psychometric properties, an objective scoring system for coding responses and a wide range of scores, thus allowing movement over time and avoiding floor effects (Dalton, 1996). The test is being employed as the primary outcome measure in a large-scale intervention study. It also has the benefit of being relatively quick to administer.

5.3 Informant-based measures

Although informant-based measures should be used cautiously within a retrospective assessment strategy, they can play a useful role when used for repeated testing over time. At present there are few measures available that have been developed specifically for those who have an intellectual disability, and which have been subjected to rigorous psychometric assessment. Two measures, the Dementia Questionnaire for Mentally Retarded Persons (DMR) (Evenhuis et al., 1990) and the Dementia Scale for Down Syndrome (DSDS) Gedye (1995), have good face validity with some assessment of reliability and could be used alongside neuropsychological assessments. A modified scoring procedure for the DMR has been proposed in order to overcome the problem that the DMR appears to be more prone to identifying dementia in the presence of a severe intellectual disability (Prasher, 1997). The need for caution when using these informant-based measures is primarily related to the appraisal of inter-informant reliability. Given that there is an inevitable change of staff over time, the issue of inter-informant reliability is more important than that of the measure's stability alone.

6 Conclusion

The diagnosis of dementia in adults who have intellectual disability presents a significant clinical challenge and the problems increase with the degree of pre-existing intellectual disability. There are psychological, health and social issues that can impede accurate diagnosis and thus promote the need for objective and specific psychological assessment. The strategy for the deployment of psychological assessment should be proactive and prospective. If this strategy is not adopted, then referrals are likely to be made at a late stage when dementia may be advanced, there is little time for future service planning and when residential resources may have been unsupported for some time, thus making placement breakdown more likely. The problems associated with informant-based measures mean that at present these measures should not be relied on in the absence of other assessments. Neuropsychological tests are a critical component of the diagnostic procedure, and the use of a small number of tests with lower floors targeting specific domains of cognitive decline is probably more beneficial than a broad-ranging battery of tests that might give results replete with floor effects. There are now a small number of neuropsychological tests that would be well supported by an informant-based approach, such as the DMR, which has a broad supportive literature. The challenge for the future remains the development of neuropsychological tests appropriate across levels of intellectual disability and the enhancement of the reliability and validity of informant-based measures. These measures will provide objective assessments against which the reliability and validity of clinical diagnosis can be judged.

REFERENCES

Aylward, E. H., Burt, D. B., Thorpe, L. U., Lai, F. & Dalton, A. J. (1997) Diagnosis of dementia in individuals with intellectual disability. *Journal of Intellectual Disability Research*, 41, 152–164.

Berg, J. M., Karlinsky, H. & Holland, A. J. (1993) *Alzheimer Disease, Down Syndrome and their Relationship*. New York: Oxford University Press.

Burt, D. B., Loveland, K. A., Chen, Y. W., Chuang, A., Lewis, K. R. & Cherry, L. (1995) Aging in adults with Down syndrome: Report from a longitudinal study. *American Journal on Mental Retardation*, 100, 262–270.

Burt, D. B., Loveland, K. A. & Lewis, K. R. (1992) Depression and the onset of dementia in adults with mental retardation. *American Journal on Mental Retardation*, 96, 502–511.

Carr, J. (1994) Annotation: Long term outcome for people with Down syndrome. *Journal of Child Psychology and Psychiatry*, 35, 425–439.

Crapper, D. R., Dalton, A. L., Skopitz, M., Eng, P., Scott, J. H. & Hachinski, V. (1975) Alzheimer degeneration in Down syndrome. *Archives of Neurology*, 32, 618.

Crayton, L. & Oliver, C. (1993) Assessment of cognitive functioning in persons with Down syndrome who develop Alzheimer disease. In J. M. Berg, H. Karlinsky & A. J. Holland (eds.), *Alzheimer Disease, Down Syndrome and their Relationship*. New York: Oxford University Press, pp. 135–153.

Crayton, L., Oliver, C., Holland, A., Hall, S. & Bradbury, J. (1998) The neuropsychological assessment of age related cognitive deficits in adults with Down syndrome. *Journal of Applied Research in Intellectual Disabilities*, 11, 255–272.

Dalton, A. J. (1996) *Dyspraxia Scale for Adults with Down Syndrome*. Staten Island: Aging Studies Consortium and Bytecraft Ltd (5 Van Cortlandt Avenue, Staten Island, NY 10301).

Dalton, A. J. & Crapper, D. R. (1977) Down Syndrome and ageing of the brain. In P. Mittler (ed.), *Research to Practice in Mental Retardation*. Vol. 3: *Biomedical Aspects*. Baltimore, MA: University Park Press, pp. 391–400.

Dalton, A. L., Crapper, D. R. & Schlotterer, G. R. (1974) Alzheimer's disease in Down's syndrome: Visual retention deficits. *Cortex*, 10, 366–377.

Dalton, A. J. & Fedor, B. L. (1998) Onset of dyspraxia in aging persons with Down Syndrome: Longitudinal studies. *Journal of Intellectual and Developmental Disability*, 23, 13–24.

Dalton, A. J. & McMurray, K. (1995) *Dalton/Murray Visual Memory Test*. Staten Island, NY: Aging Studies Consortium and Bytecraft Ltd (5 Van Cortlandt Avenue, Staten Island, NY 10301).

Devenny, D. A., Silverman, W. P., Hill, A. L., Jenkins, E., Sersen, E. A. & Wisniewski, K. E. (1996) Normal ageing in adults with Down syndrome: A longitudinal study. *Journal of Intellectual Disability Research*, 40, 208–221.

Ellis, W. G., McCulloch, J. R. & Corley, C. L. (1974) Presenile dementia in Down syndrome: Ultrastructural identity with Alzheimer disease. *Neurology (Minneapolis)*, 24, 101–106.

Evenhuis, H. M., Kengen, M. M. F. & Eurlings, H. A. L. (1990) *Dementia Questionnaire for Mentally Retarded Persons*. Zwammerdam, Netherlands: Hooge Burch Institute for Mentally Retarded People.

Eyman, R. K., Call, T. L. & White, J. F. (1991) Life expectancy of persons with Down syndrome. *American Journal on Mental Retardation*, 95, 603–612.

Gedye, A. (1995) *Dementia Scale for Down Syndrome (Manual)*. Vancouver: Gedye Research & Consulting.

Holland A. J. & Oliver, C. (1995) Down's syndrome and the links with Alzheimer's disease. *Journal of Neurology, Neurosurgery and Psychiatry*, 59, 111–114.

Hon, J., Huppert, F. A., Holland, A. J. & Watson, P. (1998) The value of the Rivermead Behavioural Memory Test (Children's Version) in an epidemiological study of older adults with Down syndrome. *British Journal of Clinical Psychology*, 37, 15–29.

Hon, J., Huppert, F. A., Holland, A. J. & Watson, P. (1999) Neuropsychological assessment of older adults with Down Syndrome: An epidemiological study using the Cambridge Cognitive Examination (CAMCOG). *British Journal of Clinical Psychology*, 38, 155–165.

Jarrold, C., Baddeley, A. D. & Hewes, A. K. (2000) Verbal short-term memory deficits in Down syndrome: A consequence of problems in rehearsal? *Journal of Child Psychology and Psychiatry*, 41, 233–244.

Jorm, A. F., Korten, A. E. & Henderson, A. S. (1987) The prevalence of dementia. *Acta Psychiatrica Scandinavica*, 76, 4465–4479.

Katzman, R. (1976) The prevalence and malignancy of Alzheimer disease. *Archives of Neurology*, 33, 217–219.

Knopman, D. S., DeKoskey, S. T., Cummings, J. L., Chui, H., Corey-Bloom, J. et al. (2001) Practice parameters: Diagnosis of dementia. *Neurology*, 56, 1143–1153.

Lai, F. (1992) Clinicopathologic features of Alzheimer disease in Down syndrome. In L. Nadel & C. J. Epstein (eds.), *Down Syndrome and Alzheimer Disease*. New York: Wiley-Liss, pp. 15–34.

Lai, F. & Williams, R. S. (1989) A prospective study of Alzheimer disease in Down syndrome. *Archives of Neurology*, 46, 849–853.

Mann, D. M. A. (1993) Association between Alzheimer disease and Down syndrome: Neuropathological observations. In J. M. Berg, H. Karlinsky & A. J. Holland (eds.), *Alzheimer Disease, Down Syndrome and their Relationship*. New York: Oxford University Press, pp. 71–92.

Martin, C., West, J., Cull, C. & Adams, M. (2000) A preliminary study investigating how people with mild intellectual disabilities perform on the Rivermead Behavioural Memory Test. *Journal of Applied Research in Intellectual Disabilities*, 13, 186–193.

Oliver, C. (1999) Perspectives on assessment and evaluation. In M. P. Janicki & A. J. Dalton (eds.), *Dementia, Aging, and Intellectual Disabilities: A Handbook*. Philadelphia, PA: Taylor & Francis/ Bruner/Mazel, pp. 123–140.

Oliver, C., Crayton, L., Holland, A. J. & Hall, S. (2000) Acquired cognitive impairments in adults with Down syndrome: Effects on the individual, carers and services. *American Journal on Mental Retardation*, **105**, 455–465.

Oliver, C., Crayton, Holland, A. J., Hall, S. & Bradbury, J. (1998) A four year study of age related cognitive and behavioural change in adults with Down syndrome. *Psychological Medicine*, **28**, 1365–1377.

Oliver, C. & Holland, A. J. (1986) Down syndrome and Alzheimer disease: A review. *Psychological Medicine*, **16**, 307–322.

Penrose, L. S. (1966) *The Biology of Mental Defect*. London: Sidgwick & Jackson.

Prasher, V. P. (1997) Dementia Questionnaire for Persons with Mental Retardation (DMR): Modified criteria for adults with Down syndrome. *Journal of Applied Research in Intellectual Disability*, **10**, 54–60.

Reid, A. H., Maloney, A. F. J. & Aungle, P. G. (1978) Dementia in ageing mental defectives: A clinical and neuropathological study. *Journal of Mental Deficiency Research*, **22**, 233–241.

Ropper, A. H. & Williams, R. S. (1980) Relationship between plaques, tangles and dementia in Down syndrome. *Neurology*, **30**, 639–644.

Saxton, J, McGonigle, K. L., Swilart, A. A. & Boller, F. (1993) *The Severe Impairment Battery*. London: Thames Valley Test Company.

Schrojenstein Lantman-de Valk, H. M. J. van, Haveman, M. J., Maaskant, M. A., Kessels, A. G., Urlings, H. F. & Sturmans, F. (1994) The need for assessment of sensory functioning in ageing people with mental handicap. *Journal of Intellectual Disability Research*, **38**, 289–298.

Thase, M. E. (1982) Reversible dementia in Down syndrome. *Journal of Mental Deficiency Research*, **26**, 111–113.

Thase, M. E., Liss, L., Smeltzer, D. & Maloon, J. (1982) Clinical evaluation of dementia in Down syndrome: A preliminary report. *Journal of Mental Deficiency Research*, **26**, 239–244.

Thase, M. E., Tigner, R., Smeltzer, D. J. & Liss, L. (1984) Age-related neuropsychological deficits in Down syndrome. *Biological Psychology*, **19**, 571–585.

Wilson, B. & Ivani-Chalian, R. (1995) Performance of adults with Down's syndrome on the Children's version of the Rivermead Behavioural Memory Test. *British Journal of Clinical Psychology*, **34**, 85–88.

Wisniewski, K. E., Howe, J., Gwyn-Williams, D. & Wisniewski, H. M. (1978) Precocious ageing and dementia in patients with Down Syndrome. *Biological Psychiatry*, **13**, 619–627.

Witts, P. & Elders, S. (1998) The 'Severe Impairment Battery': Assessing cognitive ability in adults with Down syndrome. *British Journal of Clinical Psychology*, **37**, 207–210.

Zec, R. F. (1993) Neuropsychological functioning in Alzheimer's disease. In R. W. Parks, R. F. Zec & R. S. Wilson (eds.), *Neuropsychology of Alzheimer's Disease and Other Dementias*. New York: Oxford University Press, pp. 3–80.

Zigman, W. B., Schupf, N., Lubin, R. A. & Silverman, W. P. (1987) Premature regression of adults with Down syndrome. *American Journal of Mental Deficiency*, **92**, 161–168.

CHAPTER 8

Genetic syndromes and behavioural phenotypes

Robert M. Walley

1 Introduction

The observation that certain genetic syndromes are associated with particular behavioural characteristics has been known in the literature since the 1860s when J. Langdon Down first described his observations on the children with the syndrome that later bore his name (Down, 1866). It was not until 1971, however, that Professor William Nyhan first used the term 'behavioural phenotype' to describe the self-injurious behaviour found in people with Lesch-Nyhan syndrome. He proposed that this behaviour was genetically determined rather than the result of any environmental factor.

It is interesting to consider why it took such a long time for the concept of behavioural phenotypes to be developed. A number of reasons for this have been suggested, including the negative impact of the early twentieth century eugenics movement on research and the view that if a behaviour is believed to be genetically determined, it can produce feelings of therapeutic nihilism (Holland, 1999). Holland, however, notes, 'identifying the likely genetic influences on a particular behaviour is but the starting point for both research and, in clinical situations, the development of appropriate management and treatment strategies' (p. 242).

There has been a rapid growth in interest in genetic syndromes and behavioural phenotypes since the 1970s, and this may be due to a combination of factors; the common experiences and observations of parents leading to the development of support groups; an increased knowledge of the processes involved in human genetics; greater collaboration between clinicians and researchers; developments in psychological assessment, and scanning techniques accompanied by the 'cognitive revolution' (Tager-Flusberg, 1999) in psychology.

Deciding on a definition for the term 'behavioural phenotype' is not without its difficulties. That provided by Flint and Yule (1994) suggests, 'A characteristic pattern of motor, cognitive, linguistic and social abnormalities, which is consistently associated with a biological disorder. In some cases, the behavioural phenotype may constitute a psychiatric disorder; in others, behaviours which are not usually regarded as symptoms of psychiatric disorders may occur' (p. 666).

This definition suggests, however, rather a rigid connection between the genotype (i.e. the genetic region involved in 'causing' the syndrome) of individuals affected by a particular syndrome, and the resulting behavioural phenotype; it ignores the observation that there may be considerable variability between individuals who have the same genetic syndrome. This variability may exist because of family, developmental or environmental factors as well as variability within the affected genetic region itself (Dykens, 1995; Flint, 1996; Hodapp, 1997; Tager-Flusberg, 1999). Dykens (1995) has suggested that a behavioural phenotype 'be described as the heightened probability or likelihood that people with a given syndrome will exhibit certain behavioural and developmental sequelae relative to those without the syndrome' (p. 523).

Identification of particular syndromes and associated behavioural phenotypes may occur at any stage of a person's life, though ideally the earlier the better. While psychological assessment can make an important contribution to this understanding, input from genetic counsellors and clinical genetics services, widely available in developed countries, have a critical role to play. They can provide not only specific information on the syndrome and local contacts who may offer support, but also advice to the family on the probability of further births of children with the same syndrome.

2 The Relevance of Genetic Syndromes and Behavioural Phenotypes to Professional Practice

This chapter and chapter 16 approach the subject of assessment in genetic syndromes and behavioural phenotypes from two different angles. In this chapter the utility of considering genetic syndromes and their behavioural phenotypes as an important part of assessment will be discussed. The present chapter will be of interest to professionals who have direct contact with service users in health, social care or education settings. Increasingly those providing services will be supporting people with an identified syndrome and will be expected to be informed on the characteristic behavioural consequences of the syndrome. Not only this, but as new approaches to intervention for such consequences are developed, good professional practice will require that workers are aware of such interventions and competent in undertaking them. Though we will always wish to deal with an individual with a known syndrome in a person-centred way, knowledge of the impact of the syndrome on that person will be critical. Chapter 16 discusses some of the problems inherent in choosing assessments for research on genetic syndromes and behavioural phenotypes, and will be of interest to readers who are contemplating or utilizing research in this area. Knowledge of a genetic syndrome and, where available, its behavioural phenotype can be an important part of an assessment process, and some representative examples from the domains of health, social care and education will now be considered. There are at least a thousand genetic causes of intellectual disability (Moser, 1992), but many are very rare and it is sometimes not possible to determine whether they lead to a behavioural phenotype.

2.1 Genetic Syndromes and health

It is important to appreciate that genetic problems associated with intellectual disability often have a wide influence and can lead to a number of physical health difficulties as well as an increased risk of developing a psychiatric disorder. Studies have shown, however, that people with intellectual disabilities face a number of barriers in primary and secondary health care. These include communication difficulties and a lack of understanding that service users may have particular health needs (Espie & Brown, 1998; Paxton & Taylor, 1998; Lennox & Kerr, 1997). Given that the average general practice in the UK will have only about four or five patients with intellectual disabilities, it is not surprising that primary care staff may be unaware of the particular health concerns associated with genetic syndromes. It is therefore important that carers and staff should have knowledge of particular health difficulties associated with a given syndrome in order to ensure the best quality of health care for service users with that syndrome. This should include an awareness of hearing and eyesight problems (Yeates, 1999; Warburg, 2001), which, although under-reported in the intellectual disability population, are extremely common in some genetic syndromes. Some representative examples of important health issues associated with behavioural phenotypes are presented in table 8.1.

2.2 Behavioural phenotypes and social care

2.2.1 Working with families   The purpose of this book pertains to the issues surrounding assessment of adults with an intellectual disability, but it is often the case that service providers, in working with adult service users, come into contact with their families. It can be helpful to get a sense of a parent's experience, in order to obtain a holistic picture of an individual service user. Bringing up a child with an intellectual disability is linked to higher family stress, but a heightened risk of stress may be associated with particular syndromes and behavioural phenotypes. Sarimski (1997), investigating family stress between families who have Fragile X, Prader-Willi or Williams syndrome children, found that parenting stress was elevated in each of the three syndromes, but without significant between-group differences. Sarimski found that parenting stress was related to individual coping resources and perceived levels of social support. Some studies, however, have shown significant differences in family stress between syndromes; van Lieshout et al. (1998), also investigating families with Prader-Willi syndrome, Fragile X and Williams syndrome children, found that parents who suffer stress with children with Prader-Willi syndrome report more marital conflict, lower parental consistency, and higher levels of parental control and parental anger than the other parents. They found that both parents appear to run the risk of having high levels of anger and control in order to cope with the specific problems of their child. Dykens and Cassidy (1996) draw our attention to research that shows children with Prader-Willi syndrome have a higher level of temper tantrums, which can be, but are not always, related to their hyperphagia (overeating). Dimitropoulos et al. (2001) have shown that compulsions and tantrums emerge at an early age in Prader-Willi syndrome, are at elevated levels compared to other syndromes and follow a different developmental trajectory to that found in unaffected, typically developing children. In the van Lieshout et al. study, children with Williams syndrome were found to have much higher levels of 'agreeableness' than children with Prader-Willi syndrome or Fragile X. The parents of children with Williams syndrome report lower control and lower anger than the parents of Prader-Willi syndrome.

Hodapp (1997) describes the environment–child transaction that has been called 'evocative' in the sense that some behaviours children produce tend to 'invite' positive reactions from caregivers. Hodapp, citing the work of Pitcairn & Wishart (1994), describes how

Table 8.1 Some Representative Examples of Important Health-Related Issues Associated with Genetic Syndromes

Down	Increased risk of Alzheimer type dementia with age, significantly more common in people over 50. Increased risk of thyroid problems and heart disease. Glue ear common in children and adults, and increased risk of eyesight problems.
Rett	Physical difficulties in females affected by classical Rett syndrome tend to increase with age; i.e. progression of scoliosis, muscle wasting, joint contractures, foot deformities and increasing spasticity of lower limbs. Seizure activity common, as are episodes of disorganised breathing. Difficulties in chewing and swallowing are also extremely common, and may be accompanied by choking and regurgitation.
Prader-Willi	Characterized by overeating (hyperphagia), commonly leading to obesity that may be life threatening. Dietary, management and behavioural approaches to food input are therefore very important. Increased prevalence of scoliosis and other orthopaedic abnormalities. Endocrine problems indicate that service users with Prader-Willi should have access to a physician with experience in Prader-Willi syndrome. Increased likelihood of eyesight difficulties particularly squints (Strabismus); sleep apnoea common, which may be related to obesity. Increased risk of psychiatric problems. See also Clarke et al. (1998).
Fragile X	Some individuals with Fragile X syndrome may have cardiovascular difficulties and about 20% of males may develop seizures.
Angelman	Tendency towards obesity with age in females. Scoliosis is a problem in about 10% of cases. Epilepsy is found in over 80% of cases of childhood, but tends to decrease with age. Feeding problems also common that may be accompanied by reflux.
Williams	Increased risk of cardiovascular problems. Dental abnormalities, hypertension, gastro-intestinal and kidney problems have also been reported.
Wolf-Hirschhorn	Feet deformities common that may require podiatry input. Increased risk of eyesight and hearing problems. Kidney and heart defects common. Increased risk of seizures and respiratory infections.
Tuberous Sclerosis	Increased risk of epilepsy, kidney disease, and sometimes lung disease.

Source: O'Brien & Yule (1995)

children with Down syndrome show particular interest in people rather than objects, and charming behaviour sometimes designed to distract adults working with a child on a task. They are also perceived as having a pleasant personality.

Much of the research on family stress has tended to focus on a small number of syndromes. High family stress has been associated with Prader-Willi syndrome, probably because of the externalizing behaviours such as temper tantrums that are found in this syndrome. As Hodapp (1997) observes, however, maladaptive behaviour is an important characteristic associated with family stress, and service providers should bear this in mind when working with a service user who has a behavioural phenotype, which may include aggressive tendencies.

2.2.2 Behaviour that challenges services One of the most commonly used definitions of challenging behaviour is that given by Emerson et al. (1998) as 'behaviour of such an intensity, frequency, or duration that the physical safety of the person or others is placed in serious jeopardy or behaviour which is likely to seriously limit or delay access to and use of ordinary community facilities' (p. 17).

The concept of behavioural phenotype is concerned with increased risk of certain types of behaviour. However, because a person has a genetic syndrome, it does not always mean that a specific behaviour will be found in every individual with the syndrome, or at the same intensity and frequency. A number of behavioural phenotypes do include an increased risk of behaviours that could be considered to be challenging as well as some that may be considered to be problematic, though not to the degree that they cause considerable harm, or prevent individual service users becoming involved in community activities.

Although by definition it is thought that the behaviours that comprise a behavioural phenotype have a strong genetic component, it is still important to carry out a functional analysis. It is particularly important to ascertain if the environment can be modified, in order to change the setting conditions and/or the consequences for the behaviour.

Table 8.2 presents examples of challenging and problematical behaviours that are associated with behavioural phenotypes. For a full discussion of challenging behaviour and its assessment see chapters 5 and 13, respectively.

Even extreme behaviours such as the self-injury found in the Lesch-Nyhan behavioural phenotype may vary with the environment. Anderson and Ernst (1994) found that stressful and emotional events are associated with higher rates of self-injury in people with this syndrome. Furthermore, reduction in these behaviours can be found when service users are engaged in enjoyable activities and social interactions.

Functional analysis may assist in devising interventions that are based around changing or modifying the antecedent factors to and the consequences for a behaviour. Rose and Walker (2000) describe this type of approach with a man who has Prader-Willi syndrome and hyperphagia. Their approach looked at modifying the tangible environmental factors involved as antecedents and consequences. Additionally, they attempted to change the motivation of the service user himself towards eating. The authors report that their approach led to a sustained reduction in challenging behaviour and the weight of the service user concerned.

In addition to carrying out functional analysis on behaviours occurring in specific settings, general behavioural advice can also be useful in helping to alleviate problematic behaviours. Many parent/carer groups provide advice of this type in their books, magazines and, increasingly, on websites. An example of the last is the guidelines for families and professionals on adults with Williams syndrome by Udwin, Howlin and Davies (see www. williams-syndrome.org.uk). Sudhalter and Belser (2001), for example, suggest that producing a calm and relaxing environment can reduce the tangential language that is found in males with Fragile X syndrome. The authors suggest that if these conditions are met, they will provide the right environment for training and self-control that could lead to improved language and social behaviour.

2.2.3 Future planning Planning for individual service users should take into account changing needs, and knowledge of a behavioural phenotype can help anticipate, and prepare for, potential problems. This is particularly relevant for service users with Down syndrome

Table 8.2 Some Examples of Challenging and Problematic Behaviours Associated with Behavioural Phenotypes

Syndrome	Behavioural phenotype	References
Williams	Inappropriate interpersonal skills, hyperactivity. Anxiety, low attention span/distractibility, hyperacusis; i.e. very acute hearing in response to certain sounds, can cause behavioural problems in terms of covering ears and avoiding sounds.	Udwin & Dennis (1995) in O'Brien and Yule (1995) Einfeld et al. (1997).
Lowe	Temper tantrums, stereotypy, stubbornness and obsessions/unusual preoccupations.	Kenworthy et al. (1993)
Angelman	Hyperactivity, restlessness, eating and sleep problems, fascination with water.	Clarke & Marston (2000)
Fragile X	Behaviour problems are often related to characteristic finding of social anxiety. They may be triggered by overstimulation, particularly in social situations. Features of social anxiety include gaze aversion, tactile defensiveness and ritualistic forms of greeting. Speech may be repetitive and contain a number of tangential comments. Impulsive behaviour and poor self-control have also been reported.	Udwin & Dennis (1995) in O'Brien & Yule (1995) Sudhalter & Belser (2001)
Prader-Willi	Temper tantrums, compulsive behaviour, hyperphagia (overeating).	Clarke et al. (1996) Dykens & Kasari (1997)
Smith-Magenis	Aggression, destructive behaviour, self-injurious behaviour, hyperactivity. Sleep disorders.	Udwin & Dennis (1995) in O'Brien & Yule (1995)
Cri-du-Chat	Irritability, destructiveness, hyperactivity, self-stimulatory behaviours.	Udwin & Dennis (1995) in O'Brien & Yule (1995)

who are at a high risk of developing Alzheimer type dementia (see chapters 7 and 15), but it is also important for service users with other types of genetic syndrome who may develop a greater range of disabling health problems as they age (e.g. females with classical Rett syndrome) (Kerr, 2002).

Taking into account changing needs is particularly important for adult service users who still live in the parental home, where increasingly elderly parents may find it more difficult to provide the high levels of physical and emotional support required for their son or daughter.

2.2.4 Behavioural phenotypes in the domain of education From an educational point of view it is useful to know something of the intellectual styles and potential of individuals with different syndromes, in order to ensure the right level of support is given. This includes an understanding of particular skills as well as intellectual difficulties. Given the social and increasingly inclusive nature of education, it is also helpful to know how service users are likely to relate to their peer group, and in the case of young adults, how they might

cope with the transition from school to college. Waters (1999), for example, describes the strengths and weaknesses of school and further education students who have Prader-Willi syndrome in a practical guide written for teachers and lecturers. Similar guides are available for other syndrome groups.

3   Summary

This chapter has discussed some key issues surrounding genetic syndromes and behavioural phenotypes, in particular their role as part of an assessment process. The information provided leads to a series of questions that have to be addressed during the assessment process:

- Is there an increased risk of physical and psychological health problems because of a person's syndrome?
- Is it likely that the genetic syndrome has had an effect in the shaping of family dynamics, which may influence current aspects of a service user's behaviour?
- Is there any challenging behaviour associated with the syndrome or behavioural phenotype, and, if so, have any interventions or suggestions for treatment been published?
- Where can carers/professionals obtain further information about a particular syndrome?
- What are the implications of a syndrome for education/employment?
- Are service user's needs likely to change over time because of the syndrome?

Thus the implication of a syndrome associated with a given behavioural phenotype is wide ranging, affecting every area of a person's life. Those supporting the person, both family members and paid staff, need to be aware of these implications and how best to respond to the needs that arise.

REFERENCES

Anderson, L. T. & Ernst, M. (1994) Self injury in Lesch-Nyhan disease. *Journal of Autism and Developmental Disorders*, 24, 67–81.

Clarke, D. J., Boer, H., Chung M. C., Sturmey, P. & Webb, T. (1996) Maladaptive behaviour in Prader-Willi syndrome in adult life. *Journal of Intellectual Disability Research*, 40, 159–165.

Clarke, D. J., Boer, H., Webb, T., Scott, P., Frazer, S., Vogels, A., Borghgraef, M. & Curfs, L. (1998) Prader-Willi syndrome and psychotic symptoms: Case descriptions and genetic studies. *Journal of Intellectual Disability Research*, 42, 440–450.

Clarke, D. J. & Marston, G. (2000) Problem behaviors associated with 15q-Angelman Syndrome. *American Journal on Mental Retardation*, 105, 25–31.

Dimitropoulos, A., Feurer, I. D., Butler, M. G. & Thompson, T. (2001) Emergence of compulsive behavior and tantrums in children with Prader-Willi syndrome. *American Journal on Mental Retardation*, 106, 39–51.

Down, J. L. (1866) Observations on an ethnic classification of idiots: London Hospital Report 3, 259–262. Reprinted in Down, J. L. (1990) Mental affectations of childhood and youth. *Classics in Developmental Medicine No. 5*. London: MacKeith, pp. 127–131.

Dykens, E. M. (1995) Measuring behavioral phenotypes: Provocations for the 'New Genetics'. *American Journal on Mental Retardation*, 99, 522–532.

Dykens, E. M. & Cassidy, S. B. (1996) Prader-Willi syndrome: Genetic, behavioral and treatment issues. *Child and Adolescent Psychiatric Clinics of North America*, **5**, 913–927.

Dykens, E. M. & Kasari, C. (1997) Maladaptive behavior in children with Prader-Willi syndrome, Down syndrome and nonspecific mental retardation. *American Journal on Mental Retardation*, **102**, 228–237.

Einfeld, S. L., Tonge, B. J. & Florio, T. (1997) Behavioral and emotional disturbance in individuals with Williams syndrome. *American Journal on Mental Retardation*, **102**, 45–53.

Emerson, E., Cummings, R., Barrett, S., Hughes, H., McCool, C. & Toogood, A. (1998) Challenging behaviour and community services 2: 'Who are the people who challenge services?' *Mental Handicap*, **16**, 16–19.

Espie, C. & Brown, M. (1998) Health needs and learning disabilities: An overview. *Health Bulletin*, **56**, 603–611.

Flint, J. (1996) Behavioural phenotypes: A window onto the biology of behaviour. *Journal of Child Psychology and Psychiatry*, **37**, 355–368.

Flint, J. & Yule, W. C. (1994) *Behavioural Phenotypes*. In M. Rutter, E. Taylor & L. Hersov (eds.), *Child and Adolescent Psychiatry* (3rd ed.). Oxford: Blackwell Scientific, pp. 666–687.

Hodapp, R. M. (1997) Direct and indirect behavioral effects on different genetic disorders of mental retardation. *American Journal on Mental Retardation*, **102**, 67–79.

Holland, A. (1999) Syndromes, phenotypes and genotypes: Finding the links. *Psychologist*, **12**, 242–245.

Kenworthy, L., Park, T. & Charnas, L. R. (1993) Cognitive and behavioral profile of the oculo-cerebrorenal syndrome of Lowe. *American Journal of Medical Genetics*, **46**, 297–303.

Kerr, A. (2002) Annotation: Rett syndrome: Recent progress and implications for research and clinical practice. *Journal of Child Psychology and Psychiatry*, **43**, 277–289.

Lennox, N. G. & Kerr, M. P. (1997) Primary health care and people with an intellectual disability: The evidence base. *Journal of Intellectual Disabilities Research* , **41**, 365–372.

Lieshout, C. F. M. van, De Mayer, R. E., Curfs, L. M. G. & Fry's, J.-P. (1998) Family contexts, parental behaviour and personality profiles of children and adolescents with Prader-Willi, Fragile-X or Williams Syndrome. *Journal of Child Psychology and Psychiatry*, **39**, 699–710.

Moser, H. W. (1992) Prevention of mental retardation (genetics). In L. Rowitz (ed.), *Mental Retardation in the Year 2000*. Springer-Verlag: New York, pp. 111–137.

O'Brien, G. & Yule, W. (1995) *Behavioural Phenotypes*. London: MacKeith.

Paxton, D. & Taylor, S. (1998) Access to primary health care for adults with learning disability. *Health Bulletin*, **56**, 686–693.

Pitcairn, T. K. & Wishart, J. G. C. (1994) Reactions of young children with Down's syndrome to an impossible task. *British Journal of Developmental Psychology*, **12**, 485–489.

Rose, J. & Walker, S. (2000) Working with a man who has Prader-Willi syndrome and his support staff using motivational principles. *Behavioural and Cognitive Psychotherapy*, **28**, 293–302.

Sarimski, K. (1997) Behavioural phenotypes and family stress in three mental retardation syndromes. *European Child and Adolescent Psychiatry*, **6**, 26–31.

Sudhalter, V. & Belser, R. (2001) Conversational characteristics of children with Fragile-X syndrome: Tangential language. *American Journal on Mental Retardation*, **106**, 389–400.

Tager-Flusberg, H. (1999) An introduction to research in neurodevelopmental disorders from a cognitive neuroscience perspective. In H. Tager-Flusberg (ed.), *Neurodevelopmental Disorders*. Cambridge, MA: MIT Press, pp. 3–24.

Udwin, O. & Dennis, J. (1995) Psychological and behavioural phenotypes in genetically determined syndromes: A review of research findings. In G. O'Brien & W. Yule (eds.), *Behavioural Phenotypes*. London: MacKeith, pp. 90–208.

Warburg, M. (2001) Visual impairment in adult people with intellectual disability: Literature review. *Journal of Intellectual Disability Research*, 45, 424–438.

Waters, J. (1999) *Prader-Willi Syndrome: A Practical Guide*. David Fulton: London.

Yeates, S. (1999) Hearing loss in people with learning disabilities. *Tizard Learning Disability Review*, 3, 20–28.

PART II

Strategies and instruments

CHAPTER 9

Instruments assessing quality of life

Robert A. Cummins

1 Introduction

The instruments described in this chapter measure quality of life (QOL) as broadly defined. The critical feature of all of these scales is that they elicit responses directly from the person who has an intellectual disability and they provide information about the positive side of life.

2 Method of Scale Selection

The references for this review were located by bibliographic tracking and a Psychlit search undertaken by both author name and instrument title from 1990 to 2002. In addition, personal correspondence was sent to instrument authors, where their address could be found, requesting additional information. In the descriptions of the following instruments, the following evaluation criteria will be employed:

- *Synopsis*: A brief description of the instrument's purpose and construction.
- *Scale structure*: verification of scale structure (e.g. factor analysis).
- *Reliability*: Cronbach's alpha, test–retest.
- *Validity*: convergent and divergent.
- *Sensitivity*: The ability of the scale to detect group differences.
- *Proxy data*: References to proxy data are noted but unreviewed when referring to subjective states.
- *General evaluation*: An overview of the instrument's usefulness.

Within the published literature there are 30–40 self-completion scales for people with an intellectual disability that are designed to measure QOL, broadly defined. The complete listing of these can be found in the 'Instruments' section of the Australian Centre on Quality of Life website (acqol.deakin.edu.au). Most of these scales, however, lack basic psychometric data or are limited to some component of the QOL construct. The scales selected for this chapter are those that provide a reasonably broad view of life quality, that allow self-completion in relation to subjective QOL, and have a range of psychometric data.

3 Evaluation Criteria

The evaluative criteria to be employed are derived directly from the analysis undertaken in chapter 1. They are as follows:

- The scale may measure either objective or subjective QOL.
- Objective and subjective items cannot be validly combined, but must be represented in separate scales.
- Scales must be verified by factor analysis.
- Scales must have adequate reliability, validity and sensitivity.
- Scales should be equally applicable to non-disabled people, thus ensuring normative comparisons of life quality.
- The response mode and choice of answers should reflect psychometric theory and strike a balance between reliability and sensitivity.
- The instrument should be brief, simple to administer, and easy to score.
- A pre-test must be used to establish that respondents can comprehend the questions.
- Proxy data are unacceptable when used to judge subjective states of well-being. Proxy data may be used to evaluate objective QOL.

4 Instrument Appraisal

The scales are ordered in chronological sequence of initial publication date.

4.1 Quality of Life Questionnaire (QOLQ: Cragg & Harrison, 1984), COMPASS (Cragg & Look, 1992)

Synopsis: The original 'Questionnaire on quality of life' is based on the principles of normalization (see also Donegan & Potts, 1988). It has three parts and a total of 70 questions. Part I comprises 53 questions answered by staff and residents. Part II comprises nine objective items and Part III comprises eight subjective items pertaining to accommodation standards. These are completed by the interviewer. Each item is rated on a 4- or 5-point scale and the questionnaire divides into eight subscales as follows:

- physical details of the home
- access to the community afforded by the home
- available leisure opportunities
- community integration achieved by the residents
- routines within the home
- resident education and training

- staff behaviour
- opportunities for resident choice and decision making

The COMPASS version of the scale is intended as a 'multi-perspective evaluation of quality in home life'. The questions are as before and it takes about three hours to administer.

Scale structure: Dagnan et al. (1994) performed a factor analysis on the eight subscales and claim to have found two factors. However, since four of the subscales cross-loaded at .40 or above and the analysis was based on only 18 respondents, this cannot be accepted as reliable.

Reliability: Using all items together, Dagnan et al. (1995) report a Cronbach alpha of .94, which is high enough to indicate item redundancy; an average item-total correlation of .43, which is on the low-side; and inter-rater agreement at .90, which is good.

Sensitivity: As might be expected from an instrument based on normalization, the questionnaire should be sensitive to the changed living conditions experienced by people relocating from an institution to group homes. This has been confirmed by Dagnan et al. (1995, 1996) and Fleming & Kroese (1990).

Proxy data: Proxy data are provided by Roy et al. (1994).

General evaluation: This instrument is described by the authors as measuring both 'objective and subjective indicators of quality of life' (Dagnan et al. 1995), but, in fact, most of the subjective ratings are supplied either by staff or the interviewer, and the focus on normalization is too narrow to represent a satisfactory QOL scale.

4.2 Lifestyle Satisfaction Scale (LSS: Heal & Chadsey-Rusch, 1985; Heal & Harner, 1993), Multifaceted Lifestyle Satisfaction Scale (MLSS: Harner & Heal, 1993)

Synopsis: The authors state that the LSS was developed 'to assess mentally retarded persons' satisfaction with their residence and its community setting and associated services' (Heal & Chadsey-Rusch, 1985, p. 475). However, the more recently published manual states, 'The instrument is designed to measure satisfaction with the different lifestyle components contributing to one's quality of life' (Heal & Harner, 1993, p. 4).

The original version contained 29 items divided between five subscales as community satisfaction (9), friends and free-time satisfaction (6), satisfaction with services (7), general satisfaction (5), job satisfaction (1), and three question pairs to measure acquiescent responding (1). Scoring is on the basis of interviewer ratings linked to an open-ended question that is read aloud; for example, 'How do you like your home where you live? Can you think of a better place to live? Where would that be?'

The 1993 version contains 45 items forming the following subscales: 'Community Satisfaction' (12 items), 'Recreation Satisfaction' (24 items), 'Job Satisfaction' (7 items or 1 item if unemployed), and an 'Acquiescence Scale' (14 items). The scores from the first three scales may be combined to yield 'Total Satisfaction'.

The MLSS is derived from the LSS. It contains all of the original subscales plus two new subscales as 'Recreation and Leisure' and 'Interpersonal Interactions'. The original LSS ratings were made on a 3-point scale (positive, neutral, negative). The 1993 LSS and the MLSS, however, ask for a verbal positive (+1) or negative (−1) response. In addition, the respondent receives 0 for 'ambivalences and refusals' and +2 or −2 for 'enthusiastic' responses.

A 14-item short-form of the LSS has been devised by Schwartz & Rabinovitz (2003), which correlated .89 with the original scale and has a Cronbach alpha of .85 (N = 93: Mild to Moderate). They do not provide the items they used. These authors also use an expanded 5-point response scale and flashcards containing happy–sad faces.

Theoretical considerations: Most of the items have a unique structure as follows:

- They ask a direct question (e.g. 'Do you go to parties?') The respondent answers yes or no.
- If a 'Yes' response is given, the interviewer follows with 'Would you like to spend more time going to parties?'
- If a *No* response is given, the interviewer follows with 'Would you like to go to parties?'

The result of this procedure is that a negative response to the second question is a positive indication of life quality. Thus, such items are reverse scored. The theoretical logic of this arrangement is that the intensity of a negative response is equivalent to the intensity of a positive response. This is a complex issue.

It is now generally agreed that the relationship between measures of positive and negative affect, including measures of satisfaction and dissatisfaction, can best be described by the circumplex model (see Russell & Carroll, 1999). This asserts that activated positive and activated negative affect (as measured by the LSS +2 and −2) can occur together and are not bipolar opposites. This has been empirically confirmed (e.g. Larsen et al., 2001) and refined by Schmuckle et al. (2002) who show that under conditions of high activation, positive and negative trait affect is independent but state affect is negatively correlated. This research casts doubt on the validity of the LSS procedure. If someone has high negative affect, they will express intense negativity (i.e. −2) to items. This is indicative of an angry, activated, negative personality or mood state. There is no theoretical reason to expect such responses are indicative of a high life quality when reverse scored.

There is a further difficulty in the interpretation of a negative response. If someone says 'Yes' to the question 'Do you go to parties?', and then is strongly negative to the follow-up question 'Would you like to spend more time going to parties?', this does not necessarily imply anything about life quality. The respondents may go to one party each year, enjoy that experience, but not want to have the experience more often. Moreover, since they are not actually being required to spend more time at parties, this response is irrelevant to their actual life quality.

The interpretation of the double negative response is also fraught. If someone responds 'No' to the question 'Do you go to parties?' and then strongly negative to 'Would you like to go to parties?', this only has relevance for life quality if the person was being required to attend parties. If he or she is not, once again the question has no relevance.

Reliability: Duvdevany et al. (2002) report on overall Cronbach alpha of .78 (N = 80) but a low .27 for the general satisfaction subscale (the other subscales were .48 to .70).

The test–retest reliability over an interval ranging from 7 to 29 days was 0.44 to 0.83 (Heal & Chadsey-Rusch, 1985). However, these values may be underestimates, since the first and second interviews were conducted by different interviewers. It should also be noted that these retest reliabilities are certain to be enhanced by the binary nature of the response mode, at the expense of sensitivity of measurement.

Sensitivity: Numerous authors have demonstrated that people living in institutions have a lower score on this scale than people living in flats or group homes (Heal & Chadsey-Rusch, 1985; Yu et al., 1996; Schwartz & Ben-Menachem, 1999). However, the subscales show very different degrees of sensitivity within particular studies. Two studies have found differences in 'Friends' and 'Free Time' (Yu et al., 1996; Schwartz & Ben-Menachem, 1999), two in 'Community' (Heal & Chadsey-Rush, 1985; Yu et al., 1996), one in 'General Satisfaction' (Heal & Chadsey-Rusch, 1985), one in 'Service Satisfaction' (Heal & Chadsey-Rusch, 1985), and one in 'Current Residence' (Schwartz & Ben-Menachem, 1999). Moreover, Duvdevany et al. (2002) found differences in all subscales between people living in group homes or with their parents. So it appears that all of the subscales have demonstrated sensitivity, but they exhibit different degrees of sensitivity, depending on the nature of particular studies.

The Duvdevany et al. (2002) study is additionally interesting, since the group home respondents, who scored higher than people living at home with their parents, were also more disabled in terms of activities of daily living. However, the degree of this disability did not correlate with the total satisfaction score. In terms of subscales, Perry and Felce (2003) also found no relationship between either 'Community Satisfaction' or 'Friends and Free Time Satisfaction' with adaptive behaviour. On the other hand, using their short form, Schwartz and Rabinovitz (2003) found that scores were influenced by the degree of challenging behaviour, employment setting and form of accommodation.

This set of results is not very coherent. It is not clear why the subscales are so different in terms of their sensitivity within particular studies, yet understanding the reason for these differences is important for interpreting whole-scale scores. Moreover, the apparently different co-variation of the long and short forms with objective measures of disability creates doubt as to their equivalence.

Validity: The MLSS did not correlate significantly with the first edition of the Quality of Life Questionnaire (Schalock et al. 1990). Similarly, Duvdevany et al. (2002) found no correlation with the Choices Questionnaire (Stancliffe, 1995). This lack of convergent validity is of some concern in relation to its capacity to measure subjective QOL. There are two aspects of scale construction that may contribute to this difficulty. The first is the absence of subscales measuring the key domains of health and material well-being. The second is the widely differing number of items making up the subscales, ranging from 9 (community satisfaction) to 1 (job satisfaction). This causes an unjustified subscale weighting in the calculation of an aggregate single score.

General evaluation: The question format has the potential to engender a bias towards positive responding. For example, the interviewer asks an orienting question 'What do you do in your free time?', and then follows it with a question to be scored positive or negative 'Are you happy with what you do in your free time?' Since there is no cue to the possibility of a negative response, and a negative response may be seen by the respondent as undesirable, a bias to the positive seems highly likely.

The form of presentation and scoring has both positive and negative features. Positively, it is likely to maximize response validity, since with the open-ended format the respondent is free to concentrate on the question, without being encumbered with the additional task of response selection. Negatively, the criteria for judging the difference between 'highly positive' and 'positive' will undoubtedly vary between interviewers and even within each interviewer across time. This severely limits the usefulness of the actual scale scores as a value to be compared between studies.

In terms of theory, there are clearly problems with the assumptions of equivalence between positive and negative responses. Moreover, there are doubts concerning the scale validity and the degree of equivalence between the long and short forms. This scale is not recommended.

4.3 Life Experiences Checklist (LEC: Ager & Eglington, 1989; Ager, 1990)

Synopsis: The LEC focuses on life experiences, the assessment of which 'alongside other measures, may provide a picture of the quality of life facilitated by the service' (Ager et al., 1988, p. 11). It is based on the traditions of normalization, and as such focuses on the extent to which people have the 'ordinary' experiences of life commonly judged as valuable by people in the general population (Ager, 1993a, 1993b; Ager et al., 1988). Moreover, the items have been selected on the basis that each experience being measured (e.g. 'I have a pet') is at least potentially accessible to everybody. As a consequence, the scale is equally relevant to any group of people and data can be related to general population norms.

The LEC comprises 50 objective items distributed evenly between five areas: (1) 'Home', (2) 'Leisure', (3) 'Relationships', (4) 'Freedom' and (5) 'Opportunities for self-enhancement'. Each item is either scored positive if it is true for the individual, or left blank if it is not, and the subscales can be combined to produce a total score. This instrument is designed for either self- or proxy administration.

Reliability: A test–retest procedure using 20 college students (Ager, 1990) produced a correlation of 0.93 for the scale total score, with subscales ranging from 0.91 ('Opportunities') to 0.96 ('Relationships'). While these coefficients indicate a highly satisfactory scale performance for this small sample, it remains to be established whether this also applies to self-reports from people who are intellectually disabled.

Inter-rater reliability is high. Ager et al. (1988) reported data from two unpublished studies that provided coefficients of 0.80 and 0.96. In addition, Murphy et al. (1996) reported 96% agreement between two raters, one of whom collected data at the time of interview, while the other coded data from an audiotape of the same interviews.

Validity: Ager (1990) and Ager et al. (1988) reported that the total score correlates negatively with the number of people in a ward and positively with staff–client ratios. In addition, the total score correlated 0.72 to 0.78 with the Index of Community Involvement (Raynes & Sumpton, 1986) in a deinstitutionalization study (Ager et al., 2001).

Sensitivity: Taking first the ability of the LEC to discriminate between different living environments, Murphy et al. (1996) reported the total scale score to discriminate significantly between people living with their families or semi-independently, and those in nursing homes, hostels, or hospitals. However, since a single non-parametric test of difference was applied across the three groups, it is unclear whether the scale discriminated between each of these living environments. It also appears, from their figure 1, that the people living with their families or semi-independently did not differ from the normative population data provided by Ager (1990).

In terms of subscale sensitivity, Murphy et al. (1996) reported the same pattern of difference presented above in relation to 'Freedom', 'Opportunities' and 'Relationships', but no differences with the other two subscales. 'Freedom' and 'Relationships' were also found to fall below population norms in an unpublished study involving people with profound disability living in the community (Ager, 1990), while Ager (1993b) reported only the 'Relationships' subscale to be below normal for people with an unspecified level of intellectual disability living in the community. In sum, it appears that the subscales are differentially sensitive to living environments, with 'Relationships' being the most sensitive, and 'Home and Leisure' the least.

However, other types of studies appear to show quite different patterns of subscale sensitivity. For example, Ager (1993b) and (Ager et al., 2001) reported on the resettlement of people with an intellectual disability from an institution to community homes. Both studies found a significant positive impact of relocation, but here the 'Home' subscale showed the most consistent change and the subscale of 'Relationships' the least. Another study, reported in Ager (1993b), compared people with long-term mental illness living in hospital wards with those in more normalized accommodation. They found that the differences were restricted to the subscales of 'Home' and 'Freedom'.

In summary, the whole scale score appears to display adequate sensitivity in terms of distinguishing appropriately between different living environments. The relative sensitivity of the subscales is more uncertain.

Proxy data: While the use of proxy data for subjective indices is unacceptable, in relation to objective data, the situation is less clear, but probably depends on the scope for interpretation. For example, the LEC items 'I go to the cinema or theatre at least once a month' is pretty unequivocal, whereas the item 'I have several close friends' seems open to interpretation. What is the criterion for 'close' and can a friend also be a staff member? Such issues give rise to concern regarding the validity of proxy data based on this scale.

Ager (1990) and Ager et al. (1989) addressed this issue. He reported that, in the case of the LEC, self- and proxy report data in relation to people with an ID did not differ, and that they correlated 0.80. This was confirmed by Murphy et al. (1996) in relation to the scale total score, but not in relation to the subscale scores where proxies significantly underestimated the 'Relationship' score and overestimated the 'Freedom' score. They discuss the likely reasons for this, suggesting it is a reflection of the personal biases each person brings to the rating situation. For example, clients are inclined to overestimate the number of their friends, and proxies are inclined to overestimate measures directly related to the aims of the service delivery. It would seem that deciding consistently to use one mode or the other would assist scale reliability.

Normative data: It is notable that the LEC is designed as a purely objective measure. As such, in common with all such scales, the interpretation of data depends on the availability of population norms. The author has provided such data derived from a representative sample of 410 respondents from Leicestershire, UK (Ager et al., 1988). However, the extent to which these norms are a valid source of comparison for people living in other locations or circumstances is uncertain. Other comparative data have been provided on undergraduate students (Ager et al., 1988), elderly people seeking medical attention (cited in Ager et al., 1988), a combined sample of unemployed and retired people (Hughes et al., 1996), and people with disabilities living in a variety of settings (Ager et al., 1988).

General evaluation: The LEC has utility in measuring objective differences in the circumstances of living within different environments. However, it is notable that the subscale structure has not been confirmed by formal means, such as through factor analysis.

4.4 Quality of Life Interview Schedule (QUOLIS) (Developmental Consulting Program, 1990)

Synopsis: The QUOLIS scale is a commercial product of Queen's University, Canada. Test-kits are purchased on the understanding that all raw data will be returned to the developers for inclusion in their databank. The schedule is designed primarily for people who are non-verbal or who have a severe intellectual disability (Oullette-Kuntz & McCreary, 1996). Data are provided by proxy respondents.

The manual defines QOL as 'The degree to which a person enjoys the important possibilities of his/her life' and states 'QUOLIS considers the degree to which a person enjoys the important possibilities in his/her life by considering chosen levels of participation and apparent levels of contentment' (pp. 12–13). The 'apparent levels of contentment' refers to the proxy-nature of responses. However, the phrase 'important possibilities of his/her life' does not imply that the scale measures perceived importance.

QUOLIS is a very substantial device. It measures 43 indicators grouped into 12 domains as health services, family/guardianship, income maintenance, education/training/employment, housing and safety, transportation, social and recreational, religious-cultural, case management, aesthetics, advocacy, and counselling. It is interesting that this list omits any evaluation of personal health. Each indicator is also rated on four criteria. The first, support availability, is rated on a yes/no basis, while the remainder, including access, participation and contentment, are rated on seven-point Likert scales.

In addition to these 172 measurements (43 indicators × 4 criteria), a considerable quantity of additional data are collected. These include demographic information, levels and form of communication, types and severity of disability, personal characteristics (e.g. hobbies), type and severity of recent life events, and characteristics of multiple disability. These are all investigated using both an open and closed format of question.

Then there is the 'Residential Satisfaction Questionnaire', to be answered by verbal clients only, containing some 76 questions, and as many as 34 supplementary indicators to be used with people who have additional disabilities such as epilepsy, a visual impairment, and so on.

The assessment process involves a 'semi-structured' interview of two informants, usually a staff member and a family member, who assess each indicator as follows: whether it is available, accessible, currently utilized, and 'the adult's apparent degree of contentment with the support' (p. 16). The first of these is rated on a two-point scale and the other on seven-point scales. The interviewer also composes a 'narrative report' on the adult's QOL.

The authors state that interviewers require a two-day training course in order for them to be certified as having the skills to administer the interview in the prescribed manner. The interview takes about two hours.

Reliability: Internal and inter-rater reliability data have been calculated for the contentment scale as 0.79 to 0.99 and 0.48 to 0.95, respectively (Ouellette-Kuntz, 1990; Ouellette-Kuntz et al., 1994).

General evaluation: For the purpose of QOL measurement, the magnitude of this instrument seems excessive.

4.5 Quality of Life Questionnaire (QOLQ) (Schalock et al., 1990; Schalock & Keith, 1993)

Synopsis: This is the most widely employed scale for QOL measurement for people with an intellectual disability. It has a paralleled form for school-age adolescents (Keith & Schalock, 1995) and has been constructed to operationalize the following definition: 'QOL is the outcome of individuals meeting basic needs and fulfilling basic responsibilities in community settings (family, recreational, school and work). Individuals who are able to meet needs and fulfill responsibilities in ways satisfactory to themselves and to significant others in community settings experience a high QOL in those settings' (Schalock, 1990, p. 143).

The scale itself comprises 40 questions divided equally between four subscales as: 'empowerment/independence', 'competence/productivity', 'satisfaction', and 'social/belonging/community integration'. The scale is administered by an interviewer reading aloud each question, and the respondent uses a three-point scale.

More recently, Schalock et al. (2002) has reported the creation of a new version of the questionnaire, modified in the following respects:

- A simplification of the questions. However, the new question wordings are not provided.
- A simplification of the response choice, using a flashcard containing three stylized faces. The respondent can respond to this by pointing.
- The inclusion of another 10 items to produce a subscale called *Dignity*.

A further variation on the scale is for adolescents, both for those with and without an intellectual disability (Keith & Schalock, 1995). Using a small sample, Pretty et al. (2002) found no differences in the subscale scores for these two groups.

Caveat: All subsequent comments refer to the original scale format, unless otherwise specified. Due to the wide use of this scale and the determined efforts of Rapley and his associates, considerable understanding has been gained regarding its psychometric properties. Some of the issues that have been uncovered as a consequence of such research reflect badly on the reliability and validity of the scale. However, in passing such judgement it is important to retain the perspective that other scales may well have the same judgement passed on them if they had also been the target of such investigative research.

At the most global level, there are concerns with the construction of the scale, based on the discussion in chapter 1. These are as follows:

- The subscales mix objective and subjective data.
- The questions and the response choices are complex.
- Because the scale is based on a definition of QOL that emphasizes 'basic needs and responsibilities', the scale has a low ceiling (see Cummins, 1997b, for an expanded discussion).
- Some major QOL areas, such as finance and health, are not represented.

Scale structure: The manual presents a factor analysis indicating that the items generally load appropriately on the four factors. This has been generally confirmed (Kober & Eggleton, 2002; Rapley & Lobley, 1995). However, the factorial structure presented by Kober and Eggleton is weak. It explains only 32.4% of the variance, and the authors have not used a factor-loading criterion for the acceptance of items into a factor. Thus, 5 items are reported as loading on their respective factors <.3 and 17 load <.4. In addition, complex loadings are unreported.

In this same study, the satisfaction factor (which they renamed 'life satisfaction/domestic contentment') is particularly weak. Of the 11 items loading on this factor, two did so <.3 and nine <.4. In addition, two of the items were drawn from other factors and one original item was lost to another factor. This factor also failed to show stability when the sample was randomly split into two halves, or split according to open/supported employment, or functional ability. It appears from this analysis that the 'Satisfaction' factor is not factorially robust.

The factor structure of the simplified scale has been reported by Schalock et al. (2000). However, their data set contained 19% proxy responses and so will not be further considered here.

Reliability: In the original standardization sample for the scale, comprising 450 people living in the community, Cronbach's alpha was 0.83 (Keith et al., 1986); however, Kober and Eggleton (2002) report a Cronbach's alpha of .47 for the 'Satisfaction' factor.

Validity: Construct validity has been demonstrated through higher scores for people living in independent rather than supervised accommodation (Schalock & Keith, 1993) and by strong correlations between QOLQ scores and adaptive/challenging behaviour, financial resources, integrated activities and type of accommodation (Schalock et al., 1994).

Convergent validity has been demonstrated through a 0.57 correlation with the Multifaceted Lifestyle Satisfaction Scale (Harner & Heal, 1993). However, the 'Social Belonging' subscale failed to correlate with either the objective or subjective measures of community. Moreover, the subjective scale measuring 'Sense of Community' correlated very poorly with the QOLQ subscales. Indeed, the only significant correlation was negative with the subscale of 'Competence'. Two conclusions are suggested by this. The first is derived from the fact that a high score on this subscale is mainly indicative that the respondent is employed, and for the majority of this sample 'employment' involved placement in a sheltered workshop. So it would appear that for this form of employment at least, the 'Competence' subscale is not yielding scores in the right (positive) direction. The second conclusion can be drawn from the dominance of positive correlations with objective variables. This gives rise to the possibility that the QOLQ scores are more sensitive to objective measures and client competence levels than to subjective QOL.

In another test of validity, Reiter and Bendov (1996) found virtually no relationship between the subscales of the QOLQ and the Tennessee Self-Concept Scale among young people with an attention deficit, rather than an intellectual disability. Again this does not auger well for the subjective validity of the scale, since life satisfaction is normally one of the highest correlates of self-esteem. The correlation between the QOLQ and the Arc's Self-Determination Scale, for people IQ 47–71, was a modest .25 (Wehmeyer & Schwartz, 1998).

Sensitivity: Higher scores have been reported among people living in independent rather than supervised accommodation (Rapley et al., 1994; Rapley & Beyer, 1998), and over a two-year period of community living by former institutional residents (Rapley & Beyer, 1998). In addition, people in open employment have been found to exhibit a higher overall QOL than people who are unemployed or attending a shelter workshop, although these differences were restricted to some subscales (Eggleton et al., 1999). A similar marginal difference was found in the Arc's Self-Determination Scale between groups representing high and low QOLQ scores (Wehmeyer & Schwartz, 1998).

General evaluation: The mixing of subjective and objective data is a psychometrically invalid procedure and also causes the scale to correlate more strongly with objective than subjective QOL variables. The questions and response choices are overly complex, although the new scale format may overcome these problems. Major QOL areas, such as health and finance, are not represented in the scale, and the factorial structure is weak. Convergent validity is equivocal. In summary, the published version of this scale cannot be recommended.

4.6 Quality of Life Instrument Package (Brown et al., 1997)

Synopsis: The package contains three instruments. One is to be self-completed, another for proxy respondents, and another for the assessors to record their own perspective. The instruments are based on a theoretical framework anchored by the constructs of 'Being', 'Belonging', and 'Becoming'. Each of these is then deconstructed into three parts as follows: 'Being' – physical, psychological and spiritual; 'Belonging' – physical, social and community; 'Becoming' – practical, leisure and growth. Each of these nine areas is then allocated six question topics, and each topic generally involves asking

- how important the topic is to the respondent (e.g. 'the food you eat');
- how satisfied they are with the topic;
- a series of 4–7 open-ended questions relevant to the topic (e.g. 'What do you eat for breakfast?');
- two specific questions that require a variety of response formats, depending on the topic. These may, again, require a rating of importance, but one may also ask, 'How much?', 'How happy?', 'More?' and other forms of response. The questions associated with 'Psychological Being' omit these two specific, ending questions.

The recommended scoring procedure involves multiplying importance and satisfaction, both of which are rated on five-point scales.

A short-form containing 27 items (three for each of the nine domains) is described in Brown and Renwick (1997). The method of construction involved a vote on the 'importance' of each original item by a wide variety of people, with selective deletion or addition at the researchers' discretion to create the required content.

Reliability: The Cronbach alphas for subscales are provided for both the long and the short versions (Brown & Renwick, 1997). They generally lie in the range .4 to .6. However, these data were derived from a sample comprising both verbal and non-verbal people. No pre-testing for response competence is reported. Raphael et al. (1996) report test–retest reliability of the three main constructs as .36, .51, .79, while the Centre for Health Promotion (1993) report them as .60, .67, .43.

Validity: Centre for Health Promotion (1993) report a correlation of .80 between the total scale score and the QOLQ (Schalock & Keith, 1993).

Sensitivity: Centre for Health Promotion (1993) found no age or gender differences. However, people living in supported independent accommodation scored generally higher than people living in congregate care settings.

Normative data: Centre for Health Promotion (1993) provide means and standard deviations for the 'Being', 'Belonging', and 'Becoming' subscales (N = 41).

General evaluation: The purpose of the additional questions concerning each topic in the long version is not stated and neither are any data provided. Raphael et al. (1996) report data from 41 people, whose level of intellectual disability is not stated, but who were living in a variety of settings, such as an institution, a community home, supported independent living and with their family.

There is no doubt that a great deal of information would be generated using the long version. How to use most of this information, however, is uncertain. Given the absence of a factor analysis, there are insufficient psychometric data to confirm that the lists of questions form appropriate scales. In addition, the problem of multiplying importance and satisfaction has been discussed (see part I). The authors state that administration of the long version should take about an hour, but this would seem an optimistic projection if all of the questionnaire items were administered. The single validity estimation against the QOLQ has produced an unusually high correlation of .80. Since the scales are so different from one another, and the QOLQ is so heavily weighted to objective measurement, this validity coefficient is difficult to interpret. Finally, the 'being, belonging, and becoming' constructs are novel and interesting. However, since they are not elucidated by validity data, the interpretation of their subscale scores, in quality of life terms, remains uncertain. This scale cannot be recommended for general use.

4.7 Comprehensive Quality of Life Scale (Cummins, 1997b)

Synopsis: This scale was under development over the period 1991–7. It exists in three parallel forms; for adults in the general population (ComQol-A), for adults with an intellectual disability or cognitive impairment (ComQol-ID), and for non-disabled adolescents attending school (ComQol-S). These parallel forms mean, *inter alia*, that the life quality of people with an intellectual disability can be directly compared with that reported by non-disabled people.

The scale is intended as an operationalization of the following definition:

> Quality of life is both objective and subjective, each axis being the aggregate of seven domains: material well-being, health, productivity, intimacy, safety, community, and emotional well-being. Objective domains comprise culturally relevant measures of objective well-being. Subjective domains comprise satisfaction weighted by their importance to the individual.

Each objective domain is measured through an aggregate score of three items. For example, the domain of 'health' comprises five measures of the degree of chronic medication, frequency of physician consultation, and presence of chronic disability. Each subjective domain is measured through the product of perceived importance and satisfaction.

A feature of the ComQol-ID scale is its pre-testing procedure, which evaluates the extent of Likert-scale complexity each respondent can reliably handle. This involves a three-stage process of nominating size-order among sets of printed blocks, relating block size to a printed scale of importance, and finally placing something of known high importance to the respondents (e.g. the fortunes of their favourite football team) correctly on the importance scale. The first two stages of this procedure commence with a binary choice (e.g. 'Big', 'Small') and progress to three- or five-point choices if the respondent continues to provide correct nominations. This allows the determination of the maximum number of Likert scale points each respondent can reliably use, and this degree of scale complexity is then used for all subsequent measures of subjective life quality. It also employs three pre-test questions designed to measure acquiescent responding.

Other features of the scale are the generation of scores for importance and satisfaction that can be analysed either separately or in combination. The domains can also be analysed separately or in combination, so the subjective dimension can be considered as a single aggregate score of subjective QOL, or can be analysed in terms of its component parts. The manuals contain normative scores for each of the three versions.

Scale structure: The seven domains comprising the ComQol scale have been demonstrated to represent a high level of content validity through several converging lines of evidence as follows:

- Each domain represents an area that QOL researchers generally consider is highly relevant to a definition of the construct (Cummins, 1997a).
- The aggregate score derived from the domains conforms to the 'satisfaction with life as a whole' standard of $75 \pm 2.5\%$SM for normative group means (Cummins, 1996; Hensel et al., 2002).
- The seven subjective domain scores form a single factor (Cummins, 2000).

Reliability: The ComQol-I manual provides data indicating internal reliability as follows: 'Objective' .47, 'Importance' .48, 'Satisfaction' .65, and 'Importance' $\times$ 'Satisfaction' .68. While these values are within the acceptable range (Boyle, 1991), a few of the objective items have unacceptably low item-total correlations. Two-week test–retest reliability has been reported as .87 for importance and .82 for satisfaction (Cummins et al., 1997). Further psychometric data involving ComQol-A have been reported by Cummins et al. (1994).

Validity: The strongest case for content validity is made by the data already mentioned as described by Cummins (1996). The scores have been found to be unrelated to levels of adaptive behaviour (Perry & Felce, 2003) and proxy data (Perry & Felce, 2002). Other data on construct validity have been derived in relation to the parallel versions of the scale. Using ComQol-S, Gullone and Cummins (2000) have demonstrated a negative relationship between anxiety and subjective QOL. Using ComQol-A, Yiolitis (1997) has reported that, among Greek-Australians, subjective QOL is directly related to non-Greek integration and inversely related to stress.

Sensitivity: In using ComQol-A, the scale has detected significant differences between different forms of accommodation for people who are elderly (Ferris & Bramston, 1994) and parents with or without an intellectually disabled child (Browne & Bramston, 1996). However, Perry and Felce (2003) found subscores failed to distinguish between types of accommodation that differed on a number of objective characteristics.

Parallel scales: The three forms of the scale all produce a comparable profile of domain scores (e.g. intimacy as high, community as low) and group means that lie within the normative standard of $75 \pm 2.5\%$SM (e.g. 'Intellectual disability': Hensel et al., 2002; Verri et al., 1999; 'Adolescents': Gullone & Cummins, 1999).

Cross-cultural stability: The intellectual disability version of the scale has been found to be reliable and valid when used in Italy (Verri et al., 1999), and the general population version when used in Italy (Verri et al., 1999) and Iran (Foroughi, 1997).

Normative data: Data from the satisfaction questions can be referenced to the percentage of scale maximum data (%SM) norms published by Cummins (1995). The %SM is calculated through the formula (mean score -1) $\times$ 100/(number of scale points -1) and can be used to express any Likert scale score as though it was generated by a 0% to 100% scale. Cummins (1995) reported that, when this formula was applied to life satisfaction data derived from large general population surveys conducted in Western countries, the data distribution could be described as $75 \pm 2.5\%$SM. This was interpreted to imply, *inter alia*, that 'normal' levels of life satisfaction can be considered to lie within the range 70–80%SM.

In a further development of this work, Cummins (1996) has demonstrated that when large survey data-sets are analysed using the ComQol domains, the international standard for ComQol also approximates $75 \pm 2.5\%$SM. Thus any ComQol satisfaction data set can confidently be referenced to this statistic. It is also an indication of adequate content validity.

The time of administration depends on the extent of pre-testing and whether both objective and subjective scales are employed. The pre-testing can take 5 minutes with a further 5 minutes to answer the 14 subjective questions (7 for importance and 7 for satisfaction). However, these times can be doubled in the case of some respondents in the moderate range of intellectual disability who can only marginally perform the required task. The objective scale (21 items) can normally be competed within 10 minutes. A relative or staff person who knows the consumer well can assist in this latter task.

General evaluation: Despite these favourable evaluations, I abandoned the scale in 2001. The reasons for this decision can be read in detail in the website http://acqol.deakin.edu.au/instruments/index.htm. The most compelling reason for this abandonment is the invalidity of using importance as a weighting for satisfaction (see part I). As has been discussed, measures of importance are ambiguous in their interpretation, and creating a multiplicative composite with satisfaction is a psychometrically invalid procedure. Finally, despite numerous item changes, the 21-item objective scale never factored entirely as intended.

The satisfaction scale of ComQol, however, remains as a highly useful measure. This has now been renamed, as a separate scale in its own right, as the Personal Wellbeing Index.

4.8 Personal Wellbeing Index – Intellectual Disability (Cummins, 2003)

In 2001, I abandoned the ComQol for reasons that have been detailed in my 'Caveats' web-document (http://acqol.deakin.edu.au/instruments/index.htm). The two main concerns that led to this action were that the weighting of satisfaction by importance had been shown to be invalid (see part I) and the objective subscale did not factor into seven domains as intended. From the debris of ComQol emerged the Personal Wellbeing Index.

This seven item PWI-ID scale has been derived from the satisfaction subscale of the ComQol – Intellectual Disability (Cummins, 1997b) and the Personal Wellbeing Index for adults (Cummins et al., 2003). The construction of this scale is identical to the ComQol-ID satisfaction scale with one item change. The original item on 'emotional wellbeing' has been replaced by 'future security'. The reason for this replacement is that the former term is not a conceptual 'domain' in the same sense as the other items.

The Personal Wellbeing Index is theoretically embedded, as the first level of deconstruction of 'Satisfaction with life as a whole', and the seven domains generally contribute unique variance to this higher-order construct. Numerous data are available to indicate its validity, reliability and sensitivity in general adult samples of the Australian population (http://acqol.deakin.edu.au/index_wellbeing/index.htm).

General evaluation: It is reasonable to expect that the PWI-Adult would have much the same psychometric characteristics as the satisfaction scale of ComQol-Adult. Data from general population surveys show this to be the case as evidence by the data cited above. However, the PWI-ID is as yet untested. The new scale manual is available from Cummins (2004).

5 Conclusion

It is evident that most of the scales in this section cannot be recommended, since they have either failed to meet the stated psychometric criteria adequately, or are theoretically inadequate. Moreover, even the best of these scales require much additional testing before they can be viewed as adequately meeting the basic requirements of reliability, validity and sensitivity. Future research may well be better directed at the systematic interrogation of selected current instruments, with a view to developing them into better tools, rather than at the creation of new scales.[1]

NOTE

1   I thank Ann-Marie James and Katherine Poynton for their assistance in the production of this manuscript.

REFERENCES

Ager, A. K. (1990) *The Life Experiences Checklist.* Windsor: NFER-Nelson.

Ager, A. K. (1993a) The life experiences checklist. Part 1: Applications in staff training and programme planning. *Mental Handicap,* **21**, 7–9.

Ager, A. K. (1993b) The life experiences checklist. Part 2: Applications in service evaluation and quality assurance. *Mental Handicap,* **21**, 46–48.

Ager, A. K., Annetts, S., Barlow, R., Copeland, C., Kemp, L., Sacco, C. & Richardson, S. A. (1988) Life experiences and quality of life in the general population: A study of Leicester and its environs using the Life Experiences Checklist. Mental Handicap Research Group, Working Paper 2 (Revised). Leicester: University of Leicester, Department of Psychology.

Ager, A. K. & Eglington, L. (1989) Working paper 4: Life experiences of clients of services for people with learning difficulties: Summary of findings from studies using the Life Experiences Checklist. Mental Handicap Research Group. Leicester: University of Leicester, Department of Psychology.

Ager, A. K., Myers, F., Kerr, P., Myles, S. & Green, A. (2001) Moving home: Social integration for adults with intellectual disabilities resettling into community provision. *Journal of Applied Research in Intellectual Disabilities*, 14, 392–400.

Boyle, G. J. (1991) Does item homogeneity indicate internal consistency or item redundancy in psychometric scales? *Personality and Individual Differences*, 12, 291–294.

Brown, D. R. & Renwick, R. (1997) *Quality of Life of Adults with Developmental Disabilities in Ontario: Results of the Cross-Sectional Study*. Toronto: Centre for Health Promotion, University of Toronto.

Browne, G. & Bramston, P. (1996) Quality of life in the families of young people with intellectual disabilities. *Australian and New Zealand Journal of Mental Health Nursing*, 5, 120–130.

Brown, I., Renwick, R. & Raphael, D. (1997) *Quality of Life Instrument Package for Adults with Developmental Disabilities*. Toronto: Centre for Health Promotion, University of Toronto.

Centre for Health Promotion (1993) *Reliability and Validity Study and Pilot Implementation Study*. Toronto: University of Toronto.

Cragg, R. & Harrison, J. (1984) *Living in a Supervised Home: A Questionnaire of Quality of Life*. Manchester: West Midlands Campaign for People with Mental Handicap.

Cragg, R. & Look, R. (1992) *COMPASS: A Multi-Perspective Evaluation of Quality in Home Life*. London: Authors.

Cummins, R. A. (1995) On the trail of the gold standard for life satisfaction. *Social Indicators Research*, 35, 179–200.

Cummins, R. A. (1996) The domains of life satisfaction: An attempt to order chaos. *Social Indicators Research*, 38, 303–332.

Cummins, R. A. (1997a) Assessing quality of life. In R. Brown (ed.), *Quality of Life for People with Disabilities*. Cheltenham: Stanley Thornes, pp. 116–150.

Cummins, R. A. (1997b) *Comprehensive Quality of Life Scale – Intellectual/Cognitive Disability*. Manual (5th ed.). Melbourne: School of Psychology, Deakin University, pp.1–81.

Cummins, R. A. (2000) Objective and subjective quality of life: An interactive model. *Social Indicators Research*, 52, 55–72.

Cummins, R. A. (2003) Normative life satisfaction: Measurement issues and a homeostatic model. *Social Indicators Research*, 64, 225–256.

Cummins, R. A. (2004) *Personal Wellbeing Index – Intellectual Disability*. Deakin University: Australian Centre on Quality of Life (http://acqol.deakin.edu.au/index.htm).

Cummins, R. A., Eckersley, R., Pallant, J., Vugt, J. van & Misajon, R. (2003) Developing a national index of subjective wellbeing: The Australian Unity Wellbeing Index. *Social Indicators Research*, 64, 159–190.

Cummins, R. A., McCabe, M. P., Romeo, Y. & Gullone, E. (1994) The Comprehensive Quality of Life Scale: Instrument development and psychometric evaluation on tertiary staff and students. *Educational and Psychological Measurement*, 54, 372–382.

Cummins, R. A., McCabe, M. P., Romeo, Y., Reid, S. & Waters, L. (1997) An initial evaluation of the Comprehensive Quality of Life Scale – Intellectual Disability. *International Journal of Disability, Development and Education*, 44, 7–19.

Dagnan, D., Jones, J. & Ruddick, L. (1994) The psychometric properties of a scale for assessing quality of life of people with learning disabilities in residential care. *British Journal of Developmental Disabilities*, 40, 98–104.

Dagnan, D., Look, R., Ruddick, L. & Jones, J. (1995) Changes in the quality of life of people with learning disabilities who moved from hospital to live in community-based homes. *International Journal of Rehabilitation Research*, 18, 115–122.

Dagnan, D., Trout, A., Jones, J. & McEvoy, J. (1996) Changes in quality of life following a move from hospital to a small community unit for people with learning disabilities and challenging behavior. *British Journal of Developmental Disabilities*, 42, 125–135.

Developmental Consulting Program (1990) *QUOLIS Kit for Interviewers: The Quality of Life Interview Schedule for Adults with Developmental Disabilities.* Kingston, Ontario: Author.

Donegan C. & Potts, M. (1988) People with mental handicap living alone in the community: A pilot study of their quality of life. *British Journal of Mental Subnormality,* **66,** 10–22.

Duvdevany, I., Ben-Zur, H. & Ambar, A. (2002) Self-determination and mental retardation: Is there an association with living arrangement and lifestyle satisfaction? *Mental Retardation,* **40,** 379–389.

Eggleton, I., Robertson, S., Ryan, J. & Kober, R. (1999) The impact of employment on the quality of life of people with intellectual disabilities. *Journal of Vocational Rehabilitation,* **13,** 95–107.

Ferris, C. & Bramston, P. (1994) Quality of life in the elderly: A contribution to its understanding. *American Journal on Aging,* **13,** 120–123.

Fleming, I. & Kroese, B. S. (1990) Evaluation of a community care project for people with learning difficulties. *Journal of Mental Deficiency Research,* **34,** 451–464.

Foroughi, E. (1997) The quality of life of Iranians in Iran and in Australia. Clinical Masters Thesis. Melbourne: Deakin University.

Gullone, E. & Cummins R. A. (1999) The Comprehensive Quality of Life Scale: A psychometric evaluation with an adolescent sample. *Behavior Change,* **16,** 127–139.

Harner, C. J. & Heal, L. W. (1993) The Multifaceted Lifestyle Satisfaction Scale (MLSS): Psychometric properties of an interview schedule for assessing personal satisfaction of adults with limited intelligence. *Research in Developmental Disabilities,* **14,** 221–236.

Heal, L. W. & Chadsey-Rusch, J. (1985) The Lifestyle Satisfaction scale (LSS): Assessing individuals' satisfaction with residence, community setting, and associated services. *Applied Research in Mental Retardation,* **6,** 475–490.

Heal, L. W. & Harner, C. J. (1993) *The Lifestyle Satisfaction Scale Manual* (LSS). Worthington, OH: IDS.

Hensel, E., Rose, J., Stenfert Kroses, B. & Banks-Smith, J. (2002) Subjective judgments of quality of life: A comparison study between those people with intellectual disability and those without disability. *Journal of Intellectual Disability Research,* **46,** 95–107.

Hughes, A., McAuslane, L. & Schur, H. (1996) Comparing quality of life for people with learning disabilities and people who are unemployed or retired. *British Journal of Learning Disabilities,* **24,** 99–102.

Keith, K. D. & Schalock, R. L. (1995) *Quality of Student Life Questionnaire.* Worthington, OH: IDS.

Keith, K. D., Shalock, R. L. & Hoffman, K. (1986) *Quality of Life: Measurement and Programmatic Implications.* Hastings, NE: Mid-Western Mental Retardation Services.

Kober, R. & Eggleton, I. R. C. (2002) Factor stability of the Schalock and Keith (1993) *Quality of Life Questionnaire. Mental Retardation,* **40,** 157–165.

Larsen, J. T., McGraw, A. P. & Cacioppo, J. T. (2001) Can people feel happy and sad at the same time? *Journal of Personality and Social Psychology,* **81,** 684–696.

Murphy, G. H., Esiten, D. & Clare, I. C. H. (1996) Services for people with mild intellectual disabilities and challenging behaviour: Service-user views. *Journal of Applied Research in Intellectual Disabilities,* **9,** 256–283.

Ouellette-Kuntz, H. (1990) A pilot study in the use of the Quality of Life Interview Schedule. *Social Indicators Research,* **23,** 283–298.

Oullette-Kuntz, H. & McCreary, B. D. (1996) Quality of life assessment for persons with severe developmental disabilities. In R. Renwick, I. Brown & M. Nagler (eds.), *Quality of Life in Health Promotion and Rehabilitation: Conceptual Approaches, Issues and Applications.* London: Sage, pp. 268–278.

Ouellete-Kuntz, H., McCreary, B. D., Minnes, P. & Stanton, B. (1994) Evaluating quality of life: The development of the Quality of Life Interview Schedule. *Journal on Developmental Disabilities,* **3,** 17–31.

Perry, J. & Felce, D. (2002) Subjective and objective quality of life assessment: Responsiveness, response bias, and resident proxy concordance. *Mental Retardation,* **40,** 445–456.

Perry, J. & Felce, D. (2003) Quality of life outcomes for people with intellectual disabilities living in staffed community housing services: A stratified random sample of statutory, voluntary and private agency provision. *Journal of Applied Research in Intellectual Disabilities*, 16, 11–28.

Pretty, G., Rapley, M. & Bramston, P. (2002) Neighborhood and community experience, and the quality of life of rural adolescents with and without an intellectual disability. *Journal of Intellectual and Developmental Disability*, 27, 106–116.

Raphael, D., Brown, I., Renwick, R. & Rootman, I. (1996) Assessing the quality of life of persons with developmental disabilities: Description of a new model, measuring instruments, and initial findings. *International Journal of Disability, Development and Education*, 43, 25–42.

Rapley, M. & Beyer, S. (1998) Daily activity, community participation and quality of life in an ordinary housing network. *Journal of Applied Research in Intellectual Disabilities*, 9, 31–39.

Rapley, M. & Lobley, J. (1995) Factor analysis of the Schalock and Keith (1994) Quality of Life Questionnaire: A replication. *Mental Handicap Research*, 8, 194–202.

Rapley, M., Lobley, J. & Bozatzis, N. (1994) *Preliminary Validation of the Schalock & Keith (1994) Quality of Life Questionnaire with a British Population*. Lancaster: Department of Psychology, Lancaster University.

Raynes, N. & Sumpton, R. (1986) The index of community involvement. Unpublished manuscript.

Reiter, S. & Bendov, D. (1996) The self-concept and quality of life of two groups of learning disabled adults living at home and in group homes. *British Journal of Developmental Disabilities*, 42, 97–111.

Roy, M., Collier, B. & Roy, A. (1994) Excess of depressive symptoms and life events among diabetics. *Comprehensive Psychiatry*, 35, 129–131.

Russell, J. A. & Carroll, J. M. (1999) On the bipolarity of positive and negative affect. *Psychological Bulletin*, 125, 3–30.

Schalock, R. L. (1990) Attempts to conceptualize and measure quality of life. In R. L. Schalock (ed.), *Quality of Life: Perspectives and Issues*. Washington, DC: American Association on Mental Retardation, pp. 141–148.

Schalock, R. L., Bonham, G. S. & Marchand, C. B. (2000) Consumer based quality of life assessment: A path model of perceived satisfaction. *Evaluation and Program Planning*, 23, 77–87.

Schalock, R. L., Brown, I., Brown, R., Cummins, R. A., Felce, D., Matikka, L., Keith, K. D. & Parmenter, T. (2002) Conceptualization, measurement and application of quality of life for persons with intellectual disabilities: Report of an international panel of experts. *Mental Retardation*, 40, 457–470.

Schalock, R. L. & Keith, K. D. (1993) *Quality of life Questionnaire*. Worthington, OH: IDS.

Schalock, R. L., Keith, K. & Hoffman, K. (1990) *Quality of Life Questionnaire Standardization Manual*. Hastings, NE: Mid-Western Mental Retardation Services.

Schalock, R. L., Lemanowicz, J. A., Conroy, J. W. & Feinstein, C. S. (1994) A multivariate investigative study of the correlates of quality of life. *Journal of Developmental Disabilities*, 3, 59–73.

Schmuckle, S. C., Egloff, B. & Burns, L. R. (2002) The relationship between positive and negative affect in the Positive and Negative Affects Schedule. *Journal of Research in Personality*, 36, 463–475.

Schwartz, C. & Ben-Menachem, Y. (1999) Assessing quality of life among adults with mental retardation living in various settings. *Journal of Rehabilitation Research*, 22, 123–130.

Schwartz, C. & Rabinovitz, S. (2003) Life satisfaction of people with intellectual disability living in community residences: Perceptions of the residents, their parents and staff members. *Journal of Intellectual Disability Research*, 47, 75–84.

Stancliffe, R. J. (1995) Assessing opportunities for choice-making: A comparison of self and staff reports. *American Journal on Mental Retardation*, 99, 418–429.

Verri, A., Cummins, R. A., Petito, F., Vallero, E., Monteath, S., Gerosa, E. & Nappi, G. (1999) An Italian-Australian comparison of life quality among intellectually disabled people living in the community. *Journal of Intellectual Disability Research*, 43, 513–522.

Wehmeyer, M. & Schwartz, M. (1998) The Relationship Between Self-Determination and Quality of Life for Adults with Mental Retardation. *Education and Training in Mental Retardation and Developmental Disabilities*, 33, 3–12.

Yiolitis, L. (1997) The effects of social integration and stress on the quality of life of Greek-Australians. Master of Clinical Psychology Thesis, School of Psychology, Deakin University, Melbourne.

Yu, A. L. C., Jupp, J. J. & Taylor, A. (1996) The discriminate validity of the Lifestyle Satisfaction Scale (LSS) for the assessment of Australian adults with intellectual disabilities. *Journal of Intellectual and Developmental Disability*, 21, 3–15.

CHAPTER 10

Assessment and employment of people with intellectual disabilities

Patricia Noonan Walsh

1 Introduction

These days, Jim spends about eighteen hours each week in the dining room and kitchen of a local hotel, one of a prosperous chain. He arrives early each weekday morning, changes into his uniform and reports to Nancy, who manages the dining room during the day. Jim washes his hands carefully and then checks a list of tasks agreed some months before with Nancy and with Sue, his job coach: pouring fruit juices into jugs, transferring chilled products from the refrigerator to the buffet table and filling containers with muesli and other breakfast cereals. He nods to Simon, the chef – they share a passion for football – but Jim keeps his distance from the stove and steam tables laden with cooked foods. Jim watches as people serve themselves. He refills serving dishes as needed and sometimes he shows hesitant guests how to make toast on the conveyor belt he uses to prepare a snack for his own break. Although he smiles and seems at ease, Jim doesn't say much to anyone – even to Mark, the young trainee chef who never fails to welcome Jim and also to tease him when Jim's team lose a match. After finishing his work on Friday mornings Jim signs his first name on a slip in Nancy's office and pockets an envelope with his wages. Then Jim and Sue head for the bus stop – Jim is on his way to town to do some shopping.

It has been argued (ch. 2) that *self-determination* is a disposition more readily attained if individuals with intellectual disabilities have supports of the intensity and form best suited to their needs. Assessment helps to identify needs for *support*, ideally in a way that widens the individual's zone of proximate development and helps him or her to gain a foothold and move forward. Within this paradigm, the assessment process adds value if it leads to greater self-determination (Wehmeyer & Bolding, 2001) – in securing appropriate vocational training and satisfying work, for example. But assessment offers, at best, an estimate of how an individual performs under given conditions. Assessing vocational performance does not spring fully formed, whether from a battered test case or glossy package. Rather, the steps that led to Jim's current job were rooted in factors beyond his or any other individual's say-so: the economic climate, his family's ideas about work, social attitudes, national and regional policies, agreeable employers and availability of support workers. In Jim's case, the psychologist he met assumed that Jim could work, that an ordinary job was the critical path to a satisfying ordinary life and that she could work with Jim to identify what sort of job might suit him best right now and also in the future.

When we ask 'Who should work?', we raise the question of whether people with intellectual disabilities are equipped to seek employment – assuming that there is work to be had. Adults may find that only sheltered work is available, or perhaps none at all. But the question triggers wider issues rooted in social values and policies. Is competitive employment desirable? Should it be foisted on people with complex disabilities or older folk edging nearer what would be retirement age for their peers? Do sheltered forms of work provide greater stability and companionship? Or is ordinary employment, with or without support, the defining moment for all adults, regardless of their capacities? Although often endorsed as a preferred option, it remains elusive. For example, in the wake of dozens of EU-funded demonstration projects, it is striking that a minority of Irish adults with intellectual disabilities spend some of the day in supported or other inclusive employment settings (Mulvany & Barron, 2003, table 3.9). Practitioners often lament the fact that supported employment flourishes in the wake of dedicated initiatives, but that its influence withers when project funds disappear.

This chapter does not aim to relive yesterday's absorption with pegboards and workshop norms, much less resolve global debates about the worth of human occupation. Rather, it outlines four assessment strategies to guide the decisions of those who seek employment or who support others in doing so. Within the American Association on Mental Retardation's current definition and system of classification of mental retardation (intellectual disability), assessment serves the purpose of identifying an individual's needs for support at various levels of intensity and in different life domains such as employment (American Association on Mental Retardation, 2002). This approach does not make assessment of individual performance redundant: on the contrary, it may be argued that 'Support needs and personal competence are related but distinct constructs, and both need to be adequately assessed' (Thompson, Hughes et al., 2002, p. 402).

In this chapter, sections 2 and 3 address two forms of appraisal of individual competence: measures of performance that help to determine what individuals *can do* (Emerson, 1998), and observational methods of assessment asking the question 'What is the individual doing?' To reflect the emerging practice of shaping personalized supports for people with intellectual or other disabilities, section 4 outlines assessment strategies that focus on *what the individual prefers to do*. And various strategies for assessing employment and related *life outcomes* are set within a quality of life context in section 5. Each of these sections comprises a brief review of the literature, the rationale for selecting strategies described and a description of a few specific assessment procedures. The final section suggests a guide to these strategies, and concludes with recommendations for practice and further research about what is important for the individual with intellectual disabilities in the context of the workplace and wider life experiences.

2 Measures of Performance

Typical questions posed about people with intellectual disabilities who are about to enter the workforce ask what they *can do* or are *likely to do*. For those already in work settings, it may be important to understand *why* an individual is performing in a given way. Based on the slender report at the head of this chapter, it seems that Jim is adept at setting out and serving a breakfast buffet. But it is not clear whether he would like to greet Simon with confidence, whether he depends on certain prompts to carry out his tasks, and how he reacts if he encounters a new instruction. Nor do we understand why Jim steers clear of the hot table of cooked foods. Is this a matter of choice, or the result of his employer's decision, or because of some other factor, a discouraging experience in the past, perhaps?

A familiar, low-cost method is to explore these issues by simply interviewing the individual, or an advocate, family member or support worker. A co-teaching practice in the United States, for example, engaged secondary school students with disabilities in an inclusive curriculum including life skills such as job and daily living skills – for example, job searching and job interviews (Fennick, 2001). The purpose of the curriculum was to prepare school-leavers for the world of work. But the disadvantages of simply asking people what they'd like to do, especially for elderly people, are equally familiar. Beth, aged 38 and stuck in a dreary job doing piecework, may have an elderly parent with no ambitions for how her daughter might advance her career, and silent fears for her safety if she should leave a custodial vocational centre. Jim may have had a trial stint cooking foods in a secondary-school canteen with an overbearing manager who ridiculed his efforts. Either Beth or Jim may have an employer who is gratified that an adult with intellectual disabilities is on the premises but who may harbour low expectations for their career progression through the ranks.

Various *measures of performance* can help to answer questions about what people can or might do. Traditional instruments that sample behaviour may be applied in the light of the characteristics of vocational settings. These reflect the aims of *structural* assessment, as they are approaches that categorize behaviour according to its form and use these data to make inferences about future behaviour (Sturmey, 1996). Assessors who seek standardized measures may borrow from an array of commercial instruments, some informed by industrial psychology. Individuals with intellectual disabilities may undergo formal assessment in order to enter vocational training. Typically, they must meet norms set by the authors of a standardized instrument, or by a service-provider agency. Some typical methods, using both norms and criteria to score candidates' performance, are familiar tools to many veteran practitioners. However, it is more difficult to unearth findings that reliably associate performance on such measures with long-term employment or quality of life outcomes for employees with intellectual disabilities. (For discussion of the concept of quality of life and its measurement see chs. 1 and 9.)

In his critical review of the literature about six standardized tests of values, interest, personality and aptitude, Gruber (2000) concluded that few professionally developed assessment tools of this kind may be used confidently with members of diverse groups such as people with disabilities. He endorses a comprehensive approach to assessment and recommends useful alternatives, including self-ratings, criterion assessment, ecological assessment and qualitative assessment methods. Finally, Gruber comments that since the career assessment process is for the client's benefit, assessors must find better ways to involve individuals themselves and to develop more accurate measures of interest, for example (p. 46).

2.1 Norm-referenced assessment

Norm-referenced dexterity tests have been used to assess performance of would-be employees, including those with intellectual and other disabilities. The Purdue Pegboard Test (n. d.) was developed more than fifty years ago by an industrial psychologist. It has been used to select employees for jobs requiring fine and gross motor dexterity and coordination by measuring movements needed in assembly tasks.

The Stromberg Dexterity Test measures the speed and accuracy of arm and hand coordination (Stromberg, 1985). A candidate sorts discs and inserts them into a form board as quickly as possible. After two practice trials, the candidate completes two further trials, which take only 5 to 10 minutes to complete and score. The raw score is the total number of minutes and seconds required to complete these trials. According to its publisher, the Stromberg is effective in selection for a range of jobs requiring speed and accuracy in coordination of arm and hand movements, in assessing people with various disabilities in sheltered workshops and in evaluating candidates for entrance to training programmes.

The Bennett Hand-Tool Dexterity Test measures proficiency in using ordinary mechanics tools (Bennett, 1985). This type of skill is important in many different factory and garage jobs, and in servicing home, office and other equipment. The test requires each candidate to use the hand tools provided to take apart 12 fastenings according to a prescribed sequence and to reassemble the nuts, washers and bolts into a new position on the test frame. Its author claims that the test is useful in testing candidates across a wide range of ability, including individuals with intellectual disabilities. The test manual lists percentile ranks for operatives in different occupations – maintenance mechanics and special education and vocational training students, among others.

2.2 Criterion-referenced assessment

By contrast, *Valpar* (n, d.) products rely heavily on *criterion-referenced* testing, using an objective standard of achievement. A prospective employee must demonstrate ability at a particular level by performing tasks at that degree of difficulty, not how he or she fares in relation to norms for a given group. In general, criterion-referenced approaches to assessment are a better fit to the aims of supported employment, as they try to determine whether the person can do the job at hand, not whether he or she meets group norms. When Jim decided to start work at the hotel, it was important to know what elements of food service he preferred to do, and which tasks he could perform with low-key support in a busy dining room. It was less important to know how his timed performance scores in handling cutlery in a simulated setting compared with that of thousands of other men and women with similar levels of ability.

Practitioners in Australia have described the use of Work Ability Tables (WAT) assessments that aim to quantify an individual's work-related level of function. The tables generate a profile of nine core work abilities, including the ability to report for work regularly, to communicate with others and manipulate objects, among other tasks. A candidate's numerical score determines whether the individual is referred to a disability employment service (Sutherland & Kirby, 2000).

In addition, some target groups of adults may already have accrued a work history, but find that they must change their employment or re-enter it after a period of rehabilitation following trauma or some other set of circumstances resulting in altered capacities. Transferable Skills Analysis is an assessment procedure applied in vocational rehabilitation in an attempt to quantify functional abilities (Dunn & Growick, 2000). The aim is to identify skills – often using computer software packages – that have previously been acquired, and assess their likely application in new work setting. This approach may be less costly and take less time than traditional comprehensive vocational evaluation: however, authors writing in the United States, where such methods have been developed to inform rehabilitation professionals and meet criteria of benefit systems, urge further research to determine reliability and efficacy (Darling et al., 2002).

Each of these measures offers an assessor a valid sample of an individual's performance. While useful in measuring aspects of work-related performance, these methods do not always address two issues of paramount importance to prospective employees with intellectual disabilities. First, they do not aim to predict long-term outcomes about satisfying employment or quality of life. Second, many standard tests focus on micro-skills, or activities more suited to traditional sheltered workshops – assembly work, or collating papers – rather than the skills demanded by current job opportunities in the services sector, for example. Useful as they may be in describing current skills, none stands alone to guide the individual's career decisions, even functional methods that tap motivation by taking into account the reasons why an individual performs in a certain way under given conditions.

2.3 Functional assessment

In general, functional assessment aims 'to identify specific skills (to be learned) or adaptations (to be made) which will enable the person to function more independently in real world settings' (Emerson, 1998, p. 121). This author names four stages in the process:

- conduct an ecological inventory
- identify skills the individual already possesses
- identify discrepancies between skills possessed and skills required
- identify possible adaptations in the person's natural settings

Mapping these steps on to vocational assessment implies assessment of the individual's job skills and the attributes of the working environment.

In Jim's case, functional assessment findings might reveal a poor fit between what he can do now and what he needs to do in order to serve hot foods, or take on more supervisory responsibility and earn a higher wage. Perhaps he does not always grasp new information about how to combine elements of his job, or perhaps he can learn readily from one or two friendly co-workers like Mark, but not from others. An inventory may yield a pattern to suggest that Jim is more likely to learn new skills in a dining room that features taped piano music than in a kitchen full of clatter and banter. His quiet demeanour and agreeable nature may mask any shortfall. Yet assessment may guide his employers to making some accommodation in the instructional system used in the hotel kitchen and dining room so that all co-workers check that Jim has understood any instructions.

If the assessor wishes to determine what skills the individual possesses now, or to obtain information so as to compare performance across settings and times, and, most important, to encourage self-assessment (see section 5 of this chapter), then direct observation is likely to provide this information in a useful way.

3 Observational Methods

Traditional pen-and-pencil or manipulative tests of performance were typically carried out in contrived or virtual settings rather than in the real world of work. By contrast, direct observations focus on what happens in the here and now in a natural setting. This approach lends itself to a contextual approach to work-related behaviour, helping to answer the questions 'What can the individual do?' or 'What is the individual doing?' (table 10.1). Observations also help to determine the living and working conditions in which the individual learns and performs. Two key advantages of observational methods are their coverage of real-time rather than selected episodes, and their utility in comparing individual performances over time and across settings.

Yet caution compels the would-be assessor to consider the assumptions underlying observation – for example, what behaviours are important enough to target, or the choice of direct rather than indirect methods such as rating scales (Thompson et al., 2000). Suppose that an assessor completed a hypothetical scale, 'social ease in the workplace' (SEW), and

Table 10.1 Making Decisions on Vocational/Employment Assessment Strategies

Core question	Domains for assessment	Applications
What is the individual doing?	Objective life conditions: (ex) working setting	• Standard instruments – e.g., criterion references measures of 'typical' employment conditions • Observational methods
Why is the individual doing this? What *can* the individual; do?	Self-appraisals Observed behaviour • adaptive behaviour • vocational profiling • sampling work performance in real-world settings	Functional analysis of behaviour • support intensity scales • performance measures • ability measures • transferable skills analysis
What does the individual *prefer* to do?	Person-centred planning	• various person-centred planning methods
What has been *achieved*?	Outcomes	Measures of quality of life

found that Jim's employer awarded him a score of 3 on a scale extending from 1 to 5. How helpful would this information be? By contrast, direct observation permits us to watch Jim in action – to see how he meets and greets customers and co-workers over an entire shift or some pivotal points during it, and whether he seems to smile more when Simon or Mark are around. Better still, using a video recording, Jim can watch himself in action and reflect on his performance with a trusted ally or job coach.

In other applications, observational methods were developed as the process applied to observing challenging behaviour, permitting the assessor to describe, categorize and verify how an individual behaved (Carr et al., 1994). Many studies have reported findings based on observations of how adults with intellectual disabilities behave in residential settings (e.g. Thompson et al., 2000). Earlier reports relied on samples of behaviour observed at set intervals recorded as they occurred or analysed after the fact using video recordings. But recent technological advances have enabled assessors to account for the real-time experience of individuals. For example, hand-held computers have been used to document the incidence of self-injurious behaviours among residents (Marion et al., 2003) or the social interactions of residents across different residential settings (Robertson et al., 2004). Typically, observations complement other assessment data, to permit triangulation – or, as a real-world employment provider puts it, to avoid relying on a one-off judgement.

Hughes et al. (2000) commented that while there is a considerable literature describing social interactions in the workplace, observational methods used have been written narratives, interval recording or behaviour checklists. These authors have carried out research on computer-assisted observational research programmes. Their behavioural coding system is based on extensive observations in actual settings – rather than using pre-established categories from the employment literature (p. 254).

Elsewhere, Kilsby et al. (2002) analysed job review content with discourse analysis using adjacent pair cycles. These authors used insights gained from fine-grained interactional analysis of audio-recorded job review interviews from each of three conditions reported in an earlier study (Kilsby & Beyer, 2002). Results showed an increase in task-related talk between job-seekers and job coaches after interventions (Kilsby et al., 2002).

4 A Service Provider's View

What do service providers look for in assessment reports? An answer to this question will be found in the text of an interview with an employment supports provider in Ireland (personal communication, November 2003):

> Well, first think about the attitude of the assessor – if it's someone who doesn't believe people with intellectual disabilities should work or even that they can work, the report will reflect those attitudes. For a start, I wouldn't rely on just one strategy, or just one viewpoint: I'd look for three kinds of assessment reports. First, look at real data – observations, for instance. I'd look at how the person behaves in a whole range of settings, whether a football match, or a club or an outing, not just vocational classes in school. Then I'd look for any good information on the files – it's possible that people who knew the person or who have worked with her for years have written down useful pointers about what they like to do, or how they learn best, or even completed some test of the person's ability. IQ?

We don't put much store in just an IQ – we've found that by itself it doesn't really tell you much about how the person will get on in the workplace. I have to say, too, that some older folks have aptitude scores and other information on files dating back so long that they're not much use to us today. And finally we'd like to have some idea of how the person does in different situations – in different kinds of jobs, maybe one that brings the person into more contact with the public, for example. We encourage people to try out a few and see what works for them and for the employer. I still hear talk about 'job readiness' but in my book that's a way of keeping people in dead-end training. How do you know when you're 'ready' if you don't know what the job is? And readiness shouldn't mean old-style scores for job skills – a lot of people who enter employment today have been in sheltered workshops or training centres for years and years – and where did it get them? Basically, I think that anybody who wants to, can go to work – and it's my job to make it happen.

5 Individualized Supports

Person-centred approaches to identifying optimal supports for individuals are timely and have come to dominate the human services landscape. Their premise is that what people wish to do is irrefutable. Such a view is important as it is in line with many international policy initiatives including policy in the UK, including England (Department of Health, 2001) and Scotland (Scottish Executive, 2000), as well as initiatives in Ireland to develop national standards for services for people with disabilities (www.nda.ie). These approaches could embed *self-appraisal* methods, including direct questioning of an individual regarding what he or she *wishes* to do.

Individualized approaches such as person-centred planning rest on a second premise: that each person, level of disability notwithstanding, can and should make real choices. A considerable body of evidence has accrued, addressing different aspects of making choices – comparing opportunities from the perspectives of individuals themselves with those of staff members, for instance (Stancliffe, 1995). Choice-making applies to a very wide target population, not merely those considered to have a 'mild' level of intellectual ability. It has taken its place as a cardinal element in human services offered to people with intellectual disabilities. Valid methods to assess preferences among individuals with severe or profound disabilities have been reported (Lohrmann-O'Rourke & Browder, 1998; Hughes et al., 1998). In their review of research on this topic, Lancioni et al. (1996) found that while people with severe/profound disabilities are capable of making choices and expressing preferences, doing so may well be a relatively new and limited experience.

Task preferences may be expressed in the world of work, among adults with autism in supported jobs (Lattimore et al., 2002, 2003), for instance. Kearney & McKnight (1997) provide a synopsis of assessments and interventions related to assessing choices and preferences among people with disabilities, identifying four important areas for future research:

- apply various assessment procedures in natural settings
- replicate findings among other populations
- investigate variables shown to influence choice in different contexts – school, home, community
- develop more sensitive and efficient assessment procedures

Applied to vocational assessment, these research directions could yield more focused and less costly methods of determining what work individuals would or would not like to try.

Comprehensive assessment is necessary, not only to identify individuals' preferences, but also to plan supports to meet individual needs. Applying the most recent system of definition and classification, the American Association on Mental Retardation (2002) framework for assessment names as a third type of assessment 'planning supports'. Some of the tools listed are person-centred planning tools: self-appraisal, assessment of objective life conditions measures, support intensity scales, required individual plan elements (p. 12). In the workplace, *supports* refer also to an array of measures that will help the individual to develop social networks (Schalock et al., 2002, pp. 88–89).

Within this model of individualized support, assessment of needs may be completed on a Supports Intensity Scale (Thompson, Hughes et al., 2002). This scale was based on five assumptions about the nature of support needs:

- type of support must be tailored to individual needs and preferences
- the provision of support must be flexible
- some supports are more important to individuals than others
- systematic assessment of support needs should guide the development and revision of individualized support plans
- assessment of support needs must consider multiple factors

Assessment aims at producing a plan that identifies the sources of support, the functions of each type of support provided, and the intensity of the support. These authors propose a four-component approach to support needs assessment and planning. The structure lends itself to assessing aspects of employment:

- Identify desirable life experiences and goals: a suggested method is to interview the individual across domains such as employment. Typical probes might be, 'Are you currently employed? What do you like about your job? Tell me about the jobs you've had in the past. Tell me about what kind of job you would like to have. What kind of special assistance do you need on a job?' (p. 394).
- The assessor determines the intensity of support needs in employment and seven other areas of the individual's life.
- Once needs have been assessed, a plan for building individualized supports is developed.
- The final step is to monitor progress of this plan, for instance in closing the gap between the expected and actual outcomes of the plan.

Piecemeal, the components of this approach to assessment are not novel. The unified focus of the supports intensity model on building seamless supports in employment and other life areas, however, is a new approach to intervention in the lives of people with intellectual disabilities. Yet the effectiveness of the supports intensity scale has yet to be appraised over time. Specific assessment procedures to identify personalized support needs must be widely accepted, appealing, manageable and comprehensive in scope if they are to achieve desired outcomes and have optimal impact on the person's quality of life (Thompson, Bryant et al., 2002).

6 Assessing Outcomes

Advancing quality of life is increasingly seen as the ultimate goal of interventions or services offered to people with intellectual disabilities. Using this approach, vocational assessment plays a part in helping individuals to find and keep satisfying employment if this is a valued outcome. Given the complexity of this construct and the unique profiles of prospective employees, assessing quality of life outcomes demands multiple measures. Schalock & Verdugo (2002, p. 179) suggest six methods in their *Handbook*:

- multidimensional scales
- ethnographic approaches
- discrepancy analysis
- direct behavioural
- social indicators
- individuals' self-assessment

These methods might be expressed in a range of available assessment tools – for example, *discrepancy analysis* is one outcome of functional assessment aimed at measuring the gap between what an individual does now and what he or she needs to do in a work setting. *Ethnographic approaches* might include recent attempts to represent the social interactions and patterns of discourse experienced in the workplace. Methods may be combined: *direct observation* (this chapter, section 3) has the dual merits of recording real behaviour in real time and also facilitating *self-assessment*.

Personal satisfaction is a focus of self-assessment of quality of life (Schalock et al., 2000). (Again, see ch. 1 for the inherent problems involved in self-reports of subjective quality of life.) Once employed – what are the outcomes for men and women with intellectual disabilities? While they may accrue competence and gain seniority over time, what about wider issues of social support and personal satisfaction? When older women with intellectual disabilities from 18 countries were interviewed about their previous or ongoing jobs, their responses pointed towards a working life with little elation and, at best, patchy supports. One American woman said, 'I constantly tell them I need more help, but they tell me it's a one-person job,' while an Argentinian woman commented, 'I have to use numbers to count and I don't understand numbers,' and finally, a Scottish woman said, 'I was left all alone with all the dishes to do on my own' (Walsh & LeRoy, 2004, ch. 4).

Schalock and Verdugo (2002) have proposed that indicators of quality of life related to employment cut across different ecological spheres. At *microsystem* level, employment indicates material well-being for the individual who earns an income. At *mesosystem* level, employment status indicates material well-being and aspects of the work environment as well as work status indicate social inclusion. More globally, socio-economic status and employment rates are social indicators that potentially could indicate quality of life nationally, while other measures may express socio-economic aspects of employment. Jim enjoys collecting his pay packet enormously, and his family is a bit better off because of the relatively modest income he earns. His mother is very proud to talk about his job, especially in front of his ne'er-do-well cousin. If Jim continues to expand his working week in the future, he will officially enter regional statistics as a services sector operative.

Employment status and aspects of the work environment may also be assessed. Pierce et al. (2003) describe job tenure and wages for people with intellectual disabilities and factors affecting movement from non-competitive jobs to competitive jobs. Data were collected from service agencies rather than from individuals or employers. An important finding was that competitive workers are not substantially different to non-competitive workers in many characteristics, including those often cited as barriers to employment. Nor are traditional skills of production the only factors that predict successful employment in the eyes of employers of people with disabilities (Walsh & Linehan, 1997). Elsewhere, Reitman et al. (1999) reviewed files and employment records and invited work supervisors to complete measurement scales. They found that interpersonal problems in supported employment settings were not uncommon and that these often related to sexuality.

Social interactions in the workplace are assumed to be a valuable and worthwhile outcome. Yet Ohtake and Chadsey (1999) found little social disclosure between supported employees with intellectual disabilities and their co-workers: these authors recommended strategies to train employees in order to enhance social interactions. Storey (2002) reviewed strategies for increasing interactions in supported employment settings, with a focus on four: social skills instruction, problem-solving, communication skills instruction and co-worker supports.

In practice, assessors working within a quality of life framework are likely to measure attributes of the individual but also the social and physical properties of the working environment in an attempt to forge a good fit. Various assessment strategies – measures of performance, direct observation, and individualized supports – have distinctive purposes. But they are not exclusive. On the contrary, it is more than likely that practitioners will combine approaches in pursuit of a rounded appraisal of an individual's actual and potential work-related performance. Assessors will select a strategy to meet specific requirements, perhaps at the transition from school to work, or the transfer from sheltered to supported employment, or further up a career ladder (table 10.2). Any combination of these strategies should fit comfortably within an overarching quality of life framework.

7 Conclusion

Assessment formed part of the bedrock of modern psychology, even if forgotten and silted over for decades as a remnant of an era when test results consigned people with intellectual disabilities to restricted and bleak lives. Nowadays, assessment procedures have emerged as a set of tools that may be polished and turned to a potentially useful purpose. In this chapter it is argued that assessment strategies can contribute to greater self-determination on the part of men and women with intellectual disabilities who wish to secure appropriate vocational training and satisfying work. An array of structural instruments measures aspects of work-related performance. Functional assessment, self-assessment and direct observation methods help to validate an understanding of why individuals perform as they do in a way that they themselves may grasp.

A focus on achieving desired outcomes, such as an enhanced quality of life, seems to have shifted the weight of assessment exercises away from sampling competence in favour of identifying and providing personalized needs for support. But a balanced strategy is prudent. Imaginative assessment of each of these constructs – what the person is like, and what he or

Table 10.2 Fitting Strategies to Assessment Questions: An Approach Based on the Assessor's Assumptions

Assumption	Assessment questions	Strategy/instrument
Any adult who wishes to do so, can work.	What does this individual require as supports so that he or she can work as preferred?	Intensity of supports
An individual is already working, but has experienced some difficulty or is not progressing.	What is the individual doing in the workplace?	Direct observation
	What information will increase understanding of why he or she behaves this way?	Functional analysis
A young woman is about to leave school and make a transition to work or work training.	What is this person's current repertoire of skills?	Standardized tests
	What supports will she need in the job she aspires to fill?	Interviews
Ordinary work is not a likely option for residents, but some may enter sheltered employment on-site or elsewhere.	What is this person's current performance at a key manipulative skill, and how will it change over time?	Intensity of supports Standardized tests of dexterity
	What supports will he require in the future?	Intensity of supports

she needs to do, what is preferred – will help to steer a steady course. In the domain of employment, no less than any other salient area of life, purposeful and timely assessment is not a tyrant, but rather a guide to a satisfactory landfall.

REFERENCES

American Association on Mental Retardation (2002) *Mental Retardation: Definition, Classification and Systems of Supports* (10th ed.). Washington, DC: American Association on Mental Retardation.

Bennett, G. K. (1985) *Bennett Hand-Tool Dexterity Test (H-TDT)*. San Antonio, TX: Harcourt Assessment/Psychological Corporation.

Carr, E. G., Levin, L., McConnachie, G., Carlson, J. I., Kemp, D. & Mith, C. (1994) *Communication-Based Intervention for Problem Behavior: A User's Guide for Producing Positive Change*. Baltimore, MD: Brookes.

Darling, W. T., Growick, B. S. & Kontosh, L. G. (2002) Transferable skills analysis in rehabilitation: Issues in definition and application. *Journal of Vocational Rehabilitation*, 17, 217–224.

Department of Health (2001) *Valuing People: A New Strategy for Learning Disability for the Twenty-First Century*. London: Stationery Office.

Dunn, P. L. & Growick, B. S. (2000) Transferable skills analysis in vocational rehabilitation: Historical foundations, current status, and future trends. *Journal of Vocational Rehabilitation*, 14, 79–87.

Emerson, E. (1998) Assessment. In E. Emerson, C. Hatton, J. Bromley & A. Caine (eds.), *Clinical Psychology and People with Intellectual Disabilities*. Chichester: Wiley, pp. 114–126.

Fennick, E. (2001) Coteaching: An inclusive curriculum for transition. *Teaching Exceptional Children*, **33**, 60–66.

Gruber, G. P. (2000) *Standardized Testing and Employment Equity Career Counselling: A Literature Review of Six Tests*. Employment Equity Career Development Office, Public Service Commission, Canada (http://www.psc-cfp.gc.ca/ee/eecco/intro_e.htm).

Hughes, C., Pitkin, S. E. & Lorden, S. W. (1998) Assessing preferences and choices of persons with severe and profound mental retardation. *Education and Training in Mental Retardation and Developmental Disabilities*, **33**, 299–316.

Hughes, C., Rodi, M. S. & Lorden, S. W. (2000) Social interaction in high school and supported employment settings: Observational research application and issues. In T. Thompson, D. Felce & F. J. Symons (eds.), *Behavioral Observation: Technology and Applications in Developmental Disabilities*. Baltimore, MD: Brookes, pp. 253–269.

Kearney, C. A. & McKnight, T. J. (1997) Preference, choice, and persons with disabilities: A synopsis of assessments, interventions, and future directions. *Clinical Psychology Review*, **17**, 217–238.

Kilsby, M., Bennett, K. & Beyer, S. (2002) Measuring and reducing acquiescence in vocational profiling procedures for first time job-seekers with mental retardation. *Journal of Vocational Rehabilitation*, **17**, 287–299.

Kilsby, M. & Beyer, S. (2002) Enhancing self-determination in job matching in supported employment for people with learning disabilities: An intervention study. *Journal of Vocational Rehabilitation*, **17**, 125–135.

Lancioni, G. E., O'Reilly, M. F. & Emerson, E. (1996) A review of choice research with people with severe and profound developmental disabilities. *Research in Developmental Disabilities*, **17**, 391–411.

Lattimore, L. P., Parsons, M. B. & Reid, D. H. (2002) A prework assessment of task preferences among adults with autism beginning a supported job. *Journal of Applied Behavior Analysis*, **35**, 85–88.

Lattimore, L. P., Parsons, M. B. & Reid, D. H. (2003) Assessing preferred work among adults with autism beginning supported jobs: Identification of constant and alternating task preferences. *Behavioral Interventions*, **18**, 161–177.

Lohrmann-O'Rourke, S. & Browder, D. M. (1998) Empirically based methods to assess the preferences of individuals with severe disabilities. *American Journal on Mental Retardation*, **103**, 6–161.

Marion, S. D., Touchette, P. E. & Sandman, C. A. (2003) Sequential analysis reveals a unique structure for self-injurious behavior. *American Journal on Mental Retardation*, **108**, 301–313.

Mulvany, F. & Barron, S. (2003) *Annual Report of the National Intellectual Disability Database Committee 2002*. Dublin: Health Research Board (www.hrb.ie).

Ohtake, Y. & Chadsey, J. G. (1999) Social disclosure among co-workers without disabilities in supported employment settings. *Mental Retardation*, **37**, 25–35.

Pierce, K., McDermott, S. & Butkus, S. (2003) Predictors of job tenure for new hires with mental retardation. *Research in Developmental Disabilities*, **24**, 369–380.

Purdue Pegboard Text (n. d.) <http://www.licmef.com/evaldexterity.htm>: Author.

Reitman, D., Drabman, D. D. S., Speaks, L. V., Burkley, S. & Rhode, P. C. (1999) Problem social behavior in the workplace: An analysis of social behavior problems in a supported setting. *Research in Developmental Disabilities*, **20**, 215–228.

Robertson, J., Emerson, E., Pinkney, L., Caesar, E., Felce, D., Meek, A., Carr, D., Lowe, K., Knapp, M. & Hallam, A. (2004). Quality and costs of community-based residential supports for people with mental retardation and challenging behavior. *American Journal on Mental Retardation*, **109**, 332–344.

Schalock, R. L., Baker, P. C. & Croser, M. D. (2002) *Embarking on a New Century: Mental Retardation at the End of the Twentieth Century*. Washington, DC: American Association on Mental Retardation.

Schalock, R. L., Bonham, G. S. & Marchand, C. B. (2000) Consumer based quality of life assessment: A path model of perceived satisfaction. *Evaluation and Program Planning*, 23, 77–87.

Schalock, R. L. & Verdugo, M.-A. (2002) *Handbook on Quality of Life for Human Service Practitioners*. Washington, DC: American Association on Mental Retardation.

Scottish Executive (2000) *The Same as you? A Review of Services for People with Learning Disabilities*. Edinburgh: Scottish Executive.

Stancliffe, R. J. (1995) Assessing opportunities for choice-making: A comparison of self-reports and staff reports. *American Journal on Mental Retardation*, 99, 418–429.

Storey, K. (2002) Strategies for increasing interactions in supported employment settings: An updated review. *Journal of Vocational Rehabilitation*, 17, 231–237.

Stromberg, E. L. (1985) *Stromberg Dexterity Text*. San Antonio, TX: Harcourt Assessment/Psychological Corporation.

Sturmey, P. (1996) *Functional Analysis in Clinical Psychology*. Chichester: Wiley.

Sutherland, M. & Kirby, N. (2000) *Intellectual Disability and Models of Employment: The Australian Experience*. Disability Research Unit, University of Adelaide, Australia (http://www.minds.org.sg/papers/mms22.htm).

Thompson, J. R., Bryant, B., Campbell, E. M., Craig, E. M., Hughes, C., Rotholz, D. A., Schalock, R. L., Silverman, W. & Tassé, M. J. (2002) Supports intensity scale. Unpublished assessment scale. Washington, DC: American Association on Mental Retardation.

Thompson, J. R., Hughes, C., Schalock, R. L., Silverman, W., Tassé, M. J., Bryant, B., Craig, E. M. & Campbell, E. M. (2002) Integrating supports in assessment and planning. *Mental Retardation*, 40, 390–405.

Thompson, T., Felce, D. & Symons, F. (eds.), (2000) *Behavioral Observation: Technology and Applications in Developmental Disabilities*. Baltimore, MD: Brookes.

Valpar (n. d.) <http://www.valparint.com/>.

Walsh, P. N. & LeRoy, B. (2004) *Women with Disabilities Aging Well: A Global View*. Baltimore, MD: Brookes.

Walsh, P. N. & Linehan, C. (1997) Factors influencing the integration of Irish employees with disabilities in the workplace. *Journal of Vocational Rehabilitation*, 8, 55–64.

Wehmeyer, M. L. & Bolding, N. (2001) Enhanced self-determination of adult with intellectual disability as an outcome of moving to community-based work or living environments. *Journal of Intellectual Disability Research*, 45, 371–383.

CHAPTER 11

Assessing people with profound intellectual and multiple disabilities

Carla Vlaskamp

1 Introduction

Over the past years increasing attention has been paid to the situation of individuals with profound multiple disabilities, with a clear consensus emerging for a need to develop better services. Changing perceptions and paradigms have led to significant changes in the support of individuals with profound multiple disabilities, but these changes are mostly related to material and technical improvements. Assessment of cognitive, motor, sensory and communicative functions in people with profound intellectual and multiple disabilities is still in its infancy. The present situation shows a lack of standardized instruments (Hogg & Sebba, 1986). Available assessment tools are checklists and observation scales, and a number of criterion-referenced instruments. A number of these scales and tests are based on the sensorimotor stage from Piaget's theory on cognitive development. Because of their motor disabilities, people with profound intellectual and multiple disabilities are often only partially able to score up to their real abilities on these kinds of assessment instruments. Their lack of formal linguistic code and the presence of additional sensory impairment is another reason for this inadequacy. Their non-conventional behaviours render them highly dependent on the interpretation of others, which also forms a threat to the validity and reliability of the scores.

As already stated in chapter 3, assessing abilities in a person with profound intellectual disabilities, profound motor disabilities, sensory impairments and additional physical impairments can be said to be a real feat of skill. Partly because of the multiplicity of the disabilities and the fact that each individual with profound intellectual and multiple disabilities represents a unique configuration of abilities and constraints to functioning, but also because there are not many specific instruments available. As there are insufficient research data relating to the way these profoundly disabled people develop (or can develop), it is indeed not an easy task to design and develop reliable and valid instruments. The lack of valid and reliable instruments for determining a person's abilities in the various development domains are likely to have contributed to the development of situation-based lists (observation lists, checklists) used in that particular situation only. These lists are situation-specific, but also often have as a characteristic that 'others' are involved in assessment. Parents present information as a proxy, and are informants for interpretation of results of, for example, observations. Assessment procedures are interdisciplinary: psychologists, direct-care staff, therapists – in short, all professionals (and non-professionals) involved in the care process are likely to contribute. Although these lists often fail to meet the requirements of validity and reliability, they nevertheless often prove a helpful tool to determine how the person involved can best be supported.

In this chapter, I first briefly discuss the purpose of assessment for this category of person followed by a quick review of available forms of assessment. Cognitive, motor and sensory assessment, and the assessment processes or procedures for communication are then stated. The interdisciplinary use of the information that can be gathered by these assessment procedures or processes is then discussed. A case study example ends this chapter.

2 The Purpose of Assessment

The purpose of assessment of people with profound intellectual and multiple disabilities is, in a general sense, the same as it is for any individual; namely, the derivation of information on decision-making (Simeonsson & Bailey, 1988). Several kinds of decisions are likely to be made on the basis of assessment data. Sometimes the decision is diagnostic; for example, confirming or disconfirming the level of intellectual disability. For a considerable number of people with profound intellectual and multiple disabilities the cause of their intellectual disability is unknown (van Splunder et al., 2003). To determine what level of functioning a person has is often related to the need parents and professionals have to find out what kind of perspective is feasible for the person concerned.

Sometimes, assessment is aimed at the documentation of a current status: what a person can or cannot do at a specific moment in time. If parents or professionals want to find out whether their efforts have had any result, they need to have a point of reference. Especially for those who work with people with profound intellectual and multiple disabilities, people whose progress is often so slow that it is hardly measurable, this type of information is essential in order to keep motivated. As quite a number of people with profound intellectual and multiple disabilities – due to the seriousness of their disorder – will at a certain moment not show progress, the prevention of failing abilities is also of importance and a point of reference is needed.

Another type of assessment focuses on the decision for an intervention (e.g. a program for sensory stimulation, a method for alternative communication, a therapy directed at improving motor skills). Results of assessment provide crucial information that is needed to start an intervention: how a person approaches a task, the patterns of errors made, the ability to master basic skills, the capability of response to instruction. From the assessment results one could even derive a hypothesis concerning potentially effective directions for the actions direct-support staff and other professionals should take. Without assessment, the person with profound intellectual and multiple disabilities has to rely on the clinical view of a therapist, or on the experience of teachers and direct-support people. Their findings may have far-reaching consequences, but will lack a solid basis. Without assessment, a lack of reliable assessment data may lead to a deficiency in essential personal and environmental adaptations. It is therefore essential to ensure a high-quality assessment process.

3 Methods of Assessment

The forms of assessment most often used for people with profound intellectual and multiple disabilities are checklists and criterion-referenced tests. Also, some 'alternative' forms of assessment are used, like the assessment of changes in the relative proportions of biobehavioural states. In all methods, observations are important for interpreting the behaviour of people with profound intellectual and multiple disabilities. Observations in everyday-life situations are often made to establish cognitive, communicative and sensorimotor skills. Making an observation implies that information is gathered relevant to a person's behaviour as presented. The observation is referred to as unstructured when it is unclear which aspects are relevant or not. There may be a specific area of attention (in e.g. 'communication'), but at the same time other aspects of behaviour are also observed.

In case of a structured observation, observation regulations are required and certain targeted areas for observation are formulated prior to observation. In some observation situations, use will be made of specific aids, such as momentary time sampling (Murphy & Harrop, 1994; Saudargas & Zanolli, 1990) or video recordings. These resources enhance the validity of what is being observed. A common feature is that they are very detailed. They include observations of the overall rates of behaviour and of the complexity of behaviour. They constitute an important tool for obtaining information about the behaviour of people with profound intellectual and multiple disabilities, even though validity and reliability may be considered limited.

The reliability of the observations is determined not only by setting requirements to inter- and intra-assessment reliability. The inclusion or exclusion of environmental factors may play a role concerning factors such as the extent of reliability of the direct staff, the occurrence of audible noises in the background during observation, the presence of other people and the position and posture of the person under observation (Lohrmann-O'Rourke & Browder, 1998). The use of checklists and criterion-referenced tests is of importance to increase reliability and validity of results. By using these types of instruments, it may be possible to compare results over time, or compare results between people. Nevertheless, these results still partly depend on the eye of the beholder. To some, this is considered a substantial drawback, and some researchers suggest the use of non-conventional assessment procedures – like the use of Event Related Potentials (Diaz & Zurron, 1998).

One potentially useful area of attention for assessment lies in the biobehavioural state of people with profound intellectual and multiple disabilities (e.g. Guess et al., 1988; Sternberg & Richards, 1989). The assessment of changes in the relative proportions of biobehavioural states; for example, changes in the level of alertness and wakefulness may prove valuable, especially if instruments are developed to measure these changes reliably and effectively.

Since the 1980s, professionals in the various disciplines of health care agree on the need for a 'functional approach' in assessment. The term 'functionality' cannot be defined comprehensively: it emerges as a multifarious and general notion, the different aspects of which are emphasized by different authors (e.g. Haley et al., 1994; Rothstein, 1994; Giangreco & Dennis, 1994). Still, various theoretical accounts point out what the notion of functionality should stand for. It can be said that functionality concerns engaging in meaningful activities, regarded in close relationship with contextual factors and the goal that is to be achieved. Just how the concept of functionality is eventually expressed will be different, given the generality of the principles, for each discipline, each target group and ultimately for each individual. According to the concept of functionality, behaviour is analysed in close relationship with contextual factors and the final goal to be achieved.

Until now, many of the diagnostic processes carried out lack this notion of functionality. Thus one may know if the child is able to follow a slowly moving object visually through a 180[degree] arc, but not in what position the person should be in order to make eye contact with the person sitting next to her. Because it as important to know if a person is able to grasp an object, and to know what essential features an object should have (distance, colouring, texture that can easily be grasped, favourite object etc.), future research should devote a great deal of attention and effort to developing the instruments that fit the given concept of functionality.

4 Assessment

4.1 Cognitive and developmental assessment

The most commonly used criterion-referenced scale for measuring cognitive functioning in people with profound intellectual and multiple disabilities is the Ordinal Scales of Psychological Development (Užgiris & Hunt, 1975). The scales are based on Piaget's theory on cognitive development and are applicable to individuals displaying a cognitive function corresponding to the sensorimotor stage. The reliability and validity of the scales when used for children with profound intellectual disabilities have been investigated. This instrument is sensitive enough to pick up small changes in cognitive development (Ware & Healey, 1994), but it still relies too heavily on intact motor responses. Another point of concern is the linearity of the subscales in the test. A study by MacPherson and Butterworth (1988) showed that people with profound intellectual and multiple disabilities develop at different rates in the various areas assessed by the subscales of the Užgiris and Hunt test.

Another well-known instrument with considerable differentiation in the items presented is the Behaviour Assessment Battery (BAB) (Kiernan & Jones, 1977, 1982). The main objective of BAB is to provide a differentiated and detailed report on the functioning of severely intellectually disabled people, which in turn can serve as a basis for treatment. Although in principal aiming at people with severe intellectual disabilities, the BAB has been widely used for people with profound intellectual and multiple disabilities. The BAB was initially developed as an addition to other tests by focusing on a wide range of behaviours and by including many items on a very low level. In addition, it attempts to describe the actual abilities of the sample fully by conducting a considerably flexible test. The BAB is unrelated to age. The instrument covers a wide range of domains, is carried out step by step (sufficient differentiation) and is not bound by specific rules as to administration of the assessment. The professional conducts the assessment interview from which a certain profile can be drawn up for each resident on each test component.

There are, however, some disadvantages to the BAB. For one thing, it does not take into account a person's sensorimotor impairments, and it lacks clear guidelines for describing the testing and criterion behaviours. As the items are ranked according to a hierarchy of difficulty, the instrument wrongly assumes that an insufficient result on one item implies that all the following items cannot be completed satisfactorily. People with profound intellectual and multiple disabilities repeatedly show negative scores on low-level items, which are then followed by positive scores on the ones that are more difficult (Vlaskamp, 1993). Another drawback is that the results are reflected in a large number of profiles, rendering it impossible to present a comprehensive and coherent picture of people with profound multiple disabilities. In the Netherlands, the instrument was therefore adapted by removing those items that formerly always yielded nil scores in the group of profound intellectual and multiple disabilities people. Also, clearer instructions were formulated; for example, with respect to break-off rules, attitude and position of test leader and criterion behaviour. Contextual information was taken into account. This led to a pilot version of this strongly revised observation list (Vlaskamp et al., 2000). Reliability and validity of this pilot version (renamed Behaviour Appraisal Scales [BAS]) were computed on the basis of the pilot study (Vlaskamp et al., 2002). These findings resulted in a final version consisting of 122 items, 100 of which were categorized through factor analysis into five statistically independent factors: affective expressions, receptive language behaviour, general communicative behaviour, visual behaviour and exploratory behaviour. Reliability coefficients are found to be substantially positive. A profile is made of each subject according to the quartile scores on the five factors. Considering that the factors exist independently of each other, the consequence is that a certain score on one factor does not predict the score on another factor. Inter-individual differences in quartile scores can offer starting points for support. In order to identify regression, progress and/or stabilization in a person's functioning, repeated measurements can be taken at intervals to assess the differences in quartile scores on the five factors. By recording the changes in the quartile scores it becomes possible to evaluate the form of support given and the form it is to have in future.

4.2 Motor assessment

The assessment of motor performance involves four interdependent components. Neuromotor processes, gross motor and fine motor functions, and oral motor development. Neuromotor processes involve the underlying musculoskeletal elements that support movement, such as muscle tone and joint range of motion. Gross motor function incorporates those movements, postures and skills of the large muscles, whereas fine motor function is dependent on the small muscles of the hands and arms. Oral motor function is based upon actions of the facial musculature for speech and eating.

Assessment of motor performance is mostly done by medical or paramedical staff. They can establish the presence or absence of milestones, or give a quantitative measure of the person's performance. But this type of assessment lacks the notion of functionality. The need for a functional motor assessment has been met through development of the Top Down Motor Milestone Test (TDMMT) (Bidabe & Lollar, 1990). This test consists of 74 skills falling into 16 categories pertaining to the skills of sitting, standing and walking, and the transitions between them. The 74 skills, referred to as 'motor milestones' are quantitative in nature and the items are rated according to the amount of support needed to perform certain skills. Examples to describe these skills for testing are, 'Can sit on a conventional classroom chair without prompts for at least 30 minutes,' 'Can raise head to erect position when head is tilted back while sitting with upper trunk support.' The motor milestones are sequenced according to four levels of functioning. For each of 16 categories the rater (in most cases the physiotherapist) starts with the skills on the easiest level and proceeds until the level is reached that has been mastered so far. It is assumed that the items below the entry skill still need to be mastered. If the rater is not sure about whether a certain skill has yet to be mastered, the person is put into the right position to perform that skill. In doing so, the TDMMT provides information about the amount of support needed for the motor skills of sitting, standing and walking. The functional use of these skills is considered important. For example, if the person with profound intellectual and multiple disabilities is able to stand on his own feet for just a brief moment, it will be easier to use a wheelchair and then get into and out of the car when visiting his parents. If a person is able to hold her head up in an erect position when sitting, the opportunity arises for the person to make contact with others, thus optimizing the conditions for communication.

4.3 Sensory assessment

4.3.1 Visual   Assessing vision of people with profound intellectual and multiple disabilities requires two main areas of evaluation: tests of physiological function and evaluation of functional use of vision. Each type of evaluation supplies valuable information, and neither can substitute completely for the other (Sobsey & Wolf-Schein, 1999).

The testing of vision can be part of an examination by an ophthalmologist, using objective medical tests (like an electro-oculogram, an electroretinogram or a visual evoked potential). Most non-medical tests use fixation preference or forced-choice preferential looking, using cards like the Teller Acuity Cards (Teller et al., 1974). This test consists of a series of cards, each containing a striped pattern of varying breadth. Each breadth corresponds with a certain visual acuity. The stripe patterns are presented at a fixed distance. It is observed to what extent the person is able to discern the striped patterns. Although this instrument may tell us something about the state of certain aspects of visual perception, it tells us nothing about how a person uses those visual abilities. As people with profound and multiple intellectual disability often suffer from a disorder in the visual conduction system and/or the occipital cortex (a cerebral visual impairment; see ch. 3), assessing how a person utilizes his visual abilities is not an easy task. The cerebral visual impairment (CVI) does not yield a consistent picture. Individuals are hampered by CVI in their own particular way, and even in a single person the condition may vary according to environmental factors and time of day. Establishing the extent of impairment by means of the Teller Acuity Cards provides insufficient information to help decide on the most suitable interventions.

For this reason, the functional use of vision must be evaluated. Professionals can obtain information about individuals' history from existing records and from parents or other significant others. They should also observe the person in his or her own environment in order to obtain a complete picture. Likewise, behaviour observation should take place in different situations (daytime and artificial light) and all kinds of objects and situations should be presented to determine how contrasts and colour codes are used in the spatial context. In addition, the effect of the various acoustic conditions are taken into account. In the observations the focus is mainly on the person's reactions, which are tape-recorded in order to study and rate the person's behaviour.

4.3.2 Auditory   A variety of procedures can be used to assess the hearing of people with profound intellectual and multiple disabilities. A hearing disorder can be established by using an objective hearing test, like pure tone audiometry (which identifies the threshold at which the lowest intensity of sound can be heard at various frequencies) or an auditory brain stem response (which measures changes in the electrical brain wave activity that occur when auditory stimuli are presented). Also, existing behavioural test procedures (like conditioned play audiometry or behavioural observation audiometry) can be used. These audiological tests require carefully controlled testing conditions and cannot provide direct information about the functional use of hearing in everyday situations (in the classroom, at home, during leisure, etc.). As with vision, the person's history, the observation of the person in his or her everyday life situation and the person's responses to sound in those situations are of great importance.

4.3.3 The body senses   Although there are ways to assess the capacity of a person with profound intellectual and multiple disabilities to process information from the body senses (vestibular, proprioception, touch), it is a much-neglected area in assessment. Also, it is not easy to assess the responsiveness of a person to movement of her body in relation to gravity (using the vestibular receptors in the inner ear) or to assess the sensation that muscles and joints provide about the posture and movement of that person's body (proprioception). There is great variablity, inter- and intra-personal. The consistency of the person's performance can be influenced by the degree of environmental stimulation, the emotional state of the person and the general level of arousal. Some people with PIMD have a low sensory threshold that results in hyperreactivity or sensory defensiveness. Others have a threshold that is very high, causing them to be hyporeactive to sensory input.

The assessment of the ability to register and orient to body sense stimuli includes, again, several strategies: observations of the person in his familiar environment (including the relation between the characteristics of the environment and the response of the person with profound intellectual and multiple disabilities) and interviews with parents or others well known to the person with profound intellectual and multiple disabilities. The use of standardized instruments is limited to the use of the Test of Sensory Functions in Infants (Degangi & Greenspan, 1988), which includes the subdomains 'reactivity to tactile deep-pressure' and 'reactivity to vestibular stimulation'). An instrument to assess sensory modulation in people with profound intellectual and multiple disabilities has yet to be developed.

4.4 Communication assessment

Communication is based on the activity of individuals. Communication requires that one person (a parent, a professional) must perceive and interpret the actions (e.g. breathing, blinking, posture changes, sounds) of another person (with profound intellectual and multiple disabilities), and must respond to the actions. Due to the limited behaviour repertoire of people with profound intellectual and multiple disabilities, their communicative competence is strongly influenced by the conditions of the context. The outcome of any assessment of communicative competence is therefore regulated by the transaction between the person and the environment within the context. There is a demand for checklists and criterion-referenced tests that can be used for people with profound intellectual and multiple disabilities. In some instruments (like the Vineland Adaptive Behavior Scales [Sparrow et al., 1984] or the Behavioral Appraisal Scales [Vlaskamp et al., 1999]) are subscales that could be used for assessing communicative competence. The 'Triple C – Checklist of Communication Competencies' (Bloomberg & West, 1999) is based on the assumption that the communicative development of children with profound intellectual and multiple disabilities can be compared to the communicative development of children without intellectual disabilities. Using video tapes, a person well known to the child can interpret communicative behaviour and can score the communicative level.

Whereas most people with profound intellectual and multiple disabilities lack the basic conventional communication skills, others who know them well can often more or less reliably interpret facial expressions, eye gaze, vocalizations and other seemingly 'random' forms of behaviour into meaningful communicative signs. This notion forms the principle of the Affective Communication Assessment (ACA) (Coupe et al., 1985). The ACA is a content-free assessment, based on the development of communicative competence of non-disabled children (Bates et al., 1987).

The person under observation is, at intervals, presented with stimuli or experiences that seem likely to elicit strong responses (wanting, liking, rejecting and disliking). Each response is interpreted by people who know the person well. Then, the components of the response are isolated and recorded on an 'observation sheet' to give a behavioural record of what the interpretation is based on. Having obtained these data, the next stage in the assessment is to look for any clusters of behaviours that seem fairly consistently associated with a particular response. Examples of a typical pattern may be when given orange juice (stimulus) the person reacts by lifting her head, smiling, opening her mouth, showing much activity, eyes making contact with staff member, arms reaching out and producing vocal sounds (observed behaviour). The reactions are interpreted as indicating a 'strong liking' for the stimulus. These behaviours (e.g. eye contact and increased activity of head and arms are always observed when a stimulus is presented that staff interpret as strong/like or want) are listed on the 'identification sheet'. The person is then presented with another range of experiences to check whether the behaviours that were identified can be fairly consistently associated with a particular interpretation. Using responses from the ACA, staff and other professionals can be sensitized to the idiosyncratic, though not random, responses from people with profound intellectual and multiple disabilities (Ware, 1994). The psychometric qualities of the lists have yet to be established, although practice has shown their merits.

5 The Use of Assessment Information: Multidisciplinary and Interdisciplinary

The extent and specificity of the individuals' needs lead to a situation in which a large number of different disciplines will each be involved in several different dimensions in the process

of education and support. For any one person with profound intellectual and multiple disabilities, the list of items of functional support needs is reflected in an equally long list of
involved professionals. The fact that so many professionals are involved (medical doctors,
nurses, direct-support staff, psychologists, teachers, paramedical staff, music teacher, play
therapist, welfare workers, health insurer) may lead to conflicting advice and problems in
coordination of care and support.

Not only do people with profound intellectual and multiple disabilities have to deal with
a large number of professionals as part of daily living; these professionals have all been trained
in different approaches to service provision, with one of the biggest differences being that
teachers and direct-support personnel are trained in an educational model and therapists in
a health-care model. There are philosophical, theoretical and practical differences between
these models, and most methods and models used perpetuate unidisciplinary thinking
within the system. Professionals rarely collaborate in ways that result in an effective, integrated programme. So, we may find a certain amount of information that is supplemented
from reading through files and reports and is supplied by parents and/or other carers. This
information consists of skills categories and information about everyday experience. But
behaviours, communication and needs can only be understood in terms of the total context
of events, processes, relationships and routines.

The use of interdisciplinary assessment processes is therefore an essential prerequisite to be
able to describe the status of people with profound intellectual and multiple disabilities, and
to be able to develop and evaluate individual educational and therapeutic programmes.

6 Case Study Example

Anne is a 30-year-old woman with profound intellectual and motor disabilities. She has a
cerebral visual impairment and has been living in a residential facility for 11 years. A year
ago, she moved to a community home. She lives with seven other people, and has entered a
day services centre in the neighbourhood. In this centre, she joined a group of eight people,
all of them profoundly intellectually disabled. There are two support assistants present.

To establish a day-services programme that fits the needs and desires of Anne, an assessment process has started. As a starting point, the community home is asked for information
about her intellectual, physical and sensory disabilities. They want to be informed about
her medical condition, including her use of medication. The day-services centre also asks
for a report on her social and communicative abilities, and requests a copy of the individual
educational programme (IEP). In an IEP, long- and short-term goals should be stated.

From the report of the community home, it turns out that Anne is said to be profoundly
intellectually disabled, but there is no proper medical diagnosis available in the record to endorse
this statement. Her gross and fine motor functions have been recorded by the physiotherapist a year before. Anne is able to sit without support, but is unable to stand, not even
for a transfer. She has limited use of the small muscles in her arms and hands. She needs
support when eating and drinking. She does not receive speech therapy, and has physiotherapy
only on a weekly basis.

There is a report from an ophthalmic centre, where her visual abilities have been tested.
The report states that Anne can discriminate between light and dark only, a conclusion not

supported by the direct-support personnel. The report from the community home does not state the information on which they base this conclusion. They say that Anne is able to discriminate visual stimuli when they are of interest to her, and that she can recognize even facial expressions when presented close to her (within approximately 30 cm). No assessment has been done on Anne's hearing abilities: it says that she can hear quite well. There is some suggestion of hyper-reactivity to auditory stimuli.

Staff say that Anne has good communicative skills: she cannot speak, but her facial expressions show clearly what she wants and feels, what she dislikes and when she wants to be left alone. Long-term goals are indeed available. Goals are directed at the normalization of muscle tone, at improving swallowing patterns and at 'enjoying group life' in the home. There is no common long-term goal.

The available information gives an overview of abilities and disabilities, but does not answer the questions 'Who is Anne? What is her perspective? Are there skills that need to be kept or developed? Or do we "just" want to give her a good time at the day services, and if so, how do we do that? What do her visual disabilities mean in the context of the day services, given that she is believed to use facial expressions? How can one be attentive of auditory hypersensitivity in a group with seven other people (not including two staff members)? What sensory channels does she prefer, and how can one gather information on touch, smell, vestibular sensation and proprioception? What are the preferred characteristics of stimuli that can be offered? Does she like to have a massage? Does she like or dislike soft materials? Does she like the rocking of a swing, a waterbed, or being on horseback? Under what conditions should an activity be carried out? What are the characteristics of the environment, both social and organizational that we have to take into account?'

All these questions stress the need for a more thorough assessment procedure. This procedure should start with establishing a perspective based on consensus between her living situation and day services, and that may reflect Anne's own desires and abilities. Agreement must be reached about the perspective pursued for Anne. All those concerned must agree to work from the same perspective for a given period of time. Discussions about Anne (e.g. her functional visual capacities) will improve the quality of the services, both at the day services as well as in the living unit, and during physiotherapy.

The assessment process can start with an instrument like the Behaviour Assessment Battery or the Behavioural Appraisal Scales. For example, results of the BAS lead to a profile that can be used to acknowledge her communicative strength or by optimizing her weak explorative behaviour. Also, an audiological test is needed to gather information on her hearing abilities. All information, together with existing reports, may lead to consensus on a (preliminary) perspective.

Contextual information needs to be gathered before one could start putting a day programme together. Information on the characteristics of preferred stimuli and preferred setting needs to be gathered. Again, several disciplines need to work together to acquire information on, for example, her most alert period of time during the day, the preferred-distance visual acuity, the best place for auditory attentiveness, preferred texture of materials, her preference for either swinging or rocking on the waterbed, the preferred setting for either training activities or leisure provision, her favourite music and her best friends. All information needs to be accounted for and all team members should use a consistent system of reporting and set of criteria for decision-making.

Anne's personal profile, her perspective and the preference assessment are the basis of the activity plan. Only by using interdisciplinary assessment processes is it possible to have a well-founded plan.

7 Conclusion

Even though people with profound intellectual and multiple disabilities have become more visible in society as well as in research, they are at the same time still a 'forgotten' category. This is also very clear when it comes to assessment: there are hardly any standardized instruments available, and a solid tradition of using assessment before decision-making (either diagnostic, with relation to status or to intervention) is lacking. Still, I believe that people with profound intellectual and multiple disabilities should be given optimal opportunities to function with the abilities they have in the best possible way. Due to the failure to detect positive changes by means of the instruments we have now, it may not be concluded that people with profound intellectual and multiple disabilities are incapable of showing progress, responses or increased activity. The conclusion should rather be that more sensitive and more functional instruments are required to assess people with profound intellectual and multiple disabilities. Collaboration between practitioners and researches, and between researchers from different universities in different countries, should be encouraged in order to be able to develop such instruments in the near future.

REFERENCES

Bates, E., O'Connell, B. & Shore, C. (1987) Language and communication in infancy. In J. D. Osofsky (ed.), *Handbook of Infant Development*. New York: Wiley, pp. 149–204.

Bidabe, L. & Lollar, J. M. (1990) *MOVE (Mobility Opportunities Via Education)*. Kern Country Superintendent of Schools, Bakersfield.

Bloomberg, K. & West, D. (1999) *The Triple C – Checklist of Communication Competencies: Assessment Manual and Checklist*. Melbourne: SCIOP.

Coupe, J., Barton, L., Barber, M., Collins, L. Levy, D. & Murphy, D. (1985) *The Affective Communication Assessment*. Manchester: Melland School.

Degangi, G. & Greenspan, S. I. (1988) The development of sensory functions in infants. *Physical and Occupational Therapy in Pediatrics*, 8, 21–33.

Diaz, F. & Zurron, M. (1998) Auditory evoked and event-related potentials in the mentally retarded: A review and an experimental study. *Journal of Psychophysiology*, 12, 246–260.

Giangreco, M. F. & Dennis, R. E. (1994) Dressing your IEPS for the general education climate: Analysis of IEPS goals and objectives for students with multiple disabilities. *Remedial and Special Education*, 15, 288–297.

Haley, S. M., Coster, W. J. & Binda-Sundberg, K. (1994) Measuring physical disablement: The contextual challenge. *Physical Therapy*, 74, 443–451.

Hogg, J. & Sebba J. (1986) *Profound Retardation and Multiple Impairment Vol. 1: Development and Learning*. London: Croom Helm.

Guess, D., Mulligan-Ault, M., Roberts, S., Struth, J., Siegel-Causey, E., Thompson, B., Bronicki, G. J. B. & Guy, B. (1988) Implications of biobehavioral states for the education and treatment of students with the most profoundly handicapping conditions. *Journal of the Association for Persons with Severe Handicaps*, 13, 163–174.

Kiernan, C. C. & Jones, M. C. (1977) *Behaviour Assessment Battery: Assessment of the Cognitive, Communicative and Self Help Skills of the Severely Mentally Handicapped.* Oxford: NFER-Nelson.

Kiernan, C. C. & Jones, M. C. (1982) *Behaviour Assessment Battery: Assessment of the Cognitive, Communicative and Self Help Skills of the Severely Mentally Handicapped.* Oxford: NFER-Nelson.

Lohrmann-O'Rourke, S. & Browder, D. M. (1998) Empirically based methods to assess the preferences of individuals with severe disabilities. *American Journal on Mental Retardation,* 103, 146–161.

MacPherson, F. & Butterworth, G. (1988) Sensorimotor intelligence in severely mentally handicapped children. *Journal of Mental Deficiency Research,* 32, 465–478.

Murphy, M. J. & Harrop, A. (1994) Observer error in the use of momentary time sampling and partial interval recording. *British Journal of Psychology,* 85, 169–179.

Rothstein, J. M. (1994) Disability and our identity. *Physical Therapy,* 74, 375–378.

Saudargas, R. A. & Zanolli, K. (1990) Momentary time sampling as an estimate of percentage time: A field validation. *Journal of Applied Behavior Analysis,* 23, 533–537.

Simeonsson, R. B. & Bailey, D. B. (1988) Essential elements of the assessment process. In T. D. Wachs & R. Sheehan (eds.), *Assessment of Young Developmentally Disabled Children.* New York: Plenum, pp. 25–43.

Sobsey, D. & Wolf-Schein, E. (1999) Children with sensory impairments. In F. P. Orelove & D. Sobsey (eds.), *Educating Children with Multiple Disabilities: A Transdiciplinary Approach.* Baltimore, MD: Brookes, pp. 411–451.

Sparrow, S. S., Balla, D. A. & Cichetti, D. V. (1984) *Vineland Adaptive Behavior Scales: Interview Edition – Survey Form Manual.* Circle Pines, MN: American Guidance Service.

Splunder, J. van, Stilma, J. S. & Evenhuis, H. M. (2003) Visual performance in specific syndromes associated with intellectual disability. *European Journal of Ophthalmology,* 13, 566–574.

Sternberg, L. & Richards, S. (1989) Assessing levels of state and arousal in individuals with profound handicaps. *Journal of Mental Deficiency Research,* 33, 381–387.

Teller, D. Y., Morse, R., Borton, R. & Regal, D. (1974) Visual Acuity for vertical and diagonal gratings in human infants. *Vision Research,* 14, 1433–1439.

Užgiris, I. [hach]C[/hach]. & Hunt, J. McV. (1975) *Assessment in Infancy: Ordinal Scales of Psychological Development.* Chicago: University of Illinois Press.

Vlaskamp, C. (1993) Development and evaluation of individual eductional programmes for profoundly multiple handicapped. *Issues in Special Education and Rehabilitation,* 8, 45–51.

Vlaskamp, C., Meulen, B. F. van der & Smrkovsky, M. (1999) *Gedragstaxatie-instrument GTI.* Groningen: Stichting Kinderstudies.

Vlaskamp, C., Meulen, B. F van der & Zijlstra, H. P. (2002) *De instrumentele realisering van het Gedrags Taxatie Instrument: Tijdschrift voor Orthopedagogiek,* 41, 22–31.

Vlaskamp, C., Smrkovsky, M. & Meulen, B. F. van der (2000) *Gedrags Taxatie Instrument.* Groningen: Stichting Kinderstudies.

Ware, J. (1994) *Educating Children with Profound and Multiple Learning Difficulties.* London: Fulton.

Ware, J. & Healy, I. (1994) Conceptualising progress in children with profound and multiple learning difficulties. In J. Ware (ed.), *Educating Children with Profound and Multiple Learning Difficulties.* London: Fulton, pp. 1–15.

CHAPTER 12

Commonly employed psychopathology instruments for individuals with intellectual disabilities

Lauren R. Charlot and Edwin J. Mikkelsen

1 Introduction

In this chapter, commonly used psychopathology assessment and screening tools developed for specific application with individuals with intellectual disabilities will be described. Important issues of reliability and validity in the development of such instruments will also be reviewed. The goal is to provide the assessor with a sense of which tools are best used for which clinical purposes, and also, how critically to evaluate the contribution of such instruments to the overall psychiatric assessment of an individual with intellectual disabilities.

2 Technical Aspects of Psychopathology Instruments

2.1 Reliability

Inter-rater reliability is the extent to which two people using a scale yield a similar outcome. When there is a high degree of agreement between different raters using the same scale, then the scale is said to have good inter-rater reliability. In addition to inter-rater reliability, assessment tools may be evaluated in terms of their test–retest reliability, or how stable the measure is over time. In this case, the instrument is used at time one and then repeated, under circumstances as similar as possible to its initial use, at a later time with the same patient. The extent to which these two scores match is then calculated.

Psychopathology instruments may not show good test–retest reliability because most clinical conditions they measure do, in fact, change over time (Reiss, 1994). When assessing test–retest reliability of measures of anxiety and depression, a two-week interval has been suggested, in particular when evaluating children (Costello & Angold, 1988). Internal reliability or internal consistency is an important measure in the development of a psychopathology scale, reflecting the extent to which items within a scale measure the same phenomenon. A scale has good internal consistency when items measuring the same clinical phenomenon are highly correlated. Internal consistency is affected by the number of items in the scale, and there is a positive correlation between length and internal reliability.

2.2 Validity

There are a number of different types of validity for assessment tools. In general, if an assessment tool is valid, we know the results of its use are a true representation of the clinical entity it claims to represent. For example, when an individual has a high score on the Beck Depression Inventory (BDI), we can be confident that this person is most likely to be suffering from major depressive disorder (MDD) (Beck et al., 1961). Following are brief discussions of several subtypes of validity that pertain to the use of a psychopathology screening or assessment tool.

2.2.1 Face validity An assessment or screening tool has face validity when its items appear, on 'face value', logically to represent the clinical entity that it is purported to characterize. This may be based on clinical experience and on previous research regarding the clinical phenomena described. For example, a screening tool aimed at identification of a syndrome based on the *Diagnostic and Statistical Manual of Mental Disorders, Fourth Edition-Revised* (DSM-IV) (American Psychiatric Association, 2000), such as major depressive disorder, has face validity if it contains items corresponding to the symptom criteria for this syndrome.

2.2.2 Content validity Content validity is the extent to which a scale measures all of the symptoms or aspects of the syndrome or clinical entity it is supposed to characterize. What items are placed in a scale at the outset of its construction may be affected most by the developer's point of view about the clinical entity being described. For most psychiatric syndromes, there is still some controversy over specific definitions of disorders. Sometimes content may be based on existing literature, but it can also be derived from a factor analysis of a large number of items, that are reduced to a closely related group. There has been considerable debate over the superiority of a factor-analytic or dimensional approach to the assessment of psychopathology, as compared with categorical approaches. Some researchers have advocated a combined approach (Cantwell, 1996; Charlot, 2003), pointing out there is no need to use only one or the other of these methodologies. Factor derived scales may be more useful as initial screens in multistage evaluations, suggesting more broadly that there is some clinical problem, or for measuring treatment outcomes. Structured interviews that suggest specific diagnostic categories may be more helpful in the process of generating diagnostic hypotheses. (See chapter 4, section 3.4.)

2.2.3 Criterion validity Criterion validity is a measure of the extent to which a scale correlates with theoretically related measures of the same phenomenon or to some other established criterion. For example, a criterion may be whether or not the person received a specific diagnosis based on a clinical interview. Items can be culled from the scale to improve its rate of agreement with the established criterion. Of interest is the fact that content validity and criterion validity serve opposing functions. To ensure that an assessment tool has criterion validity, as noted, only those items correlating highly with the criterion are retained. Unfortunately, in the early stages of investigating the clinical features of a syndrome using a psychopathology instrument, items that are dropped may be important to a complete understanding of the nature of the disorder within the group under study. This would be particularly true for unusual or special clinical populations in which there may be atypical features. So improving criterion validity may actually diminish content validity. Developing a comprehensive picture of the clinical phenomenology of the DSM-IV system or *International Statistical Classification of Diseases and Related Health Problems, Tenth Edition-Revised* (ICD-10) (World Health Organization, 1997) disorders (having better content validity) may be the most important goal in the early stages of building a valid classification for people with intellectual disabilities (Cantwell, 1996; Charlot, 2003).

2.2.4 Discriminant validity   It is important that an assessment procedure identifies the clinical entity we want to identify and measure, but it is also vital that the tool is specific enough that it differentiates between clinical problems, or at least between people who do and do not have a clinically significant problem. It is much less useful if a given scale score indicates that a person may have depression, when the same score is just as likely to suggest the person suffers from schizophrenia. There is a great deal of overlap between clinical phenomena in psychiatric syndromes, and most syndromes do not have 'pathognomic' symptoms (i.e. symptoms, when present, that are absolute signs of the disorder). Typically, psychiatric syndromes are identified when a specific set of symptoms occur together, are intense and persistent, and follow a usual course. Scales with good content validity, to the extent that they are measuring disorders that appear to have clear boundaries, are probably more likely to differentiate individuals experiencing one versus another disorder. Discriminant validity may also be affected by the fact that some psychiatric problems seem to occur along a continuum with normal behaviour, while others appear to be discrete. Some of the boundaries set in attempts to classify psychiatric syndromes better may be artificially imposed by the systems we currently apply (Costello & Angold, 1988).

3 Psychopathology Instruments and Psychiatric Diagnoses

A number of psychopathology instruments have been developed for specific use for individuals with intellectual disabilities, which can be used to aid in the assessment process. Although these instruments have some problems, each of the more commonly employed tools has its strengths and weaknesses. All of them can be used to aid in a more comprehensive or complete psychiatric evaluation, and none is recommended as a free-standing diagnostic tool, with the possible exception of the Psychiatric Assessment Schedule for Adults with Developmental Disabilities (PAS-ADD).

Convergent validity among these screening tools is sometimes not as great as might be expected (Rojhan et al., 1994). Another major concern is that the most commonly employed scales for use with subjects with intellectual disabilities do not contain full complements of DSM or ICD-10 diagnostic criteria. Using the example of depression, consider the Reiss Screen for Maladaptive Behavior (RSMB), one of the most widely used instruments for people with intellectual disabilities (Reiss, 1988). The RSMB has two depression scales. Even when items from both of these scales are compiled, the nine DSM diagnostic criteria for a major depressive episode are not present. Similar concerns exist with other widely employed instruments. Failure of these specialized tools to include all DSM-IV or ICD-10 diagnostic criteria for major psychiatric syndromes may lead to a high rate of false negatives (i.e. missed cases of people with various disorders because only some of the criteria are even in the screening tool). The RSMB may still be very effective in detecting many cases of depression, and as an adjunct to other diagnostic methodologies it is felt by many assessors to be an excellent tool.

Another critical concern with the prevailing instruments is the minimal attention paid to inter-rater reliability. Some authors believe that inter-rater reliability is overemphasized in the literature on instrument development, because it is too much affected by variables outside the instrument being used (i.e. motivation and training of raters) (Reiss, 1994). As noted, when using multiple informants, many of these problems can be avoided (Laman & Reiss, 1987; Reiss, 1994).

Other researchers have argued that reliability is really the cornerstone of any assessment procedure, and is particularly important if the goal is to establish psychiatric diagnoses (Costello & Angold, 1988). Use of behavioural equivalents or descriptions could enhance reliability of psychiatric assessment, but this has not been systematically studied in people with intellectual disabilities. (See ch. 4, section 2.1.) From a practical standpoint, it is likely that the more clearly and concretely the behavioural or observable manifestations of a symptom are defined, the more likely that two observers will agree about its presence or absence. Psychiatric disorders may be misdiagnosed or missed altogether because individual symptoms are incorrectly characterized or all of the symptoms that are present are not elicited. If key symptoms are frequently not identified in subjects with intellectual disabilities, the validity of a given set of diagnostic criteria cannot be established.

4 Self-Report and Informant Reports

As noted, informant reports tend to lead to an overemphasis on externalizing problems. However, there are some data that suggest informant reports may be more reliable than self-reports, when evaluating individuals with intellectual disabilities (Reiss, 1994). A serious limitation of self-report measures is the fact that many people with intellectual disabilities do not have adequate language skills to use this type of tool. Individuals who do have enough expressive language skills may still have deficits in their ability to identify and describe internal feeling states. It is always critical to attempt some interview or to conduct some direct observation of the person for a thorough psychiatric evaluation. As noted, this should be combined with other assessment strategies, including obtaining informant reports, record reviews and a review of the past medical history. Most of the scales described below have only an informant version, while the Psychopathology Instrument for Mentally Retarded Adults (PIMRA) has both a self-report form as well as an informant-report form.

5 Psychopathology Assessment Tools for People with Intellectual Disabilities

In the following section we describe well-researched instruments for assessing psychopathology in people with intellectual disabilities (sections 5.1–5.5) and note some additional instruments that have recently been reported (section 5.6).

5.1 The Reiss Screen for Maladaptive Behavior (RSMB)

The Reiss Screen is a 36-item psychopathology symptom inventory that has been widely used in the psychiatric assessment of people with intellectual disabilities. It was developed in 1988 (Reiss, 1988; Reiss, 1990) and provides assessors with empirically derived cut-off scores. The scale has been studied in large samples of people to evaluate its psychometric properties and clinical utility, including over 1,400 people with intellectual disabilities in the initial stages of its development. The Reiss Scales are also available for use with children (Reiss & Valenti-Hein, 1994). The Reiss Screen was developed for adolescents/adults aged 12 or older. The factorial stability has also been positively assessed in a large diverse sample of individuals with varying degrees of intellectual disabilities (Havercamp & Reiss, 1997).

The Reiss Screen is filled out by familiar caregivers. The scale has great practical utility, because it can be scored easily, is simple and quick to fill out, and it employs easy to understand language. Symptoms or challenging behaviours are rated on a 3-point severity scale from *no problem* to *moderate problem* to *severe problem*. A study using a modification of the instrument that added separate ratings of frequency and duration did include additional significant diagnostic information (Havercamp & Reiss, 1996). Two raters complete a form for each individual and are asked to describe behaviour or symptoms seen for a four-week period prior to the evaluation. These informants need not be trained assessors. For each item, behavioural examples and a definition are provided to assist raters in deciding if the individual did, in fact, exhibit the problem item. The Reiss Screen generates a full-scale score and also eight separate subscales, including scales for aggression, autism, psychosis, paranoia, depression, dependent personality disorder and avoidant personality disorder. There are two depression scales: one with behavioural and another with physical signs and symptoms of depression. As noted, there are recommended cut-off scores and norms based on use of the instrument with large samples of people with intellectual disabilities.

The total score of all Reiss items has been found to be a valid measure of mental health problems. The scale differentiates people with intellectual disabilities who are not seen as having a mental health problem from individuals who have been diagnosed with a disorder using the DSM system. The total Reiss Screen score was noted to have the best psychometric properties as compared with the subscales. Cronbach's alpha coefficients for the five scales ranged from .70 to .85, though one of the depression scales had a lower internal reliability. Reiss (1994) considered this was likely to be due to the low frequency of these symptoms in the sample studied. The total Reiss Screen score was found to be correlated with other psychopathology instruments for people with intellectual disabilities, including the PIMRA and the Aberrant Behavior Checklist (ABC) (Sturmey & Bertman, 1994).

There have been translations of the Reiss Screen into other languages. A study involving a Dutch version of the Reiss Screen (van Minnen et al., 1995) reported good internal consistency for most subscales, good criterion validity, but low to moderate inter-rater reliability. In a recent report, a Swedish version of the Reiss Screen had moderate to low inter-rater agreement on specific items, but good internal consistency (Gustafsson & Sonnander, 2002). However, the criterion validity analysis revealed a greater rate of false negatives, as compared to false positives (i.e. identifying some people as not having a psychiatric disorder who were diagnosed as having one by other methods). As noted, this could pose a problem in terms of the Reiss Screen being used as a 'net', to capture all possible cases of a certain syndrome, with 'caseness' being established later in the chain of assessment, using more traditional in-depth clinical assessment techniques. Reiss (1994) has suggested that the subscales are limited due to their small number of five items.

There is general agreement that the score of the Reiss Screen is a valid and reliable screening tool for people with intellectual disabilities (Kishore et al., 2004; Sturmey & Bertman, 1994; Sturmey et al., 1995), especially when used as a first step in a more comprehensive assessment. There has been some question with regard to the subscales, and a factor analytic study of which raised questions about their consistency (Sturmey et al., 1996), though Reiss (1997) has suggested that there were methodological problems with this analysis.

5.2 The Psychopathology Instrument for Mentally Retarded Adults (PIMRA)

The PIMRA (Senatore et al., 1985; Matson et al., 1984; Matson, 1997) has also been widely used in the assessment of mental health problems in people with intellectual disabilities. The PIMRA has an informant version and also a self-report form. Each form contains 56 items, and either the informant or the individual being interviewed answers 'yes' to affirm the symptom was present, or 'no' if the symptom was not present. The PIMRA is based on DSM-III and yields scores for eight diagnostic categories, including schizophrenia, affective disorder, anxiety disorder, psychosexual disorder, adjustment disorder, somatoform disorder, personality disorder and inappropriate adjustment, as well as a total score. Assessors with training in mental health assessment techniques interview a caregiver or the individual who is self-reporting symptoms. The interviewer explains each item by giving examples and may clarify the caregiver's observations. This requires that the assessor have knowledge of the DSM diagnostic framework and an ability to interpret items. Severity of symptoms is not rated, as in the Reiss Screen and Aberrant Behavior Checklist (ABC).

There have been a number of studies using the PIMRA (Jenkins et al., 1998; LaMalfa et al., 1997; Aman et al., 1986), and these reports suggest that the full-scale score does discriminate between people with intellectual disabilities with and without psychiatric diagnoses. A study involving a Dutch version of the PIMRA (van Minnen et al., 1994) indicated that internal consistency was good for the total score, but less so for the subscales. Also, the correlation between the informant and self-report form was not robust. The full-scale score has been found to correlate positively with the total score on the Reiss Screen (Reiss, 1994). As with the Reiss Screen, the total score appears to have more validity than the individual subscales (Watson et al., 1988; Sturmey & Ley, 1990). An investigation with regard to its utility for institutionalized individuals who functioned primarily in the severe range of intellectual disability indicated that the scale did have some utility for this population (Linaker, 1991).

Two of the subscales have been independently studied and appear to have particular usefulness. These are the Schizophrenia Scale (Linaker & Helle, 1994; Swiezy et al., 1995) and the Depression Subscale (Kazdin et al., 1983; Swiezy et al., 1995). Subsequent to the development of the original instrument, a subscale has also been developed to assess for psychosexual disorders in the population of individuals who function in the mild and moderate range of intellectual disabilities (Matson & Russell, 1994).

The self-report form is not very effective unless the individual has fairly strong language skills, so for many people, the informant version will be the best choice. Also, the PIMRA does not contain a full set of DSM criteria for mania and depression, so that there may be a high rate of 'false negatives', as with the Reiss Screen. Overall, despite its drawbacks, the tool is a very helpful guide to the assessor in the context of a more comprehensive evaluation, as intended by the authors.

5.3 The Aberrant Behavior Checklist (ABC)

The ABC can be used with individuals throughout the full range of intellectual disability, though it was initially devised for people with profound to moderate intellectual disabilities (Aman et al., 1985a; Aman et al., 1985b). The ABC, unlike the Reiss Screen or the PIMRA derived from factor analysis. The tool yields scores for five scales, including irritability, lethargy, stereotypic behaviours, hyperactivity and excessive speech. There are 58 items. Caregivers answer questions regarding the presence and severity of specific behaviours, circling the appropriate rating and completing the survey independently. There are instructions that multiple informants should be used. Symptoms or behaviours are rated on a 4-point severity scale, and definitions of items are available in the user manual.

The ABC authors first compiled a long list of challenging behaviours that people with moderate to profound intellectual disabilities were known to exhibit. Case records for a large number of individuals with intellectual disabilities who were receiving institutional care were reviewed. The total number of items was then reduced by evaluating occurrence in a large sample. Items endorsed by familiar informants that were seen in a minimum of 10% of the population were included in a final version of the original scale. There were 509 subjects in the second phase of the scale's development, which yielded a scale with 76 items. A principal components factoring method with iteration, followed by oblique rotation, was applied to the data from both phases of the scale.

The authors have also developed a version for specific use with individuals who reside in the community (Aman & Singh, 1994; Marshburn & Aman, 1992; Aman et al., 1995; Brown et al., 2002; Freund & Reiss, 1991). The ABC-Community item content is the same as for the ABC-Residential, except that home, school and workplace are listed as the relevant settings. The ABC-Community has been validated and norms for people with intellectual disabilities living in community-based care situations were then developed. Rater pairs including teacher and parent ratings of children in classes for children with developmental disabilities, as well as care provider ratings of adults in group homes, were assessed. The ABC form includes recording degree of intellectual disability, the individual's medical status, and current medications. Fifty-eight specific symptoms are rated and an extensive manual gives comprehensive descriptions for each assessed behaviour. The checklist can be completed by parents, special educators, psychologists, direct caregivers, nurses and others familiar with the individual.

The application of the ABC to children and adolescents has also been investigated with positive results (Rojahn & Helsel, 1991). Extensive psychometric assessment of the ABC has indicated that its subscales have high internal consistency, adequate reliability and established validity. Average subscale scores are available for both US and overseas residential facilities and for children and adults living in the community (Ono, 1996; Rojhan et al., 2003; Newton & Sturmey, 1988; Aman et al., 1987; Bihm & Poindexter, 1991).

Like the PIMRA and Reiss Screen, the ABC has been widely used. If a caregiver is completing the ABC, recommendations are made that a supervisor give directions and it has been noted that variations in the instructions can affect the reliability (Aman et al., 1987). It is a very useful adjunct to other assessment procedures, especially when there is a plan to introduce a treatment, and then repeat the ABC at a later time to evaluate the intervention. Indeed, the ABC has had its most robust application as an instrument to measure treatment effectiveness.

5.4 The Psychiatric Assessment Scale for Adults with Developmental Disabilities (PAS-ADD)

The PAS-ADD was developed to help fill an important gap in the psychiatric evaluation of people with intellectual disabilities, as there had not been any extensive clinically oriented semi-structured interviews available prior to this (Moss et al., 1993). The revised version is based on the Schedule for Clinical Assessment in Neuropsychiatry (SCAN) (World Health Organization, 1994) (Rijnders et al., 2000; Aboraya et al., 1998) and provides ICD-10 diagnoses (Costello et al., 1997).

The first version utilized a 3-point severity scale, whereas the revised version utilizes a 4-point severity scale. An advantage to the PAS-ADD semi-structured interview is its potential for greater content validity, since it yields a higher quality of clinical information. As suggested, it may be that content validity is the most critical area at present in the evolution of instruments to improve diagnostic accuracy in the psychiatric assessment of people with intellectual disabilities, especially in research studies aimed at validating psychiatric syndromes, as defined in ICD or DSM within this special clinical population.

The PAS-ADD interview is administered through the examination of a person and an informant. However, significant differences in the results obtained between respondent and informant interviews have been reported (Moss, Prosser, Ibbotson & Goldberg, 1996). The PAS-ADD is linked to the ICD-10, and diagnoses are derived from the SCAN. Psychiatric disorders based on the interview include psychotic disorders, hypomania, depression and anxiety disorders. The PAS-ADD validity studies revealed a mean Kappa of 0.65 for the ICD-10 version, when diagnoses from the interview were compared with clinical diagnoses (Costello et al., 1997).

Clinical applications of the PAS-ADD have shown reasonably good agreement between the instrument and clinical opinion (Moss et al., 1997; Moss, Prosser, Ibbotson & Goldberg,

1996). The PAS-ADD is not as lengthy to administer as one might suspect because there are a series of filter items, and the assessor can skip over areas when it is obvious that the person does not have any signs of psychopathology in that area. The authors reported that the interview for each individual could be as brief as 30 minutes or less. It is considered acceptable, however, to use only the informant interview when the individual being evaluated has severe intellectual disabilities and cannot respond to the interview.

The PAS-ADD checklist is designed for use as a screening instrument. The symptom checklist consists of 29 items that are scored on a 4-point scale. There is also a life events checklist. In addition to a total score, the instrument also yields three subscale scores: affective/neurotic, psychotic disorder and possible organic disorder. An attempt was made to use common language in the construction of the scales so that non-professionals who were familiar with the individual could complete it (Moss, Prosser, Costello, Simpson & Patel, 1996). Each of the subscales has a threshold score with further assessment being recommended for those who score above these cut-offs. Psychometric evaluations have found it to be a valid and reliable instrument (Moss et al., 1998). The instrument has also shown utility in clinical studies (Clarke, 1998; Patel et al., 1993). A recent attempt to obtain normative data for the PAS-ADD Checklist suggested that it may be overinclusive, with the rate of psychotic disorders being particularly high. However, given its use as a screening instrument, this is not necessarily a negative characteristic (Taylor et al., 2004).

A Mini-PAS-ADD has also been developed (Prosser et al., 1998). This instrument was designed, in part, to make it possible for non-professional caregivers to make decisions with regard to the appropriateness of professional evaluation for an individual. The total instrument contains 86 psychiatric symptoms. The subscales are depression, anxiety and phobias, mania, obsessive-compulsive disorder, psychosis, unspecified disorder and pervasive developmental disorder. The results indicated that by utilizing this instrument, the caregivers' assessments were similar to the expert assessors in identifying caseness. The publishers of these instruments are now making available a Mini-PAS-ADD Interview Pack, which contains the Mini-PAS-ADD Checklist (Revised), the Mini-PASI-ADD Interview Pack as well as Mini-PAS-ADD Score Forms.

5.5 The Charlot Semi-structured Interview for Individuals with Intellectual Disabilities (CSI-intellectual disabilities)

The Charlot Semi-structured Interview for Individuals with Intellectual Disabilities (CSI-intellectual disabilities) was derived directly from the DSM-IV. The interview was developed for use by skilled assessors and is intended to be a guide that helps the assessor access comprehensive clinical information from informants. The assessor interviews a minimum of two familiar informants, who spend at least 20 hours or more per week directly with the individual who is being evaluated, and they are asked to report primarily on symptoms noted over the past month.

The CSI-ID has not yet been fully validated and its reliability has yet to be studied, though the author is in the process of conducting these investigations. Pilot data have been compiled for 91 inpatients, providing some preliminary evidence of convergent validity for the CSI-ID diagnoses of anxiety disorder, manic episode and depressive episode with clinical diagnoses based on a more comprehensive evaluation. The CSI-ID has questions covering several DSM diagnoses, including depressive episode, anxiety disorder, manic episode, panic attack, obsessive compulsive disorder, psychosis, borderline personality disorder and autistic disorder. Each of the DSM-IV diagnostic criteria in the interview has several corresponding items that are behavioural descriptions for the symptom criteria. In most cases, the descriptors are meant to be possible manifestations in people with moderate to profound intellectual disabilities, though a number of items are geared for people with verbal skills as well. The assessor decides if he or she feels the symptom criteria were met, based on informant reports of observations of the behavioural manifestations. For example, an interview with informants about a person with intellectual disabilities and suspected mental health problems might go as follows:

Assessor: Has Rob seemed anxious to you lately? We are most interested in the past month. For example, have you seen him looking fearful? Does he actually say things like 'I'm afraid'?

Residential staff: He definitely has been grabbing on to people and won't do anything without staff right with him.

Vocational staff: Well, lately, he has been looking very tense, though he doesn't say 'I'm nervous' or anything like that.

Assessor: Can you tell me what you see that helps you know he is anxious?

Parent: He paces back and forth and gets very fidgety. He's like a bubble on a griddle.

Assessor: Have you suspected he is having nightmares?

Residential staff: I don't think so, though his sleep has been bad lately.

Assessor: What time does he go to sleep and wake up?

It is unclear at this time if the behavioural descriptors used in the CSI-intellectual disabilities are valid representations of the symptoms they are hypothesized to describe. The behavioural equivalents were identified from a few different sources, and have reasonable face validity. These included

- behavioural equivalents for depression and mania formerly proposed by Sovner and Hurley (1982a, 1982b), and Lowry and Sovner (1992);
- developmental or age effects on psychiatric syndromes described in DSM-IV-TR;
- a review of research on the phenomenology of psychiatric syndromes in people with intellectual disabilities;
- research regarding clinical features of DSM disorders in children from the developmental psychopathology literature;
- pilot use of the interview in the assessment of psychiatric inpatients with intellectual disabilities.

5.6 Further specific instruments

The increased interest in mental health problems in people with intellectual disabilities, coupled with dissatisfaction with existing forms of assessment, has led to a proliferation of assessment tools and rating scales. Some of them, with their associated references, appear below.

All are at an early stage of development and before using them reference should be made to the original papers to determine their scope and psychometric adequacy:

- Glasgow Anxiety Scale for People with an Intellectual Disability (Mindham & Espie, 2003) (*anxiety*)
- Mental Retardation Depression Scale (Meins, 1996) (*depression*)
- Mood, Interest and Pleasure Questionnaire (Ross & Oliver, 2002) (*depression-related*)

There have also been efforts to modify existing widely used instruments so that they can be employed for individuals with intellectual disabilities. Specific examples include the modification of the Zung Self-Rating Anxiety Scale (Lindsay et al., 1994), and the Beck Anxiety and Depression Inventories (Lindsay et al., 2004).

6 Conclusion: Using the Right Instrument in the Right Situation

In summary, all of the assessment instruments reviewed here have value, although they may vary in terms of their utility in various clinical situations. The PIMRA and Reiss screens have been well established as assessment tools that can identify people who need more in-depth psychiatric assessment and point the direction for possible areas of more significant dysfunction. The PAS-ADD structured interview may be more useful for research purposes and as a guide to a much more in-depth look for a specific mental health disorder. The CSI-intellectual disabilities is not well established, but has the advantage of being designed as a practical informant interview guide that can be used in a regular clinical practice, and may be less time consuming than the PAS-ADD structured interview tool. The CSI-intellectual disabilities also uses multiple behavioural descriptions for criteria associated with each symptom, so it has potential for enhancing reliability at the level of symptom identification. The mini PAS-ADD may function as an excellent screening tool, but like the Reiss and PIMRA, it may yield more false negatives for some syndromes such as anxiety disorder, major depression and bipolar disorder, because it contains only items that proved statistically to be highly correlated with the criterion. In some ways, this can actually place assessors at a disadvantage in the evaluation of people who are suspected to present with unusual features. The ABC is a dimensional tool that was entirely factor-derived and is probably best when used to assess treatment outcomes in people with intellectual disabilities and psychopathology.

REFERENCES

Aboraya, A., Tien, A., Stevenson, J. & Crosby, K. (1998) Schedules for Clinical Assessment in Neuropsychiatry (SCAN): Introduction to WV's mental health community. *W V Medical Journal*, 94, 326–328.

Aman, M. G., Burrow, W. H. & Wolford, P. L. (1995) The Aberrant Behavior Checklist-Community: Factor validity and effect of subject variables for adults in group homes. *American Journal of Mental Retardation*, 100, 283–292.

Aman, M. G., Richmond, G., Stewart, A. W., Bell, J. C. & Kissell, R. C. (1987) The Aberrant Behavior Checklist: Factor structure and the effect of subject variables in American and New Zealand facilities. *American Journal of Mental Deficiency*, 91, 570–578.

Aman, M. G. & Singh, N. N. (1994) *Aberrant Behavior Checklist Community Supplementary Manual.* East Aurora, NY: Slosson Educational.

Aman, M. G., Singh, N. N., Stewart, A. W. & Field, C. J. (1985a) The Aberrant Behavior Checklist: A behavior rating scale for the assessment of treatment effects. *American Journal of Mental Deficiency,* **89**, 485–491.

Aman, M. G., Singh, N. N., Stewart, A. W. & Field, C. J. (1985b) Psychometric characteristics of The Aberrant Behavior Checklist. *American Journal of Mental Deficiency,* **89**, 492–502.

Aman, M. G., Singh, N. N. & Turbott, S. H. (1987) Reliability of The Aberrant Behavior Checklist and the effect of variations in instructions. *American Journal of Mental Deficiencies,* **92**, 237–240.

Aman, M. G., Watson, J. E., Singh, N. N., Turbott, S. H. & Wilsher, C. P. (1986) Psychometric and demographic characteristics of the psychopathology instrument for mentally retarded adults. *Psychopharmacology Bulletin,* **22**, 1072–1076.

American Psychiatric Association (2000) *Diagnostic and Statistical Manual of Mental Disorders, Fourth Edition-Revised.* Washington, DC: American Psychiatric Association.

Beck, A. T., Ward, C. H., Mendelson, M., Nock, J. & Erbaugh, J. (1961) An inventory for measuring depression. *Archives of General Psychiatry,* **4**, 561–571.

Bihm, A. M. & Poindexter, A. R. (1991) Cross-validation of the factor structure of The Aberrant Behavior Checklist for persons with mental retardation. *American Journal of Mental* Retardation, **96**, 209–211.

Brown, E. C., Aman, M. G. & Havercamp, S. M. (2002) Factor analysis and norms for parent ratings on The Aberrant Behavior Checklist-Community for young people in special education. *Research in Developmental Disabilities,* **23**, 45–60.

Cantwell, D. P. (1996) Classification of child and adolescent psychopathology. *Journal of Child Psychology and Psychiatry,* **37**, 3–12.

Charlot, L. (2003) Mission impossible: Developing an accurate classification of psychiatric disorders for individuals with developmental disabilities. *Mental Health Aspects of Developmental Disabilities,* **6(1)**, 26–33.

Clarke, D. (1998) Prader-Willi syndrome and psychotic symptoms. Part 2: A preliminary study of prevalence using the Psychopathology Assessment Schedule for Adults with Developmental Disability Checklist. *Journal of Intellectual Disability Research,* **42**, 451–454.

Costello, E. J. & Angold, A. (1988) Scales to assess child and adolescent depression: Checklists, screens, and nets. *Journal of the American Academy of Child and Adolescent Psychiatry,* **27**, 726–737.

Costello, H., Moss, S., Prosser, H. & Hatton, C. (1997) Reliability of the ICD 10 version of the Psychiatric Assessment Schedule for Adults with Developmental Disability (PAS-ADD). *Social Psychiatry and Psychiatric Epidemiology,* **32**, 339–343.

Freund, L. S. & Reiss, A. L. (1991) Rating problem behaviors in outpatients with mental retardation: Use of The Aberrant Behavior Checklist. *Research in Developmental Disabilities,* **12**, 435–451.

Gustafsson, C. & Sonnander, K. (2002) Psychometric evaluation of a Swedish version of the Reiss Screen for Maladaptive Behavior. *Journal of Intellectual DisabilityResearch,* **46**, 218–229.

Havercamp, S. M. & Reiss, S. (1996) Composite versus multiple-rating scales in the assessment of psychopathology in people with mental retardation. *Journal of Intellectual Disability Research,* **40**, 176–179.

Havercamp, S. M. & Reiss, S. (1997) The Reiss Screen for Maladaptive Behavior: Confirmatory factor analysis. *Behavioral Research Therapy,* **35**, 967–971.

Jenkins, R., Rose, J. & Jones, T. (1998) The Checklist of Challenging Behaviour and its relationship with the Psychopathology Inventory for Mentally Retarded Adults. *Journal of Intellectual Disability Research,* **42**, 273–278.

Kazdin, A., Matson, J. & Senatore, V. (1983) Assessment of depression in mentally retarded adults. *American Journal of Psychiatry,* **140**, 1040–1043.

Kishore, M. T., Nizamie, A., Nizamie, S. H. & Jahan, M. (2004) Psychiatric diagnosis in persons with intellectual disability in India. *Journal of Intellectual Disability Research*, 48, 19–24.

LaMalfa, G., Notarelli, A., Hardoy, M. C., Bertelli, M. & Cabras, P. L. (1997) Psychopathology and mental retardation: An Italian epidemiological study using the PIMRA. *Research in Developmental Disabilities*, 18, 179–184.

Laman, D. S. & Reiss, S. (1987) Social skill deficiencies associated with depressed mood of mentally retarded adults. *American Journal of Mental Deficiency*, 92, 224–229.

Linaker, O. M. (1991) DSM-III diagnoses compared with factor structure of the psychopathology instrument for mentally retarded adults (PIMRA), in an institutionalized, most severely retarded population. *Research in Developmental Disabilities*, 12, 143–153.

Linaker, O. M. & Helle, J. (1994) Validity of the schizophrenia diagnosis of the psychopathology instrument for mentally retarded adults (PIMRA): A comparison of schizophrenic patients with and without mental retardation. *Research in Developmental Disabilities*, 15, 473–486.

Lindsay, W. R., Law, J. & McLeod, F. (2004) Intellectual disabilities and crime: Issues in assessment, management and treatment. In A. Needs and G. Towel (eds.), *Applying Psychology to Forensic Practice*. Oxford: British Psychological Society and Blackwell, pp. 97–114.

Lindsay, W. R., Michie, A. M., Baty, F. J., Smith, A. H. W. & Miller, S. (1994) The consistency of reports about feelings and emotions from people with intellectual disability. *Journal of Intellectual Disability Research*, 38, 61–66.

Lowry, M. & Sovner, R. (1992) Severe behavior problems associated with rapid cycling bipolar disorder in two adults with profound mental retardation. *Journal of Intellectual Disabilities Research*, 36, 269–281.

Marshburn, E. C. & Aman, M. G. (1992) Factor validity and norms for The Aberrant Behavior Checklist in a community sample of children with mental retardation. *Journal of Autism and Developmental Disorders*, 22, 357–373.

Matson, J. L. (1997) *The PIMRA Manual* (2nd ed.). Worthington, OH: IDS.

Matson, J. L., Kazdin, A. E. & Senatore, V. (1984) Psychometric properties of the psychopathology instrument for mentally retarded adults. *Applied Research in the Mentally Retarded*, 5, 81–89.

Matson, J. L. & Russell, D. (1994) Development of the psychopathology instrument for Mentally Retarded Adults-Sexuality Scale (PIMRA-S). *Research in Developmental Disabilities*, 15, 355–369.

Meins, W. (1996) A new depression scale designed for use with adults with mental retardation. *Journal of Intellectual Disability Research*, 40, 222–226.

Mindham, J. & Espie, C. (2003) Glasgow Anxiety Scale for People with an Intellectual Disability (GAS-intellectual disabilities): Development and psychometric properties of a new measure for use with people with mild intellectual disabilities. *Journal of Intellectual Disability Research*, 47, 22–30.

Minnen, A. van, Savelsberg, P. M. & Hoogduin, K. A. (1994) A Dutch version of the Psychopathology Inventory for Mentally Retarded Adults (PIMRA). *Research in Developmental Disabilities*, 15, 269–278.

Minnen, A. van, Savelsberg, P. M. & Hoogduin, K. A. (1995) A Dutch version of The Reiss Screen of Maladaptive Behavior. *Research in Developmental Disabilities*, 16, 43–49.

Moss, S., Ibbotson, B., Prosser, H., Goldberg, D., Patel, P. & Simpson, N. (1997) Validity of the PAS-ADD for detecting psychiatric symptoms in adults with learning disability (mental retardation). *Social Psychiatry and Psychiatric Epidemiology*, 32, 344–354.

Moss, S. C., Patel, P., Prosser, H., Goldberg, D., Simpson, N., Rowe, S. & Lucchino, R. (1993) Psychiatric morbidity in older people with moderate and severe learning disability. Part 1: Development and reliability of the patient interview (PAS-ADD). *British Journal of Psychiatry*, 163, 471–480.

Moss, S., Prosser, H., Costello, H., Simpson, N. & Patel, P. (1996) *PAS-ADD Checklist*. Manchester, UK: Hester Adrian Research Centre, University of Manchester.

Moss, S., Prosser, H., Costello, H., Simpson, N., Patel, P., Rowe, S., Turner, S. & Hatton, C. (1998) Reliability and validity of the PAS-ADD Checklist for detecting psychiatric disorders in adults with intellectual disability. *Journal of Intellectual Disability Research*, **42**, 173–183.

Moss, S., Prosser, H., Ibbotson, B. & Goldberg, D. (1996) Respondent and informant accounts of psychiatric symptoms in a sample of patients with learning disability. *Journal of Intellectual Disability Research*, **40**, 457–465.

Newton, J. T. & Sturmey, P. (1988) The Aberrant Behavior Checklist: A British replication and extension of its psychometric properties. *Journal of Mental Deficiency Research*, **32**, 87–92.

Ono, Y. (1996) Factor validity and reliability for The Aberrant Behavior Checklist-Community in a Japanese population with mental retardation. *Research in Developmental Disabilities*, **17**, 303–309.

Patel, P., Goldberg, D. P. & Moss, S. (1993) Psychiatric morbidity in older people with moderate and severe learning disability (mental retardation). Part 2: The prevalence study. *British Journal of Psychiatry*, **163**, 481–491.

Prosser, H., Moss, S., Costello, H., Simpson, N., Patel, P. & Rowe, S. (1998) Reliability and validity of the Mini PAS-ADD for assessing psychiatric disorders in adults with intellectual disability. *Journal of Intellectual Disability Research*, **42**, 264–272.

Reiss, S. (1988) *Test Manual for the Reiss Screen for Maladaptive Behavior*. Worthington, OH: IDS.

Reiss, S. (1990) Prevalence of dual diagnosis in community-based day programs in the Chicago metropolitan area. *American Journal of Mental Retardation*, **94**, 578–585.

Reiss, S. (1994) *Handbook of Challenging Behavior: Mental Health Aspects of Mental Retardation*. Worthington, OH: IDS.

Reiss, S. (1997) Comments on The Reiss Screen for Maladaptive Behaviour and its factor structure. *Journal of Intellectual Disability Research*, **41**, 346–354.

Reiss, S. & Valenti-Hein, D. (1994) Development of a psychopathology rating scale for children with mental retardation. *Journal of Consulting and Clinical Psychology*, **6**, 28–33.

Rijnders, C. A., van den Berg, J. F., Hodiamont, P. P., Nienhuis, F. J., Furer, J. W., Mulder, J. & Giel, R. (2000) Psychometric properties of the schedules for clinical assessment in neuropsychiatry (SCAN-2.1). *Social Psychiatry and Psychiatric Epidemiology*, **35**, 348–352.

Rojahn, J., Aman, M. G., Matson, J. L. & Mayville, E. (2003) The Aberrant Behavior Checklist and the Behavior Problems Inventory: Convergent and divergent validity. *Research in Developmental Disabilities*, **24**, 391–404.

Rojahn, J. & Helsel, J. (1991) The Aberrant Behavior Checklist with children and adolescents with dual diagnosis. *Journal of Autism and Developmental Disorders*, **21**, 17–28.

Rojahn, J., Warren V. J. & Ohringer, S. (1994) A comparison of assessment methods for depression in mental retardation. *Journal of Autism and Developmental Disorders*, **24**, 305–313.

Ross, E. & Oliver, C. (2002) The development of the Mood, Interest and Pleasure Questionnaire (MIPQ): An informant questionnaire for use in relation to adults with severe and profound learning disabilities. *Clinical Psychology Review*, **555**, 81–93.

Senatore, V., Matson, J. L. & Kazdin, A. E. (1985) An inventory to assess psychopathology of mentally retarded adults. *American Journal of Mental Deficiency*, **8**, 459–466.

Sovner, R. & Hurley, A. D. (1982a) Diagnosing depression in the mentally retarded. *Psychiatric Aspects of Mental Retardation Reviews*, **1**, 1–3.

Sovner, R. & Hurley, A. D. (1982b) Diagnosing mania in the mentally retarded. *Psychiatric Aspects of Mental Retardation Reviews*, **1**, 9–11.

Sturmey, P. & Bertman, L. J. (1994) Validity of the Reiss Screen for Maladaptive Behavior. *American Journal of Mental Retardation*, **99**, 201–206.

Sturmey, P., Burcham, K. J. & Perkins, T. S. (1995) The Reiss Screen for Maladaptive Behaviour: Its reliability and internal consistencies. *Journal of Intellectual Disability Research*, **39**, 191–195.

Sturmey, P., Jamieson, J., Bercham, J., Shaw, B. & Bertman, L. (1996) The factor structure of The Reiss Screen for Maladaptive Behaviors in institutional and community populations. *Research in Developmental Disabilities*, 17, 285–291.

Sturmey, P. & Ley, T. (1990) The Psychopathology Instrument for Mentally Retarded Adults: Internal consistencies and relationship to behaviour problems. *British Journal of Psychiatry*, 156, 428–430.

Swiezy, N. B., Matson, J. L., Kirkpatrick-Sanchez, S. & Williams, D. E. (1995) A criterion validity study of the schizophrenia subscale of the Psychopathology Instrument for Mentally Retarded Adults (PIMRA). *Research in Developmental Disabilities*, 16, 75–80.

Taylor, J. L., Hatton, C., Dixon, L. & Douglas, C. (2004) Screening for psychiatric symptoms: PAS-ADD Checklist norms for adults with intellectual disabilities. *Journal of Intellectual Disability Research*, 48, 37–41.

Watson, J. E., Aman, M. G. & Singh, N. N. (1988) The psychopathology instrument for mentally retarded adults: Psychometric characteristics, factor structure, and relationship to subject characteristics. *Research in Developmental Disabilities*, 9, 277–290.

World Health Organization (1994) *Schedules for Clinical Assessment in Neuropsychiatry Version 2*. Geneva: World Health Organization.

World Health Organization (1997) *International Statistical Classification of Diseases and Related Health Problems, Tenth Edition-Revised* (ICD-10). Geneva: World Health Organization.

CHAPTER 13

Instruments for assessing behavioural problems

Kirk Zimbelman

1 Introduction

The assessment of behavioural problems in persons with intellectual disabilities requires consideration of the person's total context, as emphasized in chapter 5. Psychometric measures such as those described below, while providing important information on the nature, causes and consequences of challenging behaviour, yield only a portion of the information needed to design comprehensive and constructional approaches to addressing challenging behaviour. Moreover, given the multi-factorial nature of behavioural problems, it would be beyond the scope of a single chapter to review all of the instruments that might contribute to a formulation of challenging behaviour. The measures and processes discussed elsewhere in this volume, including those that assess quality of life (chs. 1 and 9), competence (chs. 2 and 10), mental health problems (chs. 4 and 5), issues to do with offending (chs. 6 and 14) and some neuropsychological deficits (chs. 8 and 16) all have relevance to the assessment of behavioural problems. Moreover, the assessment instruments reviewed below rely exclusively on the recollections of key informants. As noted in chapter 5, direct observation by the evaluator, behavioural recordings by carers, and in some instances applied analysis of behaviour all have a role to play in assessing behavioural problems.

With the above caveats in mind, the instruments reviewed below can lend some objectivity to an enterprise that in many ways remains as much an art as a science. In general, assessments of behavioural problems are not on a par with the more commonly used tests of, for example, cognitive ability. Nor are they as accessible, in terms of being produced and disseminated by major publishers. Nonetheless, the instruments below were chosen because they have been published in some form and are therefore generally available. They were designed for, standardized and validated on persons with intellectual disabilities. Numerous references to them in two major databases (PsychInfo and Medline) suggest that they have been used extensively in both research and clinical settings.

The first instrument reviewed, the American Association on Mental Retardation (AAMR) Adaptive Behavior Scale: Residential and community Part 2, is probably the most readily available, being part of a commonly used global assessment of adaptive functioning. While the assignment of items to various scales is often less than intuitive, the instrument covers a broad domain of problem behaviours, and consequently is likely to be useful for problem identification. As indicated in chapter 5, the second instrument reviewed, the Aberrant Behavior Checklist, has demonstrated sensitivity to changes in challenging behaviour over time. Consequently, this broad spectrum checklist has proven useful not only in specifying the topography of challenging behaviour, but also in evaluating the effectiveness of interventions targeted at individuals and groups. The Behavior Problems Inventory addresses more extensively a narrower range of behaviours commonly seen particularly in persons with severe intellectual disabilities. Finally, the Questions About Behavioral Function Scale assesses the motivational or functional intent of challenging behaviour. The authors have taken the rather unusual step of attempting to determine whether interventions based on their scale are superior to more generic interventions.

2 AAMR Adaptive Behavior Scale – Residential and Community, Second Edition, Part 2

The AAMR Adaptive Behavior Scale – Residential and Community, Second Edition (ABS-RC:2) represents a refinement, elaboration and renorming of two earlier versions of the AAMD Adaptive Behavior Scales (Nihira et al., 1969; Nihira et al., 1975). The ABS-RC:2 (Nihira et al., 1993a) consists of two parts. The 10 Domains of Part 1 address personal independence, and evaluate coping skills required for independence and responsibility in daily living. Of relevance to this chapter is Part 2, which addresses social behaviour – or the extent to which the person being evaluated meets social expectations for appropriate behaviour and interaction with others in a variety of settings. The revised instrument was normed on a group of 4,103 residents of community facilities in 46 US states. Norms are stratified by age, and are presented for persons between the age of 18 and 74. The authors offer evidence that this group is representative of the population of US residents with intellectual disability in residential settings. While there are no norms presented for the general adult population, the authors claim, without substantiation, that the instrument can aid in the diagnosis of mental retardation (intellectual disability).

The 41 items in Part 2 are divided into 8 Domains. In fact, the 'items' on the ABS-RC:2 are groups of up to 12 items relating to one particular theme (Nihira et al., 1993b). For example, Item 30 from the Self-Abusive Behavior domain reads, 'Does physical violence to self'. Beneath this item the respondent is invited to indicate the frequency with which the person being evaluated engages in nine different self-abusive behaviours. At the end of each item there is a free text field in which the respondent can enter and indicate the frequency of one additional behaviour relating to that item. Higher raw scores indicate more behavioural difficulties. Total raw scores for each Domain are converted into Domain Standard Scores with a mean of 10 and a standard deviation of 3. Because lower raw scores earn higher standard scores, higher standardized scores on Part 2 reflect better adjustment.

The eight Domains are:

- *Social Behavior*: verbal or physical abuse, temper tantrums and antagonizing others.
- *Conformity*: rebellious behaviour, including imprudence, tardiness or absence, and misbehaviour in groups.

- *Trustworthiness*: dishonesty and lack of personal integrity, including stealing, lying, cheating and showing disrespect for others' property.
- *Stereotyped and Hyperactive Behavior*: includes making inappropriate physical contact, and displaying stereotypies.
- *Sexual Behavior*: including inappropriate masturbation, removing clothing in public, and participating in sexual activities in socially unacceptable ways.
- *Self-abusive Behavior*: self-abusive and bizarre behaviours that interfere with community integration.
- *Social Engagement*: the degree to which a person withdraws from activities and fails to respond to others.
- *Disturbing Interpersonal Behavior*: behaviour that annoys others – including overestimating one's ability, feeling persecuted and reacting poorly to criticism.

Factor analysis of Part 2 scores yields two interpretable dimensions (Nihira et al., 1993a), the scores of which can be calculated from the Profile/Summary Form. The resulting Factor Scores described below have a mean of 100 and a standard deviation of 15:

- *Social Adjustment*: the extent to which the individual evidences aggressive and antisocial behaviour, and inappropriate interpersonal relationships.
- *Personal Adjustment*: behaviours that are autistic and stereotyped, and if an affront to others, at least lack hostile intention.

The scale is completed either by the examiner, who interviews one or more key informants, or is self-administered to someone who is familiar with the individual being evaluated (Nihira et al., 1993a). The instructions stipulate that if the interviewee is unable to answer all of the questions, an additional interview with another respondent must be conducted to obtain the relevant information. The authors indicate that the test can be administered by a range of professional and paraprofessional personnel provided they have training with the scale. Interpretation of results is reserved for persons with formal training in psychometrics and in the assessment of adaptive behaviour.

The manual reports extensive reliability data, mostly based on the original norm group. Measures of internal consistency (coefficient alpha) range from .81 to .94 for Domain Standard Scores, and are .96 and .97 for the Social Adjustment and Personal Adjustment Scores respectively. The manual reports standard errors of measurement stratified by age for each of the Domain Standard Scores and Factor Scores. Test–retest reliability was established by inviting supervisors in a sheltered workshop to re-evaluate employees (N = 45) after a two week interval. Stability coefficients for Part 2 Domain Scores range from .81 to .97, and are .94 for the Social Adjustment Factor and .82 for the Personal Adjustment Factor. Because the authors claim to view inter-rater reliability as a facet of validity, they instead confine themselves to exploring inter-scorer reliability. To accomplish this, two graduate students were asked to score 16 completed protocols. Not surprisingly, this rather trivial and essentially clerical undertaking yielded reliability coefficients ranging from .97 to .99, and a coefficient of .96 for both Factor Scores.

While the authors note that the items on the ABS-RC:2 have undergone numerous modifications since the first edition (Nihira et al., 1969), they subsequently indicate that 'because the new version contains relatively few item changes, earlier [validity studies] may be of interest to researchers' (p. 33). No information to establish the equivalence of the ABS-RC:2 and earlier versions of the scale is presented in the manual (Nihira et al., 1993a).

The manual provides evidence for the construct validity of the Scale by presenting item discrimination coefficients (point-biserial correlation coefficients in which each item is correlated with the entire test). The authors conclude that this exercise, which bears an uncanny resemblance to the process of determining internal consistency rather than validity, supports the construct validity of the instrument. Examination of the instrument (Nihira et al., 1993b), however, reveals perplexing, and at times frankly misleading, assignment of items to various Domains. As an example, behaviours listed under item 29, which is contained in the Self-Abusive Domain, include 'Is overly particular about places to sit or sleep', 'Sits on anything that vibrates', and 'Is afraid to climb or descend stairs'. Indeed, only one of the three Items contained in the Self-Abusive Domain addresses what is generally considered to be self-abusive. Other item assignment seems arbitrary, and results in considerable overlap, and consequently lack of conceptual clarity, between and within Domains. For example, the behaviour 'Tells untrue and exaggerated stories about others' is contained beneath Item 3 of the Social Behavior Domain, rather than within the Trustworthiness Domain. Item 7 ('Disrupts others' activities') in the Social Behavior Domain might be more appropriately placed within the Stereotyped and Hyperactive Behavior Domain.

The manual addresses discriminant validity by demonstrating that the scores on Part 2 are unrelated to adaptive behaviour as measured by the Vineland Adaptive Behavior Scale and the Adaptive Behavior Inventory (Brown & Leigh, as cited in Nihira et al., 1993a). Lacking in the manual, however, is any attempt to establish the convergent validity of the scale with other measures of maladaptive behaviour. Walsh and Shenouda (1999) subsequently examined the convergent validity of the ABS-RC:2, the Reiss Screen for Maladaptive Behavior, and the Aberrant Behavior Checklist (ABC) with a convenience sample of 284 adults living in community settings. They found significant medium to large correlation coefficients between four of the eight ABS Part 2 Domain Scores and the Reiss Screen total score. The Disturbing Interpersonal Behavior and Social Behavior Domains showed the highest correlations with the Reiss Screen. While the Reiss Screen was designed to detect psychopathology, the ABC and the ABS-RC:2 share the common purpose of quantifying behavioural problems. Consequently, the authors found significant correlations between the ABC Irritability subscales and the majority of the ABS-RC:2 Domain scores. Relatively low correlations between the Sexual Behavior and Self-abusive areas on each instrument may reflect differences in content, or the seemingly idiosyncratic structure of certain ABS-RC:2 Domains discussed above.

Using the ABS-RC:2, Wallace et al. (2002) were able to detect higher levels of maladaptive behaviour in intellectually disabled persons infected with *Helicobacter pylori*, a primary cause of peptic ulcer and other conditions giving rise to gastric distress, than in an uninfected control group. The 112 persons in their study testing positive for the bacteria received significantly lower scores on four of the eight Domains, with scores on a further four approaching statistical significance. While the nature of the association between infection and behavioural problems was not established, the authors hypothesized that the pain and discomfort associated with gastric symptoms caused behavioural problems.

Part 2 of the ABS-RC:2 offers the advantage of being linked to a commonly used measure of adaptive behaviour. The manual is clearly written, and provides extensive normative data, including standard errors of measurement. Regrettably, independent research has yet to demonstrate the instrument's utility in the measurement of behavioural problems. While the items on the scale sample extensively a broad array of maladaptive behaviours, as noted above and observed by others (O'Brien et al., 2001) the Domains in some cases do not provide these items with a meaningful context.

3 Aberrant Behavior Checklist

The Aberrant Behavior Checklist (ABC) is a broad-spectrum assessment of challenging behaviour, the original intent of which was to assess behavioural changes resulting from psychopharmacological treatment in individuals in residential settings with moderate to profound intellectual disability (Aman & Singh, 1986). Subsequently, the authors made minor variations in wording that reflected community rather than institutional residential settings, and renamed the instrument the Aberrant Behavior Checklist – Community (Aman & Singh, 1994a). The Community version appears to have the same psychometric properties as the residential instrument, and consequently the two scales can probably function as alternate forms of the same measure.

Aman and Singh (1986) state that the instrument is empirically derived from a large pool of items reflecting problem behaviours noted in the records of 400 persons from a large residential facility. A pool of 125 items was subsequently refined and factor analysed, resulting in a 58-item questionnaire addressing five dimensions of challenging behaviour: *Irritability*, agitation, crying (15 items); *Lethargy*, social withdrawal (16 items); *Stereotypic behavior* (7 items); *Hyperactivity*, non-compliance (16 items); and *Inappropriate Speech* (4 items). Behaviours are rated on a 4-point scale from '0' (behaviour is not a problem) to '3' (the behaviour is severe). Total scores for each dimension are obtained by summing the ratings for the scale. The scores are not subject to normative interpretation.

The original manual (Aman & Singh, 1986) stipulates that the ABC can be administered to anyone who has a good knowledge of the client's behaviour. The rater should have observed the client's behaviour in more than one setting and is encouraged to ascertain the opinions of others where feasible. The instructions on the community version test blank (Aman & Singh, 1994b) imply that the instrument can be completed independently by the respondent. Respondents and interviewers are encouraged to consult supplementary definitions and examples printed in the manual (Aman & Singh, 1986). Neither of the manuals makes an explicit statement regarding user qualifications.

The psychometric properties of the ABC were initially established on a large (N = 418) group of persons in a residential facility in New Zealand. The residential manual (Aman & Singh, 1986) offers extensive information on reliability. Measures of internal consistency (coefficient alpha) range from .95 for the Hyperactivity Subscale to .86 for the Irritability Subscale. A subsequent study on a US sample revealed internal consistency of a similar magnitude (Aman et al., cited in Aman and Singh, 1986). Test–retest reliability was high, ranging from .96 to .99. Inter-rater reliability was lower, with an average of .63 across subscales (Aman & Singh, 1986).

Exploratory and confirmatory factor analyses (with a US sample) are detailed by Aman & Singh (1986). The same five-factor structure was replicated by Newton and Sturmey (1988) with a British sample of 204 intellectually disabled adults in residential facilities. They suggested that rating items dichotomously, rather than on a 4-point scale of severity, may increase reliability, while preserving the original factor structure. Aman et al. (1995) replicated the five-factor solution with the community version of the scale using a group of 1,040 residents living in community settings in the US. Coefficients of congruence ranged from .84 to .97, and measures of internal consistency ranged from .83 to .90. Ono (1996) confirmed the five-factor solution for the Japanese version of the ABC-Community on a group of 322 persons from four residential institutions. Brown et al. (2002) replicated the factor structure and verified the internal consistency of the community version on a sample of 601 children and adolescents – though the fifth factor, Inappropriate Speech, proved to be less than robust.

The ABC's criterion validity was addressed by comparing the scores of institutional residents attending available training programmes, presumably an indication of fewer behavioural problems, with those who did not have training placements, presumably having been excluded due to challenging behaviour (Aman & Singh, 1986). Those who attended training programmes had significantly lower ABC scores on all dimensions. The instrument was also able to differentiate residents with Down syndrome from other residents. Those with Down syndrome scored lower on all dimensions except Lethargy (Aman & Singh, 1986). The association of the ABC with other instruments supports its concurrent validity. The instrument was found, for example, to be correlated only moderately with IQ (Slosson Brief Intelligence Test), and was moderately and negatively correlated with adaptive behaviour scales (Vineland Social Maturity Scale, AAMD Adaptive Behavior Scale, and the Fairfield Self Help Scale) (Aman & Singh, 1986). Walsh and Shenouda (1999) found that all ABC-Residential subscale scores with the exception of Stereotypy correlated significantly with subscale scores on the Reiss Screen for Maladaptive Behavior. The authors concluded that the instrument demonstrates concurrent validity particularly in highly visible and socially mediated behaviours. As indicated in the pervious section, in the same study (Walsh & Shenouda, 1999) they determined that the ABC correlated significantly with Part 2 Domain Standard Scores of the ABS-RC:2.

While the original purpose of the ABC was to detect changes in behaviour associated with psychoactive drug treatment, researchers have used the instrument to quantify challenging behaviour and behavioural change in a variety of contexts. Chung et al. (1995) used the ABC, the Psychopathology Inventory for Mentally Retarded Adults (PIMRA), and the Disability Assessment Scale to assign formal psychiatric diagnoses to 31 patients in a residential facility. They noted that the ABC enhanced the diagnostic utility of the PIMRA by quantifying the magnitude of behavioural disturbance. Katz et al. (1997) used the ABC-Community to assess behavioural problems in older adults (N = 172) with and without intellectual disability and with and without a psychiatric disorder. Persons with intellectual disability and a psychiatric disorder scored significantly higher on three of the five subscales. Persons on psychiatric medication were rated higher on four of the five subscales. The authors concluded that the ABC-Community can be used to assess behavioural problems in older individuals with or without intellectual disability.

Clarke and Marston (2000) used the ABC to explore challenging behaviour in 73 children and adults with Angelman syndrome. They employed both profile scores and item analysis, concluding that Angelman syndrome is associated with overactivity, restlessness, eating and sleeping problems, and a fascination with water and other materials. The instrument was sensitive to age-related decline in these behaviours. Luiselli et al. (2001) used the ABC to evaluate the effectiveness of a partial hospitalization programme for 38 adults diagnosed with intellectual disability and a psychiatric disorder. The programme consisted of personal counselling and skills teaching groups. Scores on the ABC prior to involvement in the programme, and upon discharge, suggested improvement on all scales in 39% of the participants. A further 61% showed improvement on some of the scales. None of the participants showed deterioration. The authors did not comment on the statistical significance of these findings.

In summary, the ABC is a thoroughly researched instrument that has a long history of use in applied settings. Considering the array of challenging behaviour it addresses, and its sensitivity to behavioural changes, the instrument is short and quickly administered.

4 Behavior Problems Inventory

The broadband instruments described above aim to quantify a variety of behavioural problems. Their scope makes them particularly useful as screening instruments, as an aid in problem identification, and as outcome measures of interventions, such as deinstitutionalization, that are likely to impact several challenging behaviours. But as Rojahn et al. (2001) have indicated, due to the broad range of problems that they address, such instruments use only a few items to address each behavioural cluster – prompting concerns of low reliability. The Behavior Problems Inventory was designed to be a 'narrow-band' instrument that addresses in greater depth the behavioural problems commonly seen in persons with developmental disabilities. The authors suggest that the instrument can be used for a variety of purposes, including the clinical assessment of those at risk of challenging behaviour, determining the outcome of clinical interventions and exploring the epidemiology of specific problem behaviours.

The Behavior Problems Inventory was first published in German in the 1980s and was restricted to the assessment of self-injurious behaviour and stereotypies (Rojahn, cited in Rojahn et al., 2001). The instrument was translated into English in 1988 and a third dimension, aggressive/destructive behaviour was added (Rojahn et al., 1989). Substantial revision and expansion of items measuring stereotyped behaviour resulted in the most current version of the scale, which the authors refer to as the BPI-01 (Rojahn et al., 2001).

The BPI-01 contains 49 items assessing behavioural problems in three areas discussed above – with an additional item in each scale allowing the respondent to select a behaviour not addressed elsewhere in the scale (Rojahn, 2001). The authors give no indication how these open-ended items were treated in various reliability and validity studies. The wording of the instructions for the version of the scale published on the Internet (Rojahn, 2001) would indicate that the inventory can also be self-administered by persons familiar with the client. Behaviours are rated on two dimensions. Frequency ratings range from 'Monthly' to 'Hourly', and severity ratings range from 'Slight' to 'Moderate'. Fourteen items address self-injurious behaviour, 24 items address stereotyped behaviour, and 14 items address aggressive and destructive behaviour. There are no published guidelines on the minimum qualifications for administering or interpreting the instrument.

Rojahn et al. (2001) used the Behavior Problems Inventory to evaluate 432 individuals with developmental disability residing in a developmental centre. Fifty-four per cent of the participants were male, and 46% female. About half (45.6%) had a psychiatric diagnosis. While primarily adult, they ranged in age from age 14 to 91. Graduate students administered the instrument to direct-care staff who had known the client in question for at least six months. Questions were posed in an open-ended fashion, with the interviewer quantifying frequency and severity. Given that the study was conducted in a residential setting, a high proportion of the participants (84.2%) had severe or profound intellectual disability. In light of the problem areas addressed by the scale, they constituted an appropriate population to study. Measures of internal consistency (Cronbach's alpha) ranged from .61 to .82 for individual subscales, with a coefficient of .83 for the entire scale. Retest reliability (one-week interval) ranged from .61 to .76 for the individual subscales, and was .76 for the overall scale. Inter-rater reliability ranged from .59 to .96, the interclass correlation coefficient for the entire scale being .88.

A confirmatory factor analysis of the Behavior Problems Inventory conducted on adults (Rojahn et al., 2001) suggested the appropriateness of the three oblique factors: self-injurious behaviour, stereotyped behaviour and aggressive/destructive behaviour. The aggressive/destructive scale seemed slightly more homogenous and robust than the other two scales. Ross et al., (2002) used the frequency scores of the SIB to quantify the presence of stereotypic, self-injurious and aggressive/destructive behaviour in children, adolescents and young adults with Cri du Chat syndrome. The BPI-01 was used in two multi-centre, randomized, double blind, placebo-controlled investigations of the effects of risperidone on children and adolescents with disruptive behaviour disorders (Aman et al., 2002; Snyder et al., 2002). In both studies participants showed an improvement on the aggressive/destructive behaviour scale as a result of treatment with risperidone.

5 Questions About Behavioral Function (QABF) Scale

As noted in chapter 5, the most common goal for the assessment of challenging behaviour is to understand why the person is engaging in the challenging behaviour. The Questions About Behavioral Function (QABF) (Vollmer & Matson, 1995) is a 25-item questionnaire designed to assess the functions of challenging behaviour. The instrument has five subscales, each with five items, addressing the factors that most frequently maintain aberrant behaviour. The authors offer the instrument as an alternative to applied behaviour analysis, a process which they characterize as time consuming, expensive, requiring substantial specialist input and of questionable validity (Applegate et al., 1999).

Vollmer and Matson (1995) recommend that the one-page questionnaire be administered to a carer, teacher or other individual who can comment on the challenging behaviour in a variety of contexts. The respondent rates the potential causes of the target behaviour (Example: 'Engages in behavior because he/she likes to be reprimanded'.) on a 4-point Likert scale ranging from Never (0) to Often (3). An additional rating, 'Does Not Apply', is permitted, and, by implication, is treated as a 0 score. Item endorsement scores and frequency scores are summed for each scale. Irrespective of the magnitude of the score, the factor with the highest score is considered to be a likely cause of the target behaviour. The five subscales (Vollmer & Matson, 1995; Dawson et al., 1998) are as follows:

- *Attention*: positive or negative reactions from others, including as a way of initiating interaction.
- *Escape*: avoiding task demands or social interaction with others.
- *Non-social*: internalized events where the problem behaviour itself is reinforcing.
- *Physical*: pain, illness, or other discomfort.
- *Tangible*: attempting to acquire or reacting to the loss of some valued physical object.

Paclawskyj et al. (2000) report that administration of the QABF takes about 20 minutes. In their study, administration was accomplished by a graduate student examiner – though there is no clear specification regarding training required of interviewers. The mechanics of scoring and interpretation as described in the manual (Vollmer & Matson, 1995) are relatively straightforward, and could likely be accomplished by any person qualified to undertake behaviour analysis.

Matson, Vollmer et al. (cited in Dawson et al., 1998) report that the QABF has a Cronbach's alpha of .86 and a Guttman split-half reliability of .91. Internal consistency data reported subsequently (Paclawskyj et al., 2000) ranged from .90 to .93 for individual subscales, but with an alpha of .60 for the entire scale. The last statistic is not surprising considering that the scale is multi-factorial, and does not purport to measure a unitary construct.

Test–retest reliability (stability) was assessed by re-administering the instrument to 34 staff in a large institution caring for persons with severe to profound intellectual disability, after a delay of one to three weeks (Paclawskyj et al., 2000). Test–retest reliability for individual items and subscale scores were acceptable, with Spearman rank-order correlations ranged from .65 to 1.00. Inter-rater reliability was assessed in the same study. Percent agreement regarding item endorsement (with correction for chance agreement) was acceptable, with Cohen's kappa values ranging from .64 to 1.00.

Paclawskyj et al. (2000) performed an exploratory factor analysis (Principal Axis Factoring with Varimax rotation) of the scale to confirm the *prima facie* factor structure. A five-factor solution, which accounted for 76% of the variance in ratings, conformed to the factors originally stipulated by the authors (Vollmer & Matson, 1995).

Paclawskyj et al. (2001) examined the convergent validity of the QABF, the Motivation Assessment Scale (MAS), and analogue functional analysis in a small group (N = 13) displaying self-injury, physical and verbal aggression, and stereotypies. The QABF and analogue assessment agreed on the category of antecedents prompting challenging behaviour in 56% of the cases. Concordance for the MAS and analogue assessment was 44%. At 61%, concordance was highest for the QABF and MAS. Regrettably, the group studied is small, and the design of the study therefore lacks statistical power. Correlations on the MAS and the QABF on subscales presumably addressing similar functions ranged from .51 to .87.

Applegate et al. (1999) found in a group of 417 institutionalized adults that antecedents and maintaining factors specified by the QABF were associated with the most frequently hypothesized causes of a variety of challenging behaviours, including self-injury, stereotypies, aggression, pica and rumination. Self-injuring residents scored highest on the non-social (i.e. self-stimulation and automatic reinforcement) subscales. The aggression group scored highest on the escape subscale. The stereotypies, pica and rumination groups scored highest on the non-social subscale. The authors conclude that given the often disappointing results of reliability studies with the MAS (e.g. Sigafoos et al., 1994; Thompson & Emerson, 1995; Zarcone et al., 1991), the QABF may serve as a better alternative for assessing the factors initiating or maintaining behavioural problems.

Matson et al. (1999) examined whether a treatment group (N = 90) with interventions dictated by findings on the QABF demonstrated better outcomes than a control group (N = 90) that received a standard treatment plan consisting of interrupting, redirecting and blocking maladaptive behaviours. Each group consisted of an equal number of persons exhibiting self-injurious behaviour, stereotypies and aggression. Data were collected and difference scores calculated for baseline occurrence of target behaviours one week prior to intervention, and six months into the intervention programme. There is no indication that the persons administering the intervention protocols were blind to the research design or their group membership. Groups where intervention was dictated by QABF specification of antecedents improved significantly over groups where 'standard' treatment was rendered.

To date the majority of the research on the QABF has been conducted in a single long-stay institution in Louisiana, USA. These results require to be replicated in other settings. Persons evaluated have had predominantly profound intellectual impairment. Consequently, the value of the instrument remains to be demonstrated with higher-functioning individuals in community settings. The manual is dated, requiring to be updated with subsequent psychometric findings. Despite the seeming robustness of the factor structure, the basis for initial item selection is not explained, nor is it evident that item selection was the product of an item analysis. Neither the manual nor subsequent studies by the QABF authors and their colleagues stipulate whether the instrument should be administered by a trained interviewer, or self-administered by staff and carers.

6 Conclusion

As indicated at the outset of this chapter, the instruments above each address a different aspect of challenging behaviour. Other instruments, which require further investigation to establish their reliability and validity in both research and clinical applications, deserve mention. The Challenging Behaviour Attributions Scale (Hastings, 1997) invites staff to report causal attributions of challenging behaviour in response to vignettes describing either aggressive or stereotyped behaviour. Respondents are invited to rate the likelihood of 33 possible explanations of the challenging behaviour. Items load on subscales representing the following attributions: positive reinforcement, negative reinforcement, biomedical causes, emotional causes, various aspects of the physical environment, and lack of stimulation. The instrument probably has substantial heuristic value, and addresses an important aspect of the social environment (i.e. the attributions that carers assign to challenging behaviour, in terms of creating or maintaining challenging behaviour). It has been observed, however, that attributions reported in response to behavioural vignettes may bear little resemblance to attributions made in response to actual challenging behaviour (Grey et al., 2002; Wanless & Jahoda, 2002).

While Behavior Problems Inventory and the Aberrant Behavior Checklist invite the respondent to supply a one-dimensional rating of the severity of behaviour, all of the instruments reviewed above address themselves primarily either to the causes or the topography of challenging behaviour. A recently developed instrument, the Challenging Behaviour Interview, addresses in depth the impact and severity of challenging behaviour (Oliver et al., 2003). In Part 1 of the interview, respondents are asked to determine whether the client has shown any of five types of challenging behaviour within the last month. In Part 2, the respondent is asked to rate on 14 behaviourally anchored dimensions the severity of each challenging behaviour. In addition to the commonly employed dimensions of frequency and duration of behaviour episodes, the behaviour's impact in the following areas is assessed: physical health of the individual, staff, and other service users; disruption to the interpersonal environment; modifications required in the environment to accommodate the behaviour; number of staff, and degree of verbal or physical intervention required to bring the behaviour under control. While the Challenging Behaviour Interview will likely make an important contribution to quantifying the important dimension of severity and impact of challenging behaviour, to date the instrument has not been published, and is available only from the authors.

REFERENCES

Aman, M., Burrow, W. & Wolford, P. (1995) The Aberrant Behavior Checklist – Community: Factor validity and effect of subject variables for adults in group homes. *American Journal on Mental Retardation*, **100**, 283–292.

Aman, M., DeSmedt, G., Derivan, A., Lyons, B., Findling, R. & Risperidone Disruptive Behavior Study Group (2002) Double-blind, placebo-controlled study of risperidone for the treatment of disruptive behaviors in children with subaverage intelligence. *American Journal of Psychiatry*, **159**, 1337–1364.

Aman, M. & Singh, N. (1986) *The Aberrant Behavior Checklist Manual.* East Aurora, NY: Slosson Educational.

Aman, M. & Singh, N. (1994a) *The Aberrant Behavior Checklist – Community: Supplementary Manual.* East Aurora, NY: Slosson Educational.

Aman, M. & Singh, N. (1994b) *The Aberrant Behavior Checklist [record form].* East Aurora, NY: Slosson Educational.

Applegate, H., Matson, J. & Cherry, K. (1999) An evaluation of functional variables affecting severe problem behaviors in adults with mental retardation by using the Questions About Behavioral Function scale (QABF). *Research in Developmental Disabilities*, **20**, 229–237.

Brown, E., Aman, M. & Havercamp, S. (2002) Factor analysis and norms for parent ratings on the Aberrant Behavior Checklist – Community for young people in special education. *Research in Developmental Disabilities*, **23**, 45–60.

Chung, M., Corbett, J., Clarke, D. & Cumella, S. (1995) Describing challenging behaviour: A pilot study 1. *European Journal of Psychiatry*, **10**, 167–183.

Clarke, D. & Marston, G. (2000) Problem behaviours associated with 15q-Angelman syndrome. *American Journal on Mental Retardation*, **105**, 25–31.

Dawson, J., Matson, J. & Cherry, E. (1998) An analysis of maladaptive behaviors in persons with autism, PPD-NOS, and mental retardation. *Research in Developmental Disabilities*, **19**, 439–448.

Grey, I., McClean, B. & Barnes-Holmes, D. (2002) Staff attributions about the causes of challenging behaviours. *Journal of Learning Disabilities*, **6**, 297–312.

Hastings, R. (1997) Measuring staff perceptions of challenging behaviour: The Challenging Behaviour Attributions Scale (CHABA). *Journal of Intellectual Disability Research*, **41**, 495–501.

Katz, R., Berry, E. & Singh, N. (1997) Using the Aberrant Behavior Checklist to assess problem behavior in older individuals. *Clinical Gerontologist*, **18**, 5–12.

Luiselli, J., Benner, S., Stoddard, T., Weiss, R. & Lisowski, K. (2001) Evaluating the efficacy of partial hospitalisation services for adults with mental retardation and psychiatric disorders: A pilot study using the Aberrant Behavior Checklist (ABC). *Mental Health Aspects of Developmental Disabilities*, 4, 61–67.

Matson, J., Bamburg, K., Cherry, K. & Paclawskyj, T. (1999) A validity study on the Questions About Behavioral Function scale. *Research in Developmental Disabilities*, 20, 163–176.

Newton, J. & Sturmey, P. (1988) The Aberrant Behavior Checklist: A British replication and extension of its psychometric properties. *Journal of Mental Deficiency Research*, 32, 87–92.

Nihira, K., Foster, R., Shellhaas, M. & Leland, H. (1969) *American Association on Mental Deficiency Adaptive Behavior Scale*. Washington, DC: American Association on Mental Deficiency.

Nihira, K., Foster, R., Shellhaas, M. & Leland, H. (1975) *American Association on Mental Deficiency Adaptive Behavior Scale* (rev.). Washington, DC: American Association on Mental Deficiency.

Nihira, K., Leland, H. & Lambert, N. (1993a) *American Association on Mental Retardation Adaptive Behavior Scale – Residential and Community: Examiner's manual* (2nd ed.). Austin, TX: PRO-ED.

Nihira, K., Leland, H. & Lambert, N. (1993b) *American Association on Mental Retardation Adaptive Behavior Scale – Residential and Community: Examination booklet* (2nd ed.). Austin, TX: PRO-ED.

O'Brien, G., Pearson, J., Berney, T. & Barnard, L. (2001) Measuring behaviour in developmental disability: A review of existing schedules. *Developmental Medicine and Child Neurology*, 43 (Suppl. 87), 1–72.

Oliver, C., McClintock, K., Hall, S., Smith, M., Dagnan, D. & Stenfert-Krose, B. (2003) Assessing the severity of challenging behaviour: Psychometric properties of the Challenging Behaviour Interview. *Journal of Applied Research in Intellectual Disabilities*, 16, 53–61.

Ono, Y. (1996) Factor validity and reliability of the Aberrant Behavior Checklist-Community in a Japanese population with mental retardation. *Research in Developmental Disabilities*, 17, 303–309.

Paclawskyj, T., Matson, J., Rush, K., Smalls, Y. & Vollmer, T. (2000) Questions About Behavioral Functions Scale (QABF): A behavioral checklist for functional assessment of aberrant behavior. *Research in Developmental Disabilities*, 21, 223–229.

Paclawskyj, T., Matson, J., Rush, K., Smalls, Y. & Vollmer, T. (2001) Assessment of convergent validity of the Questions About Behavioral Function scale (QABF) with analogue functional analysis and the Motivation Assessment Scale. *Journal of Intellectual Disability Research*, 45, 484–494.

Rojahn, J. (2001) *The Behavior Problems Inventory (BPI-01)*. Retrieved 26 December 2003 from http://www.gmu.edu/departments/ccd/Rojahn/BPI%20-%2001.pdf

Rojahn, J., Matson, J., Lott, D., Esbensen, A. & Smalls, Y. (2001) The Behavior Problems Inventory: An instrument for the assessment of self-injury, stereotyped behavior, and aggression/destruction in individuals with developmental disabilities. *Journal of Autism and Developmental Disorders*, 31, 577–588.

Rojahn, J., Polster, L., Mulick, J. & Wisniewski, J. (1989) Reliability of the Behavior Problems Inventory. *Journal of the Multihandicapped Person*, 2, 283–293.

Ross Collins, M. & Cornish, K. (2002) A survey of the prevalence of stereotypy, self-injury and aggression in children and young adults with Cri du Chat Syndrome. *Journal of Intellectual Disability Research*, 46, 133–140.

Sigafoos, J., Kerr, M. & Roberts, D. (1994) Interrater reliability of the Motivation Assessment Scale: Failure to replicate with aggressive behavior. *Research in Developmental Disabilities*, 15, 333–342.

Snyder, R., Turgay, A., Aman, M., Binder, C., Fisman, S., Carroll, A., et al. (2002) Effects of risperidone on conduct and disruptive behavior disorders in children with subaverage IQs. *Journal of the American Academy of Child and Adolescent Psychiatry*, 41, 1026–1036.

Thompson, S. & Emerson, E. (1995) Inter-informant agreement on the Motivation Assessment Scale: Another failure to replicate. *Mental Handicap Research*, 8, 203–208.

Vollmer, T. & Matson, J. (1995) *Questions About Behavioral Function (QABF) User's Guide.* Baton Rouge, LA: Scientific Publications.

Wallace, R., Webb, P. & Schluter, P. (2002) Environmental, medical, behavioural and disability factors associated with *Helicobacter pylori* infection in adults with intellectual disability. *Journal of Intellectual Disability Research*, **46**, 51–60.

Walsh, K. & Shenouda, N. (1999) Correlations among the Reiss Screen, the Adaptive Behavior Scale Part 2, and the Aberrant Behavior Checklist. *American Journal on Mental Retardation*, **104**, 236–248.

Wanless, L. & Jahoda, A. (2002) Responses of staff towards people with mild to moderate intellectual disability who behave aggressively: A cognitive emotional analysis. *Journal of Intellectual Disability Research*, **46**, 507–516.

Zarcone, J., Rodgers, T., Iwata, B., Rourke, D. & Dorsey, M. (1991) Reliability of the Motivation Assessment Scale: A failure to replicate. *Research in Developmental Disabilities*, **12**, 349–360.

CHAPTER 14

People with intellectual disabilities who offend or are at risk of offending: assessing need and risk

Gillian Anderson

1 Introduction

In recent years there has been greater recognition of the population of people with intellectual disabilities who offend or are alleged to have offended and their attendant needs (Lindsay & MacLeod, 2001; Lindsay, 2002a; Taylor & Halstead, 2001). The importance of assessment and treatment for individuals in this population has become increasingly acute when viewed in the context of present community-oriented policies. Here least restrictive options, minimization of risk and the protection and safety of vulnerable groups are central concerns in implementing the policy.

The difficulties of defining this population and identifying its characteristics were described in chapter 6. As indicated there, the first step in providing a service such as assessing need usually involves defining the population or group for whom this service will be available. In the present situation, however, the nature and scope of the population remains diffuse, making clarity as to the nature and purpose of assessment problematical. Nevertheless, progress has been made, and in this chapter we shall examine the current situation with respect to assessment of need and risk for those who are described as having intellectual disabilities and who have offended or are alleged to have offended. We consider in turn

- identification of people with intellectual disabilities within the criminal justice system (section 2);
- assessment in relation to criminal justice proceedings (section 3);
- risk assessment and risk management (section 4);
- assessment of specific offending behaviour (section 5);
- assessment and mental health (section 6);
- assessment and gender (section 7).

There has been a move to either adapting what is available for use with other populations to the intellectual disability population (Clare, 1993; Turner, 1998), or development of specific tools for this population (Lindsay 2002b; Broxholme & Lindsay, 2003). Progress has been relatively slow for a number of reasons. The population in question is small, and it has not always been easy to discriminate them appropriately from the larger populations, respectively, of people with intellectual disabilities or of offenders. Additionally, due to some of the cognitive deficits associated with intellectual disability, many of the interventions available are too complex to be understood by the majority of this group. Assessment has to take into account the impact of intellectual impairment on understanding, as well as discriminating between who might benefit from particular interventions and who might not. This inevitably leads to the question of what can be offered to those who would not benefit from the available interventions. Does this mean such individuals should be written off as difficult or impossible to treat, or can their needs be met using a different approach or service design?

In considering issues related to assessment with specific reference to offending, it should be born in mind that this is only one facet, albeit an important one, of the total person. Wider assessments of social and health needs are also called for and should lead to enhanced support for the individual (Clare & Murphy, 1998b).

2 Identification of People with Intellectual Disabilities within the Criminal Justice System

There are various points within the criminal justice system where individuals can be identified as having an intellectual disability (Holland et al., 2002; McBrien, 2003; ch. 6 in this volume). It is important to be able to identify such individuals so that assessment of their needs can begin and diversion to appropriate services can be made. On a more fundamental note, the identification of such individuals can assist in the planning and development of appropriate services, particularly since there is a lack of coordinated, robust community services for this population.

In general it is assumed there are two groups of people with intellectual disabilities who enter the criminal justice system. There are those who already receive services via health, social work or voluntary care services because they have an intellectual disability (Lyall et al., 1995; Holland et al., 2002; McBrien, 2003). It would be fair to say that these people have already been identified, although it is the case that some such people can be arrested and detained without the knowledge of the services supporting them. Their intellectual disability can be overlooked by the authorities, leading to their needs remaining unidentified. The second group are those who are not known to services and their behaviour brings them into contact with the criminal justice system (Murphy, 2000; Holland et al., 2002; McBrien, 2003). It is largely the second group of people at whom such assessment is targeted.

Work carried out in the UK and Australia has led to the development of screening assessments that could help to identify the offender with intellectual disabilities (Hayes, 2002; Mason & Murphy, 2002). There is, however, only one published tool available for this purpose (Hayes, 2000). The Hayes Ability Screening Index (HASI; Hayes, 2000) is a tool for screening for the possible presence of intellectual disability among people in the criminal justice system. It is designed for use by individuals who do not necessarily have psychological knowledge or understanding of psychometrics. It can be administered by police, welfare workers, social workers, lawyers and medics, among others.

The tool is not a diagnostic instrument, but will indicate whether an individual possibly has intellectual disabilities and requires full assessment to ascertain this, or if a person might require special provision during police interviewing or detention. In the UK, this would be helpful in identifying those who may require the presence of an Appropriate Adult (i.e. an informed person who accompanies vulnerable individuals and supports them during police interviews). Failure to involve such a person may have serious consequences for trial proceedings (Hayes, 2002). It is also the case that unless someone's behaviour is viewed as somewhat bizarre, or they refer to medication use, possible intellectual disabilities can be easily missed, particularly due to the acquiescence of this group (Clare & Gudjonsson, 1995).

The test is quick to administer (taking under 10 minutes). It has four subtests: background, backwards spelling, puzzle, and clock drawing. The instructions are attached to the record booklet, which means it is not necessary to carry around the manual, and there are no bulky instruments that are required as part of the assessment.

While the HASI has demonstrated adequate validity and reliability, there were some differences noted in correlations between this and other tests for younger (i.e. under 18 years) Aboriginal and Strait Islander males. In its favour, this is a short, simple screen that can be administered by most professionals working in the criminal justice system and is potentially a very useful way to identify people who may have intellectual disabilities. This means that such individuals can proceed to assessment of needs at any point in the criminal justice process. The possible disadvantages are some cultural biases, although this has only been piloted in Australia.

There is other research that examines screening assessments (Mason & Murphy, 2002). The most common forms of screening include the use of an assessment of intellectual functioning. This is not commonly the full version of the WAIS-III, which would be the most reliable and valid of such instruments (McBrien, 2003). Most rely on short forms of the Wechsler Adult Intelligence Scale – Revised (WAIS-R, Wechsler, 1981) or Wechsler Adult Intelligence Scale – 3rd Edition (WAIS-III, Wechsler, 1999), or what is known as the 'Quick Test' (Mason & Murphy, 2002). Other forms of screening also use self-report and assessments of adaptive functioning, although full assessments using tools such as the Vineland Adaptive Behavior Scales (Sparrow et al., 1984) is rare (see Holland et al., 2002; McBrien, 2003).

Some of the difficulties inherent in such screening assessments are the increased numbers of false positives and the possibilities of false negatives (Hayes, 2002). The HASI has been developed to be somewhat overinclusive (greater false positives), in an attempt to ensure that vulnerable people are not missed and continue through the criminal justice process without access to the necessary services (Hayes, 2002). The HASI has also been shown to identify higher numbers of the indigenous population in Australia, which may reflect some cultural biases in the screening (Hayes, 2002). Additionally, the cut-off for intellectual functioning in intellectual assessments is often a full-scale IQ of 75–80 or below, which is above that used for the definition of intellectual disability (American Psychiatric Association, 1994).

The points in the criminal justice process where these screening assessments are likely to have the most utility are outlined below. First, when someone comes into contact with the police as a result of a complaint about their behaviour. The utility of such a screening tool is twofold in this situation. Such screening can help police identify the need for an

Appropriate Adult and it can signal the possibility of diversion from the criminal justice system to appropriate services. The other point at which such an assessment can prove useful is when the person is appearing in court. There are already some services that offer psychiatric nursing staff to identify people with mental health problems at the court stage, and this could also be provided for people with intellectual disabilities. The HASI does not require a nursing professional to complete the screening and therefore this could be done in the UK by the duty court social worker. This does not mean that such screening assessments cannot have utility at other points in the criminal justice process. This is not a service that has routinely been offered previously and there is an argument for the use of such screening in prisons and low-, medium- and high-security health settings for people with mental health problems.

The only way adequately to assess for intellectual disability is use of a valid and reliable assessment of intellectual functioning (e.g. WAIS-III; Wechsler, 1999), an assessment of adaptive functioning (e.g. Vineland Adaptive Behavior Scales; Sparrow et al., 1984) and a good developmental history. Because of restrictions on test use (WAIS-III and Vineland) and the time taken to carry out such an assessment it is important that pragmatic, quick screening tests are developed for use by those in the front line of the criminal justice service. This would allow the police, court officials and prison officers to be able to identify people likely to have intellectual disabilities, allowing them to contact, or refer to, services appropriate to the person's need. Further assessment can then be undertaken to define more adequately each individual's need.

Once this first part of the process is complete, those identified can be diverted to appropriate services if this is judged to be the best course, or can be supported appropriately within the criminal justice process.

3 Assessment in Relation to Criminal Justice Proceedings

After someone has been identified as possibly having intellectual disabilities, one of the requests often made of mental health professionals, principally psychiatrists, but increasingly clinical psychologists, is to provide an assessment and opinion of a person's competence to stand trial (Appelbaum, 1994) or their ability to provide a 'reliable statement' (Beail, 2002).

This is not technically a clinical task, but a legal one (Birgden & Thomson, 1999). However, it has been included because it is now an increasing expectation of health service staff working with people with intellectual disabilities. There are arguments to suggest that this should not necessarily be the sole domain of mental health professionals (Birgden & Thomson, 1999), but in the UK, USA, Australia and New Zealand, this is the usual route followed by those working in the justice system. In the US the issue is one of competency to stand trial (Appelbaum, 1994; Chellsen, 1986; Everington & Dunn, 1995). This is known as fitness to stand trial in Australia and New Zealand (Birgden & Thomson, 1999). In the UK, it is less clear precisely what question is being asked here. As outlined in chapter 6, in England and Wales *mens rea* is required for a person to be deemed fit to face criminal proceedings and involves intent and knowledge of the consequences of the criminal behaviour. Lawyers may also request assessments as to whether witnesses can provide 'reliable statements' (Beail, 2002), understanding of court proceedings, and the like. There may also be requests for mental health professionals to advise on support for witnesses with intellectual disabilities appearing in court, which is partly concerned with ensuring protection of vulnerable witnesses. More occasionally, assessments are requested in relation to alleged offenders' understanding of the caution and advice to police on conducting interviews. This is partly due to problems being faced in court where transcripts of police interviews have highlighted problems with leading questions, failure to recognize acquiescence and problems relating to suggestibility within this population.

There is no standard assessment or battery of assessments to determine competency. Instead, intellectual functioning is usually assessed and various clinical assessments relating to understanding of various aspects of the court proceedings undertaken. In the USA, there has been work on developing a tool – The Competence Assessment for Standing Trial for Defendants with Mental Retardation (CAST-MR; Everington, 1990; Everington & Dunn, 1995).

The test used to determine intellectual capacity is invariably the WAIS-R (Wechsler, 1981) or WAIS-III (Wechsler, 1999). Other assessments used to determine language abilities include the British Picture Vocabulary Scale – 2nd Edition (BPVS-II; Dunn et al., 1997) and Communication Assessment Profile for Adults with Learning Disabilities (CASP; Van der Gaag, 1988). Neither is specifically targeted at a person's competency with respect to legal proceedings, or their ability to give 'reliable statements'. The Gudjonsson Suggestibility Scales (GSS; Gudjonsson, 1997) are now often used in such assessments. While Gudjonsson himself advises that the GSS-I and GSS-II (the two parallel forms of the scale) are suitable for use with people with intellectual disabilities, he does caution against use of the Gudjonsson Compliance Scale (GCS) for people with an IQ below 70 (Gudjonsson, 1997). Beail (2002) has cautioned against the use of the GSS for people with an intellectual disability because of the difficulties in remembering the passage used for the assessment. Beail (2002) suggests that this assessment measures memory problems rather than suggestibility for some of this population.

The difficulty, as outlined above, is that there is no standard procedure or instrument for use with this population. Those assessments developed for different national legal systems may only have utility in their own jurisdiction. Therefore, the assessment undertaken will depend somewhat on the questions asked and the purpose for which the opinion is required.

4 Risk Assessment and Risk Management

In legal and criminological work, risk assessment has been one of the principal areas of development in recent years. The main issue here is that of predicting future offending behaviour for the purposes of disposal in legal proceedings. This process is usually carried out by forensic psychiatrists or psychologists. The main focus for such risk assessments is often the perceived 'dangerousness' of the offender (Turner, 1998), usually relating to offences involving violence. The emphasis is protection of the public from violent and dangerous offenders (see Turner, 1998). Most of the research carried out and tools available are for offenders who do not have an intellectual disability.

The terminology used can be somewhat confusing. Reference is made to risk and dangerousness, and although these are linked, they do have different meanings. It should be noted that risk does not only define the probability of the hazard or target behaviour occurring, but also should encompass the impact this hazard or behaviour might have (Taylor & Halstead, 2001). There is no legal definition of dangerous individuals in the UK law. Dangerousness is partly about propensity to cause harm and can also include a history of inflicting serious harm on others (Turner, 1998). There is an implication that dangerous behaviour can be predicted (Turner, 1998). In law, dangerousness is viewed as an intrinsic, individual, stable and consistent characteristic, which is almost diametrically opposed to the psychological definitions of dangerousness that arise from personality theory. Here, behaviour is seen as a result of complex interactions between individual and environmental factors. This would preclude any definitive prediction of dangerousness within individuals (Turner, 1998).

There are two general ways in which risk assessment is addressed by clinicians working with this population. First, existing tools, not necessarily developed for this population, are used (Taylor & Halstead, 2001). There is no research to either support or refute the assumption that mainstream forensic tools are valid for use with the intellectually disabled population (Turner, 1998). Second, attempts are made to develop specific approaches for this population (Taylor & Halstead, 2001).

Much of mainstream forensic risk assessment is concerned with prediction of future violence. Given that there is research suggesting people with intellectual disabilities are more likely to be involved in non-violent offences (Turner, 1998), it has been suggested that assessment of risk of violence may not be the most pressing need for many of this group who find themselves involved with the criminal justice system (Turner, 1998).

Turner (1998) draws three main conclusions with respect to the prediction of future risk of offending:

- There is persistent tension between legal and medical approaches. Specifically this relates back to the definition of risk, but is further complicated by the fact that it is often medical or health professionals who are involved in assessing risk for legal purposes.
- Clinical assessment may be less effective in assessing risk of re-offending than actuarial methods. However, while actuarial methods are statistically more likely to improve accuracy of prediction, they do not take into account idiosyncratic variables, and the consequences of identification of false negatives is very concerning for individual clinicians.
- The studies available show relatively poor levels of predictive power in the face of continuing refinement of assessment models.

Because there is a lack of actuarial data relating to the intellectually disabled population, and the fact that such methods are often complex and time consuming (Taylor & Halstead, 2001), clinical models and approaches tend to dominate in this field. Organizations and individual clinicians often develop their own systems of risk assessment, based on the available literature, and the population they serve. This can present difficulties in comparison of methods and the development of a more standard approach.

It is acknowledged that risk elimination is not necessarily a realistic goal of risk assessment. Instead, the goal is risk management, which partly involves manipulation of environmental factors and partly involves targeting intervention at dispositional and attitudinal aspects of the individual that might be amenable to change (e.g. mental health difficulties, alcohol use, attitudes to various groups of people). Risk assessment instruments ideally should include clinical and actuarial information. The outcome of the assessment should lead to the development of a management and intervention plan with specific methods of monitoring and evaluating the success of the plan. Two risk assessment instruments will now be considered.

4.1 The Risk Assessment Management and Audit System (RAMAS)

The Risk Assessment Management and Audit System (RAMAS) (O'Rourke et al., 1998/1999; Taylor & Halstead, 2001) provides a framework for clinical risk assessment for this population. It is suitable for use in community, institutional, hospital and research settings, providing a standardized schedule for measuring, monitoring and managing risk (O'Rourke et al. 1998/1999). RAMAS is also considered to be applicable to people with intellectual disabilities (Turner, 1998). RAMAS trainers have trained professionals working in the intellectual disability field in the use of the instrument and do not caution against use in this area. RAMAS is used to assess four areas of risk:

- dangerousness
- mental instability
- self harm/suicide risk
- vulnerability

The process uses a multidisciplinary and interagency approach. It should be integrated into routine practice, and should be agreed by all those involved. The process involves service users and should include routine feedback. The assessment and management plan should be regularly reviewed and audited, and tools for this are included in the resources given when professionals are trained.

The RAMAS cannot be used without its users first receiving training from the group who developed the assessment. Individual professionals are trained, and the training includes the whole instrument with manual, recording sheets and audit system. The RAMAS group will also train in areas where a network is being developed, but this has to fit with their own concept of how the network would be managed, audited and evaluated.

The advantages of such a system is that it includes all aspects of the risk assessment and management process, it is fundamentally multi-professional and takes a team approach. It is firmly based in the research about risk assessment and as such would be considered evidence based. There is some quality assurance built in with the training, and only registered users can provide these assessments. As with any system, it has to be acceptable to all partners in the process, and may not carry the same kind of clout as the Care Program Approach, which is enshrined in statute. Additionally, it includes a measure of vulnerability, which may be particularly relevant to people with intellectual disabilities.

The main disadvantages of the use of RAMAS are as follows. It was developed on individuals using mental health services, and as such it cannot be presumed that it will fulfil exactly the same functions for service users with intellectual disabilities. Also there may be information more pertinent to people with intellectual disability that could be overlooked in the RAMAS process.

4.2 The Taylor and Halstead framework

As mentioned above, the main approach to risk assessment in intellectual disabilities is a clinical one. Taylor and Halstead (2001) provide a framework within which such assessments can be undertaken. They note that this framework offers an approach that is based on theoretical clinical models of offending behaviour, which can be shared by practitioners irrespective of their professional background (Taylor & Halstead, 2001). In the example given in this article, a clinical model of sex offending (Finkelhor, 1986) is used to identify the steps to offending. This is used to produce a risk analysis profile of factors influencing the risk, followed by the formulation of a risk management plan. The risk management plan has two forms, addressing *static* and *dynamic* factors respectively.

This is not a standardized instrument available to use off the shelf, but given some of the difficulties noted above in the risk assessment of individuals with intellectual disabilities, it does provide a potentially valuable framework for risk assessment. It is based on clinical models of offending, and is deemed to be a transparent way of reaching clinically defensible decisions.

5 Assessment of Specific Offending Behaviour

The main purpose of assessing specific offending behaviour is to understand both the behaviour and the context in which it occurs, with the objective of minimizing its reoccurrence (Clare & Murphy, 1998b). Assessment may here involve functional analysis in order to formulate a treatment plan. Goals may be set, and treatment evaluated against a measured behavioural baseline (Lindsay, 2002b; Bowden, 1994).

Many of the current assessment and treatment approaches in mainstream forensic settings are based on cognitive-behavioural models of offending. The assessment methods here include self-report, detailed history taking, use of informants and monitoring of target behaviours, depending on the situation of the client; this could involve self-monitoring or observation and monitoring by staff. Difficulties with some of these approaches for those with intellectual disabilities include

- memory difficulties (Clare & Gudjonsson, 1993), which may affect the person's ability to recall events and give clear information on the sequence of events, although there are interviewing techniques that can assist here (Milne & Bull, 1999);
- acquiescence and suggestibility (Clare & Gudjonsson, 1993; Clare & Gudjonsson, 1995; Gudjonsson, 1997), which refers to the greater likelihood of individuals with intellectual disabilities answering closed questions in the affirmative, regardless of content, and the increased likelihood that individuals will yield to negative pressure when giving information;
- reading difficulties (Clare, 1993; Clare & Murphy, 1998a), because many of the self-report questionnaires are intended for the clients to read and complete independently;
- understanding of complex language and concepts (Clare, 1993; Lindsay, 2002b).

These difficulties have led to development of various assessment tools for use specifically with people with intellectual disabilities. The psychometric properties of most of these tools have yet to be established, and further work is required in this area. The remainder of this section will examine the developments for people with intellectual disabilities in three areas of offending: sex offending, anger management and fire raising.

5.1 Sex offending

The main areas of assessment that require to be addressed here are

- history and background;
- sexual interest/arousal (Bowden, 1994; Lindsay, 2002b; Glasgow et al., 2003);
- cognitions/cognitive distortions/attitudes and thinking (Bowden, 1994; Broxholme & Lindsay, 2003);
- sexual knowledge (Clare, 1993; Bowden, 1994);
- sociosexual behaviour (Clare, 1993; Bowden, 1994);
- interpersonal and social skills (Clare, 1993);
- mental state (Bowden, 1994).

The issue of 'counterfeit deviance' is raised (see Bowden, 1994). This refers to behaviour that apparently has a sexual element, but the basis for this may not be related to problems with arousal or attitudes specific to sexual offending. For example, lack of privacy in the living situation, side effects of medication, and a lack of understanding about how to develop appropriate relationships, due to poor education or lack of ordinary opportunities. There are few specific assessments available for use, and of those outlined below, some are still in the process of development.

Glasgow and his associates (Glasgow et al., 2003) are developing an 'Affinity' tool that could begin to answer questions relating to sexual interest. Specifically the Affinity tool may be relevant in identifying sexual interest in age-appropriate people and where offending behaviour may reflect paedophile interest rather than social or psychological deficits. This assessment has two main parts: a ranking task and a rating task, and is presented using computer technology. The ranking task uses pictures of males and females in different age groups (young, pre-adolescent, adolescent and adult). The participant is asked to sort them according to attractiveness and unattractiveness, and rank them from most to least attractive and most to least unattractive (see Glasgow et al., 2003). The rating task presents the participant with 56 pictures of males and females in the different age categories as described. Each picture is rated by the participant according to sexual attractiveness. Two things are measured here: on task latency (how long it takes the participant to make a decision about the sexual attractiveness of the person in the picture), and post-task latency (the time taken for the participant to request the next picture). The post-task latency is a covert measure. There is some evidence to suggest that time spent looking at an individual is related to the sexual interest in that individual (see Glasgow et al., 2003).

This assessment has only been used in single cases with small numbers of people. It has been used with males with mild intellectual disabilities who offend and with non-offending men and women who do not have intellectual disabilities. Thirty individuals have completed parts of the procedure, and 14 have completed the entire assessment.

The problems with using such an approach include ethical issues of individuals being unaware of the true nature of the task, although Glasgow et al. (2003) argue that there is a balancing act to be done here between the individual's target behaviour and the risk this poses. Additionally, this may be too complex a task for many people with intellectual disabilities to understand, and there may be problems with psychomotor skills and unfamiliarity with the computer technology (Glasgow et al., 2003). Therefore, the post-task latency could be measuring interest or it could be an indication of forgetting the instructions. Further study of generalizability is required and to establish indications and contra-indications to this instrument's use (Glasgow et al., 2003).

There are a number of assessment tools that can be used to measure sexual knowledge. These include the Socio-Sexual Knowledge and Attitudes Tool – Revised (SSKAT-R; Griffiths & Lunsky, 2003). There are various non-standardized packages that can be used for individual assessment, such as *Sex and the 3Rs: Rights, Risks and Responsibilities* (McCarthy & Thompson, 1998).

None of these tools is specifically designed for people who offend, but they are designed for use with people with intellectual disabilities. The main difficulty of all of these is that they do not necessarily provide a means of identifying attitudes consistent with offending, but they may be useful with respect to identifying aspects of 'counterfeit deviance' (Bowden, 1994).

With respect to cognitive distortions and attitudes consistent with offending, see the Questionnaire on Attitudes Consistent with Sexual Offending (QACSO) (Broxholme & Lindsay, 2003). The contents of this questionnaire are based on the literature relating to sex offenders who do not have intellectual disabilities. There are 92 items and six subsections:

- rape and attitudes to women
- voyeurism
- exhibitionism
- dating abuse
- homosexual assault
- paedophilia

In the preliminary evaluation of this instrument, it was shown to discriminate significantly sex offenders with intellectual disability from non-offenders (Broxholme & Lindsay, 2003). It is suggested that questions indicating particular cognitive distortions could identify and lead the intervention offered. However, it is acknowledged that for some of the questions lack of knowledge may be a factor as well as attitudes consistent with offending, and the sample is not overly representative (Broxholme & Lindsay, 2003). It is also the case that the group of offenders with intellectual disabilities had IQ measures of between 50 and 80. As outlined in chapter 5, this may have the effect of including people who do not meet the criteria for intellectual disability (see ch. 6 in this volume). No information has been given on the adaptive functioning of the participants, or indeed whether there was a developmental history of impairments in intellectual and social functioning. Nevertheless, this is a promising development that requires further testing and refinement with larger groups.

5.2 Violent and aggressive offending

There is mixed evidence relating to the prevalence of violent offending by people with intellectual disabilities (Holland et al., 2002; Murphy, 2000). The prevalence depends on population and setting, with the highest prevalence noted in more restricted and specialist settings (Taylor et al., 2002a; Taylor, 2002). Though the literature in the intellectual disability field is sparse, some work has been carried out examining use of anger management approaches with this population (e.g. Black et al., 1997; Walker & Cheseldine, 1997; Benson & Ivins, 1992). This work has not necessarily been targeted at people with intellectual disabilities who offend or are at risk of offending, although Black et al.'s work refers specifically to secure settings.

Because of the noted links between anger and aggression (Novaco, 1994), and the success of use of cognitive-behavioural approaches to anger problems in other groups (Beck & Fernandez, 1998), this approach is being developed for use with the population of people with intellectual disabilities and those who offend or are at risk of offending. Information is limited regarding the success of such approaches to populations with more complex needs, such as those with intellectual disabilities (Taylor et al., 2002a). There are difficulties in addressing the recognition of emotion in people with intellectual disabilities, as very little is known about their emotional life. Preliminary assessment needs to address what a person's understanding of emotion is, drawing on the observation that people with intellectual disabilities can recognize and identify their own emotions relatively reliably and consistently (Stenfert Kroese, 1997).

There are no specific standardized assessments for this population; instead, the main focus is on clinical assessment, which will help form a baseline against which changes post-treatment can be measured. Self-report is one of the main methods used, and developing population-specific assessments or adapting what is available can be appropriately used with this population (Kroese, 1997). Some of the types of assessments used include, usually adapted, provocation inventories (Walker & Cheseldine, 1997; Taylor et al., 2002a). Provocation inventories provide scenarios that could be described as provoking; individuals are then asked to rate how provoking these situations would be for them (e.g how angry they might feel). Self-report anger inventories have also been used (Benson & Ivins, 1992; Rose & West, 1999) and an anger management pack that included use of daily diaries to monitor feelings of anger is available (Benson, 1992). Staff or carer reports of aggression have also been employed (Rose & West, 1999; Taylor et al., 2002a). However, apart from the Taylor et al. (2002a) study, none focuses specifically on offenders with intellectual disabilities.

5.3 Fire raising

Though there has been little in the area on the assessment and treatment of people with intellectual disabilities who set fires, Taylor et al. (2002b) describe possible approaches to this group. The two main assessments used here are the Fire Assessment Schedule or Fire-Setting Assessment Schedule (FSAS) (Clare & Murphy, 1998b; Taylor et al., 2002b) and the Fire Interest Rating Scale (FIRS) (Clare & Murphy, 1998b; Taylor et al., 2002b). Both are self-report instruments. The FAS/FSAS is a structured interview schedule that looks at a person's view of the antecedents and consequences of their fire setting. It is reported to have reasonable test–retest reliability. The FIRS asks individuals to rate the excitement they believe they would experience in a variety of fire-related situations.

6 Assessment and Mental Health

The wider issues involved in assessing the mental health of people with intellectual disabilities are considered in chapters 4 and 12. Mental health issues are also involved in considering those who offend or are alleged to have offended. These need to be taken into account when providing a service to this population. Assessment of the individual's mental health status will make an important contribution to the overall assessment of the person's needs.

In addition, there is an over-representation of people with autistic spectrum disorder in the population of people with intellectual disabilities (see O'Brien, 2002). Therefore, this should also form part of the collection of information on background and history. Some individuals, including those with Asperger syndrome, will come into contact with the criminal justice system and indeed a proportion will receive custodial sentences. As with possible mental health difficulties, it is essential that where there is an indication of an autistic spectrum disorder, a full assessment is undertaken in line with agreed diagnostic criteria.

7 Assessment and Gender

With respect to gender, people with intellectual disabilities who offend show a very similar division to those without intellectual disabilities. Males clearly predominate over females with estimates in a recent review varying from 83–96% of offenders with intellectual disabilities being male (Simpson & Hogg, 2001). In Scotland in 1994 in the general population, 86% of all offenders and alleged offenders charged were male, though some offences were higher for women, (e.g. *indecency*, principally prostitution) (Anderson & Leitch, 1994). Clearly, the influence of gender is strikingly similar for offenders with intellectual disabilities as for the general population.

The issues arising for women with intellectual disabilities who offend or are alleged to have offended require particular attention. Because they are a minority, there is far less recognition of their needs and specific assessment of these needs is a pressing concern. The consequences of inadequate assessment such as placement in services with men increases their vulnerability. They are also likely to receive more in the way of pharmacological interventions (Holland et al., 2002), and their specific needs should be addressed.

8 Conclusions

The requirements of assessment for people with intellectual disabilities who have offended or are at risk of offending have features that differ in important respects from other forms of assessment. The external frame of reference (i.e. the processes involved in the criminal justice system) imposes changing requirements for assessment at its different stages. These requirements are extrinsic to typical community health and social services. While risk assessment is not unique to people in contact with the criminal justice system, assessments of the risk of behaviour recurring also points towards re-engagement with this system. Put differently, the behaviour is not such that it can and will only be dealt with in the context of social or health service settings.

As this chapter indicates, progress has been made in developing assessment approaches that affect the path taken by an individual in contact with the criminal justice system. Overall, however, there is a lack of assessment instruments for use with this population. Many of the developments being undertaken are still in the early stages, with very few published assessments with adequate reliability and validity or indeed population norms. However, the guiding community-oriented policies noted at the start of this chapter will continue to exert pressures that should ensure progress will continue to be made, enabling people with intellectual disabilities who offend or are alleged to have offended to take their place in the community, wherever feasible.

REFERENCES

Anderson, S. & Leitch, S. (1994) *Scottish Crime Survey: First results.* Edinburgh: Scottish Office.

American Psychiatric Association (1994) *Diagnostic and Statistical Manual of Mental Disorders 4th Edition.* Washington, DC: American Psychiatric Association.

Appelbaum, K. L. (1994) Assessment of criminal-justice-related competencies in defendants with mental retardation. *Journal of Psychiatry and Law,* 22, 311–327.

Beail, N. (2002) Interrogative suggestibility, memory and intellectual disability. *Journal of Applied Research in Intellectual Disabilities,* 15, 129–137.

Beck, R. & Fernandez, E. (1998) Cognitive-behavioral therapy in the treatment of anger: A metaanalysis. *Cognitive Therapy and Research,* 22, 63–74.

Benson, B. A. (1992) Teaching anger management to persons with mental retardation. Worthington, OH: International Diagnostic Systems.

Benson, B. A. & Ivins, J. (1992) Anger, depression & self-concept in adults with mental retardation. *Journal of Intellectual Disability Research,* 36, 169–175.

Birgden, A. & Thomson, D. M. (1999) The assessment of fitness to stand trial for defendants with an intellectual disability: A proposed assessment method involving mental health professionals and lawyers. *Psychiatry, Psychology and Law,* 6, 207–214.

Black, L., Cullen, C. & Novaco, R. W. (1997) Anger assessment for people with mild learning disabilities in secure settings. In B. Stenfert Kroese, D. Dagnan & K. Loumidis (eds.), *Cognitive-Behavioural Therapy for People with Learning Disabilities.* London: Routledge, pp. 33–52.

Bowden, K. (1994) 'No Control of Penis or Brain?' Key questions in the assessment of sex offenders with a learning difficulty. *Journal of Sexual Aggression,* 1, 57–63.

Broxholme, S. L. & Lindsay, W. R. (2003) Development and preliminary evaluation of a questionnaire on cognitions related to sex offending for use with individuals who have mild intellectual disabilities. *Journal of Intellectual Disability Research,* 47, 472–482.

Chellsen, J. A. (1986) Trail competency among mentally retarded offenders: Assessment techniques and related considerations. *Journal of Psychiatry and Law,* 14, 177–185.

Clare, I. C. H. (1993) Issues in the assessment and treatment of male sex offenders with mild learning disabilities. *Sexual and Marital Therapy,* 8, 167–180.

Clare, I. C. H. & Gudjonsson, G. H. (1993) Interrogative suggestibility, confabulation, and acquiescence in people with mild learning disabilities (mental handicap): Implications for reliability during police interviews. *British Journal of Clinical Psychology,* 32, 295–301.

Clare, I. C. H. & Gudjonsson, G. H. (1995) The vulnerability of suspects with intellectual disabilities during police interviews: A review and experimental study of decision making. *Mental Handicap Research,* 2, 110–128.

Clare, I. C. H. & Murphy, G. H. (1998a) The vulnerability of suspects with intellectual disabilities during police interviews: A review and experimental study of decision making. *Mental Handicap Research*, 8, 110–128.

Clare, I. C. H. & Murphy, G. H. (1998b) Working with offenders or alleged offenders with intellectual disabilities. In E. Emerson, C. Hatton, J. Bromley & A. Caine (eds.), *Clinical Psychology and People with Intellectual Disabilities*. Chichester: Wiley, pp. 154–176.

Dunn, L. M., Dunn, L. M., Whetton, C. & Burley, J. (1997) *British Picture Vocabulary Scale: 2nd Edition (BPVS-II)*. Windsor: NFER-Nelson.

Everington, C. T. (1990) The competence assessment for standing trial for defendants with mental retardation (CAST-MR): A validation study. *Criminal Justice and Behavior*, 17, 147–168.

Everington, C. T. & Dunn, C. (1995) A second validation study of the competence assessment for standing trial for defendants with mental retardation (CAST-MR). *Criminal Justice and Behavior*, 22, 44–59.

Finkelhor, D. (1986) *A Sourcebook on Child Sexual Abuse*. London: Sage.

Glasgow, D. V., Osborne, A. & Croxen, J. (2003) An assessment tool for investigating paedophile sexual interest using viewing time: An application of single case methodology. *British Journal of Learning Disabilities*, 31, 96–102.

Griffiths, D. M. & Lunsky, Y. (2003) *Socio-sexual Knowledge and Attitudes Assessment Tool: Revised*. Woodale, IL: Stoelting.

Gudjonsson, G. H. (1997) *The Gudjonsson Suggestibility Scales Manual*. Hove: Psychology Press.

Hayes, S. C. (2000) *Hayes Ability Screening Index Manual*. Sydney: University of Sydney.

Hayes, S. C. (2002) Early intervention or early incarceration? Using a screening test for intellectual disability in the criminal justice system. *Journal of Applied Research in Intellectual Disabilities*, 15, 120–128.

Holland, T., Clare, I. C. H. & Mukhopadhyay, T. (2002) Prevalence of 'criminal offending' by men and women with intellectual disability and the characteristics of 'offenders': Implications for research and service development. *Journal of Intellectual Disability Research*, 46, 6–20.

Kroese, B. (1997) Cognitive-behaviour therapy for people with learning disabilities: Conceptual and contextual issues. In B. Kroese, D. Dagnan & K. Loumidis (eds.), *Cognitive-Behavioural Therapy for People with Learning Disabilities*. London: Routledge, pp. 1–15.

Lindsay, W. R. (2002a) Integration of recent reviews on offenders with intellectual disabilities. *Journal of Applied Research in Intellectual Disabilities*, 15, 111–119.

Lindsay, W. R. (2002b) Research and literature on sex offenders with intellectual and developmental disabilities. *Journal of Intellectual Disability Research*, 46, 74–85.

Lindsay, W. R. & MacLeod, F. (2001) A review of forensic learning disability research. *British Journal of Forensic Practice*, 3, 4–10.

Lyall, I., Holland, A. J. & Collins, S. (1995) Offending by adults with learning disabilities: Identifying need in one health district. *Mental Handicap Research*, 8, 99–109.

Mason, J. & Murphy, G. (2002) People with an intellectual disability in the criminal justice system: Developing an assessment tool for measuring prevalence. *British Journal of Clinical Psychology*, 41, 315–320.

McBrien, J. (2003) The Intellectually disabled offender: Methodological problems in identification. *Journal of Applied Research in Intellectual Disabilities*, 16, 95–105.

McCarthy, M. & Thompson, D. (1998) *Sex and the 3Rs: Rights, Risks and Responsibilities* (2nd ed.). Brighton: Pavilion.

Milne, R. & Bull, R. (1999) *Investigative Interviewing: Psychology and Practice*. Chichester: Wiley.

Murphy, G. (2000) Policy and service development trends: Forensic mental health and social care services. *Tizard Learning Disability Review*, 5, 32–35.

Novaco, R. W. (1994) Anger as a risk factor for violence amongst the mentally disordered. In J. Monahan & H. J. Steadman (eds.), *Violence and Mental Disorder: Developments in Risk Assessment*. Chicago, IL: University of Chicago Press, pp. 320–338.

O'Brien, G. (2002) Dual Diagnosis in offenders with intellectual disability: Setting research priorities: A review of research findings concerning psychiatric disorder (excluding personality disorder) among offenders with intellectual disability. *Journal of Intellectual Disability Research*, **46** (supplement 1), 21–30.

O'Rourke, M., Hammond, S., Smith, S. & Davies, J. (1998/1999) *Risk Assessment, Management and Audit System: Professional Manual*. Guildford: Forensic Clinical Psychology Unit.

Rose, J. & West, C. (1999) Assessment of anger in people with intellectual disabilities. *Journal of Applied Research in Intellectual Disabilities*, **12**, 211–224.

Simpson, M. K. & Hogg, J. (2001) Patterns of offending among people with intellectual disability: A systematic review. Part 2: Predisposing factors. *Journal of Intellectual Disability Research*, **45**, 397–406.

Sparrow, S. S., Balla, D. A. & Cicchetti, D. V. (1984) *Vineland Adaptive Behavior Scales: Interview Edition, Survey Form Manual*. Minnesota: American Guidance Service.

Stenfert Kroese, B. (1997) Cognitive-behaviour therapy for people with learning disabilities: Conceptual and contextual issues. In B. Stenfert Kroese, D. Dagnan & K. Loumidis (eds.), *Cognitive-Behavioural Therapy for People with Learning Disabilities*. London: Routledge, pp. 1–15.

Taylor, J. L. (2002) A review of the assessment and treatment of anger and aggression in offenders with intellectual disability. *Journal of Intellectual Disability Research*, **46**, 57–73.

Taylor, J. L. & Halstead, S. (2001) Clinical Risk Assessment for people with learning disabilities who offend. *British Journal of Forensic Practice*, **3**, 22–32.

Taylor, J. L., Novaco, R. W., Gillmer, B. & Thorne, I. (2002a) Cognitive-behavioural treatment of anger intensity among offenders with intellectual disabilities. *Journal of Applied Research in Intellectual Disabilities*, **15**, 151–165.

Taylor J. L., Thorne, I., Robertson, A. & Avery, G. (2002b) Evaluation of a group intervention for convicted arsonists with mild and borderline intellectual disabilities. *Criminal Behaviour and Mental Health*, **12**, 282–293.

Turner, S. (1998) *The Assessment of Risk and Dangerousness as Applied to People with Learning Disabilities Considered at Risk of Offending*. Part 1: *Literature Review*. Manchester, UK: Hester Adrian Research Centre, University of Manchester.

Van der Gaag, A. (1988) *The Communication Assessment Profile for Adults with a Mental Handicap*. Glasgow: Speech Profiles.

Walker, T. & Cheseldine, S. (1997) Towards outcome measurements: Monitoring effectiveness of anger management and assertiveness training in a group setting. *British Journal of Learning Disabilities*, **25**, 134–137.

Wechsler, D. (1981) *Wechsler Adult Intelligence Scale: Revised*. New York: Psychological Corporation.

Wechsler, D. (1999) *Wechsler Adult Intelligence Scale (UK) 3rd Edition*. London: Psychological Corporation.

CHAPTER 15

The assessment of dementia in people with intellectual disabilities: key assessment instruments

Sunny Kalsy and Chris Oliver

1 Introduction

The older population of persons with intellectual disabilities has risen dramatically over recent years, and as individuals age they are at risk of developing physical and mental health problems (Thorpe et al., 2001). As reviewed in chapter 7, this has led to significant clinical and research interest in developing knowledge about how persons with intellectual disabilities age and specifically, how they may present with dementia.

The diagnosis of dementia in persons with intellectual disabilities presents a significant clinical challenge, which increases with the degree of pre-existing intellectual disability (Oliver, 1999). There are psychological, health and social issues that can impede accurate diagnosis and thus promote the need for objective and specific psychological assessment. There are a number of strategies that might be adopted with regard to the assessment of dementia in persons with intellectual disabilities (Oliver, 1999). Clinically, the most common strategy is to attempt to review past assessments that have known psychometric properties and repeat the assessment. This retrospective strategy which entails waiting for individuals to present with cognitive or behavioural change that might indicate dementia has difficulties related to the properties of tests available for repeat assessment, including a lack of appraisal of rate of change, few dementia-relevant items and the presence of floor effects (Oliver, 1999). For these reasons there have been repeated calls for a prospective strategy which ensures that adults with intellectual disabilities who are at high risk for developing dementia have a baseline assessment as they approach the high-risk age band (Burt & Aylward, 1999). In practice, this strategy probably applies only to adults who have Down syndrome as the risk of dementia in others who have an intellectual disability is similar to that in the general population (Burt et al., 1998). If a prospective strategy is adopted, then a decision needs to be taken regarding whether direct performance-based assessment is undertaken or informant-based measures are used. Consideration also needs to be given as to whether measures that are used for the general population are employed or whether adapted measures developed in the last two decades have sufficiently robust psychometric properties to be of use. The prospective strategy entails a proactive approach by service providers with the accompanying cost and labour resources. There will also be the need to rule out other potential causes that might underlie any change and the problem of floor effects is still evident. In order to offset some of the resource issues it is tempting to employ informant-based measures alone. However, the issue of inter-rater reliability combined with the change in informants over time may lead to the collection of data that are of poor quality. Given these concerns, there is a strong argument for a prospective strategy that uses neuropsychological tests alongside measures of behavioural deficits that might be indicative of dementia. If this strategy is not adopted, then referrals are likely to be made at a late stage when dementia may be advanced, there is little time for future service planning and when residential resources may have been unsupported, thus making placement break-down more likely.

In addition to the above issues, there is no currently accepted 'gold standard' for a 'true' diagnosis for Alzheimer disease among persons with intellectual disabilities, including Down syndrome (Holland et al., 1998). If it is suspected, a thorough evaluation procedure sufficient to exclude any other possible conditions or disorders together with an assessment of cognitive functioning is strongly recommended (Aylward et al., 1997). This is called for, as the diagnosis of dementia using internationally agreed criteria (e.g. DSM-IV; American Psychiatric Association, 1994; and ICD-10; World Health Organization, 1992) requires evidence of deterioration in memory and decline in one other area of cognitive functioning in association with changes in personality and/or behaviour.

The following assessment instruments have been selected to allow for the detection of decline in the functional areas required by such dementia diagnostic criteria. Preference was given to those instruments employed with persons with intellectual disabilities and which had demonstrated reliability, on samples of persons with and/or without intellectual disabilities. Issues relating to instrument availability were also considered, as was evidence that the instruments had been employed in clinical/service settings and/or relevant research studies. The instruments selected are categorized from the perspective of a clinician with limited resources working with persons with intellectual disabilities, and refer to the combined approach for the assessment of dementia using diagnostic, informant-based and neuropsychological assessments. The recommendation is that at least one assessment from each category is selected in order to make baseline and longitudinal assessments of decline and dementia in persons with intellectual disabilities.

2 Diagnostic Instruments

The diagnostic criteria for dementia, and particularly the later stages of dementia, indicate that behavioural change will continue to be evident after cognitive decline. Thus the assessment of dementia in adults with intellectual disabilities should focus on both cognitive and behavioural change. The following instruments have been designed to evaluate the specific behavioural and cognitive deficits associated with dementia on a direct-performance and informant-rated basis.

2.1 The Cambridge Cognitive Examination (CAMCOG) part of the Cambridge Examination for Mental Disorders of the Elderly – Revised. (CAMDEX-R; Roth et al., 1986; Roth et al., 1998)

The Cambridge Examination for Mental Disorders of the Elderly (CAMDEX) is a diagnostic assessment that provides a means to identify dementia and to differentiate it from other common disorders and the normal processes of ageing developed for persons without intellectual disabilities to be made available in a single standardized interview and assessment (Roth et al., 1986). The CAMDEX-R is the revised and updated version of the CAMDEX (Roth et al., 1998) enabling a clinical diagnosis of dementia to be made on the basis of internationally agreed criteria (e.g. DSM-IV; American Psychiatric Association, 1994; and ICD-10; World Health Organization, 1992). Within the CAMDEX and CAMDEX-R is the Cambridge Cognitive Examination (CAMCOG), which is a concise group of neuropsychological tests covering all areas of cognitive function that characteristically decline with the onset of dementia. The Mini-Mental State Examination (Folstein et al., 1975) is also incorporated in the CAMCOG and can be used to obtain a global estimate of stability.

Data are collected within the CAMDEX-R through structured clinical interview of an informant supplying systematic information about the presenting disorder, past and family history, present state and history. The CAMCOG is administered by a qualified clinician, defined by the test publishers as a psychiatrist, medic, psychologist, geriatrician, epidemiologist or other mental health professional working within psychogeriatrics, directly with the person being assessed using verbal and visual stimulus items. These items relate to subscales for orientation, language, memory, praxis, attention/calculation, abstract thinking and perception, thus giving subscales scores and a total score. It has been shown in a general elderly population sample that the CAMCOG total and subscales scores significantly differentiate persons with minimal and mild dementia from those without (Huppert et al., 1995). Furthermore, the instrument has been used in clinical, population-based, neuropsychological, neuro-pathological and neuroimaging studies (Hon et al., 1999). The inter-rater reliability of the CAMDEX-R in clinical samples ranged from 0.83 to 1.00 and test–retest reliability of the CAMCOG was reported as $r = .86$ (Roth et al., 1998).

While the instrument has not as yet been validated for persons with intellectual disabilities, with minor modifications, the CAMDEX-R and CAMCOG have indicated promising results in a British sample of adults with Down syndrome (Holland et al., 1998; Holland et al., 2000; Hon et al., 1999). It was concluded that whereas the modified CAMCOG was useful to assess areas of cognitive function known to decline with dementia in persons with Down syndrome, persons with pre-existing severe intellectual disability, severe sensory impairments and/or already advanced dementia may not be able to score above the 'floor level' of the test (Hon et al., 1999). Furthermore, the modified CAMDEX and CAMCOG have not been validated for use with persons with an intellectual disability, nor validated to permit a clinical differentiation among various types of dementias (Holland et al., 1998). Additionally, studies considering the early detection of dementia in persons without intellectual disabilities have suggested that CAMCOG scores are affected by age, hearing and visual deficits (e.g. decreased visual acuity and contrast sensitivity due to cataracts in addition to dementia) (Blessed et al., 1991; Hartman, 2000).

2.2 Severe Impairment Battery (SIB; Saxton et al., 1993)

The Severe Impairment Battery (SIB) was developed to assess a range of cognitive functions in persons who are too impaired to complete standard neuropsychological tests, specifically the elderly with severe dementia (Saxton et al., 1993). It gathers direct performance-based data on a wide variety of low-level tasks that take into account the specific behavioural and cognitive deficits associated with severe dementia, thereby enhancing understanding of the disease process and providing clinical information regarding the later stages of dementia. It is psychometrically reliable (inter-rater reliability $r = .99$, test–retest reliability $r = .90$ and construct validity $r = .76$), allows for repeated assessments and each subscale yields scores that are downward extensions of instruments used to assess mild to moderate dementia (Saxton et al., 1993; Witts & Elders, 1998). The six major subscales are attention, orientation, language, memory, visuospatial ability and construction and there are brief evaluations of praxis, social interaction and orienting to name. The SIB is brief, taking approximately 20 minutes to administer and is composed of simple one-step commands that are presented in conjunction with gestural cues, thus allowing for non-verbal and partially correct responses (Saxton et al., 1993). The instrument has been designed for use by chartered psychologists and those eligible for chartered psychologist status, qualified psychiatrists, qualified occupational therapists and other clinicians involved with the assessment of elderly persons with dementia.

Although not specifically designed for persons with intellectual disabilities, the SIB is appropriate for individuals who are functioning at a very low cognitive level. It has been used with a British sample of adults with Down syndrome, obtaining good test–retest reliability ($r = .89$) and the authors found that in general terms, the SIB was suitable for longitudinal assessments of deterioration in cognitive functioning associated with dementia in adults with Down syndrome (Witts & Elders, 1998).

With regard to instrument limitations with persons with intellectual disabilities, Witts and Elders (1998) noted specific difficulties relating to item responses; for example, where the failure to read aloud a printed message meant that the participant automatically failed on three successive items. Furthermore, given that the instrument has been designed for persons with severe-impairments and dementia, it may not extend high enough in task difficulty for more able persons with intellectual disabilities.

3 Direct Performance-Based Neuropsychological Assessments

The need for assessments with robust psychometric properties that can document dementia-associated change in persons with intellectual disabilities is becoming more evident as research and clinical service agendas evolve. However, the most significant problem for the assessment of specific neuropsychological deficits associated with dementia are the variability of intellectual disability and the problems associated with administering neuropsychological tests to those with severe or profound intellectual disability who may not understand verbal instructions (Aylward et al., 1997; Oliver, 1999). Furthermore, there is the issue of poor performances on neuropsychological tests that might indicate dementia, which might easily be attributable to intellectual disability. The clear implication is that sequential testing is necessary in order to identify decline in an individual from a previous baseline by the administration of standardized neuropsychological tests that assess memory, learning, orientation, language and visuospatial perception. Instruments employed for assessing dementia in the general population may not be suitable for individuals with intellectual disabilities, which has prompted the need to develop measures that are both specific and sensitive enough to assess cognitive decline in persons with pre-existing intellectual impairments. However, there are few tests that have sufficient normative data and have had validity evaluated as studies that have addressed cognitive function have all used different methods to assess memory, learning and orientation in persons with intellectual disabilities (Oliver, 1999). While this has to some extent enhanced the validity of the finding that memory is compromised, it also means that there are very limited normative data for a small number of tests.

3.1 DYSPRAXIA scale for adults with Down Syndrome (Dalton & Fedor, 1997, 1998)

Dyspraxia describes a partial loss of ability to perform purposeful or skilled motor acts in the absences of paralysis, sensory loss, abnormal posture or tone, abnormal involuntary movements, lack of coordination, poor comprehension or inattention (Lohr & Wisniewski, 1987). The purpose of the DYSPRAXIA scale is to provide a research tool for the evaluation of simple sequences of movements without requiring a 'normal' level of verbal comprehension or communication skills in persons with intellectual disabilities (Dalton & Fedor, 1997, 1998). These could be expected to deteriorate with the onset and progress of dementia among persons with mild to profound levels of intellectual disabilities who are suspected of presenting with dementia. It is a three-part, 62-item performance test, with some items adapted from the Western Aphasia Battery (Kertesz, 1982) and the Video-recorded Home Behavioural Assessment (Crapper-McLachlan et al., 1991), while other items were included that were judged to be appropriate for persons with intellectual disabilities with low skill levels in language and communication (Dalton, 1992; Dalton & Fedor, 1998).

Data are collected by the direct assessment and observation of the individual by one examiner. The assessment taps the abilities of the individual to perform simple short sequences of highly practised voluntary movements (e.g. walking, clapping hands, using a spoon, etc.) that are involved in the daily living skills. However, it does not attempt to measure language and communication skills. The authors report good test–retest reliability ($r = .96$), item-by-item reliability ($\alpha = .97$) predictive and face validity but noted that validity has not been established against neuropathological diagnoses (Dalton & Fedor, 1998). Furthermore, the instrument has an objective scoring system for coding responses and a wide range of scores, thus allowing movement over time and avoiding floor effects. It has been employed in research with community populations of people with intellectual disabilities by skilled examiners who have undergone video-training by experienced practitioners. An abbreviated version of the measure is currently being evaluated as a primary outcome measure in an international multi-centre trial of vitamin E in older persons with Down syndrome (Dalton et al., 2001).

With regard to instrument limitations, the authors note that the instrument is not a speed test but requires video-recordings of test performances to verify within-person response definitions and accurately to document deterioration of function, particularly given that there are no standardized tests for the analysis of voluntary movements (Dalton & Fedor, 1997, 1998). It can take between 20 minutes to 1 hour to complete the assessment, so test fatigue is a concern.

3.2 Dalton/McMurray Visual Memory Test: Delayed Matching to Sample Cognitive Test (Dalton, 1995)

The Visual Memory Test: Delayed Matching to Sample Cognitive Test is a computerized research instrument that assesses visual recognition memory ability in persons with Down syndrome who are at risk of developing dementia of the Alzheimer type (Dalton, 1995). The instrument is intended to provide a reliable and valid indicator of impairment associated with dementia and contributes information towards a diagnostic evaluation of individuals suspected of suffering from possible or probable Alzheimer disease. The test consists of two learning tests and two memory tests employing computer presentation of software-generated stimulus items requiring the individual to match these correctly by touching the special touch-sensitive screen, immediately and after a predetermined delay (Dalton, 1995). An individual's performance is compared against a series of standardized norms generated from a reasonably large North American sample of adults with Down syndrome, of which there are two sets, home (i.e. community) settings and institutional settings (Dalton, 1995). Data are collected through the direct assessment and observation of the individual by an examiner who has been trained in running the software and administering the tests. The employment of match-to-sample training procedures ensures that the individual is able to understand and perform the task before memory is assessed, and the information generated by the tests describes the memory functions associated with dementia among persons with intellectual disabilities (Dalton, 1995). The instrument has demonstrated its usefulness in longitudinal follow-up studies of dementia in persons with Down syndrome, up to a follow-up period of 18 years, and has a low floor with a reasonably high ceiling to maximize sensitivity (Dalton, 1995).

The measure has been validated against post-mortem neuropathological findings of Alzheimer disease in persons with Down syndrome (Dalton & Crapper-McLachlan, 1984) and memory scores indicating impairment can be observed more than three years before focal neurological signs of Alzheimer disease are detected (Dalton & Wisniewski, 1990). The tests have routinely yielded highly reproducible results and good test–retest as well as inter-rater reliability (Pearson $r = .90$) and earlier studies have indicated that test performances were not correlated to length of institutionalization or level of intellectual disability (Dalton & Crapper-McLachlan, 1984).

With regard to instrument limitations, the manual states a level of language and communication skills at about the two-year 'mental age' level is required for assessed individuals (Dalton, 1995). Furthermore, the test is not linked to any developmental theory nor any theories of memory and the experience of the authors indicated that a significant proportion of individuals with Down syndrome over the age of 40 would be unable to complete this test, noting that the measure could be 'cumbersome, requires complex equipment including a touch-sensitive screen and [was] relatively difficult to administer' (Dalton, 2001, personal communication).

3.3 The Rivermead Behavioural Memory Test (RBMT; Wilson et al., 1985, 1991)

The Rivermead Behavioural Memory Test (RBMT) was developed in order to assess the real-life memory capacities of children and adults who had sustained brain damage, but not intellectual disabilities. Its 12 subtests were designed as analogues of everyday memory situations; for example, recalling a short news-report, remembering a person's name, and so on (see Wilson et al., 1985, 1989). Two scores are available, a screening score based on a pass/fail grading of each item and a more detailed profile score. The screening score offers a simple way of estimating whether an individual is likely to have everyday memory problems or not, while the profile score offers a more sensitive measure of change. The latter would be more suitable for measuring change due to either deterioration in the person or possible improvement due to treatment. For both the adult and child versions of the RBMT, data are collected by direct assessment of the individual by qualified clinicians (e.g. chartered psychologists and those eligible for chartered psychologist status, qualified occupational therapists and qualified speech therapists). The instrument allows for repeated assessments to monitor stability, improvement or deterioration over time; and practice effects due to repeated testing could be avoided, as there are four parallel versions of the test. It has very high inter-rater reliability (100% agreement between raters) and satisfactory parallel-form reliability (exceeding $r = .67$; Wilson et al., 1989, 1991). British standardized norms for persons aged 16 to 96 years are available and the adult version is also suitable for persons aged 11 to 15 years and a modified children's version for 5- to 10-year-olds is available.

While the RBMT has not been standardized or validated for persons with intellectual disabilities, a number of British studies have indicated promising results. Wilson and Ivani-Chalian (1995) administered a modified child version (RBMT-C) (Aldrich & Wilson, 1991) with persons with Down syndrome between the ages of 19 and 44 years of age and found that the measure was suitable and could be used to monitor change over time. Hon et al. (1998) used this modified version of the RBMT-C in a population study with older adults with Down syndrome, aged between 30 and 65 years. They concluded it was a useful test of memory for those people with mild or moderate intellectual disabilities in the early but not late stages of dementia. Martin et al. (2000) administered the adult test with a clinical sample of 20 adults with mild intellectual disabilities aged between 19 and 58 years. They concluded that the instrument was a suitable test to use with this population and also reported an age effect (i.e. a poorer performance was evidenced on the memory test by older persons with intellectual disabilities). Thus, monitoring ability over time with this instrument becomes possible and may allow for the identification of changes, which could raise the question of dementia.

With regard to the limitations of the instrument, while the subtests are administered consecutively over a period of 30 to 45 minutes, the requirements of the tasks are explained verbally. The range of raw scores is small on some subtests; for example, remembering a name, providing little room for differentiation within the intellectual disability population in the adult version (Martin et al., 2000). However, Hon et al. (1998) reported a wider spread of scores on the modified children's version. Furthermore, they noted that the instrument was of limited value for individuals with severe or profound intellectual disabilities or sensory problems and that no standardized profile total scores, which offered a more sensitive measure of change than a screening score alone, could be calculated due to the lack of standardized data available for persons with intellectual disabilities.

4 Informant-Based Assessment Instruments

Caregivers, family members or professionals are important sources of information who can comment upon an individual's past performance, abilities and observed changes in everyday functioning. Although informant-based measures should be used cautiously within a retrospective assessment strategy, they are useful when used for repeated testing over time. However, as baseline measures may not be available when an individual first presents with change that might indicate dementia, this has led to a heavy reliance on informant-based measures. At present, there are few measures available that have been developed specifically for persons with intellectual disabilities and that have been subject to rigorous psychometric assessment.

4.1 Dementia Questionnaire for Persons with Mental Retardation (DMR; Evenhuis, 1990, 1992, 1996)

The Dementia Questionnaire for Persons with Mental Retardation (DMR) is a screening instrument (i.e. for the selection of persons who should be referred for further expert diagnostic assessment, for the diagnosis of early dementia in adults with intellectual disabilities) (Evenhuis, 1992). It contains 52 items categorized in eight areas: short-term and long-term memory, spatial and temporal orientation, speech, practical skills, mood, activity and interests and behaviour disturbances. It was designed for adults with all levels of intellectual disability and is one of the informant scales available for assessing orientation with normative data for adults functioning in the mild to moderate ranges of intellectual disability (Evenhuis, 1992). It can take between 15 and 20 minutes for the DMR to be completed by an informant who responds to each question as either 'normally yes', 'sometimes' or 'normally no', based on judgements of the individual's behaviour during the immediate preceding two months. Different cut-off scores for the diagnosis of dementia have been used for people with different levels of intellectual disability and the instrument has been deployed in clinical studies and research on community and institutionalized samples (Evenhuis, 1992, 1996; Prasher, 1997).

An instrument limitation is that the DMR has absolute cut-off scores for dementia that vary by 'mental age' as well as alternate cut-off scores indicating significant change from year to year for cognitive and social skills. The absolute cut-off scores are to be used with caution, as 'mental ages' obtained outside the Netherlands may differ from those in the standardization sample (Burt et al., 1998). Indeed, Prasher (1997) has proposed a modified scoring procedure in order to overcome the problem that the DMR appears to be more prone to identifying dementia in the presence of a severe intellectual disability. Furthermore, the questionnaire is designed to assess current functioning and thus on the basis of one assessment cannot indicate whether there has been change over time. Indeed, although absolute cut-off scores are provided for diagnosis on the basis of single administration, it is recommended that longitudinal administration is necessary and that cut-off scores for dementia should be used cautiously and in conjunction with information gathered from other neuropsychological instruments (Deb & Braganza, 1999; Evenhuis, 1996). Furthermore, Thompson (1994) and Evenhuis (1992) highlight the difficulty in discerning sensitivity of DMR when used with depressed individuals and recommend the use of an additional measure. Indeed, it should be remembered that the DMR is a carer-rated tool and cannot measure directly the individual's skills such as performance on specific tasks. It may show a particular individual to have global deficits but specific deficits may be pin-pointed by using a different measure. An additional limitation relates to the fact that the English translation of the Dutch original is grammatically incorrect and may be confusing for informants if completed as a questionnaire as opposed to a structured interview, the latter strategy having recently been recommended (Burt & Aylward, 1999). There is a requirement for informants to have known the person with intellectual disabilities for a number of years, which is difficult to control for, given the increasing number of persons with intellectual disabilities residing in community settings with a high turnover of staff. Furthermore, the instrument is less sensitive for assessing individuals with dementia in the severe and profound ranges of intellectual functioning who may never have been able to perform many of the skills covered by the questionnaire, resulting in high baseline scores (Evenhuis, 1996). Finally, as with all informant-based measures caution is recommended in their deployment, specifically in relation to the appraisal of inter-informant reliability. Given that there is an inevitable change of care staff over time, the issue of inter-informant reliability is more important than that of the measure's stability alone.

4.2 Dementia Scale for Down Syndrome (DSDS; Gedye, 1995)

The Dementia Scale for Down Syndrome (DSDS) was designed to assist clinicians and researchers to make a diagnosis of dementia in persons with Down syndrome on the basis of information gathered from informants on changes in the person's cognitive and daily living skills (Gedye, 1995). It is designed to be administered as an interview before dementia is suspected and to be re-administered at least every year with a six-month follow-up if there are any reported signs of dementia. Its 60 items are equally divided into three categories of early-stage, middle-stage and late-stage features of dementia, and the behaviours are scored as 'present' or 'absent over time', 'not applicable' or 'typical of that individual'. The last three responses are scored as absent, so in this way a distinction can be made between the newly developed behaviours and behaviours that have already existed in a person with an intellectual disability (Deb & Braganza, 1999; Gedye, 1995; Temple et al., 2001). Furthermore, the scale has discontinue rules at the end of each stage if a specified threshold of behaviours indicative of dementia are not reported up to that point. Thus the scale is reported for use with all individuals with intellectual disabilities, regardless of their functioning level. The informant's responses during the interview permit the generation of a cognitive score and an early-middle and late score, with different cut-offs to indicate stage of dementia (Deb & Braganza, 1999; Gedye, 1995). Furthermore, the DSDS attempts a differential diagnosis of Alzheimer dementia with depression, hypothyroidism and visual and hearing impairment and only takes into account the new behaviours that have appeared recently and have lasted for at least six months. Thus, impairments in cognitive and daily living skills, which pre-existed current difficulties, could be excluded to avoid a floor effect.

Data are collected by a psychologist administering the DSDS in interview-format to two informants over a period between 15 and 30 minutes, with less time needed if the behaviours are not present. Reliability and validity data are available for North American adults with profound and severe levels of intellectual disability with a reported sensitivity of 100% and a specificity of 98% when comparing findings of DSDS at baseline with a clinical diagnosis of dementia (Gedye, 1995). However, Deb and Braganza (1999) showed a specificity of 89% and sensitivity of 85% in their study and, with other authors, noted that the scale's sensitivity for individuals functioning at levels higher than that of the normative sample has not been documented (Burt & Aylward, 1999; Temple et al., 2001).

With regard to instrument limitations and constraints, Burt and Aylward (1999) highlighted the practical logistics and expense of administrating the instrument as stipulated by the author, to two reliable informants by a chartered psychologist, the feasibility of re-administration of the interview after six months and difficulty with applying scoring criteria based on information supplied in the manual. Furthermore, while the DSDS has the advantage of focusing on changes that would be indicative of dementia, Burt and Aylward (1999) also raised concerns regarding the reliability of such retrospective data as informant(s) are required to compare current to previously recalled levels of functioning. Other considerations relate to a disparity in diagnosis between the measure and clinical diagnosis. Huxley et al. (2000) found such a disparity when persons with mild or moderate intellectual disabilities were presenting symptoms indicative of early-stage dementia. This may be connected with the test item selection and development in that items were developed for persons with Down syndrome with severe and profound intellectual disabilities. The DSDS has good face validity with some assessment of reliability and could be used alongside neuropsychological assessments. Again, the need for caution when using informant-based measures is reiterated as issue of inter-informant reliability is more important than that of the measure's stability alone.

5 Conclusion

The diagnosis of dementia in an individual with intellectual disabilities relies heavily on direct performance-based, neuropsychological assessments and informant-based interviews. There is no test or procedure that can identify the presence of dementia before the onset of clinical manifestations. Furthermore, there is no test that adequately monitors the total range of deficits induced by dementia and no single test is useful throughout the entire course of the disease. There is also no generally accepted definition of dementia for individuals with intellectual disabilities. Thus, this diagnosis relies on procedures that have been developed for those who do not have intellectual disabilities, and extreme care needs to be taken. Variability in course and areas of decline should be expected and the possibility for improvements in functioning should not be ruled out even in those with an underlying progressive disease.

The use of only one area of functioning to define dementia (e.g. memory or adaptive behaviour), or the use of information collected at only one assessment, is not appropriate (Aylward et al., 1997; Burt & Aylward, 1999; Burt et al., 1998; Devenny et al., 1993; Oliver, 1999). Furthermore, the usefulness of large test batteries is limited to persons with relatively high levels of speech and language skills, largely absent in persons with severe and profound intellectual disabilities (Dalton & Wisniewski, 1990). The challenge of diagnosis is further compounded in persons with intellectual disabilities, as the subtle, insidious and progressive signs of dementia disease are superimposed on pre-existing limitations in behaviour, verbal and communication skills. The limitations of existing neuropsychological tests, which are insensitive to detect changes over time nor specific enough to detect dementia in the presence of pre-existing intellectual disabilities, also creates an important obstacle. The limitations associated with informant-based measures mean that at present these measures should not be relied on in the absence of other assessments. The challenge for the future remains the development of neuropsychological tests that are appropriate across levels of intellectual disability and the enhancement of the reliability and validity of informant-based measures. These measures will provide objective assessments against which the reliability and validity of clinical diagnosis can be judged.

REFERENCES

Aldrich, F. K. & Wilson, B. A. (1991) Rivermead Behavioural Memory Test for Children (RBMT-C): A preliminary evaluation. *British Journal of Clinical Psychology*, **30**, 161–168.

American Psychiatric Association (1994) *Diagnostic and Statistical Manual of Mental Disorder, 4th Edition*. Washington, DC: American Psychiatric Disorder.

Aylward, E. H., Burt, D. B., Thorpe, L. U., Lai, F. & Dalton, A. J. (1997). Diagnosis of dementia in individuals with intellectual disability. *Journal of Intellectual Disabilities Research*, **41**, 152–164.

Blessed, G., Black, S. E., Butler, T. & Kay, D. W. K. (1991) The diagnosis of dementia in the elderly: A comparison of CAMCOG (the cognitive section of CAMDEX), the AGECAT Program, DSM-III, the Mini-Mental State Examination and some short rating scales. *British Journal of Psychiatry*, **159**, 193–198.

Burt, D. B. & Aylward, E. H. (1999) Assessment methods for diagnosis of dementia. In M. P. Janicki & A. J. Dalton (eds.), *Dementia, Aging and Intellectual Disabilities: A Handbook*. Philadelphia, PA: Bruner/Mazel, pp. 141–156.

Burt, D. B., Loveland, K. A., Prmieaux-Hart, S., Chen, Y.-W., Philips, N. B. et al. (1998) Dementia in adults with Down syndrome: Diagnostic challenges. *American Journal on Mental Retardation*, **103**, 130–145.

Crapper-McLachlan, D. R., Dalton, A. J., Kruck, T. P. A., Bell, M. Y., Smith, W. L. et al. (1991) Intramuscular desferrioxamine in patients with Alzheimer disease. *Lancet*, **337**, 1304–1308.

Dalton, A. J. (1992) Dementia in Down syndrome: Methods of evaluation. In L. Nadel & C. J. Epstein (eds.), *Down Syndrome and Alzheimer Disease*. London: Wiley-Liss, pp. 51–76.

Dalton, A. J. (1995) *Dalton/McMurray Visual Memory Test: Delayed Matching to Sample Cognitive Test*. Canada: Byte Craft.

Dalton, A. J. & Crapper-McLachlan, D. R. (1984) Incidence of memory deterioration in persons with Down syndrome. In J. M. Berg (ed.), *Perspectives and Progress in Mental Retardation*. Vol. 2: *Biomedical Aspects*. Baltimore, MD: University Park Press, pp. 55–62.

Dalton, A. J. & Fedor, B. L. (1997) *DYSPRAXIA Scale for Adults with Down Syndrome*. New York: New York State Institute for Basic Research in Developmental Disabilities.

Dalton, A. J. & Fedor, B. L. (1998) Onset of dyspraxia in aging persons with Down syndrome: Longitudinal studies. *Journal of Intellectual and Developmental Disability*, **23**, 12–24.

Dalton, A. J., Sano, M. C. & Aisen, P. S. (2001) Brief Praxis Test: A primary outcome measure for treatment trials of Alzheimer disease in persons with Down syndrome. Multi-centre Vitamin E trial: Project Proposal. New York: New York State Institute for Basic Research in Developmental Disabilities.

Dalton, A. J. & Wisniewski, H. M. (1990) Down syndrome and the dementia of Alzheimer disease. *International Review of Psychiatry*, **2**, 43–52.

Deb, S. & Braganza, J. (1999) Comparison of rating scales for the diagnosis of dementia in adults with Down syndrome. *Journal of Intellectual Disability Research*, **43**, 400–407.

Devenny, D., Wisniewski, K. E. & Silverman, W. P. (1993) Dementia of the Alzheimer type among high-functioning adults with Down syndrome: Individual profiles of performance. In B. Corain, K. Iqbal, M. Nicolini, B. Woinbald, H. Wisniewski & P. Zatta (eds.), *Alzheimer Disease: Advances in Clinical and Basic Research*. New York: Wiley, pp. 47–53.

Evenhuis, H. M. (1990) *The Dementia Questionnaire for Persons with Mental Retardation (DMR)*. Zwammerdam, Netherlands: Hooge Burch Institute for the Mentally Retarded.

Evenhuis, H. M. (1992) Evaluation of a screening instrument for dementia in ageing mentally retarded persons. *Journal of Intellectual Disability Research*, **36**, 337–347.

Evenhuis, H. M. (1996) Further evaluation of the Dementia Questionnaire for persons with Mental Retardation (DMR). *Journal of Intellectual Disability Research*, **40**, 369–373.

Folstein, M., Folstein, S. & McHugh, P. (1975) Mini-Mental State: A practical method for grading the cognitive state of patients for the clinician. *Journal of Psychiatric Research*, **12**, 189–198.

Gedye, A. (1995) *Dementia Scale for Down Syndrome* (Manual). Vancouver: Gedye Research & Consulting.

Hartman, J. A. (2000) Investigation of the use of the CAMCOG in the visually impaired. *International Journal of Geriatric Psychiatry*, **15**, 863–869.

Holland, A. J., Hon, J., Huppert, F. A. & Stevens F. (2000) Incidence and course of dementia in people with Down syndrome: Findings from a population-based study. *Journal of Intellectual Disability Research*, **44**, 138–146.

Holland, A. J., Hon, J., Huppert, F. A., Stevens, F. & Watson, P. (1998) Population-based study of the prevalence and presentation of dementia in adults with Down's syndrome. *British Journal of Psychiatry*, **172**, 493–498.

Hon, J., Huppert, F. A., Holland, A. J. & Watson, P. (1998) The value of the Rivermead Behavioural Memory Test (Children's Version) in an epidemiological study of older adults with Down syndrome. *British Journal of Clinical Psychology*, **37**, 15–29.

Hon, J., Huppert, F. A., Holland, A. J. & Watson, P. (1999) Neuropsychological assessment of older adults with Down syndrome: An epidemiological study using the Cambridge Cognitive Examination (CAMCOG). *British Journal of Clinical Psychology*, **38**, 155–165.

Huppert, F. A., Brayne, C., Gill, C., Paykel, E. S. & Beardsall, L. (1995) CAMCOG – A concise neuropsychological test to assist dementia diagnosis: Socio-demographic determinants in an elderly population sample. *British Journal of Clinical Psychology*, **34**, 529–541.

Huxley, A., Prasher, V. P. & Haque, M. S. (2000) The Dementia Scale for Down syndrome. *Journal of Intellectual Disability Research*, **44**, 697–698.

Kertesz, A. (1982) *Western Aphasia Battery*. New York: Grune & Stratton.

Lohr, J. B. & Wisniewski, A. A. (1987) *Movement Disorders: A Neuropsychiatric Approach*. New York: Guildford.

Martin, C., West, J., Cull, C. & Adams, M. (2000) A preliminary study investigating how people with mild intellectual disabilities perform on the Rivermead Behavioural Memory Test. *Journal of Applied Research in Intellectual Disabilities*, **13**, 186–193.

Oliver, C. (1999) Perspectives on assessment and evaluation. In M. P. Janicki & A. J. Dalton (eds.), *Dementia, Aging and Intellectual Disabilities: A Handbook*. Philadelphia, PA: Bruner/Mazel, pp. 123–140.

Prasher, V. P. (1997) Dementia Questionnaire for Persons with Mental Retardation (DMR): Modified criteria for adults with Down syndrome. *Journal of Applied Research in Intellectual Disability*, **10**, 54–60.

Roth, M., Huppert, F. A., Mountjoy, C. Q. & Tym, E. (1998) *CAMDEX-R The Cambridge Examination*. Cambridge: Cambridge University Press.

Roth, M., Tym, E., Mountjoy, C. Q. et al. (1986) CAMDEX: A standardised instrument for the diagnosis of mental disorder in the elderly with special reference to the detection of dementia. *British Journal of Psychiatry*, **149**, 698–709.

Saxton, J., McGonigle, K. L., Swilart, A. A. & Boller, F. (1993) *The Severe Impairment Battery*. London: Thames Valley Test Company.

Temple, V., Jozsvai, E., Konstantareas, M. M. & Hewitt, T. A. (2001) Alzheimer dementia in Down's syndrome: The relevance of cognitive ability. *Journal of Intellectual Disability Research*, **45**, pp. 47–55.

Thompson, S. B. N. (1994) A neuropsychological test battery for identifying dementia in people with Down syndrome. *The British Journal of Developmental Disabilities*, **60**, 135–142.

Thorpe, L., Davidson, P. & Janicki, M. (2001) Healthy Ageing – Adults with Intellectual Disabilities: Biobehavioural Issues. *Journal of Applied Research in Intellectual Disabilities*, **13**, 218–228.

Wilson, B. A., Cockburn, J. & Baddeley, A. (1985) *The Rivermead Behavioural Memory Test (RBMT)*. Bury St Edmund: Thames Valley Test Company.

Wilson, B. A., Cockburn, J., Baddeley, A. & Hiorns, R. (1989) The development and validation of a test battery for detecting and monitoring everyday memory problems. *Journal of Clinical and Experimental Neuropsychology*, **11**, 855–870.

Wilson, B. A., Cockburn, J., Baddeley, A. & Hiorns, R. (1991) *The Rivermead Behavioural Memory Test: Manual 2nd Edition*. Bury St Edmunds: Thames Valley Test Company.

Wilson, B. A. & Ivani-Chalian, R. (1995) Performance of adults with Down syndrome on the Children's Version of the Rivermead Behavioural Memory Test: A brief report. *British Journal of Clinical Psychology*, **34**, 85–88.

Witts, P. & Elders, S. (1998) The 'Severe Impairment Battery': Assessing cognitive ability in adults with Down syndrome. *British Journal of Clinical Psychology*, **37**, 207–210.

World Health Organization (1992) *ICD-10 International Statistical Classification of Diseases and Related Health Problems* (10th ed.). Geneva: World Health Organization.

CHAPTER 16

Behavioural phenotypes: approaches to assessment

Robert M. Walley

1 Introduction

Assessment of behavioural phenotypes helps one understand the unique associations between phenotype and behaviour, and also the overlaps that are seen in behaviour between syndromes. Once differences and similarities in behaviour between syndromes have been elucidated, one can investigate their cognitive and emotional substrates, which may lead to improved methods of intervention for problematic behaviours, and support with intellectual difficulties. Additionally, by understanding the cognitive 'underpinnings' of particular skills/deficits found in behavioural phenotypes, one may learn more about how information is processed and how this may change during the lifespan. For further discussion see Flint (1996), Hodapp (1997), Holland (1999), O'Brien (2000), Dykens & Hodapp (1997, 2001), Hodapp & Dykens (2001).

Einfeld and Hall (1994) and Einfeld et al. (1999) argue that behaviour-phenotype associations can only be determined accurately by meeting the following set of criteria:

- Evidence obtained of an association from a case control study.
- Chance ruled out with tests of statistical significance and corrections for multiple comparisons.
- Where no association is found, the possibility of Type 2 error is considered. (In this context a Type 2 error means that there could be an association but it is not detected because of inadequate assessments or sample size. Alternatively, the association could be too small for it to be detected by the statistics used.)
- Confounding variables are measured or controlled.
- Ascertainment bias is reduced with attention to selection and participation.
- Measurement error is reduced and evaluated by using measures of known reliability and validity.

Einfeld et al. (1999) also note the need to replicate studies to ensure that a given behavioural phenotype is reliably determined. Although important to aim for, there are a number of difficulties associated with meeting these criteria that fall into two broad areas. First, the selection of appropriate assessments and measures. Second, the selection of appropriate control groups. With respect to the former, selection of appropriate assessments and measures, we need to consider both behavioural and cognitive assessment.

1.1 Behavioural assessment

Einfeld and Hall (1994) advocate the use of measures of known reliability and validity, though the major problem with many such measures is that they have not been standardized on groups of people with an intellectual disability. A number of measures of challenging behaviour and adaptive behaviour have now been standardized on intellectual disability populations but may not be specific enough to detect some of the particular behaviours associated with certain genetic syndromes. To overcome this problem Dykens (1995) advocates the use of some standardized measures with more detailed syndrome specific observations. Dykens for example, describes how individuals with Fragile X syndrome, Smith-Magenis and Prader-Willi syndromes share elevated perseveration scores on standard instruments, yet in fact show different types of perseverative style. In addition to the problems of standardization, many people with intellectual disabilities are unable to do cognitive tests used in adult neuropsychology and perform at floor levels.

1.2 Cognitive assessment

A further issue in the cognitive assessment of individuals with intellectual disabilities is that they may be impaired in a number of domains, which means that one should be careful about making assumptions about what a test is measuring. To some extent, difficulties of validity can be overcome by using tests that control for confounding variables and also using tests that cover a range of ability. Tests of this type may be adapted from assessments developed for children, which in turn have often been developed to measure the same abilities as their 'adult' equivalents. Examples of this type of test are the Stroop type tasks to measure attention, which now exist in various forms, and tests of verbal fluency.

Dykens (2002) points out that cognitive assessment is designed to pick up deficits, and this may mean that there are no tests available to tap particular skills that are observed in some behavioural phenotypes. Jigsaw puzzles skills have been included as supportive criteria for Prader-Willi syndrome; although tests of visuospatial ability have been developed, there are no standardized tests that purely measure jigsaw puzzle ability. Dykens (2002) describes a study investigating the ability of Prader-Willi children to solve non-standardized jigsaw puzzles and word searches as well as their abilities to perform a variety of standardized visuospatial tasks.

1.3 Selection of appropriate control groups

The second area that causes difficulties for research in behavioural phenotypes is the selection of an appropriate control group. The selection of an appropriate control group is extremely important, given many measures and tests used in research have not been standardized on groups of people with an intellectual disability. Hodapp and Dykens (2001) provide a comprehensive discussion of the issues involved in selecting a control group and discuss the advantages and disadvantages of different approaches. One common approach that is used is to select a control group of individuals with either mixed aetiology or non-specific intellectual disability. These authors point out that there is a difference between these two groups in that the latter may contain individuals with what has been described as familial or cultural familial intellectual disability and are more likely to come from poorer social economic backgrounds. They suggest that the control group should contain individuals with identified causes of intellectual disability as well as those with non-specific intellectual disability. They also caution against the overuse of individuals with Down syndrome as a control group, which is a common practice because Down syndrome is the most common genetic cause of the intellectual disability. Hodapp and Dykens (2001) point out that Down syndrome has a behavioural phenotype of its own, and if another behavioural phenotype is going to be used, it is better to compare behavioural phenotypes that are superficially similar in one domain. They cite the work of Dykens and Rosner (1999) which investigated the ways in which adolescents and adults with Prader-Willi syndrome expressed anxiety in comparison to those with Williams syndrome.

A further strategy is to compare individuals with specific behavioural phenotypes to a group that does not have an intellectual disability, but may have similar behavioural or physical profiles. Skuse et al. (1999) compared girls with Turner syndrome to girls with other short stature disorders, while Dykens et al. (1996) compared adults with Prader-Willi syndrome who show high levels of obsessive and compulsive behaviour to individuals without intellectual disability who had a diagnosis of obsessive-compulsive disorder.

2 Types of Assessments

The types of assessment instruments that have been used in behavioural phenotype research may include

- tests of general intellectual function;
- assessments of adaptive and challenging behaviour;
- assessments of personality, mood and psychiatric disorder;
- cognitive tests used in adult and/or child neuropsychology research or adaptations of these tests for individuals with an intellectual disability;
- assessments usually of the questionnaire type designed to determine and distinguish particular behavioural phenotypes.

To illustrate the variety of different types of assessment approaches used, the three behavioural phenotypes of Prader-Willi, Williams and Rett syndrome will now be considered. Prader-Willi and Williams syndrome have been chosen because they are relatively well-researched behavioural phenotypes. In addition, individuals with these syndromes are often in the mild to borderline range of intellectual disability and therefore it has been possible to use assessments and tests developed for the general adult population. In contrast, Rett syndrome has been chosen because certainly in the case of classical Rett syndrome, affected individuals are usually in the severe to profound range of intellectual disability, and are much more difficult to assess using conventional assessment instruments. As research on these syndromes has involved children as well as adults affected by the syndrome, child assessments will be mentioned.

2.1 Prader-Willi syndrome

Prader-Willi syndrome is characterized by intellectual disability, obesity, insatiable appetite, infantile hypertonia, hypogonodaism, and dysmorphic features (e.g. small hands and feet, short stature and characteristic facial features). The disorder arises from loss of the genes on chromosome 15 within the region of 15q11-13. Prader-Willi syndrome will result if there is an absence of paternally derived genes from this location, or if there are two copies of the maternal chromosome 15 instead.

Individuals with Prader-Willi syndrome have a behavioural phenotype that includes temper tantrums, impulsiveness and stubbornness (Dykens & Cassidy, 1996). Compulsive behaviour has also been found to be a feature of individuals with Prader-Willi syndrome, and it would appear that people with Prader-Willi syndrome have an increased risk of developing obsessive-compulsive disorder (Dykens et al., 1996).

2.1.1 Assessment of intellectual functioning (IQ)   Dykens et al. investigated 'correlates, and trajectories of intelligence' (Dykens et al., 1992b, p. 1125) in Prader-Willi syndrome, in a group of participants aged between 5 to 46 years. The Kaufman Assessment Battery for Children (K-ABC) (Kaufman & Kaufman, 1983) was used to assess intelligence, as well as to investigate the abilities of Prader-Willi individuals to process information sequentially and simultaneously. Receptive vocabulary in the study was measured by the Peabody Picture Vocabulary Test – Revised (PPVT-R) (Dunn & Dunn, 1981, 1997). In addition to using the Kaufman Assessment Battery for Children, the study used the Wechsler Intelligence Scale for Children – Revised (WISC-R) (Wechsler, 1973) or Wechsler Adult Intelligence Scale – Revised (WAIS-R) (Wechsler, 1981). The study indicated that subjects with Prader-Willi syndrome showed weaknesses in sequential processing relative to simultaneous processing and achievement. The authors suggested this indicated Prader-Willi subjects had difficulty with short-term memory and processing information step by step, in which stimuli are placed in linear or temporal order. The study also showed that IQ does not appear to be correlated with weight (i.e. there was no evidence of an association between low IQ and increased weight). It also pointed to stability of IQ across the life span relative to other genetic disorders such as Fragile X syndrome or Down syndrome, which may show a decline with age.

In a study investigating maladaptive behaviour differences in Prader-Willi, Dykens et al. (1999) used the Kaufman Brief Intelligence Test (Kaufman & Kaufman, 1990), which has been standardized on a intellectual disability population.

Most studies in Prader-Willi syndrome where general intellectual function is measured, however, use the Wechsler intelligence scales: either the WISC-R or the WAIS-R. Einfeld et al. (1999) investigated the behavioural and emotional disturbance in Prader-Willi syndrome using the Wechsler scales, as did a study by Roof et al. (2000) that investigated intellectual characteristics of Prader-Willi syndrome and a comparison of its genetic subtypes. Roof et al.'s study showed that the majority of individuals with Prader-Willi syndrome fell into the mild to borderline ranges of intellectual disability, but that individuals who had two copies of maternally derived chromosome 15 appeared to have relative strength in verbal IQ compared to individuals who had paternal deletions.

2.1.2 Adaptive behaviour

Very little attention appears to have been given to studying adaptive behaviour in individuals with Prader-Willi syndrome, in contrast to the number of studies that have investigated maladaptive behaviour. Dykens et al. (1993) investigated adaptive behaviour using a standardized assessment instrument, the Vineland Adaptive Behavior Scales (Sparrow et al., 1984), and found that the composite score was considerably less than expected from the subject's IQ. The Vineland Adaptive Behavior Scales assess adaptive behaviour in the domains of communication, daily living skills, socialization, and motor skills; it also contains a maladaptive behaviour section. The Vineland is one of the most widely used assessments for adaptive behaviour, and is commonly used in studies involving intellectual disability populations.

2.1.3 Maladaptive behaviour

Maladaptive behaviour in Prader-Willi syndrome is probably the most researched area of its behavioural phenotype. Einfeld et al. (1999) investigated behavioural and emotional disturbance in Prader-Willi syndrome, and studied 46 children with Prader-Willi syndrome, using the Developmental Behaviour Checklist (DBC) (Einfeld & Tonge, 1994). The Developmental Checklist is a 96-item checklist designed to assess behavioural and emotional difficulties in children and young people with intellectual disability. This study indicated that individuals with Prader-Willi syndrome had higher levels of behavioural disturbance compared to control participants, especially in antisocial behaviour.

Dykens et al. (1999) measured maladaptive behaviour in 23 individuals ranging from 6 to 42 years, and used the Child Behavior Checklist (Achenbach, 1991). This checklist contains three factors – internalizing problems, externalizing problems and total problems – as well as nine clinical subdomains; within the internalizing domain, these are withdrawn, somatic complaints, anxious, depressed; delinquent behaviour and aggressive behaviour comprise the externalizing behaviour domain; the four remaining subdomains consist of social, thought, attention and other problems. The study showed that individuals with paternally derived deletions causing Prader-Willi syndrome showed significantly higher maladaptive ratings on the Child Behavior Checklist, internalizing and externalizing and total domains than individuals with two copies of the maternal chromosome 15. The Child Behavior Checklist had also been used in a previous study by Dykens & Kasari (1997) when they investigated maladaptive behaviour in Prader-Willi children using two control groups, one comprising children with Down syndrome, the other a group of children with non-specific intellectual disability.

Clarke et al. (1996) have investigated maladaptive behaviour in adults with Prader-Willi syndrome, using the Aberrant Behavior Checklist (ABC), a 58-item structured interview which rates behaviours on a 4-point scale and gives information on five factors:

- irritability and agitation
- lethargy and withdrawal

- stereotypic behaviour
- hyperactivity
- inappropriate speech

The Aberrant Behavior Checklist was developed by Aman et al. (1985) to provide a standardized rating scale assessing the effects of drugs and other treatments on severely and profoundly intellectual disabled individuals. (For a full discussion of the Aberrant Behavior Checklist see ch. 13.)

The results of the Clarke et al. (1996) study in adults with Prader-Willi syndrome show relatively high levels of maladaptive behaviour, particularly in the domain of irritability and agitation. A similar study by Clarke and Boer (1998) investigated problem behaviours in Prader-Willi, Cri-du-Chat and Smith-Magenis syndromes and found that all three disorders were associated with higher ratings of problem behaviours (than a comparison group) on at least one domain of the checklist. Behaviours in Cri-du-Chat syndrome are reported by Clarke and Boer to be characterized by hyperactivity, restlessness and impulsiveness, inattentiveness and distractibility; Prader-Willi syndrome, by temper tantrums, inability to delay gratification, repetitive speech, lability of mood, inactivity and self-injury; Smith-Magenis syndrome, by impulsiveness, temper outbursts, distractibility, labile mood, bizarre and boisterous behaviours.

Clarke and Marston (2000) also used the Aberrant Behavior Checklist to investigate problem behaviours in Angelman syndrome, and found that the ABC scores were lower than the other syndrome groups, although associated with problems such as lack of speech, overactivity, restlessness, eating and sleep problems. Clarke and Marston also used the Reiss Screen for Maladaptive Behavior (Reiss, 1998) that is only suitable for individuals over the age of 12. (See ch. 12 for a full discussion of this scale.)

Dykens et al. (1992a) used the maladaptive behaviour domain from the Vineland Adaptive Behavior Scales; this has been used to investigate behaviour in a number of other syndromes; for example, Fragile X syndrome (Dykens et al., 1989), Lowe syndrome (Kenworthy et al., 1993) and Smith-Magenis syndrome (Dykens et al., 1993).

The compulsive behaviours seen in Prader-Willi syndrome have been investigated using a number of different instruments. Dykens et al. (1996) used the Yale Brown Obsessive Compulsive Scale (Y-BOCS) (Goodman et al., 1989). The Y-BOCS, was not developed for individuals with intellectual disability, and in the study was adapted for use in this population. This was done by making it an informant rather than a self-rated scale. The scale comprises 56 checklist items that are rated as being present in the past week. Ten additional items assess symptom severity and assess the extent to which obsessions and compulsions are distressful and cause problems in everyday life. In this study, individuals with Prader-Willi syndrome aged between 5 and 47 years were compared with a group of individuals who did not have an intellectual disability, but did have a diagnosis of obsessive-compulsive disorder. The Prader-Willi syndrome and diagnosed compulsive-disorder groups showed similar levels of symptom severity and numbers of compulsions. Compulsive behaviour in Prader-Willi syndrome has also been investigated by Feurer et al. (1998), using the Compulsive Behavior Checklist for clients with mental retardation (Gedye, 1992). The checklist consists of 25 types of compulsion that have been grouped loosely into five categories. It can be scored in two ways, either by tallying the number of compulsive behaviours or by the number of categories represented. The categories are ordering compulsions, completeness-incompleteness compulsions, cleaning/tidiness compulsions, checking/touching compulsions and deviant grooming compulsions. Feurer et al. adapted the scoring system slightly by rating the compulsions in terms of being severe, moderate, mild or not present at all.

Dimitropoulos et al. (2001) investigated the emergence of compulsive behaviour and tantrums in children with Prader-Willi syndrome in comparison with children with Down syndrome, and typically developing children. Using the Compulsive Behavior Checklist they found that the children with Prader-Willi syndrome exhibited more compulsions, skin picking and tantrums than did the comparison groups.

Other types of behaviour that have been investigated in Prader-Willi syndrome include characteristics of the eating disorder in Prader-Willi syndrome (Holland et al., 1995) and sleep disturbance (Richdale et al., 1999). The latter study used the Epworth Sleepiness Scale (ESS) (Johns, 1991) and an adaptation of the Sleep Disorders Questionnaire (Douglass et al., 1994).

2.1.4 Family stress Sarimski (1997) explored family stress in three syndromes, Fragile X, Prader-Willi and Williams syndrome, using the Society for the Study of Behavioural Phenotypes postal questionnaire (O'Brien, 1992), the Parenting Stress Index (Abidin, 1990) and the Family Functioning Style Scale (Deal et al., 1988).

2.1.5 Personality Curfs et al. (1995) investigating the personality profile of young people with Prader-Willi used a Dutch version of the California Child Q Set (CCQ; Block & Block, 1980). The CCQ consists of one hundred statements describing a wide range of behaviour and personality characteristics. Dykens and Rosner (1999) investigated personality and motivation in individuals with Prader-Willi and Williams syndrome, using the Reiss Profiles of Fundamental Goals and Motivation Sensitivities, for Persons with Mental Retardation (Reiss & Havercamp, 1998). Dykens reports that this assessment has been specifically designed to assess motivational strengths and styles in adolescents and adults.

2.1.6 Psychiatric disorder Beardsmore et al. (1998) investigated psychosis in Prader-Willi syndrome, using the Present Psychiatric Scale-Learning Disabilities (PPS-LD) (Cooper, 1997) and Mini Psychiatric Assessment Scale for Adults with Development Disabilities (Prosser et al., 1997). The PPS-LD and PAS-ADD have been specifically developed to measure psychopathology among adults with intellectual disability. Clarke (1998) used the PAS-ADD (Moss et al., 1997) to estimate the prevalence of psychotic symptoms associated with Prader-Willi syndrome. (For a full discussion of psychiatric assessment with respect to people with intellectual disabilities see chs. 4 and 12 in this volume.)

2.2 Williams syndrome

Williams syndrome is a genetic disorder that is caused by a deletion in a small area of the long arm of Chromosome 7. This area includes a number of genes including the elastin gene. Elastin is an important connective tissue protein that is found in skin ligaments, organ and artery walls. Individuals with Williams syndrome have a distinctive cognitive profile, of relatively spared language abilities compared to poor visuospatial abilities; auditory short-term memory is also a relative strength, and face perception abilities may be in the normal range (Mervis et al., 1999; Morris & Mervis, 1999; Bellugi et al., 1999). Overfriendliness is a characteristic of the behaviour of individuals with Williams syndrome, and difficulties in anxiety may also be present. Hypersensitivity to sound (hyperacusis) is also a common feature.

2.2.1 Assessment of general intellectual function and language   The unique cognitive profile of Williams syndrome has been the subject of much research, and is manifested in a typical profile, of superior verbal to performance score on the Wechsler intelligence scales. Much of the research on Williams syndrome has been carried out on children, but Howlin et al. (1998) conducted a study investigating cognitive function in adults with this syndrome. This study used the Wechsler Adult Intelligence Scale – Revised UK (Wechsler, 1986) to measure general cognitive functioning, and also the British Picture Vocabulary Scale (BPVS; Dunn et al., 1997) to assess receptive and expressive language skills. The study also included use of the Vineland Adaptive Behavior Scales – Interview Edition (Sparrow et al., 1984) to assess adaptive behaviour.

The study indicated that full-scale IQ scores were in the mild range of intellectual disability with verbal IQ scores higher than performance IQ scores. The authors noted that participants did relatively well on tests with vocabulary and abstract reasoning but performed poorly on tasks involving general knowledge, memory, numeracy and visual sequencing. It was also noted that the adaptive behaviour scores of the Vineland Adaptive Behavior Scales were relatively poorer than would be expected from the IQ scores of the group.

Mervis et al. (1999) describe a series of studies on 50 individuals with Williams syndrome, aged between 3 years 11 months to 46 years. The aim of these studies was to demonstrate a consistency and uniqueness of the profile of Williams syndrome by using a method of assessment that could be used across a broad age range. The assessment instrument the authors used was the Differential Ability Scales (DAS) (Elliot, 1990). Mervis et al. considered that the DAS was the most appropriate instrument because it offered a large range of possible standard scores, and could provide specific information about individual strengths and weaknesses across a range of intellectual abilities. The DAS includes six core subtests, which contribute to a general conceptual ability or IQ score, and also a subtest that measures auditory short-term memory. Subtests provide information on verbal reasoning and visuospatial constructive abilities. The DAS is available at two levels, a pre-school level, and a school-age level that is suitable for children and adolescents aged between 7 and 18 years. This test has not been standardized for use with adults, but the authors used the norms of the oldest age group in the standardization sample for use with adult participants. The Mervis et al. study indicates that Williams syndrome participants show a characteristic profile of high-level language abilities compared to visuomotor integration and spatial constructive abilities. They also showed relative strengths in the DAS digit recall subtest, indicating auditory short-term memory abilities.

Jarrold et al. (1998) carried out a study on 16 Williams syndrome participants aged between 6 and 28 years to examine the claim that language abilities are relatively spared compared to visuospatial abilities. This study also used the DAS and found a similar profile to other studies using the DAS and Wechsler Scales in individuals with Williams syndrome. The authors suggested the differences between verbal ability and non-verbal ability could be accounted for by a faster rate of development of some verbal abilities over some non-verbal abilities.

A considerable body of research has been produced on the language abilities seen in Williams syndrome, and Mervis et al. (1999), Bellugi et al. (1999), Morris et al. (1999) and Clashen & Temple (2003) contain good reviews on this topic. The assessments that have been used in this research include the Peabody Picture Vocabulary Test – Revised (PPVT-R) (Dunn & Dunn, 1981, 1997) which is a test commonly used to measure receptive vocabulary development. Participants are asked to choose from a set of four pictures the one that best matches a target word. The words that are tested include names for objects, actions, descriptions and abstractions. The PPVT-R was used in the Mervis et al. studies, but has been used in many other similar studies. Mervis et al. used the Test for Reception of Grammar (TROG; Bishop, 1989) as a standardized measure of grammatical comprehension.

Jarrold et al. (1998) used the British Picture Vocabulary Scale (BPVS) (Dunn et al., 1997) as a test of a receptive vocabulary. As its title suggests, the BPVS is a similar British version of the Peabody Picture Vocabulary Test. Another common assessment in the study of language in Williams syndrome that is used is verbal fluency. Verbal fluency tasks can be presented in a number of forms and Bellugi et al. (1999) describe a study where they showed that Williams syndrome participants could name more animals in a minute that Down syndrome participants. Indeed, the Williams syndrome individuals' scores were within the normal range. Bellugi et al. (1999) also describe how face processing is spared in Williams syndrome, which is perhaps unexpected given their difficulties in other areas of visuospatial cognition. In one particular test of face processing, the Test of Facial Recognition (Benton et al., 1983), not only did Williams syndrome participants perform better than Down syndrome controls, they also performed in the average range. Bellugi et al. (1999), suggest that the well-developed language abilities of Williams syndrome may not be lateralized to the left hemisphere as is commonly found in the general population and that the relative preservation of the neo-cerebellum and the frontal cortex may further account for the unusual cognitive profile observed in the syndrome.

2.2.2 Behavioural and emotional problems

Einfeld et al. (2001) describe their study on a cohort of young people with Williams syndrome, who were assessed for behavioural and emotional problems at time 1 (1990/1991) and then five years later again at time 2 (1995/1996). The assessment instrument used was the Developmental Behaviour Checklist (Einfeld & Tonge, 1994, 1995). Einfeld et al. found that individuals with Williams syndrome were more likely to experience anxiety, hyperactivity, pre-occupations and inappropriate interpersonal relating. They also found a significant increase in the rates of other symptoms, including sleep disturbance and hyperacusis. Einfeld et al. (2001) found that after five years there was still substantial persistence of the overall levels of behavioural and emotional problems. The control participants in both studies were young people with intellectual disability recruited from an epidemiological register. Other assessment instruments that have been used include the Child Behavior Checklist (CBCL) (Achenbach, 1991). Greer et al. (1997) used the CBCL, and consistent with other studies, found that Williams syndrome children had elevated scores on the attention problem scale of the CBCL.

Van Lieshout et al. (1998) using the California Child Q Set (CCQ) (Block & Block, 1980) found that subjects with Williams syndrome, scored as high on agreeableness as controls but relatively more poorly on conscientiousness and motor activity. Along with the other syndrome groups being studied (Prader-Willi and Fragile X), Williams syndrome participants showed less emotional stability and openness than controls. All three syndrome groups showed higher irritability than typically developing children, although there were no significant differences between the syndrome groups.

2.3 Assessment of Rett syndrome

Rett syndrome, in its classic form, is characterized by a pattern of apparently normal development in girls up to the age of approximately 12 months, followed by an acute period of regression between one and two years, which involves a reduction in skills, particularly in hand and speech use. Repetitive hand movements appear, and walking, if achieved at all, is usually characterized by an awkward gait. Respiratory rhythm becomes irregular and seizures are extremely common. Recently the underlying genetic cause of Rett syndrome has been ascribed to mutations on the MECP 2 (methyl CpG binding protein 2) gene at Xq28 (Amir et al., 1999). Recent reviews on Rett syndrome can be found in Kerr (2002) and Mount et al. (2002, 2003). The majority of studies of Rett syndrome have been carried out on girls with the classic form of Rett syndrome who become profoundly intellectually disabled, and, as described above, have extremely limited language abilities and hand use. Kerr (2002), however, draws our attention to the range of severity in Rett syndrome and points to research that indicates boys with Rett syndrome may be able to survive. The incidence of classic Rett syndrome in the UK has been estimated at one in ten thousand female births. Kerr and Burford (2002) describe some of the health concerns associated with Rett syndrome, but also discuss suggestions for therapeutic work that may be carried out, particularly in communication and music therapy.

2.3.1 Assessments of general intellectual function and adaptive behaviour

Perry et al. (1991) investigated adaptive behaviour in a group of girls with classic Rett syndrome aged between approximately 3 years and 19.5 years. Instruments that were used in this study were the Vineland Adaptive Behavior Scales and the Cattell Infant Intelligence Scale. The mean mental age that the participants performed on the Cattell was three months; significantly the Cattell scores did not correlate with the Vineland scores that came out at significantly higher means, ranging from the daily living skills domain with a mean of 16.9 months to socialization with a mean of 25.9 months. Perry et al. (1991) suggested that the scores on the Vineland may reflect issues such as parental bias and the difficulties in scoring the test, but do not necessarily reflect higher functioning.

Given the profound level of intellectual disability found in girls with Rett syndrome, together with their lack of motor abilities, it is very difficult to carry out standardized assessments on them. Woodyatt and Ozanne (1993) have investigated cognitive skills and communication in children with Rett syndrome using an assessment based on Piaget's sensorimotor stages, and have shown that the majority of girls with classic Rett syndrome are at a pre-intentional level of communication. (For a full discussion of Piagetian assessment see ch. 11.)

2.3.2 Assessment and behavioural and emotional behaviour Mount et al. (2001)

carried out a literature search with the aim of identifying behavioural and emotional features that might be candidates for specific behaviours in Rett syndrome. A study by the same group of researchers (Mount et al., 2003) used the Developmental Behaviour Checklist (Einfeld & Tonge, 1994, 1995) to compare 143 girls aged between 4 and 18 years with Rett syndrome, compared with 85 girls with severe to profound intellectual disability with mixed aetiology. The authors were careful to control for the effects of Rett syndrome related physical disability and found that the Rett syndrome girls presented more 'autistic relating' and fewer anti-social behaviours. Analysis of the data indicated that the Rett syndrome group do not present with classical autistic features but had other social relating deficits. It is of note that Mount et al. (2003) used the Developmental Behaviour Checklist not only because of its track record in behavioural phenotype research, but also because in a study of children with severe intellectual disability and autism, the factor structure and psychometric properties of the Developmental Behaviour Checklist were shown to be robust (Hastings et al., 2001). Mount et al. noted, however, that one concern with respect to use of a standardized instrument such as the Developmental Behaviour Checklist was its lack of specificity (it did not detect some of the behaviours seen in Rett syndrome). Mount et al. (2002) have built on the earlier work using the Developmental Behaviour Checklist by developing a normative checklist of characteristic Rett syndrome behavioural and emotional features, the Rett Syndrome Behaviour Questionnaire (RSBQ). These authors report that the RSBQ requires full validation to confirm its discriminatory power and reliability with more independent samples of individuals with Rett syndrome and control groups of girls with severe intellectual disabilities. The RSBQ was based on behaviours found in children, as there were difficulties in obtaining an appropriate adult comparison group. The authors report, however, that the RSBQ has good psychometric properties, including scale and subscale internal consistency in test–retest reliability. Specific behaviours found in Rett syndrome include hand behaviours and breathing problems. Additional behaviours found more frequently in the Rett syndrome group included fluctuations in mood and signs of anxiety/fear, inconsolable crying and screaming at night, repetitive mouth and tongue movements and grimacing.

3 Conclusion

Some of the difficulties involved in selecting assessments to investigate behavioural phenotypes have been reviewed and discussed, while a number of the assessments that have been used to investigate Prader-Willi syndrome, Williams syndrome and Rett syndrome have been described. Attention has been drawn to the wide range of instruments relevant to such assessment.

REFERENCES

Abidin, R. (1990) *Parenting Stress Index*. Charlotesville: Paediatric Psychology Press.
Achenbach, T. M. (1991) *Manual for the Child Behavior Checklist/4–18 and 1991 Profile*. Burlington: University of Vermont, Department of Psychiatry.
Aman, M. G., Singh, N. N., Stewart, A. W. & Field, C. J. (1985) The Aberrant Behavior Checklist: A behavior rating scale for the assessment of treatment effects. *American Journal of Mental Deficiency*, **89**, 485–491.

Amir, R. E., VanDen Veyver, I. B., Wan, M., Tran, C. Q., Franke, U. & Zoghbi, H. (1999) Rett syndrome is caused by mutations in X-linked MECP2, Encoding methyl CpG binding protein 2. *Nature Genetics*, **23**, 185–188.

Beardsmore, A., Dorman, T., Cooper, S.-A. & Webb, T. (1998) Affective psychosis and Prader-Willi syndrome. *Journal of Intellectual Disability Research*, **42**, 463–471.

Bellugi, U., Mills, D., Jernigan, T., Hickok, G. & Galaburda, A. (1999) Linking cognition, brain structure and brain function in Williams syndrome. In H. Tager-Flusberg (ed.), *Neurodevelopmental Disorders*. Cambridge, MA: MIT Press, pp. 111–136.

Benton, A. L., Hamsher, H., Varney, N. R. & Spreen, O. (1983) *Contributions to Neuropsychological Assessment*. Oxford University Press: New York.

Bishop, D. (1989) *Test for the Reception of Grammar* (2nd ed.). Manchester, UK: Chapel.

Block, J. H. & Block, J. (1980) The Role of ego-control and ego-resiliency in the organisation of behavior. In W. A. Collins (ed.), *Development of Cognition, Affect and Social Relations, Minnesota Symposia on Child Psychology*, vol. 13. Hillsdale, NJ: Erlbaum, pp. 39–101.

Clarke, D. J. (1998) Prader-Willi syndrome and psychotic symptoms: A preliminary study of prevalence using the Psychopathology Assessment Schedule for Adults with Developmental Disability checklist. *Journal of Intellectual Disability Research*, **42**, 451–454.

Clarke, D. J. & Boer, H. (1998) Problem behaviors associated with deletion Prader-Willi, Smith-Magenis and Cri Du Chat syndromes. *American Journal on Mental Retardation*, **103**, 264–271.

Clarke, D. J., Boer, H., Chung, M. C., Sturmey, P. & Webb, T. (1996) Maladaptive behaviour in Prader-Willi syndrome in adult life. *Journal of Intellectual Disability Research*, **40**, 159–165.

Clarke, D. J. & Marston, G. (2000) Problem behaviors associated with 15q-Angelman syndrome. *American Journal on Mental Retardation*, **105**, 25–31.

Clashen, H. & Temple, C. (2003) Words and rules in children with Williams syndrome. In Y. Levy & J. Schaeffer (eds.), *Language Competence Across Populations*. Hillsdale, NJ: Erlbaum, pp. 323–352.

Cooper, S.-A. (1997) Epidemiology of psychiatric disorders in elderly compared with younger adults with learning disabilities. *British Journal of Psychiatry*, **170**, 337–380.

Curfs, L. M. G., Hoondert, V., Lieshout, C. F. van, M. & Fryns, J.-P. (1995) Personality profiles of youngsters with Prader-Willi syndrome and youngsters attending regular schools. *Journal of Intellectual Disability Research*, **39**, 241–248.

Deal, A., Trivette, C. & Dunst, C. (1988) Family Functioning Scale. In C. Dunst, C. Trivette & A. Deal (eds.), *Enabling and Empowering Families: Principles and Guidelines for Practice*. Cambridge, MA: Brookline, pp. 179–184.

Dimitropoulos, A., Feurer, I. D., Butler, M. G. & Thompson, T. (2001) Emergence of compulsive behavior and tantrums in children with Prader-Willi syndrome. *American Journal on Mental Retardation*, **106**, 39–51.

Douglass, A. B., Bornstein, R., Nino-Murcia, G., Keenan, S., Miles, L., Zarcone, V. P., Guilleminault, C. & Dement, W. C. (1994) The Sleep Disorders Questionnaire 1: Creation and Multivariate Structure. *Sleep*, **17**, 160–167.

Dunn, L. & Dunn, L. (1981) *Peabody Picture Vocabulary Test – Revised*. Circle Pines, MN: American Guidance Service.

Dunn, L. M. & Dunn, L. M. (1997) *Peabody Picture Vocabulary Test – Revised*. Circle Pines, MN: American Guidance Service.

Dunn, L. M., Dunn, L. M., Whetton, C. & Burley, J. (1997) *The British Picture Vocabulary Scale* (2nd ed.). Windsor: NFER-Nelson.

Dykens, E. M. (1995) Measuring behavioral phenotypes: Provocations from the 'New Genetics'. *American Journal on Mental Retardation*, **99**, 522–532.

Dykens, E. M. (2002) Are jigsaw puzzles skills 'spared' in persons with Prader-Willi syndrome? *Journal of Child Psychology and Psychiatry*, **43**, 343–352.

Dykens, E. M. & Cassidy, S. B. (1996) Prader-Willi syndrome: Genetic, behavioral and treatment Issues. *Child and Adolescent Psychiatric Clinics of North America*, **5**, 913–927.

Dykens, E. M., Cassidy, S. B. & King, B. (1999) Maladaptive behavioral differences in Prader-Willi syndrome due to paternal deletion versus maternal uniparental disomy. *American Journal on Mental Retardation*, **104**, 67–77.

Dykens, E. M., Finucane, B. M. & Gayley, C. (1993) Neuropsychological and behavioral profiles in individuals with Smith-Magenis syndrome. Poster presentation at the Annual General meeting of the American Society of Human Genetics. New Orleans.

Dykens, E. M. & Hodapp, R. M. (1997) Treatment issues in genetic mental retardation syndromes. *Professional Psychology: Research and Practice*, **28**, 263–270.

Dykens, E. M. & Hodapp, R. M. (2001) Research in mental retardation: Toward an etiologic approach. *Journal of Child Psychology and Psychiatry*, **42**, 1–3.

Dykens, E. M., Hodapp, R. M. & Leckman, J. F. (1989) Adaptive and maladaptive functioning in Fragile-X males. *Journal of the American Academy of Child and Adolescent Psychiatry*, **28**, 427–430.

Dykens, E. M., Hodapp, R. M., Walsh, K. & Nash, L. J. (1992a) Adaptive and maladaptive behavior in Prader Willi syndrome. *Journal of the American Academy of Child and Adolescent Psychiatry*, **31**, 1131–1136.

Dykens, E. M., Hodapp, R. M., Walsh, K. & Nash, L. J. (1992b) Profiles, correlates and trajectories of intelligence in Prader-Willi syndrome. *Journal of the American Academy of Child and Adolescent Psychiatry*, **31**, 1125–1130.

Dykens, E. M. & Kasari, C. (1997) Maladaptive behavior in children with Prader-Willi syndrome, Down syndrome and nonspecific mental retardation. *American Journal on Mental Retardation*, **102**, 228–237.

Dykens, E. M., Leckman, J. F. & Cassidy, S. B. (1996) Obsessions and compulsions in Prader-Willi syndrome. *Journal of Child Psychology and Psychiatry*, **37**, 995–1002.

Dykens, E. M. & Rosner, B. (1999) Refining behavioral phenotypes: Personality – motivation in Williams and Prader-Willi syndromes. *American Journal on Mental Retardation*, **104**, 158–169.

Einfeld, S. L. & Hall, W. (1994) When is a behavioural phenotype not a phenotype? *Developmental Medicine and Child Neurology*, **36**, 463–470.

Einfeld, S. L., Smith, A., Durvasula, S., Florio, T. & Tonge, B. (1999) Behavior and emotional disturbance in Prader-Willi syndrome. *American Journal of Medical Genetics*, **82**, 123–127.

Einfeld, S. L. & Tonge, B. J. (1994) *The Manual of the Developmental Behaviour Checklist.* Sydney and Melbourne: University of New South Wales / Monash University.

Einfeld, S. L. & Tonge, B. J. (1995) The Developmental Behaviour Checklist: The development and validation of an instrument for the assessment of behavioural and emotional disturbance in children and adolescents with mental retardation. *Journal of Autism and Developmental Disorders*, **25**, 81–104.

Einfeld, S. L., Tonge, B. J. & Rees, V. W. (2001) Longitudinal course of behavioral and emotional problems in Williams syndrome. *American Journal on Mental Retardation*, **106**, 73–81.

Elliot, C. D. (1990) *Differential Ability Scales.* San Diego, CA: Harcourt, Brace, Jovanovich.

Feurer, I. D., Dimitropoulos, A., Stone, W. L., Roof, E., Butler, M. G. & Thompson, T. (1998) The latent variable structure of the Compulsive Behavior Checklist in people with Prader-Willi syndrome. *Journal of Intellectual Disability Research*, **42**, 472–480.

Flint, J. (1996) Behavioural phenotypes: A window onto the biology of behaviour. *Journal of Child Psychology and Psychiatry*, **37**, 355–368.

Gedye, A. (1992) Recognising obsessive–compulsive disorder in clients with developmental disabilities. *Habilitative Mental Healthcare Newsletter*, **11**, 73–77.

Goodman, W. K., Price, L. H., Rasmussen, S. A., Mazure, C., Delgado, P., Heninger, G. R. & Charney, D. S. (1989) The Yale-Brown Obsessive Compulsive Scale. Part 1: Development, use and reliability. *Archives of General Psychiatry*, **46**, 1006–1011.

Greer, M. K., Brown, F. R., Pai, G. S., Choudry, S. H. & Klein, A. J. (1997) Cognitive, adaptive and behavioral characteristics of Williams syndrome. *American Journal of Medical Genetics*, **84**, 521–525.

Hastings, R. P., Brown, T., Mount, R. H. & Cormack, C. F. M. (2001) Exploration of psychometric properties of the Developmental Behaviour Checklist. *Journal of Autism and Developmental Disabilities*, **3**, 423–431.

Hodapp, R. M. (1997) Direct and indirect behavioral effects on different genetic disorders of mental retardation. *American Journal on Mental Retardation*, **102**, 67–79.

Hodapp, R. M. & Dykens, E. M. (2001) Strengthening behavioral research on genetic mental retardation syndromes. *American Journal on Mental Retardation*, **106**, 4–15.

Holland, A. J. (1999) Syndromes, phenotypes and genotypes: Finding the links. *Psychologist*, **12**, 242–245.

Holland, A. J., Treasure, J., Coskeran, P., & Dallow, J. (1995) Characteristics of the eating disorder in Prader-Willi syndrome: Implications for treatment. *Journal of Intellectual Disability Research*, **39**, 373–381.

Howlin, P., Davies, M. & Udwin, O. (1998) Cognitive functioning in adults with Williams syndrome. *Journal of Child Psychology and Psychiatry*, **39**, 183–190.

Jarrold, C., Baddeley, A. D. & Hewes, A. K. (1998) Verbal and non-verbal abilities in the Williams syndrome phenotype: Evidence for diverging developmental trajectories. *Journal of Child Psychology and Psychiatry*, **39**, 511–524.

Johns, M. W. (1991) A new method for measuring daytime sleepiness: The Epworth Sleepiness Scales. *Sleep*, **14**, 540–545.

Kaufman, A. & Kaufman, N. (1983) *Kaufman Assessment Battery for Children*. Circle Pines, MN: American Guidance Service.

Kaufman, A. & Kaufman, N. (1990) *Kaufman Brief Intelligence Test*. Circle Pines, MN: American Guidance Service.

Kenworthy, L., Park, T. & Charnas, L. R. (1993) Cognitive and behavioral profile of the oculo-cerebrorenal syndrome of Lowe. *American Journal of Medical Genetics*, **46**, 297–303.

Kerr, A. (2002) Annotation: Rett syndrome: Recent progress and implications for research and clinical practice. *Journal of Child Psychology and Psychiatry*, **43**, 277–289.

Kerr, A. M. & Burford, B. (2002) Towards a full life with Rett disorder. *Paediatric Rehabilitation*, **4**, 1–12.

Lieshout, C. F. M. van, De Mayer, R. E., Curfs, L. M. G. & Fryns, J.-P. (1998) Family contexts, parental behaviour and personality profiles of children and adolescents with Prader-Willi, Fragile-X or Williams syndrome. *Journal of Child Psychology and Psychiatry*, **39**, 699–710.

Mervis, C. B., Morris, C. A., Bertrand, J. & Robinson, B. (1999) Williams syndrome: Findings from an integrated program of research. In H. Tager-Flusberg (ed.), *Neurodevelopmental Disorders*. Cambridge, MA: MIT Press, pp. 65–110.

Morris, C. A. & Mervis, C. B. (1999) Williams syndrome. In S. Goldstein & C. R. Reynolds (eds.), *Handbook of Neurodevelopmental and Genetic Disorders in Children*. New York: Guildford, pp. 555–590.

Moss, S., Prosser, H., Costello, H., Simpson, N. & Patel, P. (1997) *PASS-ADD Checklist*. Manchester, UK: Hester Adrian Research Centre, University of Manchester.

Mount, R. H., Charman, T., Hastings, R. P., Reilly, S. & Cass, H. (2002) The Rett syndrome Behavior Questionnaire (RSBQ): Refining the Behavioral Phenotype of Rett syndrome. *Journal of Child Psychology, Psychiatry and Allied Disciplines*, **43**, 1099–1110.

Mount, R. H., Hastings, R. P., Reilly, S., Cass, H. & Charman, T. (2001) Behavioural and emotional features on Rett syndrome, *Disability and Rehabilitation*, **23**, 129–138.

Mount, R. H., Hastings, R. P., Reilly, S. & Cass, H. & Charman, T. (2003) Towards a behavioral phenotype for Rett syndrome. *American Journal on Mental Retardation*, **108**, 1–12.

O'Brien, G. (1992) Behavioural phenotypes and their measurement. *Developmental Medicine and Child Neurology*, **34**, 365–367.

O'Brien, G. (2000) Behavioural phenotypes. *Journal of the Royal Society of Medicine*, **93**, 618–620.

Perry, A., Sarlo-McGarvey, N. & Haddad, C. (1991) Brief Reports: Cognitive and adaptive functioning in 28 girls with Rett syndrome. *Journal of Autism and Developmental Disorders*, **21**, 551–556.

Prosser, H., Moss, S., Costello, H., Simpson, N. & Patel, P. (1997) *The Mini PASS-ADD: An Assessment Schedule for the Detection of Mental Health Problems in Adults with Developmental Disabilities.* Manchester, UK: Hester Adrian Research Centre, University of Manchester.

Reiss, S. (1998) *Reiss Screen for Maladaptive Behavior Test Manual.* Worthington, OH: IDS.

Reiss, S. & Havercamp, S. M. (1998) Toward a comprehensive assessment of fundamental motivation: Factor structure of the Reiss Profiles. *Psychological Assessment*, **10**, 97–106.

Richdale, A. L., Cotton, S. & Hibbit, K. (1999) Sleep and behaviour disturbance in Prader-Willi syndrome: A questionnaire study. *Journal of Intellectual Disability Research*, **43**, 380–392.

Roof, E., Stone, W., MacLean, W., Feurer, I. D., Thompson, T. & Butler, M. G. (2000) Intellectual characteristics of Prader-Willi syndrome: Comparison of genetic subtypes. *Journal of Intellectual Disabilty Research*, **44**, 25–30.

Sarimski, K. (1997) Behavioural phenotypes and family stress in three mental retardation syndromes. *European Child and Adolescent Psychiatry*, **6**, 26–31.

Skuse, D., Elgar, K. & Morris, E. (1999) Quality of life in Turner syndrome is related to chromosomal constitution: Implications for genetic counseling and management. *Acta Paediatricia*, **88** (Supplement 428), 110–113.

Sparrow, S. S., Balla, D. & Cicchetti, D. (1984) *Vineland Adaptive Behavior Scales.* Circle Pines, MN: American Guidance Service.

Wechsler, D. (1973) *Wechsler Intelligence Scale for Children – Revised.* New York: Psychological Corporation.

Wechsler, D. (1981) *Wechsler Adult Intelligence Scale – Revised.* New York: Psychological Corporation.

Wechsler, D. (1986) *Wechsler Adult-Intelligence Scale – Revised UK.* London Psychological Corporation.

Woodyatt, G. C. & Ozanne, A. E. (1993) A longitudinal study of cognitive skills and communication behaviours in children with Rett syndrome. *Journal of Intellectual Disability Research*, **37**, 419–435.

INDEX